Business Research Solutions Series

NEW SERIES TITLES IN PREPARATION

INTRODUCTION TO ONLINE ACCOUNTING & FINANCIAL RESEARCH

Editor and Contributor Susan M. Klopper

INTRODUCTION TO ONLINE COMPANY RESEARCH

Editor and Contributor Chris Dobson

INTRODUCTION TO ONLINE INVESTMENT RESEARCH

Editor and Contributor Jan Davis

INTRODUCTION TO ONLINE LEGAL, REGULATORY & INTELLECTUAL PROPERTY RESEARCH

Editor and Contributor Genie Tyburski

INTRODUCTION TO ONLINE COMPETITIVE INTELLIGENCE RESEARCH

Editor and Contributor Conor Vibert

Produced by The Benjamin Group

THOMSON

TEXERE

EDITORIAL ADVISORY BOARD

The following group of national experts on business and financial information formed an Editorial Advisory Board to work with editors and contributors to ensure content quality control and related professional research standards:

DIRECTORY OF CONTRIBUTORS*

Melissa Barr
Cuyahoga County Public Library

Mary Ellen Bates
Bates Information Services, Inc.

Kathy Biehl
Independent Researcher

Polly D. Boruff-Jones
IUPUI University Library

Meryl Brodsky
Consultant

Helen P. Burwell
Burwell Enterprises

Cindy Carlson
Fried, Frank, Harris, Shriver & Jacobson

Margaret Metcalf Carr
Carr Research Group

Elena Carvajal
Ernst & Young

Donna Cavallini
Kilpatrick Stockton LLP

Dudee Chiang
Amgen, Inc.

Naomi Clifford
Consultant

Lynn Ecklund
SEEK Information Services, Inc.

Wes Edens
Thunderbird School of International Management

David Ernsthausen
Kenan-Flagler Business School

Michelle Fennimore
Competitive Insights

James Galbraith
Columbia University

James Harrington
Fujitsu Network Communications

Michelle Hartstrom
Columbia Financial Advisors, Inc.

Jean M. Heilig
Jones International University

Karl Kasca
Kasca & Associates

Wendy S. Katz
Factscope LLC

Hal P. Kirkwood, Jr.
Purdue University

Jan Knight
Bancroft Information Services

Margery A. Mackie
Mackie Research LLC

William S. Marriott
Marriott Research and Recruitment

Matthew J. McBride
Information Consultant

Karin Mohtadi
KZM LLC

Kathleen Morley
Independent Researcher

Rita W. Moss
University of North Carolina—Chapel Hill

Robin Neidorf
Electric Muse

Judith M. Nixon
Purdue University

Judith Parvez
Tax Analysts

Marcy M. Phelps
Phelps Research

Vicky Platt
Willamette Management Associates

Brenda Reeb
University of Rochester

Jan Rivers
Dorsey & Whitney LLP

Mary Rumsey
University of Minnesota Law School

Roger V. Skalbeck
George Mason University School of Law

Ann Spoth
A.T. Kearney

Kent A. Sutorius
Informed Solutions, Inc.

Jen Venable
Purdue University

Patricia A. Watkins
Thunderbird School of International Management

Susan F. Weiler
Weiler Information Services

Samuel Werberg
FIND/SVP, Inc.

Kim Whalen
Emory University

Morgan Wilson
Hamline University School of Law Library

* See Appendix D for more detailed biographies of most of the contributors.

Introduction to Online Market & Industry Research

SEARCH STRATEGIES, CASE STUDY, PROBLEMS, AND DATA SOURCE EVALUATIONS AND REVIEWS

Editor and Contributor Cynthia L. Shamel
Shamel Information Services

Produced by The Benjamin Group

THOMSON
TEXERE™

Australia · Canada · Mexico · Singapore · Spain · United Kingdom · United States

THOMSON

TEXERE

Introduction to Online Market & Industry Research: Search Strategies, Case Study, Problems, and Data Source Evaluations and Reviews
Cynthia Shamel, Editor and Contributor

Vice President/ Editorial Director:
Jack Calhoun

Vice President/ Editor-in-Chief:
Dave Shaut

Acquisitions Editor:
Steve Momper

Channel Manager, Retail:
Chris McNamee

Channel Manager, Professional:
Mark Linton

Production Editor:
Todd McCoy

Production Manager:
Tricia Matthews Boies

Manufacturing Coordinator:
Charlene Taylor

Compositor:
GEX Publishing Services

Printer:
Phoenix Color Corp.
Hagerstown, MD

Design Project Manager:
Stacy Jenkins Shirley

Cover Designer:
Knapke Design
Mason, OH

Cover Photo:
Getty Images

For permission to use material from this text or product, contact us by
Tel (800) 730-2214
Fax (800) 730-2215
http://www.thomsonrights.com

For more information contact South-Western, 5191 Natorp Boulevard, Mason, Ohio 45040.
Or you can visit our Internet site at:
http://www.swlearning.com

Library of Congress Cataloging in Publication Data has been applied for.

PREFACE

Read the preface. That's what I always told my reference services and materials students in library technology school. The preface will tell you why the book exists; what's in it and how it got there. It will tell you what the book can do for you and what it can't. Read the preface.

The Business Research Solutions Series is intended to make online business and legal research easier to understand and practice. Taken together, all of the volumes serve both as a training tool and a reference resource for entry-level corporate personnel, undergraduate and graduate students of business and law, corporate academic librarians, and market researchers.

Online Market and Industry Research specifically addresses information gathering related to understanding any industry and the marketplace within which that industry operates. For the researcher seeking the best source of information and a workable strategy to access the content of that source, this volume should provide valuable guidance.

This volume is organized in four parts to provide background, instruction, and reference to sample solutions and key sources. The researcher should consider reading Chapters One and Two in total. They lay the groundwork and provide context for understanding search strategies, particularly as they relate to market and industry research. Chapters Three and Four work well as reference sources for understanding specific types of research questions and choosing appropriate sources.

1. RESEARCH STRATEGIES: This chapter introduces the reader to business research strategies and procedures. It also provides a plethora of practical advice and recommendations on better research techniques, dependable data sources, and industry best-practices;

2. RESEARCH CASE STUDY: The second chapter takes an involved, multilevel research project and traces the solution from initial strategy to final data analysis and reporting. This provides real insight to the reader on professional research methodology and practices from an industry overview to specific market research needs;

3. **RESEARCH PROBLEMS AND SOLUTIONS:** The third chapter presents sixteen detailed, worked out research problems and their solutions. They apply to market and industry research with practical advice on data source selection and content.

4. **RESEARCH DATA SOURCE EVALUATIONS AND REVIEWS:** In this volume the sources fall into one of five categories. The Big Three Database Aggregators includes large database aggregators offering massive amounts of information on a wide range of topics. The Big Three are deep and broad. The Government Information sources provide information, data, and statistics gathered and compiled by government agencies. The section on Aggregators and Portals contains sources of information compiled by information entrepreneurs specifically for business researchers. The Individual Databases generally represents one source or product covering multiple industries and markets, and Subject Specific Special sources provides detailed coverage of a specific type of information.

5. **APPENDIX:** The four-part appendix contains valuable reference material that will be useful to any researcher. Included is a data source directory with contact names and the combined results of data source evaluations and ratings for the 102 business research sources that are (or will be) reviewed in this seven-volume series.

The topics, problems, solutions, and sources featured in this book were identified through the editor's experience, through the business literature, through the input and guidance of other series editors, and through the wise contributors who rely on their professional research skills and experiences every day to meet their customers' and clients' information needs.

Dozens of highly competent, motivated research professionals banded together to produce this volume. Their names appear either as members of the Editorial Advisory Board or as Contributors in the front matter. I am most grateful for their advice and assistance, both of which were always delivered in kind spirit and with good humor. Detailed biographies of these experts appear in the Appendix of this volume. I would especially like to thank the editors of the other volumes in this series for their unfailing support and their willingness to share ideas and content. Thanks also go to Bill Benjamin for his encouragement and confidence, and to Helene Segal for phenomenal attention to detail. Finally, thanks to Blair for demonstrating how to apply passion and elbow grease to a worthwhile project.

A word is in order about the selection of online sources to be reviewed. Each editor provided a listing of key online data sources and the publishers were then contacted to ask for temporary passwords to assign to a specific reviewer and editor. Although most of the publishers responded, we were surprised at the lack of interest on the part of several important business data sources, and hence there are some unavoidable omissions that the editors regret.

In the near future, all of the content for all of the books in the series will appear online as well as in print with the fervent hope that more and more useful material (as well as revisions) will be made available on a continual basis. A number of additional volumes are planned for inclusion in this series so as to eventually address all special aspects (and vertical applications) of business research that cover international as well as domestic practices.

The Benjamin Group of Santa Barbara, California, developed the concept of this series with considerable help from the volume editors and the Advisory Board. We will appreciate any and all suggestions for improvement in future editions and, of course, regret any shortcomings in the current content for which we are responsible.

Cynthia L. Shamel
Editor

The Editor

Cynthia L. Shamel, entrepreneur and small-business owner, founded Shamel Information Services in 1998, offering competitive-intelligence and business research to clients ranging from sole proprietors to multinational corporations. She served as a college reference librarian and taught in a library technology program before launching her research business. Ms. Shamel obtained her Master of Library Science degree from Indiana University in 1990, and holds a B.A. in geography. Ms. Shamel has spoken at industry and information professional conferences on marketing and competitive intelligence and has been published in *Searcher Magazine, FreePint, Connections,* and *Community & Junior College Libraries.* She is a member of the Special Libraries Association and 2003-2004 president of the Association of Independent Information Professionals.

TABLE OF CONTENTS

Definition and Strategy

Imagine trying to run a profitable business without reliable market research. It would be like trying to drive a car blindfolded. You sit in the driver's seat with your hands on the wheel, but you can't see the potholes, the curves, or any part of the road ahead. You can't see what kind of traffic is coming toward you, and you can't tell what the other drivers are doing. To arrive safely at your destination would require either incredible luck or nothing short of a miracle.

Market research offers business managers a picture of the environment in which they operate. It is the eyes and ears, the map and the traffic report of the entrepreneur. Market research gives decision makers an awareness of the road and the traffic; it tells them what cross streets to anticipate, which turn to take at the intersection, whether the traffic copter is circling overhead and what to do about it, and what kind of weather to expect for the journey. Good market research can thus facilitate informed decision making.

What does market research cover? Broadly speaking, it covers the market and the industry. Markets are "all people who have a specific, unsatisfied need or want and are willing and able to purchase a product or service to satisfy that need."[1] An industry includes those organizations striving to meet the needs of a market. In his 1980 classic book called *Competitive Strategy: Techniques for Analyzing Industries and Competitors,* Michael Porter defines an industry as "the group of firms producing products that are close substitutes for each other."[2] Within an industry, importers, suppliers, manufacturers, and distributors (all of which generally manifest themselves as companies) come together to bring goods and services to the target market or target customer. To understand a

---

1. Nitin Nohria, *The Portable MBA Desk Reference,* 2nd ed. (New York: John Wiley & Sons, 1998), 245.
2. Michael Porter, *Competitive Strategy: Techniques for Analyzing Industries and Competitors* (New York: Free Press, 1980), 5.

target market, the researcher must understand the industry within which it fits. Conversely, to understand an industry, the researcher must comprehend the markets that the industry serves. Figure 1-1 illustrates how the pieces of the industry/market puzzle come together in one particular case.

Product managers, sales representatives, market researchers, competitive-intelligence professionals, business development specialists, and technical writers, as well as presidents, chief executive officers, chief financial officers, and investor relations personnel all need market and industry research. Who gathers this market and industry information depends on the situation; librarians, market research personnel, and competitive-intelligence professionals within companies all conduct market and industry research. At one time or another, however, most business professionals do their own market or industry research. This book provides workable search strategies and valuable source information that can facilitate research in just about any industry, whether you are a novice or a seasoned researcher. You can use the techniques outlined here to guide any market search, and ideally, they will lead you to the most useful and cost-effective sources.

Market and industry research is used within companies and enterprises to enlighten tactical decision making and to develop longer-range strategic marketing plans, which in turn guides product development, business development, product positioning, product price, technology, distribution, and promotion. This volume will help you conduct effective market and industry research to facilitate informed decision making in your organization.

Chapter One offers an overview of the issues surrounding good market and industry research, and puts the research process into a larger context by explaining the types of sources available and how information is gathered and distributed. In this introductory chapter you will discover how to define the research problem and identify the questions that require answers. You will learn search strategies based upon the type of information you need and where that information might be found. You will learn about major information suppliers and gain insights into how to choose between them, as well as how to create an effective search statement for each of the online environments you search. The chapter concludes with guidance on how to assemble the search results and illustrates what a final report might look like.

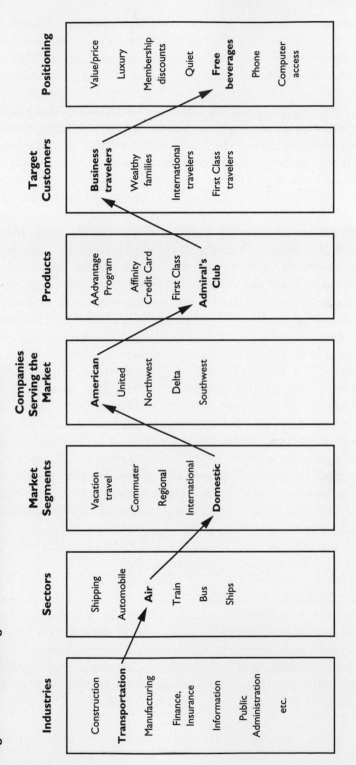

Figure 1-1. Market Segmentation: American Airlines—Admiral's Club

Industries	Sectors	Market Segments	Companies Serving the Market	Products	Target Customers	Positioning
Construction	Shipping	Vacation travel	American	AAdvantage Program	Business travelers	Value/price
Transportation	Automobile	Commuter	United	Affinity Credit Card	Wealthy families	Luxury
Manufacturing	**Air**	Regional	Northwest	First Class	International travelers	Membership discounts
Finance, Insurance	Train	International	Delta	**Admiral's Club**	First Class travelers	Quiet
Information	Bus	**Domestic**	Southwest			**Free beverages**
Public Administration	Ships					Phone
etc.						Computer access

Chapter Two offers a detailed case study. In this chapter, the researcher recounts an actual research project from the initial request through the final report. In an interesting narrative the researcher describes the initial request, the project definition process, and the step-by-step research process. The information was used to guide a country club board of directors (the client) on how to better serve their members (the customers), how to attract new members, and how to best manage the club's physical plant. The board of directors and president wanted to understand the industry and the marketplace as they set policy and developed plans for their organization. The case study illustrates the processes described in Chapter One.

To illustrate practical solutions to real-life research problems, Chapter Three presents a series of detailed problems, each with a proposed solution. These problems come from the experience of professional business researchers, and they reflect the choices and strategies made to keep the project on time and within budget. The problems and solutions included in Chapter Three illustrate how to research many of the topics outlined in Helen Burwell's industry study template (described in Chapter One).

Seasoned researchers know that there are hundreds of online sources that can help answer market and industry research questions. Chapter Four contains valuable descriptions and assessments of the most frequently used sources. This final chapter serves as a reference that may prove useful as you select the best sources for specific types of information in your future research.

Together, these chapters provide a wide range of tools for market and industry researchers, from general principles to specific examples and tips. Now, let's turn to an outline of the research process.

THE RESEARCH CYCLE

In *Online Competitive Intelligence,* Helen Burwell offers an excellent Industry Study Template that can serve as a checklist for an industry study or overview. Burwell's template[3] is reproduced here to illustrate the types of information needed to develop an understanding of a market and the industry within which that market operates.

---

3. Helen P. Burwell, *Online Competitive Intelligence* (Tempe, Ariz.: Facts on Demand, 1999), 228–229. Reprinted with the permission of Facts on Demand.

- Status of the Industry
  - Relative size and scope of the industry—growing, stable, or declining?
  - History of industry
  - Trends in industry
  - Forecasts regarding size of the industry
  - SIC or NAICS codes
- Customers for Products or Services
  - Customers
  - Size of market
  - Potential new buyers
  - Directions in the market
  - Import penetration
  - Forecasts for market
  - Distribution methods
- Market/Marketing Issues
  - Scope of products
  - Brand loyalty
  - Product leader description
  - Product differentiation
  - Alternate products/services
  - Complementary products
  - Quality continuum
  - Marketing media used
  - Price structure
  - Price margins
- Manufactured Goods Issues
  - Technology in use
  - Technological trends
  - Industry innovations
  - Emerging technologies
- Service Business Issues
  - Scope of services
  - Level of services
- Fiscal Matters
  - Changes that may affect supplier prices
  - Legislation/regulations
  - Availability of raw materials
  - Other sales by major product type

- Productivity-Related Matters
  - Manufacturing Rates
  - Efficiency levels
  - Product innovation

This is a lot of information! How does the market researcher get a handle on it all, much less find it, assess it, organize it, and present it? The Research Cycle, shown in Figure 1-2, illustrates the market research process. Generally, the first thing to happen is that someone in the company (the client) identifies an information need. Through the steps that follow (either formally or informally), the research question must be clearly understood by the researcher. A search strategy is created and implemented, and the results are reviewed. Then, as the project progresses and interim results are gathered, an assessment determines whether or not the search should continue. Interim results might indicate that some of the assumptions underlying the research are incorrect. In that case, the researcher will want to reevaluate the search strategy to make any necessary changes. Because this process is cyclical and can require more than one iteration, it is appropriate to call it "re-search."

Figure 1-2. The Research Cycle

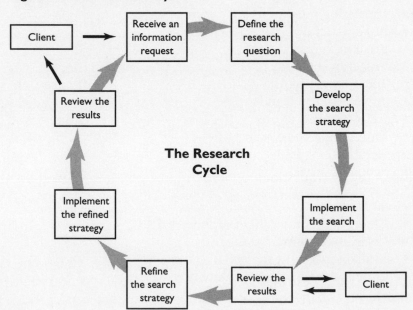

RECEIVING THE REQUEST AND
DEFINING THE QUESTION

Once the researcher has received an information request, the researcher needs to carefully define the question to be answered and understand who wants to know and why. On that foundation, the researcher plans the search strategy.

Questions do not come up out of the blue or without reason. Typically, someone in the organization needs to make a business decision and wants information that will facilitate a good decision. Within a company, the executives, the marketing department, the business development department, and the legal department commonly need information. Occasionally manufacturing, human resources, and finance also require market or industry-related information. Because all these requestors can have different perspectives on the market, understanding who wants to know (your client) is an important step in defining a research question.

Besides simply guiding the search, knowing the client can help the researcher tailor the results or the look and feel of the final report. For example, will the client be satisfied with a conclusion drawn from published reports, or will backup tables and data be expected? What sources will the client trust, and how much validation and cross-checking will suffice? Of course, you yourself may very well be the "client," the person who wants to know. But that does not change the steps in the process. It is still important to think through the purpose of the research.

It would be hard to overstress the importance of communicating with the client. To deliver usable research results, you must be clear about what is needed, why it is needed, when it is needed, whether there are cost limitations, and what the end product should look like. Whether you will use the results yourself or deliver them to someone else, you should think through or get answers to these questions. A clear understanding of these points will help focus the search in a most useful and cost-effective way.

The Client Interview

How and when does this communication take place? The client interview is the best place to get your answers. A typical client interview includes some version of the following questions:

• Who wants to know?
• How will the information be used?

- When does the client need the information?
- What does the client already know?
- Are there budget constraints?
- What should the end product look like?

How you organize the client interview depends upon the situation, but as a general rule, face-to-face conversations are best. An in-person interview allows you to obtain information not only from what is said, but from body language and demeanor as well. Telephone conversations are also effective. E-mail is useful for keeping in touch, but it does not work as well for the initial conversations. If possible, have this conversation directly with the client, rather than with an assistant or other intermediary, to avoid serious miscommunications. Working through people other than your client can turn into something like the "telephone game," where a message starts on one end of a line of people and gradually changes (sometimes disastrously!) as it is whispered down the line.

Do not be afraid to ask questions. By asking questions you help the client define, think through, and verbalize the information need. Clients do not always ask for exactly what they need. Sometimes they try to help the researcher by "simplifying" the question. They ask for what they *think* might be out there rather than what they really need. Clients sometimes use broad or general terms because they are afraid you don't know the jargon or might miss something if they define the question too specifically. For instance, a client might ask: "Can you find some articles on bottled water?" But after the initial questioning you realize that what the client really needs is market share for carbonated and noncarbonated bottled water in the United States! To make sure you understand the client's request, restate it and ask for clarification if you need it. Don't worry about sounding uninformed or bothersome. Generally, people are happy to explain a topic that is near and dear to them, and they appreciate your interest.

In *Building and Running a Successful Research Business*, Mary Ellen Bates suggests that you ask the following types of questions to help identify the client's underlying need:

- What do you mean by _____?
- What do you already know about _____?
- What do you expect me to find?
- Are there any sources you have already checked, or that you would recommend?
- Are there any other terms used to describe _____?

- I'm not familiar with _____ . Can you explain it to me?
- If you were writing an article about this, what would the headline be?
- If I can't find exactly _____ , what would be second best?[4]

Asking this kind of question during the client interview will help you get the information you need to develop your research strategy. Keep in mind that as a result of the interview, you should be able to list the objectives of the research and articulate clearly the questions to be answered.

Define the Research Questions

One way to clarify the research questions is to ask how the information will be used. Use the client interview to find out what business opportunity is being explored. What problem or situation is being evaluated in this process? What are the actions that might be taken as a result?

Suppose this question comes to you from a client: *How big is the market for event-related travel?* To obtain information that is useful to the client, wouldn't it help you to know that he or she is thinking of creating a service that would allow conference and meeting goers to book air travel and room reservations online from the event sponsor's Web site? If you know your research will support this decision, you will be able to refine the scope to include a look at air travel to conferences, hotel accommodations at conferences, number of travelers, number of conferences, trade shows, and exhibitions, and so on. Knowing what your client plans to do with the information allows you to translate the original question—*How big is the market for event-related travel?*— into a set of more specific questions—*How are travelers currently making these plans? How many event-related travelers are there? If we offer an easy online solution, how many customers are likely to use it?* This level of understanding will help you realize when to end the search. You will be better able to determine if the need has been met.

Another way to focus the research questions is to ask clients whether they have already done any research on the topic or what experience they may have had in the field. Suppose your client is the company's marketing manager, who previously worked for

---

4. Mary Ellen Bates, *Building and Running a Successful Research Business* (Medford, N.J.: CyberAge Books, 2003).

a competitor and wants to develop a marketing strategy for a new product. This client already has industry background and is thoroughly familiar with the industry. Understanding this background will help you formulate your research strategy, building upon rather than repeating what is already known. In this case, the scope of the project will likely focus more on details related to the competing products than on a broad overview of the industry.

Identify the Search Constraints

The factors most likely to constrain a given search are time and money. Your ability to research as deeply as your client requires will depend a great deal on these two factors, so you will need to know up front what the deadline and budget are. Of course, it is music to the researcher's ears to hear "I don't care how much it costs or how long it takes, just get me that information!" But it is the rare project indeed that has no budget and no deadline. More typically, financial and time concerns guide the project in one way or another.

Sometimes, time and cost concerns are in direct conflict, as time-saving research methods often carry the highest out-of-pocket costs. Make sure your client is aware of this, and be ready to discuss at least a rough estimate of time and money requirements for their research request at the client interview. You may have to negotiate a bit as the conversation continues, and as the research progresses you'll need to keep the client informed if it looks like more time or money is required.

Plan for the End Product

Once you have completed a research project and are comfortable that you have either obtained the information you need or that it cannot be found with the resources at hand, you need to convey the information to your client. Delivery of information takes many forms. A quick e-mail or telephone call may suffice. Some people prefer a "rip-and-ship" approach, where you simply deliver the downloaded material—unedited. Some projects require an analysis and summary of the information with conclusions outlined for the reader. Chapter Three includes a sample problem and solution that required the researcher to create a database to sort and evaluate the research findings. The end product options range from a short answer delivered verbally to a multipage report with an executive summary, charts, tables, and supporting documentation. It is important to understand in advance what kind of end product will meet the client's needs, so that the search strategy employed and the time allotted for report preparation can be structured accordingly.

After the client interview, put the agreed-upon research objectives and questions and any time and budget limitations in writing for yourself and/or the client. This can help to ensure that you are on the right track. Then, as the project progresses, check back as needed to review and report on interim results and explore alternative avenues of research, if needed. Sometimes a course correction is in order. Interim results might indicate that some of the assumptions underlying the research are incorrect.

DEVELOPING THE SEARCH STRATEGY

After the client interview, the researcher should have a clear understanding of the questions to be answered, what end product is expected, what is already known about the topic, and the time and budget constraints. As we've seen, the information gathered in the client interview provides the groundwork for planning the research. The next step in the process is developing a research strategy, which outlines the steps required to get from your list of objectives and questions to the information that offers the answers. To develop an effective and appropriate search strategy, you need to look at your questions and constraints in light of what you know about the research process. How will you answer the research questions in the time required? Which sources will you start with? Are any key sources that will strain your budget? If so, are there any alternatives? These are the sorts of questions your search strategy will address.

Define the Research Depth

To plan your research, you'll need to know how much information you should be looking for. In other words, how much is enough? The client interview should have defined the research questions rather specifically, and you should have a good idea how the information will be used. Now it's time to look at these questions and objectives in terms of the sources available to you.

Let's look at three research examples, including the situation, opportunity, or problem that prompted the request, the decision to be made, and the research questions:

1. Situation: A new product requires a competitive warranty package.

    Decision to be made: What will our warranty package look like?

    Research Question: What are the competing products? What kinds of warranty do they offer?

2. Opportunity: Your client is a high-technology computer peripherals company. The competition's color printers seem to be gaining market share.

    Decision to be made: Should we rethink our target market or should we redesign the printer?

    Research Questions: How is the competition positioning its printer in the marketplace? What are the features and benefits of their printer compared with ours? How does the competition advertise and promote its product?

3. Problem: Sales for one of your client's products have gone flat.

    Decision to be made: Do we reposition the product, or identify a new target market?

    Research Questions: How has the competition positioned its product for the market? What is the target market? What are the characteristics of this market in terms of size and demographics? How does the target market perceive the product?

Each of these examples suggests a different project depth. Look at the research questions. Is the information required general or specific? How many different areas of research would you need to investigate in each case? The greater the number of distinct research topics, the deeper your research needs to be. The first example, for instance, is relatively straightforward, requiring specific research into a fairly focused area. Your research will need to identify competing products and describe the warranty packages they offer. The second example is a bit more complex: it requires you to do some general research to identify competing printers, and some specific research on features, benefits, advertising, and promotion. The third example is relatively focused on the market, but it requires the deepest research: you'll need to identify the market, describe the market, and research the market response to the product in question.

Looking at your research questions in this way allows you to start planning your research. A relatively simple research question may be answered in a short period of time, using only a handful of key resources. More complicated questions require more time, and you'll need to look at a broader variety of sources. As we will see, the more you know about your sources, the better able you'll be able to define your strategy at this point.

To define the research depth, you'll also need to consider your time and budget constraints. In planning your search strategy you will sometimes need to consider whether time constraints outweigh cost concerns, or vice versa. In many cases, the tradeoff between paying more and obtaining the information quickly is worth it.

For instance, let's say a pharmaceutical company CEO asked her research librarian to comprehensively search the medical literature for references to a specific antibody and what disease states were being associated with it. The client wanted to broaden her own thinking about therapeutic applications in time for a meeting two days later. The researcher could have chosen to search free sources, such as PubMed,[5] or printed indexes such as Biological Abstracts,[6] with the only expense being her time. But given the short deadline, she instead conducted a simultaneous online search of three huge medical/pharmaceutical bibliographic databases (citations and abstracts only, no full text articles), with duplicates automatically removed. The search yielded a highly relevant list of references, formatted and delivered within a couple of hours. This approach left plenty of time for the client to scan the list, obtain the full text, and prepare for the meeting. The results, using the Dialog Corporation[7] databases, cost about five hundred dollars, with most of the expense attributed to the large number of hits downloaded. In this case the research librarian developed a research strategy that favored speed over low cost, paying the fees associated with the online aggregated databases to ensure a broad search that could be completed in a short period of time.

---

5. PubMed, at *http://www.pubmed.gov*, is a service of the National Library of Medicine that provides access to more than twelve million MEDLINE citations back to the mid-1960s.

6. Biological Abstracts indexes articles from more than four thousand life sciences serials each year, with archives back to 1969. The online version is called BIOSIS.

7. The Dialog Corporation, at *http://www.dialog.com*, is a business of The Thomson Corporation. Dialog provides more than twelve terabytes of information from authoritative publishers worldwide.

There may, of course, be situations in which cost concerns outweigh time constraints. In such a case, your research strategy may include free databases and Web pages, free library access, and time to format your results so that the client can use them. Whether it is time, money, or the nature of the required results, always consider the project constraints when planning the search strategy.

Conceptualize the Information You Need

In developing the research strategy, it can help to conceptualize the information you need to address the questions. Ask yourself, what, exactly, am I looking for? Try to picture the answer, or even the report that you will eventually deliver. Will it contain statistics, copies of articles, charts, tables, or all of these? If your question involves trends or forecasts, will you need a table of statistics to illustrate the answers? What kind of data would fill that table? Ask yourself, if you haven't already asked your client, to imagine the ideal article that would address your questions. What would be the title of that article?

By conceptualizing the information you need and what the answers might look like, you can begin to identify possible sources for that information. If you think the answer will come from published articles, you can search the databases containing that type of information. If data and statistics will answer the questions, you can identify statistical sources and plan to search there. Later portions of this chapter elaborate on how to construct a search string to retrieve information from online databases.

Consider Who Might Have the Information You Need

In developing your research strategy, it helps to know something about the origin, assimilation, and distribution of the information you're looking for. Where, for example, does online information come from? Who compiles it and makes it available? If you have an image of the information stream in mind, it is easier to picture where and how to jump into that stream. As Leonard Fuld points out, "Each business transaction reveals data. By understanding the transaction, you can locate the intelligence source."[8] Fuld gives an example from the banking industry:

---

8. Leonard M. Fuld, *The New Competitor Intelligence* (New York: John Wiley & Sons, 1995), 29.

Table 1-1. The Information Stream from a Business Event

EVENT	ACTORS	PUBLIC SOURCES	INTELLIGENCE REVEALED
Announcement of new cash-management product	Bank; corporate end-users; financial reporters	Trade news; conferences; written proposals	Features; pricing

Leonard M. Fuld, *The New Competitor Intelligence* (New York: John Wiley & Sons, 1995), 29. ©1995, John Wiley & Sons. This material is used by permission of John Wiley & Sons, Inc.

In this case, the bank, the intended customers, and journalists covering the banking industry participate in announcing a new product. It is reported in the trade news, discussed at conferences, and outlined in written proposals. As this example shows, knowing something about the actor and the sources early in your search will help you access the needed information more efficiently. If you know the target industry well, you are probably already well acquainted with the actors and the sources.

To illustrate where to find certain types of market and industry information, let's revisit Burwell's industry study template. The augmented version in Table 1-2 includes possible sources.

Table 1-2. Sources for Industry Studies

GENERAL INFORMATION CATEGORY	SPECIFIC INFORMATION	POSSIBLE SOURCES
Status of the Industry	Relative size and scope of the industry—growing, stable, or declining?	Industry overviews
	History, trends, and forecasts for the industry	Trade publications and associations
	SIC or NAICS codes	U.S. Census Bureau (*http://www.census.gov/epcd/www/naics.html*)
Customers for Products or Services	Customers, potential new buyers, and size of market	Trade publications, news sources, SEC filings, statistical sources
	Directions in the market	Market research reports and trade publications
	Import penetration and distribution methods	Trade associations and publications
	Forecasts for the market	Market research reports and trade publications

Table 1-2. Sources for Industry Studies (*cont.*)

GENERAL INFORMATION CATEGORY	SPECIFIC INFORMATION	POSSIBLE SOURCES
Market/Marketing Issues	Scope of products	News sources, company Web sites, catalogs
	Brand loyalty	News and trade publications
	Product leader description and market share	Company Web sites, news and trade publications, market research reports
	Product differentiation, alternate products/ services, complementary products	Advertising sources, trade publications, company Web sites
	Quality continuum	Trade publications
	Marketing media used	Advertising industry sources
	Price structure, price margins	Investor analysts reports, trade publications
Manufactured Goods Issues	Technology in use, technological trends, industry innovations, emerging technologies	Trade publications and associations, technology information databases, regulatory agencies, market research reports
Service Business Issues	Scope and level of services	Industry overviews, news sources, trade publications
Fiscal Matters	Changes that may affect supplier prices	World economic news sources, general news sources, trade associations
	Legislation/regulations	Regulatory agencies, government sources, law sources
	Availability of raw materials	News and economic sources in jurisdiction of material source, general news sources, U.S. government sources
	Other sales by major product type	Government sources, trade publications
Productivity-Related Matters	Manufacturing rates, efficiency levels, product innovation	Trade publications and associations

Adapted from Burwell, Helen P. *Online Competitive Intelligence* (Tempe, AZ: Facts on Demand, 1999), 228–229. Reprinted with the permission of Facts on Demand.

Note that in almost every case the industries' trade publications and association Web sites are of value. Also, many industries have industry-specific databases that contain unique and detailed information. Again, the more you know about the industry in question, the better able you will be to identify and assess the possible information sources.

Consider How Information Is Organized

The more you know about how the information is gathered, organized, and retrieved, the more effective your search strategy will be. As a researcher, you will search many collections of information. A great deal of the information market and industry researchers need can be accessed through a portal or a database.

Portals have become very popular with the growth of the World Wide Web. Portal developers bring together on one Web site a variety of resources, including links to other Web sites, subject-oriented directories of relevant sources, and searchable databases. Alacra, described in more detail below and in Chapter Four, is a good example of a portal. Databases have long been the fundamental resource for the online searcher. These are highly organized collections of information labeled and categorized to facilitate retrieval. Databases are generally searched using a command language designed for that database.

Knowing your way around online databases is an important key to successful searching. Databases contain records that are tagged and indexed by fields. To better understand this, think of your bank check register as a database. Each check is a record. Each check has fields in which to place information, and each of these fields has a name or "tag." So the field tagged *Payee* is the place in the record where you will find information about who received the money accounted for by this check. The field tagged *Amount* contains information on how much money the Payee received. The field tagged *Date* contains information on what day and year the check was written.

Similarly, in an online database, you might find records organized into fields tagged *Title* or *Author* or *Journal Name*. These tags facilitate powerful and precise searching through the terabytes of information available online. The search software for each online database service is set up to allow searchers to target specific fields. For instance, you could search for all references to a certain author in the *Author* field and retrieve the list of articles written by that author. Each database has its own way of organizing its records—from the way it obtains its records, to the field names it uses, to the search interface design you see on the screen. Let's look at one example.

A great deal of information is revealed in the normal course of doing business, information that agencies and organizations then gather and make available to the public. For instance, information from vessel manifests and U.S. Customs data tapes on U.S. imports are gathered in the Port Import Export Reporting Service (PIERS),[9] produced by Commonwealth Business Media, Inc. Reporters throughout the country gather export information from bills of lading at all U.S. ports. The data is compiled, indexed, and put into an electronic format for online searching. Search fields include such things as *Country of Port of Origin, City of Exporter,* and *Company Name of Importer.* PIERS makes this data available for a fee through their Web site (see Figure 1-3) and through information aggregators such as LexisNexis[10] and Dialog.

Figure 1-3. Sample PIERS Record

```
IMPORTER: INTL TURBINE RESEARCH
PACHECO, CA

SHIPPER:
 DAN CONTROL ENGINEERING
 ODENSE, DENMARK,

NOTIFY NAME :

COMMODITY DETAILS
 MANIFEST COMMODITY DESCRIPTION: WIND TURBINE
 JOC STANDARD COMMODITY DESCRIPTION AND CODE
 7 DIGIT : TURBINES; WATER, PARTS, NOS (6607000)
 4 DIGIT : TURBINES, MISC (6607)
 HARMONIZED COMMODITY DESCRIPTION AND CODE
 6 DIGIT : NO DESC()
 4 DIGIT : ()

 DIRECTION : I SHIP LINE: MAER VESSEL : LOUIS MAERSK
 VOYAGE NUMBER : VESSEL CODE:
 ARRIVAL DATE AT U.S.PORT: 90/05/04
 U.S.PORT & CODE : OAKLAND (2811)
 FOREIGN PORT & CODE : BREMERHAVEN (42870)
 ORIGIN POINT & CODE : COPENHAGEN (40948)
 COUNTRY & CODE : (409)
 US FINAL PORT CODE: FOREIGN FINAL PORT CODE:
```

9. PIERS, Commonwealth Business Media, *http://www.piers.com.*
10. LexisNexis, at *http://www.lexisnexis.com,* is a division of Reed Elsevier. It provides business, legal, news, public records, tax, and regulatory information.

```
CARGO PARTICULARS
 PACKAGING QTY/TYPE : 64 PKG 4,237 CU FT
 CONFLAG: C CONTAINER QTY/SIZE: 3 ZZ
               6.00 TEU S 34.84 METRIC TONS
     $0 ESTIMATED VALUE THIS TRANSACTION
     BILL OF LADING: MANIFEST NUMBER:
 RECORD NUMBER : 08743792 AVAILABLE FROM PIERS AS OF:
90/06/08
```

Reprinted with the permission of Commonwealth Business Media, Inc.

The organizations that gather and publish information seem almost endless. Another database developer is a U.K. company called PJB Publications,[11] which uses reporters and telephone interviewers to gather progress reports on new pharmaceutical projects. Their Pharmaprojects[12] database contains indexed and searchable entries online, allowing those interested in the pharmaceutical project pipeline to monitor projects of interest.

The Gale Group,[13] which is a large company owned by Thomson, an even larger company, produces hundreds of reference works and databases. Very popular is the Gale database PROMT,[14] which covers companies, products, markets, and technologies for all industries. PROMT includes documents from trade and business journals, papers, business publications, newsletters, studies, analysts' reports, news releases, and annual reports.

Information Sources, a small private company, produces Soft-Base: Reviews, Companies, and Products.[15] This database covers products in the information technology industry, gathering information from business, computer, technical, trade, and consumer publications and adding value through indexing and abstracts.

---

11. PJB Publications, at *http://www.pjbpubs.com*, provides business news and information in the pharmaceutical, biotechnology, device and diagnostic, crop protection, animal health, and brewing industries.
12. Pharmaprojects is published by PJB Publications and reports on new pharmaceutical products in all stages of development.
13. Gale Group, at *http://www.gale.com*, is a business unit of Thomson Learning, a division of The Thomson Corporation. Gale is known for its intelligent organization of full-text newspaper and magazine articles.
14. PROMT is published by Gale Group and provides international coverage of companies, products, markets, and applied technologies for all industries.
15. Information Sources, Inc., at *http://www.searchsoftbase.com*, produces SoftBase: Reviews, Companies, and Products, which incorporates review, product, and company information designed to track emerging technology and the evolution of technologies into products and services.

When organizations such as PIERS, Gale Group, and Information Sources compile information, they add value to it by tagging fields, applying indexing, and putting it online to facilitate retrieval. These examples illustrate the range of organizations and agencies that collect, compile, organize, and disseminate information. Understanding the information-gathering industry can help the researcher plan an effective search strategy.

Move from the General to the Specific

Research sources vary in the depth of the information they offer. There are general, broad-based sources that tend to include a little bit of information on a lot of things (such as a Dun & Bradstreet company directory), and there are very specific sources that might contain in-depth information on fewer things (such as the 369-page directory that covers only companies providing library automation software). In developing your search strategy, plan to move from the general sources to the more specific. This is one of the most important principles of the research process: move from the general to the specific. Preliminary research in a general source should help you to get "the big picture" and to learn relevant market or industry jargon, acronyms, vocabulary, and keywords.

You probably remember this research principle from your writing courses in college, where many students learn the basic research strategy model. Student researchers might start with a general or subject-specific encyclopedia article to obtain background and an overview. They might then move to a search of magazine, newspaper, and journal indexes for more references to articles with information, different perspectives, and expert opinion. Often, the next step is to pursue details, facts, statistics, and verification by searching directories and statistical sources for further detail.

Market and industry research works pretty much the same way. Do the background work that it takes to understand the structure of the industry in question. Familiarize yourself with the jargon, keywords, industry association names, and key players. A good industry overview helps identify issues and trends and points you in the right direction. As necessary you can then move to subject-specific databases for articles and analysis. Even if your ultimate goal is only a specific piece of market data, background knowledge on the industry within which that market operates will help you put that bit of market data in context. This context often allows you to provide better, more useful information to your client.

STANDARD INDUSTRIAL CLASSIFICATIONS AND NORTH AMERICAN INDUSTRY CLASSIFICATION SYSTEM.   Doing the background work to begin an industry profile should include a look at the industry's Standard Industrial Classifications (SIC) codes or North American Industry Classification System (NAICS) codes. These codes reveal how the industry is classified and compared with other industries. The SIC codes were created by the federal government's Office of Management and Budget to provide "the statistical classification standard underlying all establishment-based Federal economic statistics classified by industry."[16] Many business and industry online databases include the SIC field in their index for precise searching by industry.

In 1997 the Office of Management and Budget published the newly developed NAICS codes. Developed in cooperation with Mexico and Canada, the NAICS codes "provide a consistent framework for the collection, analysis and dissemination of industrial statistics used by government policy analysts, by academics and researchers, by the business community, and by the public."[17] These codes give special attention to new and emerging industries, service industries in general, and industries engaged in the production of advanced technologies.[18] Many database creators add indexed fields for both SIC and NAICS codes, so searchers can use them to narrow or target search results.

For industry research, general sources include industry overviews from government sources such as the U.S. International Trade Administration.[19] Following the leads from an industry overview will direct your research to the appropriate subject-specific media, statistical, organization, and business sources for the next level of detail. As a follow-up to general sources, you can move to a more specific source, such as the subject-related govern-

---

16. *Standard Industrial Classification Manual,* 1987, Executive Office of the President, Office of Management and Budget, p. 3.

17. Economic Classification Policy Committee, *North American Industry Classification System* (Washington, D.C.: Office of Management and Budget, 1997), 1.

18. Ibid., p. 3.

19. The U.S. International Trade Administration provides information that helps U.S. businesses participate in the global marketplace, working through four units: Commercial Service, Trade Development (which provides industry sector specialists), Market Access and Compliance, and Import Administration.

ment agency (e.g., the U.S. Department of Energy or Transportation). For market research, begin with an aggregator[20] such as MarketResearch.com[21] and move to the more specific firm that focuses on your industry.

The following lists contain some key general sources for market and industry research. Table 1-3 lists key resources for researching specific markets.

GUIDES TO INDUSTRY RESOURCES

- Baker Library Industry Guides (*http://www.library.hbs.edu/industry*) lead researchers to excellent resources in thirteen industry sectors.
- Cole Library Rensselaer at Hartford (*http://www.rh.edu/library/industry/industry.htm*) points researchers to sources of information on twenty-three industries.
- Industry Information (*http://www.ita.doc.gov*) from the U.S. International Trade Administration provides industry statistics and data and also offers a guide to resources such as key trade associations, market research companies, and trade publications for selected industries.
- Valuation Resources (*http://www.valuationresources.com*) has created a guide to industry resources and reports, covering information available from trade associations, industry publications, and research firms.

PORTALS TO INDUSTRY OVERVIEWS

- Current Industrial Reports (*http://www.census.gov/ftp/pub/cir/www*) offers data on production and shipment of selected products, focusing on manufacturing of commodities such as textiles, chemicals, primary metals, computer and electronic components, industrial equipment aerospace equipment, and consumer goods.
- First Research Industry Profiles (*http://www.1stresearch.com*) offers more than 140 industry profiles, updated quarterly. The profiles cover recent developments and changes, business and credit risks, trends, opportunities, and financial benchmarking information.

---

20. Aggregators gather information from outside sources and generally make it available through one search interface. Dialog, LexisNexis, and Factiva are aggregators. They license information from hundreds of database developers and make it searchable through their own proprietary software. MarketResearch.com is an aggregator of market research reports, making them simultaneously searchable.

21. MarketResearch.com is a privately held company originally dounded in 1998 as Kalorama Information.

- Hoover's (*http://www.hoovers.com*) provides company information arranged by industry.
- Trade Association Research (*http://research.thomsonib.com*) offers industry-specific statistics, economic indicators, analysis, trends, and forecasts from 202 trade associations worldwide, covering every major industry.
- Standard & Poor's Industry Surveys (*http://www.netadvantage. standardandpoors.com*) cover fifty-two major U.S. industries and include data, forecasts, and trends.
- U.S. Business Reporter (*http://www.activemedia-guide.com*) is a private company that prepares and sells business information reports, including industry overviews.
- *U.S. Industry and Trade Outlook* is an annual publication from the U.S. International Trade Administration (Department of Commerce) and McGraw Hill. It contains industry overviews and descriptions and includes trends, forecasts, and references for further research. Efforts are under way to bring the latest edition to the Web.

GUIDE TO MARKET RESEARCH ON THE WEB

- KnowThis.com (*http://www.knowthis.com*) is a "marketing virtual library" edited by Paul Christ, Ph.D., associate professor in the Marketing Department of West Chester University of Pennsylvania. This site offers a directory of topic-specific marketing resources carefully chosen from the vast realm of the World Wide Web.

PORTALS TO MARKET RESEARCH REPORTS

- Alacra (*http://www.alacra.com*) provides access to market research reports from publishers such as Datamonitor, Freedonia, Multex Research, and Thomson Financial MarkIntel.
- ECNext Knowledge Center (*http://www.ecnext.com/commercial/ knowledgecenter.shtml*) has compiled 250,000 sources from five hundred publishers into a searchable and browseable collection of market intelligence.
- *Findex 2002* is an 850-page directory to global market research reports available in print from MarketResearch.com.

- MarketResearch.com (*http://www.marketresearch.com*) has gathered more than fifty thousand publications from more than 350 market research companies, including Aberdeen Group, Datamonitor, Economist Intelligence Unit, Frost & Sullivan, Jupitermedia Corporation, Kalorama, and *The Wall Street Transcript.*
- MindBranch (*http://www.mindbranch.com*) provides research in more than 130 industry segments from leading publishers such as Dun & Bradstreet, eBrain, Freedonia, Frost & Sullivan, Grey House, Parexel International, Sage Research, and The Yankee Group.
- OneSource (*http://www.onesource.com*) provides industry and market information from sources including the *Financial Times,* ProQuest, Phillips, Thomson Gale's Business & Industry database, Freedonia, and *U.S. Industry and Trade Outlook.*
- Profound (*http://www.profound.com*) provides global market research, company information, country data, and analysts' reports.
- Thomson Research (*http://research.thomsonib.com*) is very strong for company information but also provides access to market research from MarkIntel, Datamonitor, IDC, Gartner, Espicom, and TowerGroup.

DATABASES CONTAINING MARKET INFORMATION

- ABI/Inform from ProQuest (*http://www.umi.com*)
- Business & Industry from Thomson's Gale Group (*http://www.galegroup.com*)
- PROMT from Thomson's Gale Group (*http://www.galegroup.com*)
- Trade & Industry from Thomson's Gale Group (*http://www.galegroup.com*)
- Wilson Business Abstracts from the H.W. Wilson Company (*http://www.hwwilson.com*)

Table 1-3. Market-Specific Sources

MARKET	SOURCES
All	Business Monitor International, Global Industry Analysts
Agriculture	Market and Business Development, IBISWorld, Harris InfoSource, Icon Group International, Key Note Publications, Euromonitor International, Market Share Reporter

Table 1-3. Market-Specific Sources (cont.)

MARKET	SOURCES
Automotive	Auto Business, Chemquest, Datamonitor, Diagonal Reports, Economist Intelligence Unit, IAL Consultants, IMR Research, J.D. Power, Market Share Reporter, MIRA Reports, Reuters Business Insight
Biotechnology	Business Communications Company, CenterWatch, Datamonitor, Decision Resources, Frost & Sullivan, IAL Consultants, PJB Publications, POV Incorporated, Theta Reports
Broadcasting, Media	Baskerville Communications, Communications Industry Researchers, Goulden Reports, Information Gatekeepers, Primary Research Group, Screen Digest, SCRI International, Simba Information, SMI Newsletters, Veronis, Suhler & Associates
Chemicals	BRG Townsend, Business Communications Company, Business Trend Analysts, Economist Intelligence Unit, Freedonia Group, Frost & Sullivan, Gobi International, IAL Consultants, Informa Global, Richard K. Miller & Associates, SRI Consulting
Computers and Information Technology	Aberdeen Group, AMI Partners, AMR Research, Bloor Research, Communications Industry Researchers, Electronic Trend Publications, Faulkner Information Services, GartnerGroup's Dataquest, Giga Information Group, IntelliQuest, International Data Corporation, Jupiter Communications, Jupiter Media Metrix, META Group, PAC Group, Red Herring Research, Sageza, Semico Research, SRI Consulting, Strategy Analytics, Summit Strategies, Technical Insights, Wintergreen Research, Yankee Group, Zona Research
Construction, Real Estate	BRG Townsend, Leading Edge Reports, Market Share Reporter
Consumer Goods	AC Nielsen, Beverage Marketing Corp., Business Trend Analysts, Datamonitor, IMR Research, The Information Network, J.D. Power, Euromonitor Major Market Profiles, Mediamark Research, Packaged Facts, RoperASW, Snapshots International
E-Commerce	ActivMedia Research, AMR Research, Datamonitor, eMarketer, Forrester, IDC, Reuters Business Insight
Electrical and Electronics	Business Trend Analysts, Decision Resources, Electronic Trend Publications, Euromonitor, Faulkner Information Services, Forecast International, Frost & Sullivan, Gobi International, Goulden Reports, Semico Research Corp., Simba Information, SRI Consulting, Strategy Analytics, Technical Insights

Table 1-3. Market-Specific Sources (*cont.*)

MARKET	SOURCES
Finance, Accounting, Banking, Insurance	Cerulli Associates, Datamonitor, eMarketer, Lafferty Publications, Market Share Reporter, Reuters Business Insight, Thomson Financial, TowerGroup
Food and Beverage	ACNielsen, Beverage Marketing, Business Trend Analysts, FIND/SVP, Frost & Sullivan, Leatherhead Food Research, Packaged Facts, Specialists in Business Information
Furniture, Wood Products	AKTRIN Furniture Research, Verdict Research
Health and Beauty Aids, Packaged Goods, Paper Products	ACNielsen, Corporate Intelligence on Retail, Diagonal Reports, Economist Intelligence Unit, Euromonitor Major Market Profiles, IMR Research, Packaged Facts, Verdict Research
Health Care	Business Communications Company, Datamonitor, Decision Resources, Freedonia Group, Frost & Sullivan, IAL Consultants, Informa Global Pharmaceuticals & Healthcare, Marketdata Enterprises, Medical Strategic Planning, POV Incorporated, Theta Reports, Wintergreen Research
Heavy Industry	Freedonia Group, Global Industry Analysts, Gobi International, IBISWorld, Impact Market Consultants
Metals and Minerals	Roskill
Niche Industries (such as fertility clinics/adoption agencies, carpet cleaning, stress management programs and products, child care, and funeral homes)	Marketdata Enterprises
Oil, Petrochemicals, Energy, and Utilities	Forecast International/DMS, Goulden Reports, Reuters Business Insight, Richard K. Miller & Associates, SRI Consulting, Thomson Financial
Pharmaceuticals, Medical Devices, and Diagnostics	CenterWatch, Datamonitor, Decision Resources, Espicom Business Intelligence, Euromonitor, IAL Consultants, IMS Health Publications, Kalorama Information, Medical Data International, Medical Strategic Planning, Nicholas Hall & Company, PJB Publications, POV Incorporated, Reuters Business Insight, SMG Marketing Group, Theta Reports
Plastics	BRG Townsend, Global Industry Analysts, Gobi International
Retail	Corporate Intelligence on Retail, eMarketer, Euromonitor, FIND/SVP, Market Share Reporter, Planet Retail, Seymour-Cooke Food Research International, Verdict Research
Service Industries	TowerGroup, Worldwide Videotex, Gardner Publications, Global Advertising Strategies

Table 1-3. Market-Specific Sources (*cont.*)

MARKET	SOURCES
Technology	Aberdeen Group, Baskerville Communications, Business Trend Analysts, Cahners, Datamonitor, eMarketer, Espicom Business Intelligence, Frost & Sullivan, IDC, SRI Consulting, Worldwide Videotex, Yankee Group
Telecommunications	Baskerville Communications, Cahners, Communications Industry Researchers, Datamonitor, Decision Resources, Economist Intelligence Unit, EIU Pyramid Research Newsletters, Electronics International Reports, Espicom Business Intelligence, Fuji-Keizai USA, GartnerGroup's Dataquest, Gobi International, Goulden Reports, IDATE, Information Gatekeepers Newsletters, Insight Research Corporation, Jupiter Communications, Jupiter Media Metrix, Paul Budde Communications, Reuters Business Insight, Semico Research, Simba Information, SRI Consulting, Strategis Group, Strategy Analytics, Technical Insights, Telecommunications Reports International, Warren Publishing, Wintergreen Research, World Information Technologies
Transportation (including aerospace, aircraft, and shipping)	Drewry Shipping Consultants, Forecast International/DMS, Freedonia Group, Jane's Information, J.D. Power, SMI Newsletters, Thomson Financial
Travel, Tourism, Leisure, and Recreation	Economist Intelligence Unit, J.D. Power, Specialists in Business Information
Waste Management	Business Communications Company, FIND/SVP, IAL Consultants, Leading Edge Reports, Market Strategy Group, Richard K. Miller & Associates

TYPES OF INFORMATION

Information comes from a multitude of sources and generally can be characterized as proprietary (protected and shared), public (fee based and free), primary, and secondary. The information industry has its structure, technology, suppliers, distributors, customers, products, and price structure, just as any other industry does. By understanding the variety of online information products and their distribution systems, the researcher is in a better position to identify the source most likely to have the desired information. Understanding the types of information facilitates the development of an effective search strategy. Figure 1-4 illustrates the various types of information.

Figure I-4. Types of Information

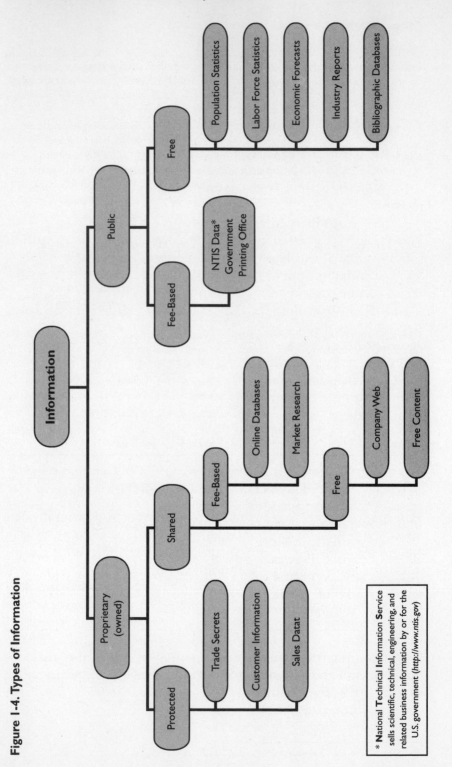

Proprietary vs. Public

Proprietary information is owned or protected in some way, and it may be inaccessible if it is closely guarded or kept secret by the owner. Individual companies generally control their internal information carefully. For instance, certain market data such as internal sales data or customer profiles should be available internally to a company's market research department but are not likely to be available to outside researchers. The trade secret behind the formula for Coca-Cola is a good example of proprietary information that you can assume is not available through ethical research methods.

Some proprietary information is shared with the public. This information is furnished by people and businesses with the understanding that it will likely be published and generally available. Such information might be found in a directory, on a company Web site, in a press release, or in a book or journal.

Public information comes from fulfillment of government requirements to file records or documents or from government agencies that gather and disseminate information. Public information is generally available for free from the agency that collected or produced it. Occasionally a fee is required to cover the costs of printing or distribution.

ETHICAL STANDARDS FOR RESEARCHERS

Information professionals and competitive-intelligence researchers are all governed by a code of ethics. These codes guide the researcher in conducting legal and ethical research for the good of the profession and with respect for the clients and subjects of research.

The Association of Independent Information Professionals Code of Ethical Business Practices can be found on the AIIP Web site (*http://www.aiip.org*), and the Society of Competitive Intelligence Professionals Code of Ethics can be found on the SCIP Web site (*http://www.scip.org*).

"Those records maintained by government agencies that are open without restriction to public inspection, either by statute or by tradition"[22] are considered public records. *Black's Law Dictionary* further illuminates public records as "those records which a

---

22. Burwell, *Online Competitive Intelligence*, 97.

governmental unit is required by law to keep or which it is necessary to keep in discharge of duties imposed by law."[23] Filings submitted to governmental agencies and records kept by governmental agencies are, for the most part, public. Public records include everything from building plans filed at the county land-use office to corporate registrations filed at the secretary of state's office.

For the purposes of this book, think of public records as those coming from sources at all levels of government. Organizations and agencies are often required to file reports or records of transactions with the appropriate governmental regulating agency. Similarly, governmental agencies gather and compile information in accordance with some law or for their own purposes and make it available to the public. Examples include the decennial census of the population, labor and economic statistics, agricultural census data, and public health data. Government employees within the gathering agency compile reports from the raw data. These reports are often published and posted on the Internet, distributed to local libraries for their government documents collections, or sold through the Government Printing Office.[24] The tables and charts created as a result of the decennial census, for instance, can be accessed through computer tapes, downloadable files, and printed reports. The U.S. Census Bureau (*http://www.census.gov*) offers one of the most comprehensive and information-intensive Web sites in existence. This is the kind of public records information that proves invaluable to the market and industry researcher.

There are also companies in the business of gathering and selling information. Some conduct primary research, others compile information from secondary sources (see "Primary vs. Secondary"), and others offer a combination of both. They own and protect the information but make it available for a fee through online information aggregators, Web sites, CD-ROMs, or print publications. PIERS, which as we've seen compiles import and export data, exemplifies the companies that compile information from primary sources, adding value through organization and indexing. PJB Publications, Information Sources, and

---

23. Henry Campbell Black, *Black's Law Dictionary,* 6th ed. (St. Paul, Minn.: West, 1990), 1231.
24. The Government Printing Office (GPO) is part of the legislative branch of the federal government. The Public Printer, who serves as the GPO's chief officer, is nominated by the president and confirmed by the Senate. The GPO operates under the authority of the public printing and documents chapters of Title 44 of the U.S. Code.

Gale Group, also mentioned earlier, are a few of the companies that gather, compile, and index information from secondary sources for distribution.

Primary vs. Secondary

Primary research involves going to "the source" for information—primary sources being just that, the first or primary source, or where the data or information originates. Thus primary sources include interviews, surveys, and focus groups held to obtain information directly from affected parties. Secondary research involves "secondhand," previously published information—analyses, descriptions, and opinions given in response to primary source material by people not directly involved. Secondary sources can include newspaper and magazine articles, trade journal articles, newsletters, technical analyses, brokerage reports, and all other forms of information that interpret or otherwise "massage" data or events. In short, primary source materials are firsthand accounts of something, and secondary source materials reveal people's perspectives about a fact or event.

Conventional wisdom indicates that a market researcher begins with secondary research and fills in the missing pieces with primary research. For comprehensive market research studies, however, it is common to assume that secondary and primary market research will go on simultaneously and in sort of a "dialog" as answers come together.

Primary research is required when you need specific quantitative or qualitative information on a target market. Examples of questions needing primary quantitative market research include the following:

- What kind of music do the people who visit my coffee shop prefer to listen to?
- How many visitors to the San Diego Zoo arrive there by public transportation?
- How many users of personal digital assistants (Palm Pilots, for example) would prefer a keyboard to the "graffiti" style of data entry?

Examples of questions needing primary qualitative research include these:

- How satisfied might current pantyhose wearers be with the look and feel of a newly developed brand?

- Knowing that customers are having trouble using a technically advanced copy machine, what does the machine/user interaction look like?
- Can consumers taste any difference between regular cheddar cheese and the new, low-fat cheddar cheese?

Do market/industry researchers engaged in searching secondary sources online ever conduct primary research? Generally, no. Although conducting primary research is a huge part of the market/industry research profession, most online researchers rely on published sources. If extensive primary research is required, it is common to contract with a primary research firm to conduct the survey or hold a focus group. It is not unusual, however, for an online researcher to make a phone call to verify data or seek opinions and further information from experts. Readers will notice in Chapter Three, Problems and Solutions, that researchers often use a combination of secondary and primary research to meet an information need. Industry, media, and market experts are an important source of information and can offer useful, specialized information not available online. For an in-depth understanding of interviewing techniques, read *Super Searchers Go to the Source* [25] by Riva Sacks. The tips in this book apply even when the project requires only one interview, especially if the interview subject has a unique perspective on the topic.

Researchers can also take advantage of information from primary sources by searching for copies of speeches, letters to stockholders, results from association surveys, and data from syndicated data sources. Company CEOs or presidents make speeches directed at stockholders or analysts that can sometimes be downloaded from the Internet or read in the company's annual report. They also write letters to the stockholders that are included in the annual report. Associations commonly conduct surveys and compile statistics about members. For example, the American Medical Association[26] publishes a series of books containing detailed demographic information on member specialties, incomes, education, type of practice, age, geographic location, and size of practice. The Special Libraries Association[27] publishes an annual salary survey of its members.

---

25. Risa Sacks, Super Searchers Go to the Source: The Interviewing
26. The Web site of the American Medical Association can be found at *http://www. ama-assn.org.*
27. The Web site of the Special Libraries Association can be found at *http://www.sla.org.*

No matter what, researchers seeking a comprehensive look at a topic or issue will want to consult a wide variety of sources. This strategy offers the opportunity to verify and check facts, to assimilate a variety of viewpoints, and to uncover valuable details. Moving from the general to the specific, the researcher can drill down for the data that is needed while building an accurate picture of the market or industry. For a detailed examination of secondary sources see Chapter Four and Appendix 1.

Fee vs. Free

Another way to understand information is to distinguish between commercial online database services and free, open Web sources. Each has its place and its function, but how do you know which to use and when?

For market and industry researchers, important sources of information include trade associations, government agencies, magazines and journals, and market research reports. Obtaining information from these sources involves at least two steps: (1) determining the source in which the information resides and (2) obtaining access to that information. Given the widely diffuse information environment, there are times when it is possible to search for free and to obtain the information for free. Then there are times when searching is free, but obtaining the information requires a fee. Of course sometimes searching and obtaining the information both incur a cost. How does this work, and how should the searcher manage it?

First let's look at some of the advantages and disadvantages of the various types of sources.

TRADE ASSOCIATIONS AND GOVERNMENT AGENCIES.   The Web is a primary conduit for information from trade associations and government agencies. The organization's Web site is often the first place to look for background, overviews, statistics, and reports. If you do not know the name of the relevant trade associations, consult an online database such as Gale's *Encyclopedia of Associations,* available on Dialog as File 114 and on LexisNexis as ENCASSC. You can also search the American Society of Association Executives Web site (*http://www.asaenet.org*) for free, but this source is not as comprehensive as the *Encyclopedia of Associations.*

Using a search engine to search the open Web can sometimes uncover links to trade associations. Or, to simultaneously search for publications across several trade associations, access Trade Association Research through Thomson Research (*http://research. thomsonib.com*).

If you think a government agency might provide useful information, but do not know which one to research, there are a couple of strategies to try. One is to search FirstGov (*http://firstgov.gov*) for federal government information, or State and Local Government on the Net (*http://www.statelocalgov.net/index.cfm*) for appropriate (state or local) jurisdictional Web sites. Because government Web sites can be so large, be prepared to use the site's own search engine, or the Google toolbar search-within-site capability to track down the appropriate Web pages within the site.

Table 1-4. Trade Associations and Government Agencies

	COSTS TO SEARCH	COSTS TO VIEW	ADVANTAGES (+) AND DISADVANTAGES (–)
Trade Association Web sites	Free (unless membership is required)	Free for most items	+ Access sometimes restricted to members only + Excellent source of information otherwise unavailable + Telephone assistance and experts often available
Government Agencies	Free	Free	+/– Reliable information, but not always current – Sometimes challenging to locate appropriate agency

TRADE MAGAZINES, JOURNALS, AND NEWS SOURCES. Searching the open and free Web is rarely a good option when you need magazine and journal articles. An indexed database, whether you go through an online database service or a library, will virtually always offer better results. Although free to access, collections such as Findarticles.com have limitations, because their archives and titles are limited. You get what you pay for when it comes to searching magazines, journals, newsletters, trade publications, and news sources. Unless you know which publication you want to search, it is more cost-effective to use a value-added database such as PROMT or ProQuest,[28] or an aggregator such as Factiva.

---

28. ProQuest Information and Learning, at *http://www.proquest.com*, provides access to full-text information back to 1986.

Searching the commercial fee-based services is a significant time-saving strategy. By using an online database service you can search hundreds of publications at once. For example, is the best analysis of American Airlines' position in its industry in *Aviation Week & Space Technology,* the *New York Times,* the *Wall Street Journal,* the *Los Angeles Times,* or the *Dallas Morning News*? Unless you know, you will need to search each publication individually—or you can search them all at once on Factiva. Although the current issue of many publications is available for free on the Web, increasingly publishers charge for access to archival issues. Additionally, most publication-specific sites have rudimentary search capabilities. You may, therefore, waste significant time sorting through dozens of articles on dozens of Web sites of only marginal interest.

One could also ask, "Why should I pay for a subscription to an online database service when I can find thousands of documents by searching Yahoo or Google?" The answer is because your client needs reliable information on which to base an important decision. Web search engines do not discriminate—unless they accept fees for listings and placement in results lists. You may find articles from reputable publications and government documents through a search of the Web, but you will also find documents from special interest groups, undergraduate papers, individual opinions, and carefully disguised advertising.

Although everything published is not necessarily true, editors of reputable publications do make an effort to check the accuracy of articles submitted to them. For much of the material on the Web there are no editors. You will find terrific, well-researched articles written by people with academic credentials with no discernable date. The article may be so old that the conclusions are no longer valid. You will find papers presented at conferences with no indication of the sponsor or date of the conference. Before you let a client rely on any information you gather, you must be able to tell the client who wrote the article, when they wrote it, and why they wrote it. You do not want an investment decision, for example, to be based on the opinions of a biased salesperson whose only goal is to sell a new stock issue.

Table 1-5. Trade Magazines, Journals, and News Sources

	COSTS TO SEARCH	COSTS TO VIEW	ADVANTAGES (+) AND DISADVANTAGES (−)
Publisher's Web Site	Free	Sometimes free, but more commonly by subscription or per article	− Time consuming, since sites can be searched only one by one − User needs to know which site to search − Site's search engines are often inefficient and limited
Open Web via search engine such as HotBot[29]	Free	Free	− Most content in the open Web is not indexed − No assurance of quality
Aggregator of open Web such as Findarticles[30]	Free	Free	− Limited archives (Findarticles goes back to only 1998) + More targeted than an open Web search + Broad subject coverage − Limited number of publications
Commercial aggregator such as Dialog and LexisNexis	Fee	Varies, but there will virtually always be some cost	+ Ability to search multiple sources simultaneously + Full indexing, facilitates precision and good recall − Can require training and practice for effective searches
Commercial aggregator such as Factiva[31]	Free	Always a fee	+ Ability to search multiple publications simultaneously + Full indexing facilitates precision and recall + No costs incurred until articles are downloaded
Public library databases	Free	Free	− Access generally restricted to library cardholders − Database availability changes with budgets + Can often be accessed remotely
Academic library databases	Free	Free	+ Wide variety of quality databases − Must access from on-site if not faculty, staff, or student

---

29. Hotbot, a Lycos company at *http://www.hotbot.com*, offers Internet searching through Inktomi, Teoma, Google, and Fast.

30. Findarticles.com is an archive of articles developed by collaboration between Look-Smart and Gale. It dates back to 1998 and offers articles from three hundred magazines.

31. Factiva, at *http://factiva.com*, is a joint venture of Dow Jones and Reuters providing global news and business information.

MARKET RESEARCH REPORTS. The open Web would be a good place to start when looking for market research reports only if you are feeling very lucky. A Web search might turn up the occasional commentary or quote from a market research report, but not the report itself. Remember, market researchers spend substantial sums to create these reports in order to sell them at a profit to interested parties. Little, if any, current information from a market research report is likely to be available for free.

If you know who the publisher is and want to obtain a specific report, the publisher's Web site can serve as a good starting place. In fact, the only way to access some information is through the publisher. The publisher may also be the only source if you need a recently released report. To protect their products, some publishers embargo them so that they do not go out to the aggregators until sixty to ninety days after being published. Note, however, that occasionally some interesting facts and figures can be gleaned from the press release announcing the report's availability.

Recent additions to the market research landscape are Web-based aggregators such as MarketResearch.com, MindBranch,[32] and the Thomson Research site. These information suppliers offer content on a variety of subjects and from a variety of publishers, allowing free searching, subject directories, and the opportunity to purchase information by the page or section. It is important to remember that no one source is going to have everything, so be prepared to search these sites as well as others. Even if some reports can be obtained in more than one of your sources, producing an "overlap," remember that individual suppliers have individual embargo periods and specific report availability. Having multiple sources is essential to provide good coverage of published market research reports.

The market research reports collected and made available by value-added aggregators such as Dialog and Profound offer yet another access point for this type of information. These aggregators offer very broad, deep coverage with powerful search capabilities that can assist the researcher in targeting specific bits of information or combinations of search criteria. Although the costs can be significant, the material is often of high value, since it may not be available elsewhere.

---

32. MindBranch, Inc., at *http://www.mindbranch.com*, publishes market research reports online from approximately 130 sources.

Table 1-6. Market Research Reports

	COSTS TO SEARCH	COSTS TO VIEW	ADVANTAGES (+) AND DISADVANTAGES (−)
Publisher's Web site	Free	Fee	+ Quick and generally easy to search − User needs to know which publisher to search − Reports not always available "by the slice"
Open Web via search engine (e.g., Google)	Free	Free	− Most market research is not going to turn up in a free search of the open Web − Results retrieved (if any) not generally vetted and may be unreliable
Web aggregator such as Thomson Research or MarketResearch. com (for a more complete list, see Table 1-3)	Free	Fee	+ Ability to search multiple publishers reports simultaneously + User can browse directories by subject + Generally available "by the slice"
Commercial aggregator such as Dialog or Profound[33]	Fee	Fee	+ Wide selection of reputable reports + Contain material not available elsewhere + Available "by the slice" + Can search multiple sources simultaneously

Evaluating Web Sources

It is extremely important to you and to your client that you use credible sources with reliable information. When you search the fee-based databases from major vendors, you have some assurance that the information has been compiled from credible sources. Even so, you will want to check multiple sources to verify what you find. In the case of Web sources, it gets more complicated. On the open Web, no one is vetting the information for you in advance.

---

33. Profound, at *http://www.profound.com,* is a product of The Dialog Corporation offering market research, company reports, country data, and brokerage analysts' reports.

You, the user, must assume that responsibility. The key axiom to employ here is "know your source." When assessing Web sources, you must determine the following:

- Who sponsors the Web site? This will tell you something about who paid for the information you find there, and this in turn can tell you something about any potential biases.
- Who wrote the information? The author should have some knowledge or credibility in the subject area. For example, the author could be a journalist specializing in the industry or market, an academic who teaches and studies that area, or a corporate executive who works in the industry. In each case the author is likely to have some knowledge of the subject. But the author can just as easily be a disgruntled employee with an ax to grind, so it's best to do a little research before you take anyone's word for it.
- When was it written? Timing is everything, and if currency matters, you will need to know when the material was written and when it was last updated.

Most college and university Web sites offer tutorials and checklists to help you evaluate Web sites. Examples include sites published by Cornell University (*http://www.library.cornell.edu/okuref/research/webeval.html*), Widener University (*http://www2.widener.edu/Wolfgram-Memorial-Library/webevaluation/webeval.htm*), and University of North Carolina–Chapel Hill (*http://www.unc.edu/cit/guides/irg-49.html*). For a detailed look at evaluating information on the Web, consult *Web of Deception: Misinformation on the Internet*,[34] edited by Anne Mintz.

IMPLEMENTING THE SEARCH

Once you've chosen your information source, it's time to figure out how to search that source for the information you need. For online sources, this means constructing an effective search statement.

Regardless of how you will perform the search, you must have a clear and concise statement that describes the question. You must start out with a sentence, not just keywords. A sentence indicates the relationship between the keywords, a critical element in

---

34. Anne P. Mintz, *Web of Deception: Misinformation on the Internet* (Medford, N.J.: Information Today, 2002).

developing a search strategy and in evaluating what you retrieve. If your client gives you keywords, write them down, and then ask your client to describe what he or she needs in complete sentences.

There are two ways to construct a search statement: using natural language or using basic search syntax. Which you select depends on the nature of your question and on the search engine you will be using.

Natural Language

Search engines for the free Web use sophisticated algorithms to determine what words in a search statement are important, what possible synonyms exist for those words, and which of the thousands of potential documents on the Web contain information related to the search statement. The result of a Web search is a list of sites ranked by relevance. The sites with the best information, as calculated by the search engine, are listed at the top. If the search engine is operating properly, you should need to review only a page or two of sites, not the thousands that are actually retrieved by a search.

For many search engines, searchers must use natural language search statements. In practice, natural language is not exactly the way people speak. Most search engines ignore prepositions, conjunctions, and other small words such as "how" and "why" that may be key elements in your description of the question. You may be able to force the search engine to see an important word by using a plus sign (+) before it, but this sometimes makes the search engine place too much importance on these connector words and can skew the results. As a general rule, natural language search statements should contain all the significant words from your description of the research question. Word order does have an effect, so place the most important concepts at the beginning of your search statement.

One of the weaknesses of natural language search engines is that they do not accommodate synonyms. Even if you are not sure whether an industry's direction would be described as "trends," "forecasts," or "future," you must still select only one. If you use all three, the search engine will look for documents containing all three words. The search engine may be programmed to know that "trends" and "forecasts" are closely related terms, but it may give priority to the term you actually use. To make sure you get the greatest number of possible hits, you must repeat the search using another search term.

Let's look at an example showing how different terms and word order affect a search on Google, Teoma,[35] and AlltheWeb.[36] The client wants to know about trends in the wearable microdisplay industry. At this point, the client simply needs an overview to see what technologies and companies are involved.

Phrasing the request as a question, we ask, "What are the trends in the wearable microdisplay industry?" The best communication with the Web search engine will be unambiguous keywords. "Trends," "wearable," and "microdisplay" all have synonyms, however, so let's see how different word choices affect the results. Table 1-7 illustrates synonyms from which to choose in creating a search string.

Table I-7. Synonyms for Sample Search Terms

INITIAL TERM	SYNONYMS
Trends	Forecasts
	Industry overview
Wearable	Near to eye
	Head mounted
Microdisplay	Screen

From these keywords, we develop three search strings:

- Search String A: *trends wearable microdisplay*
- Search String B: *forecast wearable microdisplay*
- Search String C: *"industry overview" wearable display*

Screen shots from Google show that each search returned entirely different results within the first page of hits. Search String A returned a promising hit in number two on the list (see Figure 1-5). From the United States Display Consortium (USDC), it addresses "bring to eye designs" and "near eye display." These could serve as additional synonyms, if we need them. The USDC's mission is to be a "neutral forum," so we conclude that it is a reliable, unbiased source.

From Search String B, the third hit looks pretty good (see Figure 1-6). It is a directory page assembled by a professor at the University of Ghent in Belgium. Search String C produced only three hits (see Figure 1-7). Two are from commercial Web sites and

---

35. Teoma, at *http://www.teoma.com*, was acquired by Ask Jeeves, Inc. in September 2001. It is a search engine built on subject specific communities.
36. AlltheWeb, at www.alltheweb.com, comes from Fast Search & Transfer, at *http://www.fastsearch.com*.

one is from an academic institution. One of the commercial sites, an industry overview from a venture capital site, offers some useful information. The document on the academic site also offers some objective information about the industry, and the academic connection gives it a measure of reliability.

Searching on Teoma with the same search strings yielded different results. This time the University of Ghent site came up second on the list using Search String A. On AlltheWeb, Search String B yielded much better results than Search String A, with two hits from a manufacturer's Web site at the top, and the Ghent professor's page coming in third. The first two were useful, keeping in mind the natural bias of a product manufacturer. With Search String A, the first two hits were for a commercial search service that would like to help you monitor the microdisplay market, and for this search those were not particularly helpful.

Figure 1-5. Google Search: *trends wearable microdisplay*

Trends de **wearable** computer
... PC Mobiel nummer 01-1999. **Trends** de **wearable** computer. ... De '**wearable**' PC:
links de headset met de **microdisplay** en rechts de TrackPoint. ...
www.fnl.nl/pcmobiel/mobielarchief/ 1999/01/pcm_1999_01_27.htm - 24k - Cached - Similar pages

[PDF]DISPLAY **TRENDS** DISPLAY **TRENDS**
File Format: PDF/Adobe Acrobat - View as HTML
DISPLAY **TRENDS** DISPLAY **TRENDS** IN THIS ISSUE: Introduction ... bring to eye designs or
wearable headsets ... Clearly, **microdisplay** near eye displays offer the only path ...
www.usdc.org/newsroom/newsletters_downloads/ displaytrends2.PDF - Similar pages

Wearable Computers and their Usage
... ARM processors; **Wearable** links; **Wearable** Computing **Trends**; ... Liteeye **Microdisplay** Systems;
eShades HMD; Canon display; ... Linux **wearable** video grabber; HMD report; Virtual ...
www.iptel-now.de/PROJECTS/WEARABLE/wearable.html - 57k - Cached - Similar pages

Wearable Computing
... Picard Industries; Pomona Electronics; Power **Trends**; Ramsey Electronics; ... TekGear
- Products for **wearable** computing; The **MicroDisplay** Corporation; Virtual ...
cliffleong.com/links/wearable.html - 24k - Nov. 17, 2002 - Cached - Similar pages

[PDF]COMPANY RELEASE eMagin and Virtual Vision Demonstrate OLED- ...
File Format: PDF/Adobe Acrobat - View as HTML
... emitting diode (OLED) on silicon **microdisplay** and proprietary ... 8, 2001, Gartner analysts
named **wearable** computers as ... four key emerging technology **trends** for the ...
www.emagin.com/pressreleases/wpr111501.pdf - Similar pages

Reprinted with the permission of Google, Inc.

Figure 1-6. Google Search String: *forecast wearable microdisplay*

<u>AMEX EMA Press Release</u>
... of the OLED device for **microdisplay** applications. ... use in future products, such as **wearable** computers and ... worldwide OLED display market is **forecast** to increase ...
www.emagin com/pressreleases/prcov.htm - 8k - <u>Cached</u> - <u>Similar pages</u>

   <u>AMEX EMA Press Release</u>
   ... are driving a high-growth **forecast** for this ... on its campus in East Fishkill, NY **Wearable** and rrobile ... system design and full-custom **microdisplay** system facilities ...
   www.emagin.com/pressreleases/prkodk.htm - 10k - <u>Cached</u> - <u>Similar pages</u>
   [<u>More results from www.emagin.com</u>]

<u>The **Microdisplay** Page</u>
... conference will focus on the technologies behind **wearable** computing and ... number of interesting reports, like the **Microdisplay** Module **Forecast** Report and ...
Description: Guide to **microdisplay** development information.
Category: Ccmputers > Hardware > Systems > Wearables
www.elis.rug ac.be/ELISgroups/tfcg/microdis/ - 67k - Nov. 17, 2002 - <u>Cached</u> - <u>Similar pages</u>

[PDF]<u>Insight Media Catalog-4-02</u>
File Format: PDF/Adobe Acrobat
... cameras, visualization/simulation procucts, 3D and **wearable** PC's ... System Integration (section only) $ 995 2001 **Microdisplay** Module **Forecast** Report Insight ...
www.insightmedia.info/ Insight%20Media%20Catalog-4-02.pdf - <u>Simi ar pages</u>

Reprinted with the permission of Google, Inc.

Figure 1-7. Google Search String: *"industry overview" wearable microdisplay*

<u>TFS</u>
... **Industry Overview**. ... Potential near-term **microdisplay** applications include use in office projection ... pagers, and PDAs as well as in **wearable** computing equipmen: ...
www.smallcapreview.com/tfs.htm - 84k - <u>Cached</u> - <u>Similar pages</u>

[PDF]<u>Copyright</u>
File Format: PDF/Adobe Acrobat - <u>View as HTML</u>
... Before the Forum, all participants receive the **industry overview** and white papers that provide market and technical background on the techno ogy areas to be ...
cosmos.ot.buffalo.edu/aac/aac-final.PDF - <u>Similar pages</u>

<u>Bandwidth Market, Ltd. -- SEC Filings</u>
... **INDUSTRY OVERVIEW** Liquid Crystal Displays Prior to the ... and head mounted displays or **wearable** computers XGA ... markets for our LCoS **microdisplay** products will be ...
www.bandwidthmarket.com/resources/sec:Three-Five_Systems,_Inc/ 0000950153-01-500104.txt - 101k

Reprinted with the permission of Google, Inc.

When you fail to find useful material through a Web search engine, there are several possible explanations:

1. You did not use the right combination of search terms.
2. You did not use the search terms in the correct order.
3. You did not use the right search engine.
4. None of the search engines crawled the site with the information you need. (The process the search engines employ to find and index Web sites is called crawling).
5. The information is not available on the free or open Web.

Basic Search Syntax

Using the tools of basic search syntax, the researcher has the opportunity to tell the computer exactly what to look for and how to look for it.

The most commonly used tools are Boolean logic, truncation, proximity operators, and nesting. Boolean operators (AND, OR, and NOT) link terms to define how the computer will look for the terms you have used.

AND means that all terms linked using AND must appear in the document retrieved.

OR means that as long as either term is there, the document will be retrieved.

NOT means that documents containing that particular term should *not* be retrieved.

So for instance a search for *price AND toothpaste* will retrieve documents containing both the word "price" and the word "toothpaste."

Truncation helps account for the various endings of a word root, so that the searcher can broaden a search by truncating selected terms. A search for *pric? AND toothpaste* would retrieve documents containing the word "toothpaste" as well as variations on "price," including "pricing" and "prices." The truncation symbol varies according to the database:

Database	Truncation Symbol
Factiva	$
Dialog	?
LexisNexis	!
PubMed	*

Proximity operators allow the searcher to limit the results to documents where the selected terms are near each other in some way. The search string *price w/3 toothpaste* would find documents in which "price" was within three words of "toothpaste," regardless of word order. "Market share" is an example of a term that benefits from using proximity operators, since *market w/5 share* would retrieve documents containing "market share" as well as those containing "share of the market." As with truncation symbols, proximity operators vary, depending upon the search service you are using, so check the help screens.

Nesting is simply a way to help the computer search for terms in the order you specify. A nested search string resembles an algebraic expression. Let's examine this search statement:

market w/5 share and (toothpaste OR tooth powder OR dentifrice)

The parentheses tells the computer to look for records that contain the word "toothpaste," or the phrase "tooth powder," or the word "dentifrice," then to examine that set of records and limit it to those that also contain the word "market" within five words of "share."

WHICH SERVICES DO YOU REALLY NEED?

Selecting the sources you need access to might be a straightforward process. But selecting the services you will use to access those sources can be a daunting task. Again, it helps to know your sources.

A number of special-purpose online database services provide particular types of information on markets and industry. For example, MarketResearch.com and MindBranch supply market research reports from a number of contributing companies. Trade Association Research, available online from Thomson Research, compiles overviews from 202 trade associations worldwide, and *The Wall Street Transcript* provides industry overviews compiled by independent researchers, including CEO interviews. Remember, although many sources have similar or overlapping information, there are often subtle differences in the actual content.

There are also online database services that offer a wide range of information, incorporating many of the special-purpose services. Services such as Dialog, Factiva, and LexisNexis are known as aggregators. All provide access to databases produced by

Investext[37] and to the reports available from Thomson Research or Thomson Financial.

In some cases, special-purpose online database services incorporate information from the aggregators. For instance, Hoover's,[38] which provides industry profiles, includes selected news articles from Factiva and links to Dun & Bradstreet reports.

To select the service or services that best meet your information needs, you will need to analyze pricing and interface options as well as take a close look at content. Commercial, fee-based online database services are available through several avenues. These options are illustrated in Figure 1-8. Online database services are often available at no cost to cardholders of many public libraries, by credit card, through transactional accounts where you are charged for each use, and by subscription. Some services offer several of these options. Which access option you select will depend on how critical the service is to your information needs, how much the service will be used, and who within your organization will use it.

Public Access

Many public libraries now offer remote access to online database services. Usually a library card number is required. For details, check the Web sites of the libraries in your area. Some may require that you visit the library and provide proof that you are a resident of the city or other jurisdiction that funds the library. Some will have more liberal definitions of residence than others. Others may allow you to sign up for a card online. If you are just beginning to do online market and industry research, if you are not sure what publications and databases you will need, and if you have no idea how much research you will actually do, using the databases available through the library is an excellent option.

Public libraries generally have online database services that can be used for market and industry research. These are periodical databases such as ProQuest or InfoTrac.[39] Some libraries have the RDS Business Suite with Gale's Business & Industry (B&I)

---

37. Investext from Thomson Financial is a compilation of analysts' research from more than 950 firms.

38. Hoover's, at *http://www.hoovers.com*, acquired in March 2003 by Dun & Bradstreet, is a directory of company and industry information.

39. InfoTrack is a databse of full-text articles develped by the Gale Group and owned by Thomson Learning.

Figure I-8. Comparison of Online Database Access Options

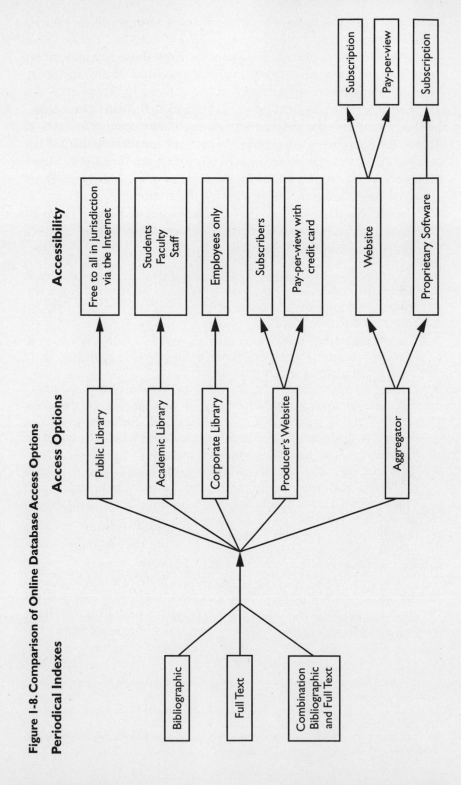

database and TableBase.[40] B&I has articles from trade magazines and newsletters, the general business press, regional newspapers, and international business newspapers. TableBase includes tables of information covering markets and market share, brands, products, industries, and companies.

There are also "hybrid" sources that include access to a selection of business databases, such as the Gale Group Business & Company Resource Center (*http://www.gale.com/BusinessRC*). This suite of products offers General BusinessFile ASAP, Market Share Reporter, press releases, and market research reports from Datamonitor International.

Online database access through the public library has two significant advantages: no cost and the absence of contracts. There are also significant disadvantages:

- *Uncertain long-term access.* Libraries constantly evaluate their electronic collections based on usage and budgetary considerations. Portions or all of an online database service may be eliminated without notice.
- *Content variability.* Because vendors provide a number of packages to libraries, you may have difficulty determining what publications are covered by a service.
- *Limited interface options.* The basic interface may be suitable for very simple searches when you first use an online database service, but as you become experienced you may want the flexibility and power of an advanced interface. Most public libraries provide only the simplest interface.
- *Technical difficulties.* Public libraries periodically have network problems and unresolved technical issues with vendors. In some cases their contracts may limit the number of concurrent users for a particular online database service. When you are unable to connect to a service through the library, your only option is to try again later.
- *Absence of training.* The major online database services provide a variety of training opportunities to customers that explain the resources available, advanced search techniques, and ways to take advantage of the information available. Library access does not include access to training.

---

40. TableBase is a Gale Group database that focuses on tabular and statistical data with references to the originating text when available.

Credit Card Accounts

Several of the online database services allow pay-as-you go research with a credit card. As with access through a public library, credit card access does not entitle you to training, and interface options are limited. Using a credit card is reasonable if you know that an article you need is available on a service for which you do not have an account. In general the credit card option allows searching for free; your card is charged only when you view a record. But you should not attempt a complex search on an unfamiliar service. Charges can mount quickly when an imprecise search strategy yields dozens of potential articles. Titles are not always indicative of article content.

If you have an unusual request and you believe the information is available through an online database service for which you do not have an account, your best option is to contact the Association of Independent Information Professionals (AIIP) at *http://www.aiip.org*. The AIIP Referral Program can provide the name of an experienced researcher who subscribes to the online database service and knows how to search it. Although you will pay for the researcher's time, you will have the assurance that a skilled professional has executed the search.

Transactional Accounts

If you are the only researcher in your organization, transactional accounts should be your initial choice if they are available from the online database services you need. With the exception of an account set-up fee for some services, you pay only when you use the service. In general fees are closely related to the amount of information you retrieve. Searches that do not yield results are free or very low cost. Many services allow you to enter a client name or number so that your invoice indicates the amount spent by project, making charging the cost of research to the clients' departments virtually effortless. When you have established an account you will receive regular updates on changes and enhancements to the service and you will be entitled to group and/or individual training. Many of the online database services have account representatives with research experience who show customers how to search the services effectively. With a transactional account you usually have access to all the interfaces available from the vendor so that you can migrate to a more advanced and flexible interface as your expertise increases.

Subscriptions

If several individuals in your organization will search the online database services or if you find that your usage is substantial, you should consider an annual subscription. Some services are available only by subscription. Subscriptions offer several advantages over transactional accounts:

- *Predictable costs.* With a subscription you can establish a budget for information services; with transactional accounts your expenditures may vary widely from month to month.
- *The freedom to err.* With a subscription, you incur no extra cost if you download documents in the wrong format or select the wrong documents, whereas such errors can involve substantial costs with a transactional account.
- *Customization.* Several of the online database services offer sophisticated tools that allow subscribers to customize what those in the organization see when they log on to the service, including industry news and predefined searches.

The disadvantage of a subscription is the substantial initial payment that is wasted if you do not use the service as much as you anticipated.

For a comprehensive look at options for access to the major aggregators' online services, refer to Mary Ellen Bates's article "Can Small Businesses Go Online?: The Professional Online Services Flirt with Mom and Pop."[41] The full text of this article has been reprinted in Appendix B of this chapter. Bates covers Dialog, Factiva, LexisNexis, and divine's Northern Light in some detail, facilitating the choice of your best small-business resource.

REVIEWING THE RESEARCH RESULTS

In almost any research project, you could conceivably continue forever. When do you stop? Knowing when to stop and review your results is a key research skill. There are a few signals that will tell you when to stop looking. When you begin finding repeated references to the same article, author, or statistic, it is safe to conclude that you have been fairly comprehensive in your approach. At this point it becomes less and less likely that you will find anything new if you continue searching. Another signal is

---

41. Mary Ellen Bates, "Can Small Businesses Go Online? The Professional Online Services Flirt with Mom and Pop," *Searcher* 11, no. 1 (January 2003): 16–25.

when you have exhausted all possible sources. Whether or not you have found what you had hoped to find, it is probably time to stop looking. Finally, when you run out of either time or money, you will need to stop the search.

It is a good idea to review the results once or more along the way, while you still have time and money to supplement or verify the results if needed. First, take the time you need to compare the information you have gathered against the questions you're trying to answer. You may realize that a few of the data points have appeared in multiple sources, whereas some data points remain missing. Second, begin writing up your summary and plugging data into tables as you review, before you finish the research. This process sometimes reveals gaps or inconsistencies that require a bit more searching to clarify.

Another strategy useful in reviewing your results is to compare the steps of your search against the sources you know you need to consult. Occasionally a key source gets overlooked in the process, and a review of results would reveal that omission. Ideally you still have the time and the budget to pick up additional sources, as needed.

ORGANIZING AND REPORTING THE RESEARCH RESULTS

The information you have found through diligent and skilled research techniques brings the most value to your organization when it is analyzed, summarized, and organized into a useful report. Analysis should begin with the retrieval of the first bit of research results and continue throughout the process. As a researcher it is your responsibility to evaluate the information you retrieve to determine its validity and relevance for the questions you are trying to answer. In the end, you will analyze the information you have collected to identify the components that help answer the questions at hand. Look for patterns, trends, quotes, and statistics relevant to your project.

A useful research report contains an executive summary. This is usually a one- to two-page discussion of the analysis and the findings. A summary can include recommendations, observations, and suggestions for future research. The summary is supported by the attached articles and reports that were found during the course of the research effort. A carefully written summary adds significant value to the research report, since it helps the reader get to the bottom line. Although you may be totally immersed in the particulars of the topic and think every detail is important, the client may simply want to know "What does this mean to me?"

Formatting for function and readability is important; in fact, it can almost be considered a courtesy to the reader. Type sizes should be large enough to read easily. Try to avoid going below 10 point, unless it is required to maintain formatting of a table or a downloaded article. In some cases a fixed-width font is required for proper formatting, in which case Courier New works well. Times New Roman is a traditional variable-width font that most people can read easily in 12 point.

White space on a report offers visual relief. You can achieve white space by using one-inch margins and bullet points when appropriate. Your report will likely include bibliographic citations and full-text articles or tables. Watch how these things fall at the end of a page, so that you don't have to split a table or place the first few lines of a citation on one page with the rest on the next page. Insert page breaks as necessary to begin new articles or main topics on a new page. (Hint: To easily insert a page break in Microsoft Word, press Ctrl-Enter.)

Reports with more than two or three articles benefit from a table of contents. This helps the reader see what the report contains and how it is organized. Plus, newer versions of most word-processing programs will create links from the table of contents to that point in the document. If you use this feature and use headings for article titles, those titles become part of the table of contents. The reader can then click from there directly to the beginning of the article in question.

Packaging is an important component of the reporting process. If your company has a corporate style guide, letterhead, or document template, then it should be used as appropriate. If not, consider creating one. As a researcher in your company you may want to create a brand for yourself or your department. You do this by making each report look similar—using the same font, headers, footers, logos, and style for each report you produce. By making each report visually consistent, you begin to create a brand so that clients and users recognize the source of the information in hand.

SAMPLE REPORT OUTLINE AND TEMPLATE

Client:
Researcher:
Date:
Topic:

Background

Here you will restate the research questions, specifying what you were looking for. For example:

We need to understand the United States market for blood oranges, including where they are grown, how many are grown in terms of boxes or pounds, what products use blood oranges, who buys them, and what the market trends are.

Research Results Summary

Here you will summarize the findings. This section includes the executive summary and generally consists of no more than two or three pages. For example:

The United States market for blood oranges is growing. Last year xxx acres were in production, yielding yyyy pounds of oranges, compared with ten years ago, when . . .

Table of Contents

The contents page lists the main headings present in the report. For example:

Background
Research Results Summary
Table of Contents
Research Results
    Organgina Rouge Light Sparkling Fruit
    Carbonates: Losing Fizz?
    Frieda's Moro (Blood) Oranges: Gift Box
    1998 California Citrus Acreage Report
    Stonewall Kitchen Dessert Topping
    Earthbound Farm Organic Fruit

Research Results

This section would include the full text of selected articles. For example:

"Orangina Rouge Light Sparkling Fruit," *International Product Alert* 19, no. 23 (December 2, 2002). ISSN: 1086-1238.

Word has arrived from the United Kingdom on the launch of Orangina Rouge Light. This Sparkling Fruit Drink . . .

Riley, Lisa "Carbonates: Losing Fizz? They've Taken a Hit from the Growth of Water and Fruit Juices, but Don't Write Carbonates Off Yet. (Soft Drinks): Overview of Carbonated Soft Drinks Sector in UK," *Grocer (The)* 225, no. 7552; 54, no. 2 (May 4, 2002). ISSN: 0017-4351.

Carbonates have been the star of the soft drinks market for decades, their growth outstripping virtually all the other segments each year without fail. Even as recently as 2000, carbonates accounted for over 60% of total market value share, and sales were growing significantly faster than still's . . .

"Frieda's Moro (Blood) Oranges—Gift Box," *Product Alert* 33, no. 3 (February 11, 2002). ISSN: 0740-3801.

Touted as being a perfect gift, Frieda's Moro (Blood) Oranges are presented in a 3 lb. "pack 'n stack" Gift Box. Available for . . .

1998 California Citrus Acreage Report, U.S. Department of Agriculture, May 12, 1999 <*http://www.nass.usda.gov/ca/rpts/acreage/citrus/905citac.htm*>. (May 26, 2003).

RESULTS: The California Agricultural Statistics Service recently conducted a Citrus Acreage Survey to estimate the 1998 acreage of citrus standing in California. The results of that survey are shown below . . .

CONCLUSION

If you've ever taught someone to ride a bicycle, then you have some idea what's involved with teaching cost-effective and successful online market and industry research. Once you know how to ride a bicycle, you can do it almost without thinking—based upon learning, doing, and practicing. The components of a successful bike ride become second nature. You understand the parts of a bicycle and how it works so that you can mount, balance, pedal, steer, brake, coast, stop, and dismount pretty much automatically.

Breaking down those components into a step-by-step process for the learner is another matter. Describing to a learner the particular details of how to put one foot on a pedal, leave the other foot on the ground, push down on the pedal, swing the other foot over the bike, steer straight ahead while putting the second foot on the second pedal and then pushing on that pedal while still steering straight ahead and picking up enough speed to balance makes things sound complicated. The only hope for the learner is to assume there may be a few false starts, and to practice, practice, practice.

So it is for the online searcher. A book such as this can give you all sorts of information that will develop full meaning only with application and practice. Most likely you have already done some online searching, so you know that it is both an art and a science. There is a science to picking a source that contains the information you need, but there is an art in knowing how to approach that source to extract the information it contains. There is a science to developing a search strategy as you follow the rules of syntax for the online system you are searching, but there is an art to honing that search strategy using synonyms and proximity operators to communicate the meaning you have in mind. Extracting data from a database is a science, but evaluating that data for relevance is an art.

In this chapter I have described the rules of online searching while touching on the role of creativity and language manipulation to achieve the best possible results. As you begin to practice what you have learned here, refer to this chapter regularly to improve and refine your skills as they develop. Continue to watch for new sources of information and stay abreast of changes in the sources you become comfortable using. Soon you will be able to smoothly negotiate the multitude of online sources with skill and ease, almost without thinking.

APPENDIX I: SECONDARY SOURCES

Government Sources

Government sources can be one good place to begin a search. These resources are often available free of charge and are searchable on the Web. Various government sources produce statistical information, data analysis, reports on current and anticipated situations, and projections of economic and labor situations. There may not be a government report that addresses your questions directly, but you should always check them to make sure. Vast quantities of information are available through these sites, and most likely something will prove useful and insightful. Government sources are especially strong for statistics. They also offer overviews and analysis largely free of the slant that may come from a specific company or industry source.

SEARCH TOOLS AND DIRECTORIES

- FirstGov (*http://www.firstgov.gov*): This is your first click to the U.S. government and the official U.S. gateway to all government information. This site, administered by the U.S. General Services Administration, also includes links to all state home pages, as well as county, city, and tribal government home pages.
- Access (*http://www.access.gpo.gov*): This is the site of the U.S. Government Printing Office for government information products, including access to the GPO Online Bookstore.
- FedWorld (*http://www.fedworld.gov*): The FedWorld Web site is a gateway to government information managed by the National Technical Information Service as part of its information management mandate.
- State and Local Government on the Net (*http://www. statelocalgov.net/index.cfm*): This site serves as a convenient directory to state and local government servers.
- NASCIO (*http://www.nascio.org/stateSearch*): NASCIO's State Search site represents chief information officers of the states, with information arranged by topic.

FEDERAL GOVERNMENT DEPARTMENTS: DEPARTMENT OF COMMERCE

- Economics and Statistics Administration (*http://www.esa.doc. gov/508/esa/home.htm*): The ESA produces, analyzes, and disseminates some of the nation's most important economic and demographic data.
- The Bureau of Economic Analysis (*http://www.bea.gov*): The BEA provides the most comprehensive statistical picture available of the U.S. economy. Resources at this site include gross domestic product by industry and input-output data, which show how industries provide input to and use output from each other.
- U.S. Census Bureau (*http://www.census.gov*): Known as "the nation's fact finder," the Census Bureau conducts the decennial census of population and housing, demographic and economic censuses, and more than two hundred annual surveys, many of them for other government agencies. Reports from the Economic Census are available for a small fee (the 2002 census was under way at the time of this writing). Reports from this census include the Industry Series, which includes reports on mining, construction, and manufacturing.
  - *Statistical Abstract of the United States* (*http://www.census. gov/prod/2002pubs/01statab/stat-ab01.html* and *http://www. census.gov/index.html*): This is an excellent starting place when looking for statistics. It is comprehensive and easy to use. It contains a collection of statistics on social and economic conditions. For example, in the 2001 edition, Table 1123, Information Technologies (IT)—Employment and Wages, shows that computers and equipment wholesalers employed 367,000 people in 1998 with annual wages per worker at $69,000. The 2001 edition contains more than 1,390 tables of data.
- The International Trade Administration (*http://www.ita. doc.gov*): The ITA is the lead unit for trade in the Department of Commerce. It promotes U.S. exports of manufactured goods, nonagricultural commodities, and services. The ITA Web site includes valuable industry analyses under the heading "Industry Sector Data." These tables have been prepared using statistics from the Annual Survey of Manufacturers published by the Census Bureau. The data are presented according to the North American Industry Classification System (NAICS); tables are available for each a three-, four-, five-, and six-digit NAICS manufacturing code. The tables include data for 1997 through 2000 for industry and product shipments, total employment, number of production workers, and capital expenditures.

Import and export data derived from the merchandise trade statistics for 1997 through 2001 are also provided.

- *U.S. Industry and Trade Outlook*, 2000, offers an industry-by-industry overview of the U.S. economy. It includes historical data on shipments, imports, exports, and employment; discussions of industry trends, technology, and international competition; one-, two-, and five-year forecasts; recent trade patterns and major country markets; graphs highlighting domestic and international trends; and reference lists for further research. It is available only in print or on CD-ROM. For ordering information go to *http://www.ita.doc.gov/td/industry/otea/outlook*.

- The Bureau of Labor Statistics (*http://www.bls.gov*): The BLS focuses on collecting and disseminating data related to labor economics. From the BLS home page you can link directly to "Industries at a Glance," "Research Papers," "Import/Export Price Indexes," and "Career Guide to Industries." This is a very rich data source. The *Occupational Outlook Handbook*, demographic characteristics of the labor force, and import/export prices illustrate the kind of information useful to the market/industry researcher.

- The Securities and Exchange Commission (*http://www.sec.gov*): The SEC seeks to protect investors and maintain the integrity of the securities markets. "To achieve this, the SEC requires public companies to disclose meaningful financial and other information to the public, which provides a common pool of knowledge for all investors to use to judge for themselves if a company's securities are a good investment." To do this, the companies file reports with the SEC. In recent years, these reports have been filed electronically and are available through EDGAR, the Electronic Data Gathering, Analysis, and Retrieval system. For market and industry research, the most interesting SEC filings are the annual (10-K) and quarterly (10-Q) reports, along with the 8-K, which are reports of unscheduled material events or corporate changes, deemed of importance to the shareholders or to the SEC. (See Source Evaluation sections of the Web site for options for accessing electronic filings to the SEC.)

For additional industry-specific information from government sources, go to the agency or department that oversees that industry. For example, within the Department of Energy, the Energy Information Administration maintains official energy statistics for the U.S. government. The Food and Drug Administration offers pharmaceutical industry information, and so on. Use Firstgov.com to assist you in finding the relevant agency.

Industry Sources

The industry players themselves are an extremely valuable source of information about the trends, forecasts, companies, products, and statistics of an industry. Trade, professional, and industry associations are one avenue to pursue in tracking down this information. Trade associations generally represent businesses operating within that industry. Professional associations represent the workers within an industry, and industry associations represent the industry itself, or the subject of interest within that industry. For example, the Biotechnology Association is a trade association; the American College of Cardiology is a professional association; and the American Heart Association is an industry or subject-specific association.

Virtually all industries and professions are represented by some kind of association. What value do these organizations bring to the market/industry researcher? The members represent the collective wisdom and key participants in the field. Their staff and executive directors are steeped in the issues, expertise, and knowledge of the industry. Their publications carry insights and information not found elsewhere. The trade and industry associations tend to focus on the companies and organizations that function within that industry. These companies and organizations are members of the association. There are also professional associations to which individual practitioners within the industry belong. The fewer organizations there are representing a given market or industry, the more concentrated the information will be within the existing associations. After you have done your homework and have begun to understand the nature of the industry and its issues, a call to the association headquarters for further information can be very effective. Association publications can be accessed through the association Web site or through commercial sources such as Gale Group's Trade and Industry Database.

SEARCH TOOLS AND DIRECTORIES

- *Gale Encyclopedia of Associations*
- Gateway to Associations (*http://www.asaenet.org/main*)
- Trade magazines by industry
  (*http://tradewriter.freeservers.com/maglists.htm*)
- Fuld & Company Internet Intelligence Index
  (*http://fuld.com/i3/index.html*)

Company Sources

Recall that BRSS includes an entire volume on company research. That is your source for detailed information on researching all aspects of public and private companies. For the purposes of this volume it is important to be aware of the information a company generates that sheds light on the marketplace and the industry as a whole. Annual reports from companies include a letter to shareholders from the CEO. This sometimes contains an announcement of new strategies, or an explanation of current strategy that sheds light on the company's plans. Companies also share industry and market insights through press releases. These can usually be viewed at the company's Web site or found through searches of the newswire databases.

SEARCH TOOLS AND DIRECTORIES

- 10k Wizard (*http://www.10kwizard.com*)
- FreeEDGAR (*http://www.freeedgar.com*)
- The target company Web site
- Newswires

Journalist Sources

Journalists write for the full range of news sources, including the trade and industry publications mentioned previously. They also write for the general purpose news outlets, such as broadcast media, local and national newspapers, business newspapers, and news magazines. Any source that includes news coverage will provide access to the information being generated by journalists.

SEARCH TOOLS AND DIRECTORIES

- Bizjournals for local business papers
  (*http://www.bizjournals.com*)
- Library of Congress Lists of Newspapers, Periodicals and News
  Resources (*http://lcweb.loc.gov/rr/news/lists.html*)
- Television News Archive at Vanderbilt University
  (*http://tvnews.vanderbilt.edu*)
- U.S. News Archives on the Web maintained by the News
  Division of the Special Libraries Association
  (*http://www.ibiblio.org/slanews/internet/archives.html*)

Special Interest Groups

Special interest groups include industry watchdogs and activists. These groups often organize with the intention of providing a point of view distinct from that of the industry spokespeople.

SEARCH TOOLS AND DIRECTORIES

- Environmental Defense (*http://www.environmentaldefense.org/home.cfm*)
- The Scorecard (*http://www.scorecard.org*)
- Guidestar, a national database of nonprofit organizations (*http://www.guidestar.org*)

Environmental Defense, particularly through its Scorecard Web site, will lead the researcher to information about how industry pollutes or affects the environment. The viewpoint available from Environmental Defense will likely take a different slant from what the industry and participating companies might offer. Many other nonprofit organizations are well funded and have the opportunity to gather data and publish reports that comprise an important addition to the wealth of sources covering market and industry information. The information produced by such organizations can serve to validate, refute, or expand upon the information coming from those participating directly in a market or industry. Special interest groups are an important source of industry and market information for the comprehensive search.

Academics and Research Groups

Knowledge of current and ongoing research efforts can reveal industry trends and patterns. In some industries, by the time the information hits the trade or industry literature and indexes, it is "old news." In the pharmaceutical industry, for instance, universities, corporations, and clinical trial groups present research results at conferences long before those results make it into a fully developed journal manuscript. The conference presentation might consist of a poster, an abstract, or a scientific session.

SEARCH TOOLS

- The National Technical Information Service (*http://www.ntis.gov*): According to its Web site, NTIS is "the central source for U.S. government scientific, technical, and business information." The material comes from federal agencies, industry and university contractors, and "a worldwide compendium of research and development organizations."
- Inside Conferences is produced by the British Library and available through Dialog in File 65. According to the Dialog Bluesheet, this database contains references to "papers given at every congress, symposium, conference, exposition, workshop, and meeting received at the British Library Document Supply Centre (BLDSC) since October 1993."
- Research Centers and Services Directory: File 115 on Dialog, this directory covers more than 27,500 organizations that conduct research worldwide.

For-Profit Researchers and Publishers

The information sources discussed so far tend to represent organizations and agencies that fulfill a mission or mandate. They exist to carry out laws, conduct business or trade, report the news, lobby for a cause, or advance knowledge through research. The information they produce and distribute is a by-product of their primary mission.

This last group of information sources includes those whose mission is to compile information and then market that information as a product. These information sources include market research reports, brokerage reports, directories, credit/financial reports, and subject-specific databases.

SEARCH TOOLS AND DIRECTORIES

- *Encyclopedia of Business Information Sources,* published by Gale
- *Directory of Business Information Resources,* published by Grey House
- *Market Research Reports.* Because there is a constant need for market research in all industries, companies have been developed to meet this need. They are in the business of creating market research reports for sale. Examples include Forrester

Research, specializing in technology, Jupiter Research, specializing in business and technology market research, and Freedonia Group, covering a wide range of industries. Augmenting these companies are the market research aggregators who gather information from a multitude of market research firms and sell the reports in full or in sections. Generally there is an embargo period imposed by the publisher, so the information coming through the aggregator may have been published thirty to ninety days before it is available from anyone other than the publisher. Aggregators include Profound, Dialog, DataStar, MarketResearch.com, Thomson Research, Alacra, and MindBranch.

- *Brokerage house reports.* Also called analysts' reports, these reports come from securities firms. These companies have a vested interest in keeping up to date on the strengths, weakness, and trends within an industry, since they are recommending the buying and selling of securities within that industry. Recently, analysts' reports have come under criticism for inaccuracy. As always, the careful researcher needs to verify information by checking a number of sources. MultexInvestor.com compiles reports from a wide range of contributors, including Merrill Lynch, U.S. Bancorp, Piper Jaffray, and Webush Morgan. They do not filter or evaluate the reports, but offer them for sale. The MultextInvestor Web site also offers instruction on how to use and understand analysts' reports. Investext, available through Research Bank Web, "features current research reports from more than 630 investment banks, brokerage houses, and research firms worldwide."

- *Directories* are such a valuable and useful tool to the researcher that Gale has produced *Directories in Print,* which contains 15,500 active rosters, guides, and other print and nonprint address lists published in the United States and worldwide. Useful directories for market and industry researchers include lists of companies, manufacturers, associations and organizations, industrial codes, journals, and membership lists. Lists are helpful when you are trying to understand a market or an industry. Directories can help answer questions like "How many companies do screen printing to create labels on CD-ROMs?" or "Who are the major mall owners?" *The Green Book* is a worldwide directory of companies that supply more than four hundred types of marketing research services. The *Thomas Register of American Manufacturers* is a good example of a directory. According to their Web site, "Thomas Register is the most comprehensive online resource for finding companies and products manufactured in North America." Dun & Bradstreet, which now includes Hoover's, has been recognized for years as a prime source of company information. They produce a number of directories available through LexisNexis and Dialog that contain basic company data, executive names and titles, and corporate linkages.

- *Subject-specific sources.* The search tools given here will assist in locating subject-specific sources of information. There are whole companies that participate in an industry not by developing, manufacturing, selling, or distributing its products, but rather by gathering and publishing information about that industry. Until your own research proves otherwise, it is safe to assume that there is an online database dedicated to your current subject of interest. It is important to know how to find and access these databases as needed. Examples of subject-specific databases include PIERS, discussed earlier in Chapter One, which contains data on U.S. imports and exports. Another database is IMS Health, which provides pharmaceutical information. According to its Web site, IMS Health "tracks and analyzes every phase of the product life cycle." PIRA (Packaging, Paper, Printing and Publishing, Imaging and Nonwovens Abstracts) provides comprehensive coverage of the literature of the pulp and paper, packaging, printing, publishing, imaging and nonwovens industries. INSPEC is the database for physics, engineering, and computing. These are just a few examples, but you can see how subject-specific a database can be.

APPENDIX 2: ARTICLE REPRINT
CAN SMALL BUSINESSES GO ONLINE?:
THE PROFESSIONAL ONLINE SERVICES FLIRT
WITH MOM AND POP

By Mary Ellen Bates
Principal
Bates Information Services

I've been around the online world a while—a quarter-century, if you must know—and it's been interesting to see how the professional online services have changed their customer focus over the years. When I first went online, back in the 1970s, it was a lovely relationship. We information professionals and small-time researchers had the online vendors' full attention. Well, it's true that LexisNexis and Westlaw dated lawyers too, but we always knew we were their main squeeze.

Then, of course, along came the Internet—that brazen hussy—and all of a sudden, we were no longer the apple of the vendors' eye. Why worry about selling the sold when you had that mass of humanity out there with computers and modems and credit cards just dying to buy information, right? Well, that passed, too, and the vendors realized that they needed to focus on the corporate world, with all those big budgets and big spenders. Traditional online vendors have done that quite successfully, and, of course, many of us information professionals have been the keepers-of-the-budget in those big corporations. Now, lo and behold, the professional online services are again offering some tempting options to small companies which can't afford the usual four- or five-figure monthly flat-fee costs for subscription access.

Who You Callin' Small?

Before I started looking into the deals being offered to the less-than-big spenders in the corporate world, I realized that I had to define what I meant by "small business." Good U.S. taxpayer that I am, I headed over to the U.S. Census Bureau's Web site to see how it defined small business. There I discovered that "the Census Bureau does not define small or large business." Oh, thanks. However, it does provide all kinds of stats on business sizes—by number of employees, sales, and form of business—so I could at least give myself some guidelines [*http://www.census.gov/epcd/www/smallbus.html*].

Looking through the stats, I see that of 7 million total businesses, over 80 percent have fewer than 100 employees and account for 29 percent of total sales generated. Looked at another way, over 80 percent of all businesses generate less than $1 million in revenue. Sure, each company isn't going to be much, but we're talking about close to 4 million businesses here. That's a lot of revenue for an online vendor, although it'll come in much smaller chunks than a nice, juicy, enterprise-wide contract with one of the international accounting firms.

Then I did a little more poking around and looked through the Business Enterprise section of that old favorite, Statistical Abstract of the United States [*http://www.census.gov/statab/www*]. I found a great table, combining information from the U.S. Internal Revenue Service and "unpublished data," that broke out corporations by industry and revenue-size. According to the IRS (and who would know better than the tax man?), 95 percent of all corporations have annual revenue of under $5 million. Scanning the list, I see that the construction, manufacturing, wholesale, and retail trade, professional, scientific, and technical services, and healthcare and social services industries all have a large number of small corporations that together generate a healthy amount of revenue.

My hunch is that most businesses with under $5 million in revenue won't be interested in committing to a $1,000-a-month contract with any of the professional online services. These businesses are more vulnerable to the buffeting of the economic tide and need the flexibility of ad hoc purchasing of information, rather than the predictable burden of a flat fee. So, let's see what some of the major players offer the small business community.

CALLING IN THE CAVALRY

Some time you may need more than what you can find from these online vendors. You might need a more sophisticated search on some of the unique Dialog sources than you can run through its Open Access credit-card option, but you don't want to get roped into an annual contract. Or you may just feel that you're not finding enough information yourself and want to hand this research off to someone who has more expertise in online research and/or access to specialized online sources that you can't tap into yourself.

It's time to call an independent information professional. Those of us who offer research services for a fee often work with clients who do their own research when the topic is straightforward, but who farm out the more complex jobs or ones that require access to the power tools of one of the online services. The Association of Independent Information Professionals (AIIP), an international group of over 700 independent researchers, provides a free referral service through which you can request contact information for members who have the subject expertise you need. You can also browse the online membership directory and contact individual members directly. Links to both the referral service and the membership directory are under the "About" tab at *http://www.aiip.org.*

The Many Flavors of Dialog

Dialog [*http://www.dialog.com*] has been known for its obscure command language that only an info pro would love. I mean, is s solar(6n)power??(6n)(vehicle? ? or auto? ? or automobile? ? or car? ?) intuitive? But Dialog offers a good selection of options for the occasional searcher who needs access to Dialog's broad collection of sources and who is willing to forfeit the power search tools that the full-featured subscribers use.

In fact, Dialog has several channels for small business users; at times, I feel like I need a map to keep track of Dialog's latest offerings. For all of these choices, you are limited to the database groupings that Dialog presents you with. These offerings all use pre-built search forms tailored to specific content areas (e.g., pharmaceutical research or current news), so in general you can only search the databases that Dialog has programmed into that form. On the other hand, you also have predictable prices for your budgets. In fact, both DialogSelect and Dialog1 offer entirely per-document pricing, freeing customers from the need to think about DialUnits or connect-time costs.

DIALOG SELECT AND OPEN ACCESS. DialogSelect actually includes two offerings — one for existing Dialog subscribers [*http://www. dialogselect.com*] and the other for ad hoc credit card payment [*http://openaccess.dialog.com*], called Open Access. Same sources (with a few exceptions), same screens . . . you just use different Web sites and different pricing. The DialogSelect.com site is a nice option for regular subscribers who need to search a database they're not familiar with or who don't use Dialog enough to remember the command syntax. The search screens have fill-in-the-blank forms that prompt you for the appropriate information, specific to the type of search underway—words in the title for articles; company name for directory databases; patent numbers for intellectual property research; government agency name for government regulations; and so forth.

For small business owners who need occasional access to Dialog, the Open Access program is probably the best choice. You don't have to subscribe—which means you don't pay the $168/year service fee—all you need is a credit card. Charges are entirely output-based; there are no DialUnit or connect-time costs. The per-record price is about 25 percent higher in the Open Access product than in DialogSelect for subscribers, for the obvious reason that Dialog wants to give its occasional users under Open Access an incentive to sign up as a subscriber. And that means that you'll pay more than you might expect for articles—over $4 for most industry publications, and $3.40 for newspaper articles.

Speaking of prices, here's a great deal—if you're a subscriber and use DialogSelect.com, you're charged the same per-document price that you'd pay on DialogWeb or DialogClassic, but without the DialUnit or connect-time charges! Even if you're a long-time Dialog searcher, if you've got a simple search to run, you'll pay less if you use DialogSelect than if you use any of the full-featured flavors of Dialog. When asked about this, a Dialog spokesperson said:

The Dialog pricing strategy is all based on value. Information professionals, such as yourself, use Dialog for its precision searching, speed and depth and breadth of content. . . . With our end-user products, such as DialogPRO or Dialog1, the searcher does not have the freedom to target certain fields or to capitalize on a special indexing code. The information returned is valuable to the end-user, whereas the searching itself is not valued as much. Therefore, we have a different pricing mix for those products.

Fair enough, but I'll take DialUnit-free searching when I do simple searches, thank you.

Figure 1-9. Doing a pharmaceutical search in DialogSelect

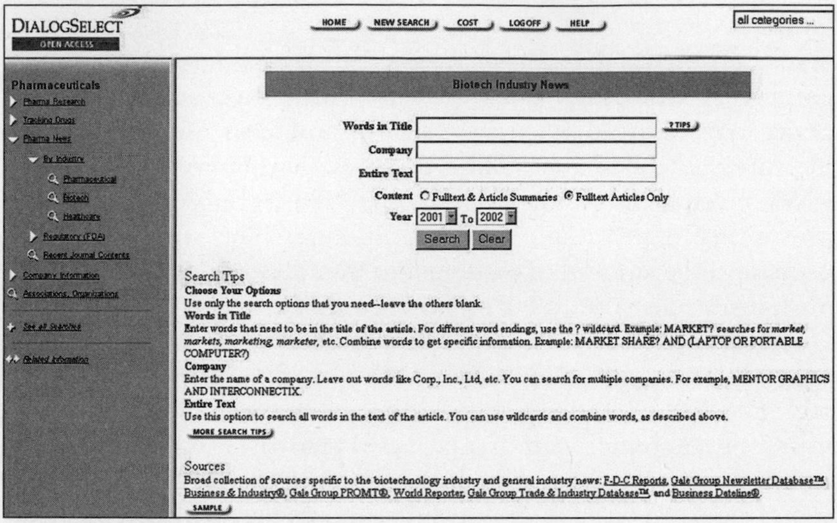

Search categories in DialogSelect and Open Access include Business, Chemistry, Energy, Food and Agriculture, Government, Intellectual Property, Medical, News, Pharmaceutical, Reference, and Technology. Figure 1-9 above shows the search screen for one of the Pharmaceutical searches. The search tips are tailored to the specific search form and, while you do have to understand basic search syntax (the question mark for truncation, Boolean operators and parentheses for nested logic, etc.), you don't have to deal with the more arcane Dialog language. Sources are clearly listed at the bottom of each search form.

Search results include title, source, date, and cost. One annoying feature is that search results of more than 500 records aren't sorted by either date or relevance. That's going to confuse searchers accustomed to the automatic relevance ranking of search engines and every other online service.

DIALOGPRO (PREDICTABLE RESEARCH ONLINE). The "Predictable" in this service offering refers to the predictable price; Dialog-PRO is a flat-fee subscription, but at a much lower level than what is offered to most subscribers. In fact, Dialog has revenue size limits for who can subscribe to DialogPRO that vary by country. If you're too big, you can't play in this sandbox.

This service [*http://dialogpro.dialog.com*] rolled out early in 2002. [For a thorough discussion of DialogPRO, see Barbara Quint's NewsBreak of February 25, 2002, at *http://www.infotoday. com/newsbreaks/nb020225-3.htm.*] As with DialogSelect, it includes content-specific modules, in this case biotech, competitive intelligence, consulting, defense, advertising, and news. Four more modules are scheduled for release during 2003. Subscribers choose which module they want and then pay a flat-fee subscription. Price points vary, depending on the module you select, the number of users, and the amount of content you want, but we're talking about $200 or less per month for one or two users.

Each module offers three pricing levels, depending on the number and type of sources available. The Primary package includes the essentials; the Plus package includes additional sources that contain commentary and analysis; the Premier package includes the most complete selection of sources. Note that subscribers can buy content outside their package, priced on an ad hoc basis.

Bottom line? DialogPRO is a good option for small businesses with enough experience on Dialog (using Open Access, for example) to have established usage patterns and to know what sources they need. The predictable flat fee is attractive for searchers who anticipate a reasonably consistent need for information throughout the year.

DIALOG1. Yet a third version of forms-based searching is Dialog1 [*http://www.dialog1.com*], a product designed for existing Dialog subscribers who need a simpler way to search Dialog files. Dialog1's channels include biotech, business intelligence, chemical, energy, engineering, intellectual property, marketing, pharmaceuticals, world news, and the NewsRoom product. These forms resemble DialogSelect's, but—in my eyes, at least—seem to go into more detail. For example, there's a search form specifically for finding articles discussing marketing to specific age groups. (See Figure 1-10.) This version of Dialog works well if you really aren't sure where to start.

Figure 1-10. Forms-based searching on Dialog1

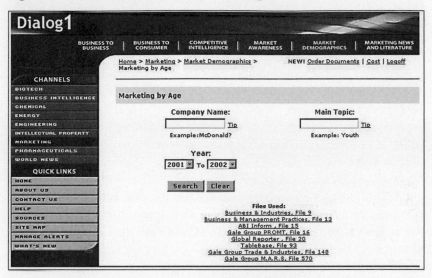

As with DialogAccess, and unlike DialogWeb and DialogClassic, there are no charges for searching—yup, neither DialUnits nor connect-time charges. Instead, you just pay a per-record fee, which is the same price as the full format for regular subscribers.

And if you're a subscriber, when do you use Dialog1 and when DialogSelect? A Dialog spokesperson explained the distinction this way:

Dialog1 is the easiest level of searching. For example, Dialog1 allows users to retrieve patent families from Derwent World Patent Index by just typing in the respective patent number. A search script executes behind the scenes in order to retrieve the related documents. DialogSelect operates under the assumption that users have some knowledge of Dialog and its content, because the search forms use specific indexing and search fields, such as the "corporate source" field in some of the research databases. Also, many of the forms in DialogSelect have multiple fields, allowing for more sophisticated searches to be conducted.

The distinction seems pretty clear, although I wish it were more apparent when looking at the two interfaces.

DIALOGWEB GUIDED SEARCH. A final option, although probably not the most appropriate for small businesses, is the Guided Search version of DialogWeb [*http://www.dialogweb.com*]. (If your default is Command Search, you'll see a button when you first log on that sends you to Guided Search.) This interface is for regular subscribers; you can't use a credit card to purchase records ad hoc, and DialogPRO subscribers can't use their ID and password to access DialogWeb. Unlike any of the other forms-based services, Guided Search includes all Dialog databases and lets you mix and match the files you want to search. On the other hand, this can be a bit overwhelming for the occasional searcher. Plus, you're charged connect-time or DialUnit fees, which tend to make the search experience too expensive for the average small business user. Of course, the Guided Search does offer some pre-formatted search forms just like the other options listed here, as well as "dynamic search."

My main objection to the Guided Search is that while it displays the per-record cost when you see the search results screen, it doesn't remind users of the additional DialUnit or connect-time charges accruing in the background. All in all, this isn't the best option for the budget-conscious small business, particularly given the other choices available.

Factiva's Small-Biz-Friendly Options

When Factiva.com [*http://global.factiva.com*], the successor service of Dow Jones Interactive and Reuters Business Briefing, rolled out in 2001, the only subscriptions offered were flat-fee contracts, starting at $1,000 per month. In fact, the page explaining pricing said that although user pricing is based on per-record fees, "There is no pay-per-article plan for Factiva.com." However, beginning in March or April of 2003, Factiva will roll out a transaction-based subscription plan similar to the old transaction plan of Dow Jones Interactive. For an annual subscription fee of $69, billed to your credit card, users will be able to search the Factiva.com sources at no charge and pay $2.95 per article. Other content, such as company profiles, investment analysts' reports, and corporate credit reports, will price separately—most will probably run between $5 and $15.

Searchers can toggle between two search interfaces—Standard and Advanced—on Factiva.com using the Preferences tab. The Advanced search interface could intimidate first-time searchers, particularly those accustomed to a simple search engine. The Standard interface, however, is straightforward and does not require understanding of search rules such as truncation, Boolean operators, and nested logic. You can select the industry, company, and/or subject you want to research and use free-text search terms as well as the Factiva controlled vocabulary. See Figure 1-11 for an example of a search for articles about advertising.

Figure 1-11. Searching on Factiva.com for articles about advertising

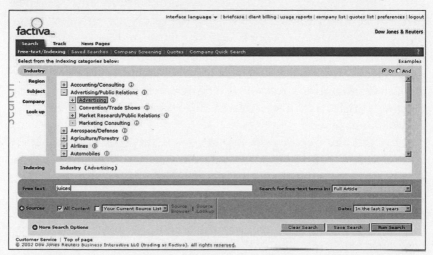

What I particularly like about Factiva is that it's applied consistent subject terms to all the bibliographic records, regardless of the original source of the content. This means that I can search for the bicycle industry and know that I'll find relevant articles, whether coming from Gale Group, Responsive Database Services, or even directly from a publisher.

Selecting Factiva.com's transaction-based pricing has one drawback. It limits you to the most current two investment analyst reports on a given company or industry. Given that some analyst reports can consist of nothing more than a rehash of the latest quarterly financial report, this is a real limitation. If you want more, you'll have to shop elsewhere (or pony up that $1,000 a month flat-fee subscription).

Factiva VP and director of Global Marketing, Pat Sabosik, noted that this latest offering is still in development. Factiva may roll out additional offerings or features later in the year. She also said that Factiva expects to add training efforts to raise the understanding of its non-info-pro users of the wealth of information resources and how to use these sources in a decision setting. Of the four vendors covered here, Factiva is the most focused on business users and business information needs; its user support and training modules reflect that emphasis.

LexisNexis—Not Just for Law Firms

Let's face it: LexisNexis has never been known for its user-friendly pricing. It has always focused on the large (or at least large-budget) organizations which will pay hefty flat-fee subscription prices. In fact, just trying to find pricing information at lexis.com or nexis.com won't work. That said, LexisNexis offers some unique pay-as-you-go options, including a daily or weekly pass in which you pay a set rate for all you can download from a selected subset of the Nexis database.

To find the credit-card payment options, go to *http://www. nexis.com* and click the link at {Not a Subscriber}. This takes you to the menu page where you can select which option you want. The "pay as you go" choice lets you select the general type of research you plan to do—legal, news, company and financial information, or public records—and pay per document. Articles are $3 each; company and financial information runs from $4 to $12 per record. You can also purchase a 1-day or 1-week "pass" to a selected subset of Nexis' holdings. If you plan on conducting intensive but infrequent research, this can be a very cost-effective option. Prices range from $30 for a day's worth of searching 50 major newspapers to $250 for a week's searching in company and financial files and a wide selection of bibliographic databases. Be sure to check the source list before you select any of these options; they're not comprehensive, and some sources include selected documents only.

You do lose some search functionality with credit-card access. See Figure 1-12, the search screen for an industry news search under the one-day-pass access. As noted at the bottom of the screen, an all-day pass limits you to the latest 50 articles that match your search criteria. And search tools are fairly simple—a mandatory "topic" search box, an industry type, and then the option of including "additional terms" and restricting by date. On the other hand, you can try as many searches as you want, since there's no additional charge for searching or downloading material. You may get your best results by trying your search using several different search screens. Depending on which channel of content you select, you have the option of searching for "Industry News," "Company News," "Products in the News," and so on. Each of these search screens differs slightly. For example, "Industry News" has a pull-down list of industries; "Products in the News" lets you limit your search by product name; and "Company Financial Information" includes a pull-down list of SEC filing forms.

Figure 1-12. Credit-card access through Lexis Nexis loses some functionality

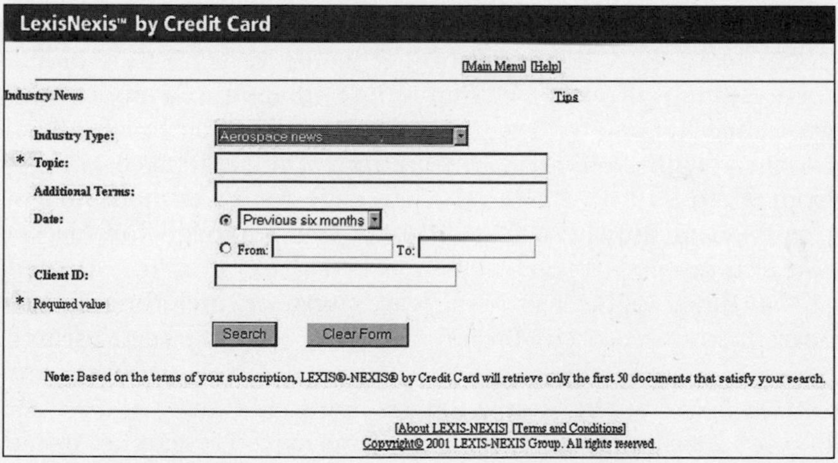

Downloading the full text of retrieved materials is a bit tedious with the all-day pass (my cynical mind suspects a plot to slow down any feeding frenzy with all-you-can-eat buffets). You can review headlines, but you have to click on each headline separately to view and download the full text. The pay-as-you-go search results screen, on the other hand, has check boxes; you select all the items you want, confirm that, yes, you want to pay for 'em, and then download the results.

divine's Northern Light: Moving from Free to Fee

At the beginning of 2002, Northern Light declared that it was leaving the free search engine space and focusing on providing transaction-priced access to its "Special Collection" content, with access to its Web search functions available only to enterprises. In fact, as of late 2002, searchers who go to *http://nlresearch. northernlight.com* still have free access to the Northern Light search engine by selecting "World Wide Web only" on the search source box. Note, though, that a recent study by Greg Notess of Search-EngineShowdown.com suggested that the index is getting pretty stale, and my quick survey of search results confirms that Northern Light hasn't refreshed its index in quite a while.

In any event, Northern Light—now owned by divine—does offer pay-as-you-go access to its "Special Collection," which includes full-text and abstracted articles, investment reports, and market research reports. Although the search options aren't as powerful as you might get through some of the other online services, this is the only e-content vendor that offers a money-back guarantee. If you aren't happy with something you bought from Northern Light, you can ask for a refund. The per-item cost ranges from $1 to $4 for articles, $10 per page for investment analyst reports, and anywhere from $14 to $50 per page for market research reports.

Northern Light has several search screens, including Simple Search, Power Search, Business Search, and Market Research Search, all of which are accessible from *http://nlresearch. northernlightcom.* The Simple Search option is actually too simple for even a basic searcher; even an inexperienced researcher would have no problem using the Business or Market Research Search interfaces. See, for example, Figure 1-13 to view the Business Search screen. You've got lots of options—limit the search to title words, select type of document or industry, even limit the search to a specific market research publisher.

Figure 1-13. Northern Light's Business Search screen

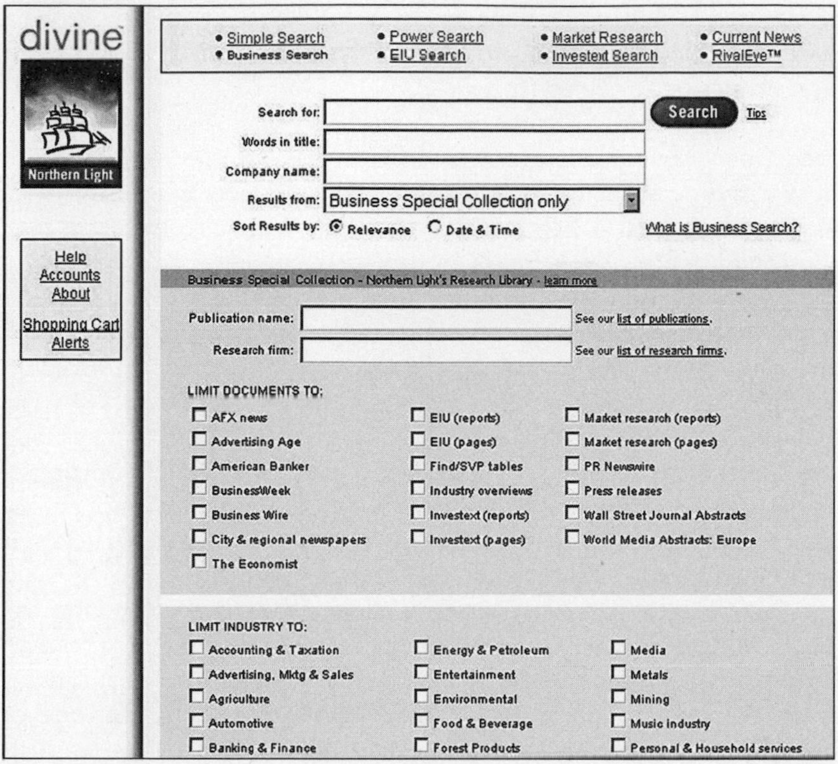

Search results can be sorted by date or relevance and also organized by Custom Search Folders, created on the fly. You can purchase documents one at a time or you can click an "Add to Cart" link to add them to a shopping cart to pay at the end of your search. It's an easy way to purchase and download all the articles you want, from multiple search searches, at the end of your search session.

WHAT CAN I DO WITH THIS INFO?

Many small business searchers will use the material they download from an online vendor only for internal use, to drive product planning, marketing campaigns, sales efforts, or strategic planning. But some small businesses, such as advertising agencies and consultants, may want to pass along individual articles to clients. What kind of restrictions do the aggregators place on redistribution?

Dialog's Standard Terms and Conditions, which apply to DialogSelect, Open Access, DialogPRO, and Dialog1 users, specify, "Except as authorized pursuant to Service commands (e.g., Dialog ERASM [Dialog's redistribution and archiving service]) under no circumstances may Customer, or any party acting by or through Customer, copy or transmit data received from Service in machine-readable form, or retain such data in machine-readable form other than temporarily for purposes of making a single human-readable copy thereof, except as may be expressly authorized in advance by the information provider." Now, I'm not a lawyer, but this sounds like users are prohibited from passing along any material to a third party. Note, too, that even the ERA program restricts redistribution to others within the subscriber's own organization. Looks like you're out of luck if you want to pass along an article you found on Dialog to your client.

Factiva states that subscribers may "review and download Information ... for their own use; and include in internal reports and/or reports to customers, on an occasional and infrequent basis, individual articles from the Information, provided that such articles (or portions of articles) are attributed to the relevant author or provider of such article." It's heartening to see official recognition of the fact that users will occasionally send an interesting article to a friend or colleague; now I know that at least the Factiva Copyright Police won't be kicking my door in any time soon. In fact, Factiva has a nifty feature called On Demand E-Mail, which lets you e-mail selected articles from a search results screen to anyone. There's a system limit of 100 documents at once, which seems to me like a tacit acknowledgement that sometimes information does want to be free and wander from person to person.

As one might expect from a service with a legal background, LexisNexis' Terms & Conditions are comprehensible only to a lawyer. See if you can use the following as a guideline for deciding if you can forward an article to a client or colleague:

With respect to all Materials other than Authorized Legal Materials and Authorized Patent Materials, the right to retrieve via downloading commands of the Online Services and store in machine-readable form for no more than 90 days, primarily for one person's exclusive use, a single copy of insubstantial portions of those Materials included in any individual file to the extent the storage of those Materials is not further limited or prohibited by the Supplemental Terms for Specific Materials.

To the extent permitted by applicable copyright law and not further limited or prohibited by the Supplemental Terms for Specific Materials, you may make copies of Authorized Printouts and distribute Authorized Printouts and copies.

Right, I can't figure that out either.

Northern Light's user-friendly Terms of Service clearly gives permission for a user to pass along an article to a client or colleague. There's a catch, though. "The purchaser may dispose of that single copy in any way the purchaser sees fit (such as give it away, sell it, summarize it, or quote from it with attribution). The purchaser may not, however, make or distribute multiple copies, create modified versions of the purchased document, or engage in any other acts inconsistent with the principles of copyright protection and fair use as codified in 17 U.S.C. Sections 106-110. Further, the purchaser may not give away or sell a purchased copy and still retain a separate copy as well." So, if you send an article to someone else, you must delete your own copy. (I wonder if Northern Light expects us to delete copies of our sent mail from e-mail servers....)

Picking Your Best Small Business Resource

All of these sources provide options that fit the needs of small businesses. Which one you rely on will, to a certain extent, depend on whether you expect your information and research needs to become more sophisticated or more frequent within the next year or so. Dialog clearly offers the best options for moving from simple, forms-based research to searching that utilizes power tools not available in the other online services. And Dialog covers the most vertical markets and subject areas by far. You'll find patent databases, obscure sci-tech databases, and academic journal databases on Dialog that won't appear on LexisNexis, Factiva, or Northern Light.

If, on the other hand, you think that you'll never spend 5 or 10 hours a week searching an online database, your best choice may be Factiva or Northern Light. Both have relatively low-priced per-article charges and both offer simple search interfaces with plenty of advanced tools when you need them and a streamlined purchase and download function.

LexisNexis would be the most appropriate source if you have an occasional need for in-depth research. Its daily and weekly passes offer a good value, particularly if you can batch several research projects and run them all during the period of time you purchase. The downloading options leave something to be desired, but having a set fee for a given time period sure is nice.

Source: Bates, Mary Ellen. "Can Small Businesses Go Online? The Professional Online Services Flirt with Mom and Pop." *Searcher* 11, no. 1 (January 2003): 16–25. Reprinted with the permission of Information Today, Inc.

2

Research Case Study on Rocky Mountain Country Club

Chapter One introduced the research process and examined the issues, strategies, and concepts that facilitate effective online market and industry research. Now the reader has the opportunity to see how all of this theory fits into a real-life research project. By following this case study from the initial information through project definition and step-by-step information gathering to a detailed explanation of how the project questions were answered, the reader will see the research process unfold. The case study in this chapter illustrates each step along the way, and a strategic narrative explains just what the researcher did and why.

In this detailed case study, market and industry researcher Marcy Phelps looks closely at the recreational industry, and private country clubs in particular. The club in question has a long and respected history but needs to make some hard choices to ensure that it will remain successful in the future. The research results provided in this case study should lay the foundation for good decisions by the club's board of directors.

This study required a close look at trends and practices in country club facilities planning and management. Selected club policies were evaluated and benchmarked, with special attention to their effect on member recruitment and retention. In short, Chapter Two illustrates the thought processes and the steps involved in putting together the pieces of an information puzzle in order to see the bigger picture.

This is a case study of an actual research project. However, to protect the identity of the country club, the club name and description, the researcher's name, and some of the circumstances surrounding the project have been changed.

Contributor Marcy Phelps is principal researcher and founder of Phelps Research. She specializes in providing clients with industry profile reports and has particular expertise in online database searching.

CASE STUDY BACKGROUND

Established in 1921, the Rocky Mountain Country Club (RMCC) is in a suburb west of Denver, Colorado. Nestled in the foothills of the eastern slope of the mountains, RMCC offers a beautifully designed and maintained golf course with spectacular views of both the mountains and the Denver skyline. Steeped in tradition, RMCC admitted women as voting members nine years ago. The membership roster includes 425 regular members, with 418 men and 7 women. Other membership categories, with reduced privileges and no voting rights, serve 132 additional families.

In addition to its exceptional golf facilities, RMCC possesses many strengths. The family-oriented club boasts a one-of-a-kind Juniors Program for the children and grandchildren of members. The close proximity to both downtown Denver and the mountains attracts people from the entire metropolitan area. Renovated five years ago, and with an excellent reputation for fine food and service, the banquet facilities remain booked a year in advance.

Regular (voting) members elect the seven-member board of directors for three-year terms. The board sets policy and hires the general manager, who implements policy and runs day-to-day operations. In its recent history, the club has experienced considerable turnover in its leadership. Not only do the board terms rotate, so that three new members are elected every year, but in the past ten years, the club has seen five managers come and go. In addition, the club never developed a long-term plan. This operating mix has resulted in frequent policy changes and, in some cases, little follow-through.

Accustomed to a full membership with a waiting list, the club experienced decreased membership numbers in the last two years. With nine member vacancies, RMCC was in better shape than other area clubs, but it still needed more members. The aging facility made this difficult. The old building and equipment contributed to poor service and made it difficult to offer new services. The out-of-date decor did not appeal to prospective members.

A decline in membership naturally leads to declining revenues, but in this case, revenues were decreasing at a disproportionately high rate. Many of the club members, including some on the board, blamed the decrease on recent changes in club dress policy. Although a golf course dress policy was always enforced, the board had recently instituted a clubhouse dress policy. This policy prohibited jeans of any kind in the dining and banquet facilities. The membership became divided over the policy during the last year. Some thought the new dress policy was necessary to maintain the image of the club. Others thought it was unnecessary because RMCC had always maintained a more casual and relaxed atmosphere than other area clubs and Denver was more casual than most cities. The new rules, they claimed, turned away members.

Further, some on the board thought that club members, affected by the economic downturn, were spending less time and money at the club. Others blamed the club for not promoting activities that might attract new members and keep current members active. They suggested that recent cutbacks in services and events, instituted in response to low participation, were perhaps alienating the membership.

To address these issues and to institute a formal procedure for decision making, the board had recently created the Strategic Planning Committee. The seven-member committee took on the task of developing a plan for leading the club through the next twenty-five years. To carry out this task, committee members thought they needed more information and came up with several key questions: What were similar clubs doing to increase membership and revenues? What kind of facility would they need to operate effectively during the next twenty-five years? What services would attract new members and restore member loyalty? After consulting with the committee and the club manager, the board decided to hire a professional to undertake the research. One of the board members was able to recommend Elaine Myers, a researcher he had recently contracted in his management consulting business.

THE CLIENT INTERVIEW

As the first order of business, Elaine met with the board of directors and club manager. The purpose of this meeting was to identify the club's information needs, discuss possible solutions, and determine if there was interest in going ahead with the project. As discussed in Chapter One, in client interviews researchers ask questions designed to identify exactly what the clients want to know, when they want it, and in what format they want it. Key interview questions always include the following:

1. Who needs the information?
2. What is your research goal? (How will you be using the information?)
3. What information will help you reach that goal?
4. What information do you already have?
5. What budget do you have in mind?

Additional questions will, of course, uncover additional needs. In the interview, researchers generally make suggestions about possible research methods, sources, and so on. By asking new questions about each suggestion, researchers hope to understand how these different research options might answer their clients' needs.

In this case, the client interview revealed that both the board of directors and the Strategic Planning Committee would be using the information at their meetings throughout the year—mainly to help them make decisions about the club's future. For example, they would use the industry research to help them decide whether to scrap the facility and start over, do a major remodel, or continue the Band-Aid approach. In addition, the board and manager were aware of the weaknesses in the current system for setting policy and wanted to explore alternatives. Finally, they hoped the research would help them decide how to effectively market the club's facilities and programs to current and potential members. Not only was there a need for more revenue to see the club through the coming years, but many on the committee and the board wanted to "bring back the fun" they had once enjoyed at RMCC.

The club leadership had already done some primary research on its own. RMCC staff had collected data about similar clubs in the Denver Metro area, including information about membership numbers, dues, dress policies, facilities, and programs. A lengthy survey had been conducted within the past six months to help identify club strengths and weaknesses from the members' perspective. Finally, the club manager had purchased a report from the Metro Denver Chamber of Commerce's Information Store that covered the regional economy, including historical and current economic conditions and the outlook for the area. No industrywide research had been done.

To help clarify the scope of the project, Elaine asked the group to list specific questions for which they wanted answers, and she had them prioritize the list. After some deliberation, a basic list of four questions was compiled:

1. How do similar clubs attract and retain members?
2. What are the current trends in clubhouse policies such as smoking and dress?
3. What are the current trends in clubhouse building and design, and which architectural firms are the top players?
4. What roles do country club managers and boards play in setting and implementing policy?

At this point, Elaine assured the group that, in addition to the sources they had already used, there were a number of other logical places to look for this type of industry information. In an attempt to answer their questions, she would search trade, business, and regional publications as well as newspapers and association research reports. She also offered format options for the final report. Did they want a compilation of articles, or a report summarizing her findings? To facilitate the use of the research in committee meetings, the board thought a report would be the best.

The next meeting was in three weeks, so the board requested the report in two weeks. In light of what the board was willing to spend on this project, Elaine suggested a twelve-hour project for the research and report with a do-not-exceed budget. If she needed to use the full budget, she would make recommendations for any additional research in her report. The club could then decide whether to stop there or approve a budget for additional research. A letter of agreement outlined the details of the project, including research questions, budget, report format, and delivery dates (see Figure 2-1).

Figure 2-1. Letter of Agreement

January 10, 2003

This letter confirms our agreement regarding the country club industry research project.

- Online research using the Internet and online database services will attempt to answer the following questions:
  - How do similar clubs attract and retain members?
  - What are the current trends in clubhouse policies such as smoking and dress?
  - What are the current trends in clubhouse building and design, and which architectural firms are the top players?
  - What roles do country club managers and boards play in setting and implementing policy?
- The budget for this project is $1,200 plus $200–$250 for expenses.
- Research results will be compiled in a full, footnoted report, including an executive summary and table of contents.
- An electronic version (MS Word) will be e-mailed on or before January 17, 2003. A print report and all full-text documents will be delivered to RMCC by January 17, 2003.
- Payment terms require $500 in advance and the balance within fifteen days of delivery.
- Please sign and fax this letter of agreement with a credit card number to 303-555-5555.

I look forward to working with you and researching this topic. Thank you for this opportunity.

RESEARCH STRATEGY

For most market and industry research projects of this type, the researcher starts with Internet research and then moves to online database services. After reviewing and organizing the results, the next step is to fill in the gaps with additional research. With an awareness of time and costs, the research typically moves from the general to the specific, building more direction and focus throughout the process, with stops along the way to decide whether to do more research or move on. Only after completing this process can data analysis begin. Outlined, the research strategy looks like this:

1. Internet Research
   a. Search engines
   b. Bookmarks, directories, and free databases
   c. Packaged research
2. Review Internet Research—Do You Have Enough?
   a. If no, go back to step 1
   b. If yes, go to step 3

3. Online Database Research
   a. Profound
   b. Factiva
   c. Dialog
4. Review Online Database Research—Do You Have Enough?
   a. If no, go back to step 3
   b. If yes, proceed with data analysis

Step 1: Internet Research

The purpose of Internet research is to become better acquainted with the industry. This part of the process helps researchers add search terms to their vocabulary and gain an understanding of the industry and its issues. Internet research identifies industry associations, which can be excellent sources of both free and fee-based information. Other sources for articles and industry reports can also be uncovered during this phase.

Internet research will generally involve three types of resources:

1. General or subject-specific search engines
2. General or subject-specific directories and free databases
3. Packaged research, including market research reports and off-the-shelf industry profiles

Unfortunately, this stage of research can eat up more than its share of time because the Internet is not well organized and has mostly unsophisticated searching capabilities.[1] To avoid wasting too much of the budget, the researcher sets an Internet time limit based on the topic, budget, and total time involved. Once this time limit is reached, the researcher "takes stock"—reviews what has been found, makes purchases, and confirms that it is time to move to online database searching. For this project, a one-hour limit was set.

SEARCH ENGINES. In this project, the first stop on the Internet was the popular search engine Google (*http://www.google.com*), which, according to the site, searches more than three billion pages. Researchers find it to be fast and thorough and appreciate the clutter-free interface. Elaine generally uses the advanced search

---

1. For a discussion of the "costs" of the public Web, see *Free, Fee-Based, and Value-Added Services*, part of the *Factiva 2002 White Paper Series* at *http://factiva.com/collateral/files/whitepaper_feevsfree_032002.pdf*.

page and has already set the preferences that work most effectively for her own purposes (see Figure 2-2).

Figure 2-2. Google Preference Page

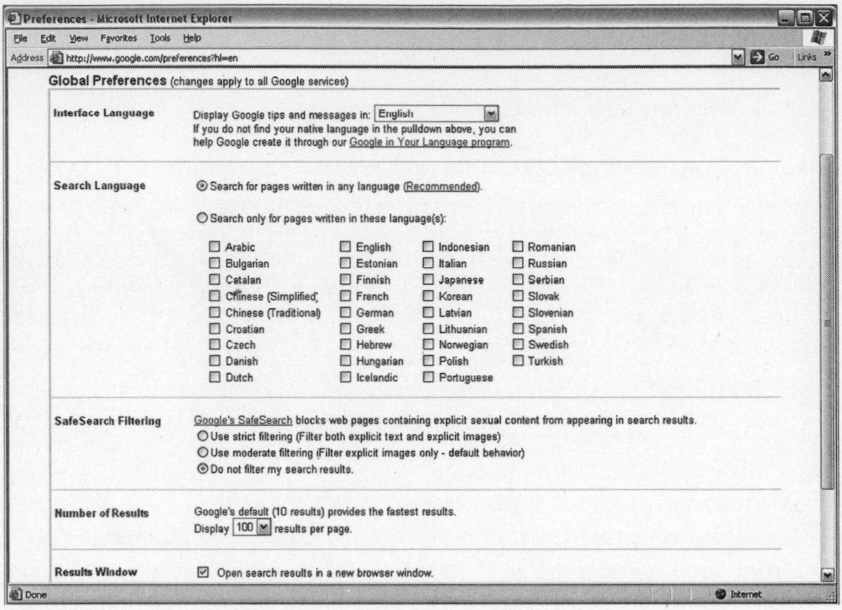

Reprinted with the permission of Google, Inc.

SETTING PREFERENCES

To set preferences in Google, start at the main page, *http://www. google.com*, and click Preferences. From there, select language preferences, filtering levels, and number of results per page, and indicate whether Google should open search results in a new browser window.

Most search aids allow site visitors to set similar preferences, and this feature can save Internet searchers a lot of time. Options will vary, but, whenever possible, set to display the greatest number of results per page to avoid loading extra pages. Having your results open in a separate window allows you to go back to your results list quickly, and it minimizes the chances of "getting lost" online.

KNOW YOUR SEARCH ENGINE

For effective, time-saving Internet research, get to know the leading search engines. Most offer a link to search tips; here you find out how to search phrases, exclude or combine terms, limit searches, and perform other advanced techniques. Two excellent sites offer comparisons of search engine features:
- Search Engine Showdown, at
  http://www.notess.com/search/features/byfeature.shtml
- Search Engine Watch, at
  http://www.searchenginewatch.com/facts/ataglance.html

In using Internet search engines it is important to choose search terms carefully and be prepared to try alternate strings of terms. In this case, the initial search term was *country club industry*. This search resulted in only eighty-one hits, a very small amount in the world of Google. The researcher scanned the results for relevant links, looking for associations, articles, guides, or other authoritative resources. The scan turned up a five-year-old article from *Restaurants USA* covering club restaurant trends. The emphasis was on service—nothing new here. Another article, published by an attorney in 2000, detailed how contracts can minimize risk in country club design, construction, and renovation. Again, nothing useful for the research project, and no new search terms were identified.

One item from the initial search did seem worthwhile, though: an organization called the National Club Association (NCA), at *http://www.natlclub.org*. The NCA, which represents the "interests and well-being of private, social and recreational clubs," offered a Fax on Demand program for members, sending free full-text articles on finance, IRS issues, compliance reminders, human resources, membership and marketing, risk management, legal issues, regulatory issues, and operations. A quick phone call to RMCC revealed that the club was not an NCA member, but it did belong to the Club Managers Association of America (CMAA).

The CMAA Web site (*http://www.cmaa.org*) was retrieved with another search term in Google, *country club management*. According to the site, the association is dedicated to "advancing the profession of club management by fulfilling the educational and related needs of its members." Elaine made note of the page describing the CMAA Fax on Demand topics (*http://www.cmaa.org/pr/ FODonweb.htm*) in case she needed them later. There was no free information here. One publication did catch her eye, however. The **Education** link provided a list of books and other publications that the association offered for sale. The *CMAA 2001 Economic Impact Report* included information on "club revenues and employee payrolls, national averages on staff benefits, smoking policies, informal and formal dining, dress code policies and actions clubs have taken to attract families to the club and how these changes have affected the bottom line." This was definitely on track with the project goals, so she made a copy of the Web page and added it to her file of possible resources. Another publication, the *CMAA 2002 Club Operations Survey*, looked very content-rich, although not entirely relevant. Just to be safe, she added it to the possibilities as well.

The search term *country club management* also retrieved a site called The Virtual Clubhouse (*http://www.club-mgmt.com*). Presented by the publishers of *Club Management* magazine, this site offers selected articles, arranged by the following topics: GM, Dining Room, Board Room, Golf Course, and Sports/Fitness. Some titles appeared relevant (e.g., "The Changing Face of Club Kitchens" and "Room for Change: Consumer Trends Give Bathroom Renovations Appealing New Direction"). Elaine noticed the articles did not include publication dates, so she looked at the URLs, since the date for online periodical articles will frequently be part of the URL. Sure enough, the URLs indicated that these articles probably came from the August 2001 and September 2002 issues. The Web site's search function was pretty ineffective, so she skimmed the lists and printed the two mentioned articles, another on swimming pool renovation, and a survey of clubhouse renovation costs and financing. These looked very worthwhile for answering the client's question on current trends in clubhouse building and design and would perhaps offer some information about the leading architectural firms.

Experienced researchers know that, no matter how great a search engine is, it doesn't cover everything, or even close to everything. In fact, there is surprisingly little overlap in search engine indexes. So, for in-depth research, it is important to consult more than one search engine. For this project Elaine chose AlltheWeb (*http://www.alltheweb.com*), a comprehensive search engine that indexes 2.1 billion Web pages. On the main search page, she entered the phrase *country club industry*, but found that the quotation marks were not needed because of the search engine's built-in phrase-searching feature.

Scanning a couple of pages of hits revealed little except commercial sites. Using another search term, *private club management*, yielded some educational sites with a career-development slant. So Elaine went back to Google with this phrase (remember, different search engines yield different results) and found additional educational resources, as well as more commercial sites. One appeared to be worth a closer look. A site called Club Report (*http://www.resourcesforclubs.com*) offered *The Guide to Membership Marketing* (*http://www.resourcesforclubs.com/custom/Ourpublications. html# marketing*). What attracted her interest, in addition to the marketing angle, was the section on the role of the clubhouse architect. The cost of an interactive CD containing this report was $74. Elaine suspected some bias in this publication, compiled by a club marketing consulting company, but she added it to her file of resources for later consideration.

THE GOOGLE TOOLBAR

Google offers its own browser plug-in[2] that allows you to add Google search functionality to Internet Explorer (at the time of this writing, the toolbar will work only with IE version 5 or higher). From wherever you are on the Web, you can search the Web or a specific site. To download the Google Toolbar, go to *http://toolbar.google.com* and follow the directions.

The screen shot below shows the Google Toolbar just below the address bar, with the results of a Business 2.0 site search for "country club management."

---

2. A plug-in is a software module that adds a specific feature or service to a larger system.

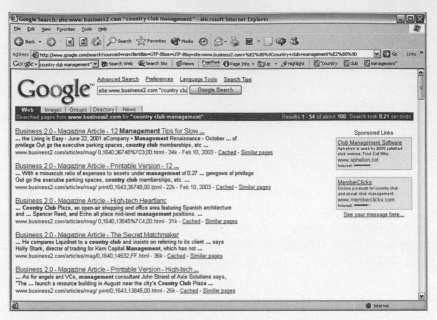

Reprinted with the permission of Google, Inc.

Google lists all the pages where the phrase was found and saves all recent searches in the drop-down menu. To set your toolbar preferences, use the drop-down menu under the word Google and go to Toolbar Options. Here you can have Google open your search results in a new window, adjust search box size, change button labels, and more.

BOOKMARKS, DIRECTORIES, AND FREE DATABASES. The next step was to check out previously bookmarked Web sites.[3] Most researchers keep a file of bookmarks, also called "favorites," for Web sites they use on a regular basis. In this case, the researcher's bookmarks offered access to industry publications, associations, news sources, and academic sites. For example, the Harvard Business School Baker Library site, at *http://www.library.hbs.edu/industry/*, offers an extensive list of guides to industry research. Although some of the resources are password protected, these guides contain many free resources and provide a valuable overview of industry information resources. The subjects are broad and tend to focus on industries of broad interest. As it happens, none of the Baker Library research guides were relevant to the country club industry.

---

3. These are Web sites that the user saves within the Web browser, called "Favoritess" in Internet Explorer and "Bookmarks" in Netscape.

Another bookmarked site, the *McKinsey Quarterly* (*http://www.mckinseyquarterly.com/home.asp*), publishes excellent industry information, available with free registration. Country, golf, or private clubs did not show up, though. Still another frequently used site for industry overviews is Business 2.0 (*http://www.business2.com/webguide*). The site does not have sophisticated searching, and again, the country club industry did not fit into any of the listed subject headings, so Elaine decided to use the Google Toolbar to search the site. A site search for *country (club OR clubs)* was too general, and neither *country club management* nor *private club management* turned up anything useful.

Associations are a worthwhile starting point for finding articles, research reports, and industry profiles, as well as for identifying experts. Directories of associations are a good place to start. For this project, Elaine went to the local public library Web page to search the online database services available there. Library cardholders can use these databases for free via the Web. The list includes *Associations Unlimited*, a Galenet database containing information for approximately 460,000 international and U.S. national, regional, state, and local nonprofit membership organizations in all fields.

Unsure of how to best construct the search, Elaine decided to use a method called "backward searching" or "pearl building." By looking at a resource you *know* is relevant, it is possible to identify indexing terms or codes, then search those terms or codes to find similar resources. For this search, the starting place was the entry for CMAA, found by searching *Associations Unlimited* for the association name (see Figure 2-3).

Figure 2-3. Search Results for CMAA in *Associations Unlimited*

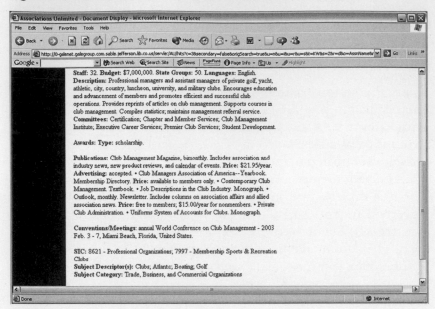

Reprinted with the permission of Gale Group.

The bottom of this entry includes reference to the SIC code 7997 (Membership Sports and Recreation Clubs) and the subject descriptor "clubs." Using the SIC code and the descriptor to search backward (the Subject/Any Word search screen), the researcher found that they were too broad—all kinds of private clubs came up, including trout fishing and polka dancing. By replacing "clubs" with "golf," another descriptor, the directory results showed that the only relevant associations were NCA and CMAA.

To check for additional associations, Elaine went to the Internet Public Library: Associations on the Net Web site (*http://www.ipl.org/div/aon*). The Internet Public Library (IPL) is a "public service organization and a learning/teaching environment at the University of Michigan School of Information," and the Associations on the Net section offers a guide to Web sites of prominent associations and organizations. Site visitors can search by keyword or browse by subjects and subheadings. Under each subheading, you find an annotated list of links.

The researcher found that the country club industry didn't seem to fit directly into any of the subjects. Next, she looked under Business & Economics, then Industry (IPL explains what each subject heading and subtopic means). Since neither "country clubs," "private clubs," or even "recreation clubs" appeared on the list of industries, Elaine clicked Other Industries. Again, there was nothing for country clubs. Without phrase-searching capabilities, it was difficult to specify the information needed, so she just entered *club*, which searched titles, annotations, and keywords. A quick scan did not turn up anything relevant.

Another source for associations is the American Society of Association Executives (ASAE). Through the association Web site (*http://www.asaenet.org/main*), Elaine accessed a gateway to associations at *http://info.asaenet.org/gateway/OnlineAssocSlist.html*. Again, searching can be difficult, but by using *club* as a keyword, she found an organization called the Association of Country Club Executives. The link to the association Web site did not work, however. Nothing else looked worthwhile, and since only fifteen minutes remained of the one-hour time limit for Internet research, she decided not to spend any more time on this.

PACKAGED RESEARCH. Packaged research comes in the form of market research reports and off-the-shelf industry profiles. Market research reports can be valuable sources of market and industry information, and Elaine thought they might be useful in this project to identify trends, marketing strategies, and demographic information. Packaged market research can be found on the Internet or through online database services, but she preferred to scan the Internet first, to get an idea of what was available.

Unfortunately, going to each market research company can be time consuming. Aggregators such as MindBranch (*http://www.mindbranch.com*) and MarketResearch (*http://www.marketresearch.com*) collect reports from market research firms, allowing you to search a wide range of resources, but even searching the aggregators can take a substantial amount of time. That's why a good first stop for this kind of information can be ValuationResources (*http://www.valuationresources.com*), which has a collection of resources for business appraisers. The site offers Industry Resources Reports (*http://www.valuationresources.com/Industry Report.htm*), which lists "resources available from trade associations, industry publications, and research firms which address subjects such as industry overview, issues, trends, and outlook, financial benchmarking, compensation surveys, and valuation resources." These fee-based resources are arranged according to SIC code, so if you have an SIC code for your industry, this site could be a time-saver.

Elaine had found the SIC code in *Associations Unlimited* (see Figure 2-3). Under Services, Industry Resources Reports listed SIC Code 7997, Private Clubs / Country Clubs. This section contained seventeen annotated links to packaged reports, association white papers, surveys, financial statements, and more. The first and second items on the list turned out to be reports from the CMAA that she had already set aside for possible purchase. The others were a variety of off-the-shelf reports, mostly financial. Unfortunately, none really stood out, and it would take too much time to go to each site and search for relevant reports, even using the Google Toolbar.

Researchers often incorporate off-the-shelf industry profiles into online industry and market research. A good starting place for this is generally First Research (*http://www.1stresearch.com*). This subscription-based site contains industry profiles that are updated quarterly. The profiles provide insight into industry trends, including recent developments, business and credit risks, industry issues, and selected industry resources. First Research offers 140 profiles that can be purchased on a transactional basis for $99 per profile, rather than through a subscription. But the company does not advertise the per-profile option, and finding the page for the transactional rate can be challenging. (This is why Elaine keeps the page bookmarked at *http://industryprofiles.1stresearch.com.*)

Unfortunately, nothing was listed for the country club industry. A profile of the golf course industry, including a free summary, was available under Services. The summary revealed little relevance to the facilities end of the industry. This illustrates a common problem with packaged research. Often, you will find a limited number of industries, and the industries are usually broad and not vertical. They frequently do not fit the bill.

After spending the allotted time on Web searching, Elaine decided it was time to add breadth as well as focus to the research. Before searching online database services, however, she needed to take stock: review what she had found so far, access what was still needed, and decide what to purchase before moving on.

ALL THIS IN AN HOUR?

To search the Internet quickly and effectively, professional researchers maintain an "arsenal" of skills and tools:

- Stay up to date on new sources of information and changes in familiar sources.

- Maintain a system for finding these sources (e.g., Bookmarks or Favorites).
- Learn to quickly scan Web pages to find the information you need.
- Using the Google Toolbar, do a site search rather than clicking through pages of a Web site.
- Use the command Ctrl F to find your keyword or keywords on a Web page.
- Know when to stop your search. You can always go back later to look for more.

Step 2: Review Internet Research—Do You Have Enough?

Before spending time and money for online database searching, it generally helps to take a few minutes to look at the information collected so far and determine what has been learned from the Internet research. After using search engines, bookmarks, directories, and free database access, and after searching for packaged research, our researcher came to the following conclusions:

- This was not an industry with a lot of easy-to-find resources.
- Additional search terms had been identified:
  - Private club management
  - Private club industry
  - Private golf club
  - Club management
  - Club membership
- When talking about clubhouse facilities, the following terms frequently appeared (any resources covering golf facilities were eliminated, as these were not part of the scope of the project):
  - Kitchen
  - Bathroom
  - Dining
  - Locker room
  - Banquet
  - Fitness centers
  - Bars/lounge
- Frequently mentioned issues within this industry included
  - Marketing
  - Technology
  - Programs and services
  - Maintenance

- Some associations had been identified, but only one with a content-rich Web site (*http://www.cmaa.org*).
- Four articles from *Club Management* showed promise:
  - "The Changing Face of Club Kitchens"
  - "Room for Change: Consumer Trends Give Bathroom Renovations Appealing New Direction"
  - "Swimming Pool Renovation: Know What You Are Doing Before You Jump In"
  - "A Survey of Clubhouse Renovations: Costs and Financing"
- Three resources for possible purchase had been noted:
  - *CMAA 2001 Economic Impact Report*
  - *CMAA 2002 Club Operations Survey*
  - *Club Marketing Report*

After looking at the information she had about these resources and comparing it with the client's original research questions, Elaine considered ordering the *2001 Economic Impact Report*. She called the order department, asking about this resource and the *2002 Club Operations Survey*. According to the descriptions, the *Economic Impact Report* fit the needs of this project. She contacted her client for approval, and the report was ordered for the $60 member price, plus $20 for next-day delivery. Having the report in hand would help her to assess what had been accomplished so far and to determine what still needed to be done for this project.

Once the report arrived, however, Elaine discovered that it did not match its description. It contained no information about how changes in dress policy had affected revenues. Nothing was mentioned about informal versus formal dining, except for a brief mention of dress restrictions. The only discussion related to attracting families was focused on children's programs and how they had affected the bottom line. She had expected more discussion on different methods of attracting members.

This purchase illustrates a common problem with buying information, especially full text—you do not always get what is advertised. Experience indicates that this could actually work both ways. Sometimes you don't get what you want, and sometimes you get an unexpected treasure. This situation included both outcomes. Although there was no information on dress codes, informal versus formal dining, or attracting families, the report did contain some extra data on male/female members, technology investments, smoking policies, compliance with the Americans with Disabilities Act, credit cards, and defibrillator usage.

To get answers about the missing information, Elaine again called the order department, where it was explained that she would need to call the association directly with this type of question. The order department suggested that she contact Ron Rosenbaum, director of Premier Club Services. She left a voice message with Mr. Rosenbaum, who called back within the hour. He courteously handled her questions about the misleading product description and emphasized that he would do whatever necessary to correct the situation. (She had not told Mr. Rosenbaum that she was writing an account of her experience that would be published.)

Elaine detailed the information needed and explained what had been expected from the report, given its description on the Web site. She explained that although some of the information in the report would be very useful, she had purchased it mainly because the description said the report contained information about dress policy changes and how they affected revenues. Mr. Rosenbaum agreed that the description on the Web site was inaccurate and promised that it would be corrected (the Web site was, in fact, changed that very day). He said the association did not have any information on the effect of dress policies, and he was not sure it could be measured (although they apparently measured the effect of smoking policy changes). He recommended information from the *2002 Club Operations Survey*. After further discussion of the information needed, Mr. Rosenbaum agreed to fax sections he thought would be relevant. He also invited Elaine to call back if she needed anything else.

The faxed documents did provide insight into minimum spending requirements, food and beverage pricing and sales, dress code at informal dinners, and profit and loss in dining operations. But Elaine was still frustrated by the lack of information about programs and services for attracting members. She realized that Mr. Rosenbaum also might be able to direct her to information about establishing policy, so she gave him another call. Although he was leaving for the association's annual conference the next day, he again took the time to listen to her request. He thought that he could find some more relevant sections in the *2002 Club Operations Survey*. However, his association kept no statistics on setting policy, and he knew of no source for this type of information.

After the phone call, Mr. Rosenbaum faxed additional statistics on facilities and programs offered by clubs. Elaine found this information useful and decided that it made up for what was lacking in the original report. This trade-off assured that the RMCC got its money's worth in purchasing the report. In addition, she was impressed by Mr. Rosenbaum's integrity. She found association people to be generally helpful, but Mr. Rosenbaum clearly went out of his way to ensure that this situation came out favorably and that the inaccuracy was corrected.

How might one prevent this sort of thing from happening? Online researchers can't really eliminate the risk involved with buying information, but they can minimize the risk by knowing their products. Do your homework ahead of time, always keeping an eye on the budget, and ask as many questions as possible. It often pays to dig around for further information on a product:

- Going beyond the order department or customer service representative, as illustrated here, can be beneficial.
- Company or association Web sites generally provide e-mail links or phone numbers for getting more detailed information about products.
- Considering the price of many of these products, asking for a table of contents is not out of line.
- Following up on misunderstandings usually helps. Most company representatives are eager to solve customer complaints, and it's important to avoid those who aren't helpful.

Finally, this experience illustrates the value of complementing online market and industry research with some primary research. Even with secondary research, taking time to talk briefly with someone who is willing to share some industry expertise can uncover different options for getting to the right information. Besides getting the misunderstanding corrected, the researcher in this case tapped into Mr. Rosenbaum's expertise. As a result, statistics from the survey that did not at first seem relevant took on new meaning. In addition, learning that this expert had no suggestions for answering some of her client's questions raised a red flag for the researcher. She would have to dig deeper. Satisfied with the information found and the report purchased through her Internet research, she was ready to move to online database services.

Step 3: Online Database Research

Many researchers subscribe to a number of online database services to execute comprehensive, targeted, cost-effective research. Some services charge to search, while offering downloads for free. Others offer free searching, while charging for downloads. Still others charge for both. Faster searching and the availability of a broad range of resources can outweigh costs for these services. Another advantage of online database services is their sophisticated search options, which can pinpoint hard-to-find information. For more discussion of online databases and options for access, see Chapter One.[4]

Deciding which online database service to use depends on the topic, the budget, and the schedule. For this project, the researcher accessed three online database services—Profound, Dialog, and Factiva, as described below.

PROFOUND. The researcher used Profound, a Dialog product, because it offers ResearchLine, one of the largest online collections of market research. Rather than go to the various market research Web sites and search each separately using their bare-bones search pages, many researchers prefer the more professional search capabilities of this product. And pricing is reasonable. Not only does the researcher's subscription allow for free searching, but market reports can be purchased by the section, saving money. Experiences with this product have resulted in some useful, inexpensive resources for industry research.

Although Profound offers access to many of the Dialog databases with an easy-to-use format, Elaine prefers to use Profound mainly to access market research reports. For other information such as company information and news, she usually goes elsewhere. Profound may have free searching, but time can be eaten up by not having full content or command searching capabilities.[5] Also, in her experience, the Profound Web site seems to run slowly.

To get to ResearchLine from the Profound home page, click WorldSearch. From this search page, the ResearchLine database has been set as the default database. Profound allows searchers to indicate how many results to display on a page. Always select the highest amount, so you will have fewer pages to click through. For the most relevance, Elaine opted to search the title field and to limit the search to the United States. Any other terms or fields might be too limiting for such a narrow industry. After reviewing the Search Tips page, she used the following search string: *country*

---

4. For an overview of products offered by online database services, see Mary Ellen Bates, "Can Small Businesses Go Online?" *Searcher*, January 2003.

5. Command searching, used by experienced searchers, allows you to type your search using the online database service's command syntax, instead of checking or filling in boxes, which is necessary with many Web-based products.

club*, private club* —using the asterisk (*) to search for "club" as well as "clubs." (The comma signifies "or.") This caused an error message, however, and it turned out that the asterisk does not work within quotation marks. After taking another look at the tips, Elaine realized that the quotation marks were not necessary for phrases, so the revised search was used: *country club*, private club** (see Figure 2-4). This retrieved one report, *US Golf and Country Clubs 2001*, from Snapshots International, USA.

Figure 2-4. Profound (ResearchLine) Search Page

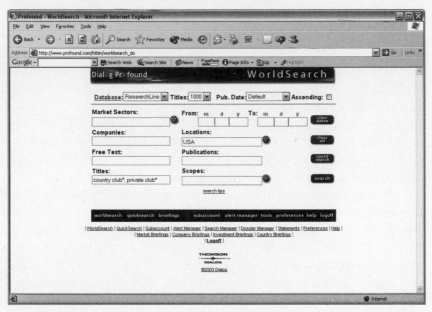

2003® Dialog, a Thomson business, *http://www.dialog.com*. Reprinted with permission of the publisher.

After Elaine clicked the title, Profound displayed links to the tables of contents and prices for the full report as well as for individual sections, highlighting those sections that contain the search terms (see Figure 2-5).

Figure 2-5. Item Details in Profound

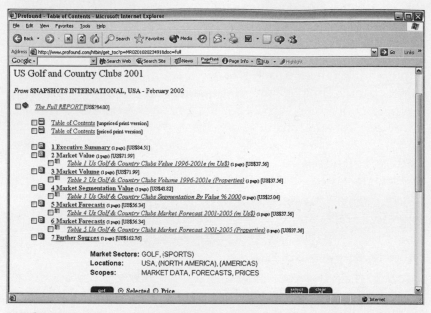

2003® Dialog, a Thomson business, *http://www.dialog.com.* Reprinted with permission of the publisher.

US Golf and Country Clubs 2001 contained sections on market value, market volume, and segmentation value, as well as market forecasts and further sources. The page for further sources came with a relatively high price tag, and Elaine wondered what this could possibly contain. She decided to call customer service since they could usually describe more fully the contents of market research report sections. According to the customer service representative, the Further Sources page offered links to additional Snapshot reports, organized under sixteen related SIC codes. This was not something for which Elaine was willing to spend $162.76. Even though the report did not seem relevant at this point, she made a copy of the table of contents for future reference. Hoping other resources would yield better results, she decided to search Factiva next.

FACTIVA. An online database service covering news and business topics, Factiva also contains company reports. The Factiva.com product, accessing nearly eight thousand newspapers, magazines, newswires, and media programs, offers a comprehensive tool for looking at current trends. With free searching, researchers can explore different approaches to the research and perhaps identify new keywords. In addition, downloaded documents from Factiva are reasonably priced at $2.95 each, and the Web interface generally seems fast and reliable.

Our researcher had already set her preferences for date, sources, languages, and where the terms were to be searched. At the search screen, she entered the phrase *country club industry or private club industry or club management* (see Figure 2-6). In Factiva, quotation marks are not necessary for phrase searching.

Figure 2-6. Factiva Search Page

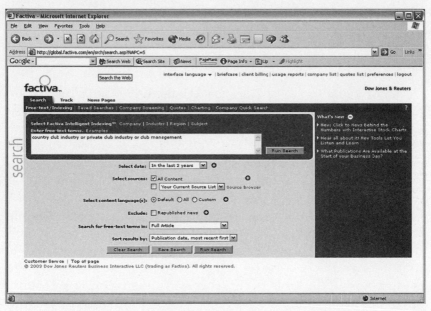

Factiva separates results into four sections: Publications, Pictures, Web Sites, and Reports. For this search too many of the results dealt with nightclub management, so Elaine recast the search term without "club management." All of the resulting twenty-nine publications looked relevant, but four seemed especially on target. She used the Save Search option, a helpful feature in case you need to run a search again.

With Factiva, you must purchase an article to get its indexing terms, which makes backward searching difficult. So Elaine tried the More Like This link. It moved very slowly at this point, and most of the two-thousand-plus results were not at all "Like This"! So she decided to purchase the four articles from her saved search. Factiva offers options for receiving documents via e-mail, printing them out, and formatting and saving them. She saved them as RTF documents and returned to the headlines listing.

To dig a little deeper, Elaine entered the search term *club management and facilit**. Even though she had removed "club management" from her first search, she thought the results might come out better if the term was paired with "facility" or "facilities." This brought up nearly 300 hits, and it was hard to find the relevant articles, so she revised the search term to "club management and facilities." This resulted in 159 hits, and she was able to skim these quickly. Three looked especially good. One article mentioned *Club Management* magazine's annual issue highlighting clubhouse facilities, *2002 Design Showcase*. The other two articles were "Membership Development: A Necessity for Today's Clubs" and "A Survey of Clubhouse Renovations: Costs and Financing," both from *Club Management* magazine. She decided to purchase the first two, remembering that the clubhouse renovation article was one of the four articles she had downloaded from the magazine Web site during her Internet research.

After looking at the article from the *Design Showcase*, Elaine decided to look at the table of contents for the whole issue. She looked around the search page and checked the help section, but she could not find how to pull up all the articles in the issue. After a few failed search attempts, she decided to try customer service. She found a customer service link on the Factiva home page and selected the 24/7 call option (see Figure 2-7).

Figure 2-7. Factiva Customer Service Page

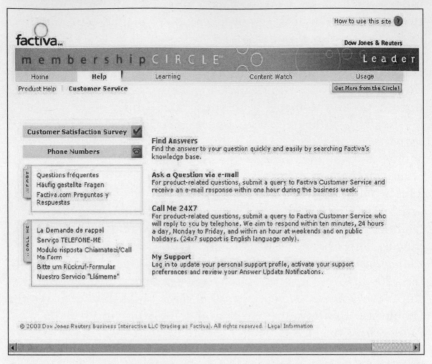

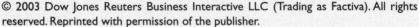

After the query form was completed and submitted, a Factiva representative called within the promised ten minutes. The representative advised Elaine to go back to the Source Browser, highlight the title, click View Source Details, and note the source code, which was ACLM. Closing this window, Elaine returned to the search screen and entered SC = ACLM. Again, she entered 12/1/02 into the date limiters, and this time the results listed all thirty-one articles from that issue. (She later found that entering the source name also works: "sn=club management.") Twelve of those thirty-one articles spotlighted individual clubs, and she had already retrieved three others. Of the remaining articles, six looked very relevant. At $2.95 per article at Factiva, Elaine thought it was worth a look at the magazine Web site to see if these could be retrieved for free.

Using the Google Toolbar, Elaine searched the site for "smokers," a title word of one of her selections. The article appeared, but the format was different from the other articles she had retrieved from the site. She noted from the URL that this article came from another section of the site. She tried to find the section by deleting the last part of the URL and found that it was a forbidden section. Elaine guessed that this article came from the subscribers-only area of the site. No other articles could be found at the site, but she did copy an article from 2001 highlighting a renovation for a country club outside of Chicago. She selected this over other articles of this type because RMCC, too, was outside a large city. Because that left five articles plus the twelve that spotlighted a single club (which she thought might offer insight into trends as well as architectural firms), Elaine made a call to the RMCC manager. He did, in fact, have that issue, and Elaine would pick it up the next day.

It was time to take stock and decide whether to search some more on Factiva or move on. So far, article retrieval had cost $17.90. At this stage, Elaine looked at each of the eight articles she had, compared them with the client's questions, and decided how the articles might answer the questions. She marked relevant sections, highlighted new keywords and terms, and then wrote at the top of each article subject words that corresponded to the client questions. She found that some of the articles did not exactly respond to the client questions, but she thought they were relevant to concerns revealed in the client interview. For example, the survey of renovation costs and financing did not reveal much about building trends, but she thought it would help the board decide whether to renovate or build.

The researcher decided to mark the highly relevant articles with an asterisk and the articles that had no value with an X. Out of the eight articles, one had an X. Of the remaining seven, four covered membership development and three discussed clubhouse facilities, trends, or construction. Three articles had an asterisk. She did not have any articles about club policy, and no information on who sets and implements policy or current trends in policies (such as smoking or dress policy). Searches using *club policy*; *smoking polic**; and *dress code* or polic** seemed to go nowhere. Elaine made the decision to move to Dialog.

DIALOG. Some research projects can be completed by looking at a small, focused set of resources. However, when your search is broad and multifaceted, a comprehensive resource is invaluable. Researchers use the Classic Dialog product because it combines extensive content with powerful command searching and time-saving tools. With the Classic product, you can select from hundreds of databases (called "Files" in Dialog). In addition,

Classic Dialog allows you to create and combine search terms, refine searches, and retrieve documents faster because you type the commands instead of clicking options and filling in boxes, as you do with many Web-based products. Indexing is powerful, and Dialog allows you to view indexing terms without purchasing the entire document. In addition, many researchers prefer Dialog's DialogLink software to Web-based products, because it is fast and reliable (see Figure 2-8).

Figure 2-8. DialogLink Interface

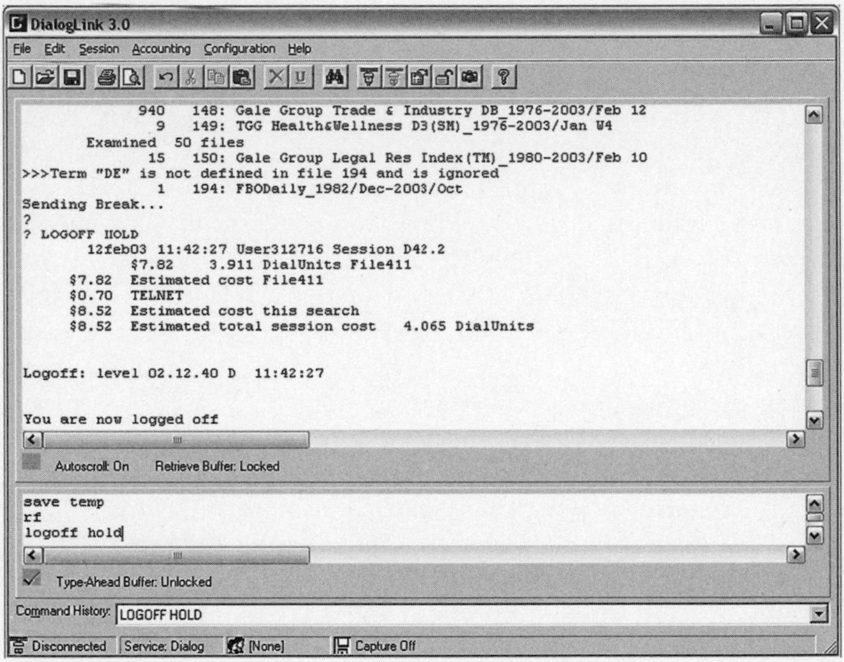

2003® Dialog, a Thomson business, *http://www.dialog.com*. Reprinted with permission of the publisher.

It takes time to learn command search techniques and file management in Dialog, but this product makes it possible to execute cost-effective yet comprehensive research, providing the information that market and industry researchers need.

LEARNING DIALOG

To get the most out of Dialog, it is essential to learn not only command language but the specifics of hundreds of files. The more in-depth knowledge you have, the greater your chances of finding and retrieving the best information possible in the shortest amount of time, without costly errors. Dialog offers a selection of search aids, training opportunities, publications, and customer support options, and it is in the searcher's best interest to take full advantage of them.

- Go to *http://support.dialog.com/searchaids/dialog* to find the search aids. Here you will find access to the Dialog Bluesheets, which include details about content, pricing, formats, special features, and more. Bluesheets are the key to learning about each of the Dialog files. Dialog has posted the electronic versions of the user guides, along with information about interfaces, alerts, and other options. Database-specific search aids contain descriptors, codes, newspaper lists, and other information about the individual files.
- Go to the training Web page (*http://training.dialog.com*) for links to online courses, tutorials, workbooks, free practice, and other training opportunities.
- Dialog publications such as *Chronolog* and *OpenDialog* offer search tips and keep searchers up to date on Dialog products and services. You can find these publications at *http://support.dialog.com/ publications*.
- Finally, use Dialog's Online Support Center (*http://support.dialog.com/ searchaids/dialog*), where support options include e-mail forms, telephone help, and more.

The research completed up to this point showed that there was not a lot of information available on the topic of country club management and policy making. Elaine concluded that a targeted search might eliminate relevant articles and decided to start with a broad search instead, pulling in as much information as possible and narrowing as needed. It is a good strategy to use a more general search and scan three to four hundred hits, looking at titles, indexing terms, and keywords in context to identify the relevant articles. With this method, you cover your bases while quickly ruling out hits that are not relevant to your search, called false drops.

The search began in File 411, DIALINDEX, which covers all Dialog databases. This reveals how many times the search terms occur in selected files. Elaine thought the best files for this search would be newspapers and business, so she set DIALINDEX to the OneSearch Group supercategory ALLBUSINESS. The search looked like this:

```
            B 411
SF ALLBUSINESS
S (COUNTRY OR PRIVATE)()CLUB?/TI,DE
SAVE TEMP
RF
LOGOFF HOLD
```

This search allowed Elaine not only to identify files with the required search term, but also to save the search and arrange the list of files according to number of items (RF is the command to rank the files according to the number of hits). Limiting the search to references where the search terms appeared in the title or descriptor fields (/TI,DE) eliminated articles that mention the term only once or twice in the text.

Figure 2-9. Search Results in Dialog

```
411b - Notepad
File  Edit  Format  View  Help

      - Enter P or PAGE for more -
?p
!Your last SELECT statement was:
   S ((COUNTRY OR PRIVATE)()CLUB?)/TI,DE

Ref        Items    File
---        -----    ----
N11           88    553: Wilson Bus. Abs. FullText_1982-2002/Dec
N12           69    583: Gale Group Globalbase(TM)_1986-2002/Dec 13
N13           59    211: Gale Group Newsearch(TM)_2003/Jan 31
N14           46    160: Gale Group PROMT(R)_1972-1989
N15           39     13: BAMP_2003/Jan W2
N16            9*   624: McGraw-Hill Publications_1985-2003/Feb 03
N17            5    745: Investext(R) PDF Index_1999--2003/Jan W4
N18            5    766: (R)Kalorama Info Market Res._1993-2000/Aug
N19            4    637: Journal of Commerce_1986-2003/Feb 03
N20            2    112: UBM Industry News_1998-2003/Feb 03
   22 files have one or more items; file list includes 42 files.
   * One or more search terms are invalid in this file

      - Enter P or PAGE for more -
?p
!Your last SELECT statement was:
   S ((COUNTRY OR PRIVATE)()CLUB?)/TI,DE

Ref        Items    File
---        -----    ----
N21            2    514: DIALOG Investment Res. Index_1995-2003/Jan 27
N22            1*   628: Ctry Risk & Forecasts_2003/Jan W4
N23            0    192: Industry Trends & Anal._1997/Jun
N24            0    481: DELPHES Eur Bus_95-2003/Jan W4
N25            0    563: Key Note Market Res._1986-2001/Aug 03
N26            0    564: ICC Brit.Co.Ann.Rpts_1984-2003/Feb 02
```

2003® Dialog, a Thomson business, *http://www.dialog.com*. Reprinted with permission of the publisher.

The search results (see Figure 2-9) revealed a large number of references in the business files, such as Wilson Business Abstracts, Gale Group Globalbase, Newsearch, and PROMT, so Elaine decided to move in that direction. Although you can search multiple files in Dialog and remove any duplicate records, including all of the likely business resources at once would still yield too many results, making it difficult to scan. To keep the search results more manageable, she executed the search in two files, 16 (Gale Group PROMT) and 148 (Gale Group Trade & Industry Database).

After removing duplicates, there were still too many results to scan, so Elaine added *PY>1999*. This narrowed the results to material published after 1999. The remaining eight hundred hits were still too many to scan, so other terms were added: *(dress OR smoking)()(policy OR policies),* which produced zero hits, and *club()management,* which produced four. Elaine requested these in format 8, k to show titles, publication dates, word counts, indexing terms, and keywords in context. One article looked good, so she pulled up the full text, saved the search, and went to Logoff Hold. This command saves the search on Dialog's server and allows the user to log back on and return to that place in the search.

A quick scan of the article revealed a great resource. It discussed trends resulting from the heavy competition private golf clubs were facing. In addition, it included valuable target market information, such as a lengthy 1999 article from the *Wall Street Journal* that talked about the state of the industry, which Elaine decided to look for. Finally, she identified some keywords and phrases from this article: "trends," "club members," "member retention," and "attract new members."

The researcher decided to take a closer look at some of the other hits from the search *(country OR private)()club?/TI, DE AND PY>1999*. She requested the first one hundred hits in format 6, a free format with titles, but again failed to find anything worthwhile. By saving the search, she was able go back into the files and quickly combine this search with additional terms: *facilities() planning* produced no hits, but *trends* produced some. Two articles viewed in format 8, k looked worthwhile, so she downloaded these. One was a brief article about hotel golf courses. The other covered Canadian private clubs and trends but also offered insight into marketing strategies in general. Elaine decided this would add value to her report. She thought she was on the right track, so she opted to try these saved searches in the other business databases she had selected.

Elaine chose File 635, Business Dateline, a business news database. She used the same technique as with the searches in Files 16 and 148:

- Scan about two hundred titles from the general search *(country OR private)()club?/TI,DE AND PY>1999*.
- Run this search with the additional terms.

- Remove duplicates.
- Look at free formats for titles, indexing terms, and keywords in context.
- Download relevant articles.

This search produced many articles on specific clubs and their renovation projects. Elaine had expected to find such results in File 635 because of its regional focus. She decided to put off printing these articles for later, because she may have already had more than enough of this type of article from *Club Management* magazine. The search also yielded three additional articles mentioning trends. After printing these, Elaine found that one was on target, with information about demographics and trends in facilities and marketing. The second wasn't bad, and the third not worthwhile at all. Again, sometimes you just can't tell until you purchase the article. You try to minimize your risk by knowing the databases, looking at free formats, and perhaps paying to view an abstract, but sometimes you have to take the good with the bad.

Elaine thought she was finally getting somewhere with the Dialog research. So far her information included some mention of trends in club policies, but nothing about who was setting and/or implementing policy. So she needed to look for additional information on setting policy. Since the budget was sufficient, she decided to execute the same search in the remaining Dialog business databases.

This next step in the search covered the rest of the business databases all at once since, according to the DIALINDEX search, the results would probably be smaller and more manageable than with the previous files. Also, Elaine was not going to use any field searching other than title and descriptor. Because Dialog includes databases from a number of providers, indexing is not always consistent. When projects call for field searching, it is helpful to combine databases that use the same indexing terms. For this project, though, limiting too much by field or index term might result in a level of specificity that would exclude valuable references.

Using her saved searches, she searched the remaining business databases from her DIALINDEX search, Files 9 (Business & Industry), 15 (ABI/Inform), 13 (Business & Management Practices, BAMP), and 570 (Gale Group Marketing & Advertising Reference Service, MARS). This resulted in three articles that seemed worthwhile, although none contained anything about setting policy. One highlighted member retention issues and answers, another offered a useful discussion on trends, and a third turned out to be an abstract of an article from File 15 about club restaurant service. File 15 is a database of citations, abstracts, and full-text documents, but you can limit your search to full-text documents. Elaine chose not to do this—again, to avoid eliminating any possibilities. At this point, on-target abstracts would be just fine.

In an effort to zero in on information about setting policy, Elaine checked *Fulltext Sources Online*, a print resource for identifying databases that contain specific publications. Here she found that *Club Management* magazine was contained in Dialog News-Room (Files 990, 993, 994, and 995). Perhaps there would be similar resources or maybe an article in that publication that she had missed. It seemed to be the best bet for information on club management issues.

Elaine used the original search, *(country OR private)()club?/TI,DE,* without the date limits, since NewsRoom goes back only to 2000. She combined this search with additional terms in every possible way she could imagine: *board(2W)directors*; *decision()making; (set OR implement? OR setting)(2W)(policy OR policies);* and finally, *club()(manager? OR management).* This retrieved four articles, one from the *board(2W)directors* search and three from the *club()(manager? OR management)* search. At this point, she noted that she was getting too close to the budget limits, as nearly $140 had been spent on Dialog searching. It was time to review her search—look at what had been accumulated to this point, see what information was still needed, and decide where to go from there.

Step 4: Review Online Database Research—Do You Have Enough?

Our researcher had used three online database services for finding articles and market research: Profound, Factiva, and Dialog. Profound had produced nothing, but the Factiva and Dialog searches were productive. Factiva seemed to work best for more general searches and Dialog for more focused or targeted searches. The searches turned up a lot about trends in membership development and facility design. Just a few articles mentioned dress and smoking policies, and nothing was found on setting/implementing policy. Elaine then looked at the search terms she had used for her online database research (see Appendix 1 at the end of this chapter).

Because there were so many terms, and expenses were close to the limits outlined in the letter of agreement, Elaine decided to stop searching the online database services. First, she needed to retrieve the *Wall Street Journal* article that she had noted earlier. Again, she consulted *Fulltext Sources Online* and found that this publication could be accessed through Factiva. After logging on, she found the source code for the publication, entered the date of the article into both date fields, and included the term *country clubs* in the title field, since the article was titled "Country Clubs Get Snubbed." She purchased the article, found it contained some information about trends, and added it to her collection of articles. It was time to analyze the data that had been collected from the Internet research and online database services.

DATA ANALYSIS

Researchers analyze their data throughout the project to evaluate products and services, devise strategies, and find patterns. At this point, though—after completing the planned search strategies—the researcher analyzes each piece of information and determines not only how it answers the client questions, but also how it will be used in the report. In addition, this is the time to decide whether to stop searching or go back to the Internet or online database services.

To analyze the resources she had accessed and the content they uncovered, our researcher again looked at each article and made notes about how that article answered the client questions. She then identified any holes in her search: the questions that had not been answered. She also took a closer look at the kind of information the client had not explicitly requested but that still might be useful in some way. Finally, she looked for possible bias, inconsistencies, or obvious errors in the retrieved articles and reports. This would help identify the need for any additional research, as well as any recommendations she could make to her client.

The analysis revealed that the research had provided ample information about building design trends and projects, including a long list of architectural firms. The articles also provided adequate information on attracting new members and retaining current members. The researcher found only small mention of smoking and dress policies, but she decided that when these were added to the statistics from CMAA, it might add up to enough information for the report.

The largest hole in the research results had to do with who sets and/or implements policy. The CMAA contact, Mr. Rosenbaum, had said he did not know of any source for this information. None of the resources set aside for possible purchase would fill this gap. All Elaine had was an article about insurance that mentioned that the board of directors usually makes the decisions. She thought that primary research would probably be the best way to get at this type of information and made a note to add this suggestion to her report. Because this question ranked lowest among the client's prioritized questions, Elaine thought that a recommendation, rather than further research, would be appropriate.

She then reevaluated the articles and statistics that, on first glance, had not seemed to fit the research questions. When compared with the results of the client interview and with other information that had been retrieved, some of these documents now seemed quite relevant to the client's needs. For example, the CMAA reports included data about dining minimums, something that was not addressed in her client's questions. An article pulled from Factiva, however, mentioned dining minimums as a drawback when trying to attract younger members. In this context, association statistics about dining minimums at other clubs would probably be worthwhile to RMCC. The client interview had also revealed that the club's Strategic Planning Committee would be using parts of the report at their meetings. Elaine decided that the committee would probably be interested in this piece of information for effective decision making, and she made a mental note to include the CMAA statistics in her report. In addition, two articles mentioned target markets in the club industry, something that did not show up in the client's questions. Elaine concluded that these articles might help the board make marketing decisions.

By looking at the data retrieved, Elaine found that most of the information had come from three sources: the business press, *Club Management* magazine, and CMAA. Research to this point had not really uncovered another industry publication or association. The *Wall Street Journal* article and some others painted a negative picture of the country club industry, whereas some sources took a more positive tone. In this respect, Elaine thought there was a fair balance.

As a result of this analysis, Elaine decided to make another call to Mr. Rosenbaum at CMAA. She hoped that he could help her identify other publications, associations, or experts, or at least direct her to someone who could. She also thought it would be worthwhile to again ask about information on setting and implementing policy. This strategy would allow some time to follow up and perhaps do additional research.

The call to Mr. Rosenbaum turned up some possible leads and additional insight into the issue of setting and implementing club policy. He suggested the *Boardroom* magazine and a newsletter, "The Private Club Advisor" (he even provided the publisher's phone number). Also, he described the National Golf Foundation (NGF), an association for both public and private facilities, as a "survey-oriented" organization that might offer some other resources. Policy setting, he said, varies from club to club, but generally speaking, except for decisions about staff and day-to-day administration, the general manager makes recommendations and the board of directors votes on and sets policy. He added that the question had been asked before, and that perhaps CMAA would undertake a survey on it in the future.

A Google search turned up the Web sites for the *Boardroom* and "The Private Club Advisor." Both offered selected articles, but none was relevant. A check for more articles from these sources through *Fulltext Sources Online* and *Ulrich's Periodicals Directory* (a print directory of periodicals that Elaine uses at her public library) turned up nothing, nor did they show up in Publist (*http://www.publist.com*), an online index of periodicals. Elaine called the publisher of the *Boardroom* and asked if they were indexed anywhere, or if they had their own index. It turned out that they were not indexed anywhere, nor were they willing to share their index with a nonsubscriber. She asked about possible resources for information on setting and implementing policy, and the publisher gave her the name of a club manager who taught at a university in California. Finally, a quick look at the NGF Web site showed that this association focused on the golf side of the industry, with little else that could be of use.

The additional primary research necessary for follow-up did not fall within the scope of this project, but the information Elaine had gathered thus far could be added to the report. She had used her allotted budget for research and needed the remaining time to prepare her report.

FINAL REPORT

A high-quality report helps clients who did not participate in the research process understand and use the information gathered. Most decision makers do not want to go through dozens of resources to get to what they need. The final report condenses the information into an understandable and useable format. For most research projects, the format takes shape according to the questions asked and what the research uncovered. For this project, report sections were based on the four questions identified by RMCC. The researcher added a section for recommendations, or "Next Steps," as well as standard sections on copyright, document delivery, and disclaimers.

To answer the questions, Elaine scanned each article or note and summarized the key points in bulleted lists under the appropriate headings, with footnotes to reference the research sources. Evidence from both the secondary and primary research was included, and recommendations for further research were made for the one question that had few answers—setting and implementing policy. To summarize the answers to the client's questions, Elaine drafted the following executive summary:

EXECUTIVE SUMMARY

- The average age of country club members is in the early fifties, a decline of about ten years over the past years. Many clubs are targeting younger, more family-oriented potential members.
- The country club industry, faced with increased competition from public, semiprivate, and resort golf clubs, has launched aggressive marketing campaigns, including open houses, radio advertising, and refundable deposits.
- Retaining members and encouraging them to refer new members is the most effective way to add to membership rosters. Keys to retaining these members include improving service by letting staff know the dollar value of a membership, involving members in activity planning and promotion, and generally improving members' emotional ties to the club.
- Both younger and older members are asking for more casual dining dress policies, and clubs have been responding by adding casual evenings and/or dining areas.

- In a survey of clubs, 73 percent require collared shirts at informal dinners. Sixty-one percent do not allow jeans/denim; 8 percent require a jacket; 61 percent allow golf attire; and 21 percent do not allow shorts.
- According to an industry survey, more than 53 percent of the respondents reported that they had made changes to their club's smoking policy in the past five years.
- Almost half of the clubs that allow smoking throughout the clubhouse said they have made changes to accommodate nonsmokers—most often the establishment of nonsmoking areas.
- According to an industry expert, in most clubs the board of directors sets policy with input from the club manager. The club manager is responsible for implementing policy. No statistics appear to have been collected on this topic.
- Most country clubs choose renovation over scrapping and rebuilding the clubhouse facility.
- Trends in clubhouse design incorporate casual gathering space, including lounges and dining areas, fitness facilities, and dining rooms with open cooking areas. Modern designs and materials are replacing traditional décor.

Satisfied that the information had been adequately distilled and organized, the researcher created the table of contents and edited, printed, and bound the report. The electronic version was e-mailed to the board president, and the print version was hand delivered before the agreed date.

CONCLUSION

The project took the anticipated twelve hours, and the expenses totaled $235.65, making the total cost of the project $1,435.65. The country club board was pleased with the final report and the depth of research, and they decided against any additional research at this point.

Changing the way club policy was set had become a lower priority. Once they realized that their outdated facility had been impeding membership development, the board of directors decided to focus their strategic planning efforts on a clubhouse renovation plan that would include replacing the aging and often-patched swimming pool. The club survey indicated that members appreciated this family-friendly area of RMCC, and board members thought a new pool would help them target new members with young families. With the help of the list in the final report and input from club members, the board immediately contacted five architects.

In light of what they had learned from the research, board members eliminated the no-jeans clubhouse dress policy and started to include members in planning club activities, a practice they had eliminated five years earlier. The general manager updated staff job descriptions to include promotion of club events. The newsletter staff rescheduled its deadlines to include information about activities earlier, starting two months in advance.

The Strategic Planning Committee drafted and approved the plan ahead of schedule. With a renovated facility, renewed interest in the club among current members, and an updated vision and marketing plan to attract new members, leaders thought RMCC was on its way to financial recovery and ready to bring back the fun.

APPENDIX 1: SUMMARY OF SEARCH TERMS

SEARCH ENGINE OR DATABASE	SEARCH TERMS
Google	*country club industry*
	country club management
	private club management
AlltheWeb	*country club industry*
	private club management
Profound	*country club*, private club* (limited to USA)*
Factiva	*country club industry or private club industry or club management*
	country club industry or private club industry or club management
	country club industry or private club industry
	club management and facilit*
	club management and facilities
	sc=aclm 12/1/02–12/1/02
	sc=j 1/30/99–1/3099
Dialog	*(country or private)()club?/ti, de*
	(country or private)()club?/ti, de and py>1999
	(dress or smoking)()(policy or policies)
	club()management
	facilities()planning
	trends
	board(2w)directors
	decision()making
	(set or implement? or setting)(2w)(policy or policies)
	club()(manager? or management)

APPENDIX 2: SUMMARY OF RESOURCES

AlltheWeb	*http://www.alltheweb.com*
American Society of Association Executives (ASAE) Gateway to Associations	*http://info.asaenet.org/gateway/OnlineAssocSlist.html*
Associations Unlimited	*http://www.galegroup.com*
Business 2.0	*http://www.business2.com/webguide*
Club Management	*http://www.club-mgmt.com*
Club Management Association of America	*http://www.cmaa.org*
Dialog	*http://www.dialog.com*
Factiva	*http://www.factiva.com*
First Research Industry Profiles	*http://industryprofiles.1stresearch.com*
Fulltext Sources Online	*http://www.infotoday.com/FSO/default.htm*
Google?lz?*http://www.google.com*	
Google Toolbar	*http://toolbar.google.com*
Harvard Business School Baker Library Industry Guides	*http://library.hbs.edu/industry*
Internet Public Library Associations on the Net	*http://www.ipl.org/div/aon*
The McKinsey Quarterly	*http://www.mckinseyquarterly.com/home.asp*
Profound	*http://www.profound.com*
Publist	*http://www.publist.com*
Ulrich's Periodicals Directory	*http://www.ulrichsweb.com/ulrichsweb*
ValuationResources.com	*http://www.valuationresources.com/IndustryReport.htm*

3

Market and Industry Research Problems and Solutions

The preceding chapter examines a complex, multilayered research project, with numerous sources consulted to answer several questions. In this chapter we extend the application of research strategies to a series of shorter research problems, with worked-out solutions, that provide even more professional insight into the online market and industry research process.

Each of the market or industry research problems and solutions in this chapter is divided into the same developmental sequence: (1) problem definition, (2) research budget, (3) strategy employed, (4) research results, and (5) solution summary. Each entry includes a list of useful research tips directly related to the search questions and sources used.

Taken together, the wide range of research problems presented examine typical market and industry research situations. The problems also serve to illustrate professional research strategies used to find the industry information identified in Helen Burwell's industry study template, described in Chapter One. The sample problems and solutions contained here examine ways to meet the need for information on industry trends and forecasts, customers, market size, market directions, product differentiation, price structure, suppliers, marketing media, technology use and technological trends, emerging technologies, and regulations.

Each contributor has addressed the research question using available resources and search strategies based on their experience. As a rule there is more than one way to approach any question, and none of the solutions presented here represents the sole means to accomplish the research. Each case, however, presents sound research advice.

This chapter's expert contributors are Jan Knight, Robin Neidorf, Kent Sutorius, Margaret Metcalf Carr, Wendy Katz, Jan Davis, Cynthia Shamel, and Karl Kasca. Their research problems are drawn from this editor's experience and from their own business practices, representing typical questions and concerns likely to arise in the workplace.

In Problem 1, Janet Knight looks at a company expanding into a new market and seeking to understand the dynamics of that market. The company has targeted cell culture laboratories and needs information on key suppliers, market size, and how suppliers market to the labs. Knight's research illustrates the value of a company's annual report in revealing marketing, selling, and advertising methods. She also points out how much information can be gleaned from the executive summary of a study, even without purchasing the complete study. In Problem 5, Knight takes a look at one segment of the market for software designed to teach foreign languages. The client wants information to support the assertion that there is a continual and increasing need for this type of training in the military and government market. Because government programs are so well documented on the Internet, the researcher in this case is able to find the desired information from the government and military Web sites, from the National Foreign Language Center, identified via Internet searches, and from the sites of competitors.

Robin Neidorf takes a multifaceted look at the competitive landscape for Web-based financial services in Problem 2. Her research strategy is methodical and thorough. She makes effective use of cached Web pages to compare competitors' current strategy with past strategies, and illustrates when and how to buy market research information "by the slice" rather than in full reports. In Problem 7, Neidorf describes the research challenge of the marketing director at a large publishing firm. Because the company's primary customers are public agencies at the state level, the director needs to determine how these customers will cope with major budget cuts anticipated for the next fiscal year. This case provides excellent insights into researching government information at the state level and demonstrates the importance of leaving adequate time and resources in the project budget to compile the final report.

In Problems 10 and 11, Wendy Katz offers a unique insight into some of the sources generally used by market and industry researchers. She takes a single research request and conducts the research twice. She first uses the Dialog databases to explore trends in digital projectors for commercial theaters, and then she repeats the search using LexisNexis. She clearly and expertly outlines the databases searched, the strategies and terms used, and the research outcomes. These solutions should prove very useful to online database searchers, as they provide a template that models simultaneous, multi-database searches. In Problem 13, Katz helps researchers navigate government regulations from the Food and Drug Administration. Highly regulated industries such as pharmaceuticals must remain current on any changes at the regulating agency. Katz shows how to use a combination of industry news sources and government Web sites to put together a picture of the regulatory environment.

Kent Sutorius demonstrates some excellent strategies for finding facts related to the profitability of a retail bicycle shop (Problem 3) and very specific statistics on the incidence and prevalence of prostate cancer (Problem 4). The case of the bicycle shop points out the value of using trade and professional associations as a source of industry overviews and statistics. The question on prostate cancer represents a common task in biomedical and pharmaceutical company marketing research, since disease statistics often reflect potential market size. In Problem 8, Sutorius takes on a broader search for overviews and trends. His strategy begins in the selection of a general source, Webopedia, which offers definitions of computer technology terms and links to other relevant sources. This demonstrates the much-touted "general-to-specific" approach advocated for most online research projects.

Researcher Peggy Carr has contributed three solutions (Problems 6, 9, and 12) that address product positioning, pricing strategies, and market trends. In the product-positioning case, a small manufacturer seeks to understand industry trends and the current market positions of other producers. Carr describes a general-to-specific strategy that begins with a broad search of general news sources for "current events" in the industry, then moves to industry and trade publications for more specific information, and finally fills in the blanks with telephone interviews of competing manufacturers. The researcher managed the $1,000 budget by interviewing as many people as possible and stopping when the funds ran out. In Problem 9 Carr describes how product-pricing research can assist a client in evaluating product-pricing options. Again Carr mixes online research with personal interviews and demonstrates the value of government and public records sources for commerce-related information. In searching for market information on a tight budget, Carr illustrates in Problem 12 how to balance the "fast" research strategies with the "cheap" research strategies. She also shows how to go beyond the information publicly available on a trade association Web site by searching the trade literature for editors' expert insights.

In Problem 14, volume editor Cynthia Shamel describes research into the digital whiteboard market to illustrate strategies for finding market share statistics. Marketing department directors and product managers often seek to understand how their product fits into the mix of available products, as well as to better understand the competition. This search demonstrates the value of proximity operators in online searching.

Jan Davis presents a scenario in Problem 15 in which a knowledge worker within an accounting firm is charged with finding executive salary information for the engineering industry. Davis recommends an Internet directory compiled by librarians to find high-quality, reliable sources of salary and compensation surveys, again demonstrating the wisdom of moving from the general to the specific. To stay on budget, Davis's researcher follows the common practice of compiling a report for her client that includes all of the relevant free information, along with a list of additional reports available for a fee.

Karl Kasca takes an interesting approach to finding customer data in Problem 16. In this case the objective is to identify potential new customers for C-clamps. Kasca uses traditional sources such as the Internet and Dialog, plus some creative sources such as Internet discussion groups. He takes a unique approach to analyzing the information using a database tool called askSam.

A sincere thank-you to each and every contributor for constructing this series of realistic problems with clear and workable solutions. Your efforts have resulted in a collection of excellent teaching materials that offer value to experienced and novice searchers alike.

PROBLEM NUMBER 1: REACHING POTENTIAL CUSTOMERS: MARKET SIZE, SUPPLIERS, MARKETING PRACTICES, AND INDUSTRY TRENDS FOR THE CELL CULTURE LABORATORY MARKET

RESEARCH BACKGROUND: LabWorks, a technology company, has created a new product to be used in a specific type of laboratory: its product will be marketed and sold to laboratories that perform "cell culture" work, the biotechnological process of growing cells outside of living organisms. To revise its business and marketing plan to incorporate this new product, LabWorks is looking for information on this relatively small niche within the pharmaceutical industry. The marketing manager already knows that a limited number of cell culture laboratories exist in the United States and that numerous vendors sell other products to this market. He wants a researcher to determine (1) approximate potential market size, (2) current key suppliers to this market, (3) how these laboratories purchase these products, and (4) any trends that are being discussed in this industry.

RESEARCH BUDGET: The marketing manager does not have access to any fee-based databases and does not want to take the time to perform his own Internet research. He is willing to hire an independent researcher to spend ten to fifteen hours researching and writing up the findings, as well as to pay for database fees ranging from $150 to $175.

RESEARCH STRATEGY EMPLOYED: The researcher knows that cell culture work takes place primarily within the pharmaceutical (drug) industry, and that it also exists within other biotechnology areas such as genetic and chemical engineering. To expand his limited understanding of the industry, he first conducts a simple Internet search using the phrase *cell culture* in Google (*http://www.google.com*). This allows him to identify pertinent industries, basic information on the potential market size, and a selection of companies that are already selling to this market. Additional searches take place using the search phrase *cell culture* combined with other search terms such as *suppliers, buyers guides, vendors, market size, pharmaceutical industry,* and *drug industry.* The Web sites of the vendors are reviewed for information on how their marketing and sales operations are set up as well as for hints on any strategic company news that might help to identify trends.

The researcher uses a "reverse look-up" of suppliers' Web sites to identify potential strategic partners as well as to find additional resources and buyers' guides where LabWorks might advertise. There are a number of ways to do this, but the easiest is to use the following search term in a search engine: *Link:www.companyname.com* (with "companyname" referring to the company's Web site address). This search retrieves a list of Web sites that link to the Web site entered in the search.

For example, to search for companies that link to Invitrogen's Web site, simply enter the search term *link:www.invitrogen.com.* The results include a listing described as "Laboratory Suppliers," an example of a buyers' guide.

A subsequent search to find out more about marketing to this niche industry is then performed using a combination of terms, such as *marketing OR advertising AND "life scientists."* This latter term was chosen after reviewing various Web sites of companies who sell to cell culture laboratories and determining that a major group of customers are academic researchers who are often referred to as "life scientists."

In addition to searching the Internet via a search engine, the researcher reviews another site, MarketResearch.com, to see if any market research studies on the cell culture industry are available for a fee. Although the budget doesn't allow for the purchase of market research reports, reviewing what is available can often provide an idea of just how much study there has been in a particular area or industry. It is often possible to review the table of contents of such reports and possibly purchase small sections "by the slice."

To determine what is being reported about the industry as a whole, the researcher then conducts an article search of newspapers, magazines, and trade journals. He chooses this strategy rather than turning to an industry search in an online database because he knows that cell culture is a small niche within a larger industry, and that this subject would be too small for most commercial databases that provide information by industry topic. Such predefined industry searches typically focus on larger industries such as "pharmaceuticals" or "engineering."

The search for articles takes place within the two subscription databases of Dow Jones Interactive and Hoover's. In Dow Jones, the researcher turns to the Publications Library, where he conducts keyword searches including the aforementioned terms, along with the addition of the keyword *trends*. In Hoover's, it is first necessary to search by company name for each of the identified suppliers. If articles are available for the company selected, they can then be found under the section "Current Stories Mentioning **Company X**" within the News & Commentary section.

RESEARCH RESULTS: The searches described above are useful for identifying potential LabWorks customers (cell culture laboratories), vendors who sell to these laboratories, and examples of how these vendors market and sell their products. It has also provided some background information on potential market size and trends. The results are summarized below:

- **Names of Other Suppliers.** The initial Internet search and review of buyers' guides provides names of major suppliers to the cell culture market: Invitrogen, Irvine Scientific, Hyclone, Bio Whittaker, and Cambrex. This is not an exhaustive list of suppliers, but from reviewing the resources, the researcher concludes that it includes the key players. The reverse look-up of links in the suppliers' Web sites provides additional examples of buyers' guides.

- **Selling and Marketing.** The annual reports and Web sites of these identified suppliers provide information on their customer base, typically both academic and private laboratories, and further review finds information on specific methods used for selling and marketing their products and services. The search using *"life scientists" AND marketing* immediately provides information on a company called BioInformatics, a company that describes itself as "an innovative market research and consulting firm supporting marketing and sales executives in the life science, medical device and pharmaceutical industries" (*http://www.gene2drug.com*). The BioInformatics Web site provides executive summaries of surveys, such as "Marketing to Life Scientists: Keys to Success," "Marketing to Life Scientists: A Comparison of the Industrial and Academic Segments," "Advertising to Life Scientists," and "Support and Service for Life Science Products: Creating Loyal Customers." Other surveys listed on the Web site reveal additional information. The search in Dow Jones also provides a citation for a 2002 article in a journal called *Chemical Week*: "Suppliers to the Drug Industry Are Trying to Stay Ahead of Competitors, Customers, and Technologies." This article provides additional general information on the suppliers, their concerns, and their methods of marketing.

- **Trends.** The Dow Jones and Hoover's article searches provide a number of citations for review. Two articles from the journal *Genetic Engineering News* are highlighted to report on. One is titled "Current Trends and Innovations in Cell Culture," and the other is "Survey of Market Trends for Cell Culture Media." Both are written in 2001 and outline a number of trends and events in the cell culture industry.

- **Market Size.** Initial searches discovered a 1997 study from PhorTech International, a company that conducts marketing research and technology assessment for life science research companies. The data are probably not current enough, and subsequent searches do not produce newer statistics on the same subject. However, the PhorTech Web site also provides a more recent 2002 study on "Global Laboratory Product Usage," which includes some useful information that, combined with the older data, satisfies LabWork's need for information about the potential market size.

SUMMARY OF SOLUTION: The researcher reviews the Web sites, and in some cases the annual reports, of the suppliers he has identified, looking for specific information on marketing, selling, and advertising methods. The review shows that a combination of direct mail, trade show attendance, articles, and print advertising in trade journals and Web sites are some of the key methods used by suppliers to reach this specific market.

The BioInformatics reports include a wealth of information on the purchasing preferences of scientists, including information about how they learn about vendors, products, and services and make purchasing decisions. The reports also show that good customer service is critical in scientists' choice of suppliers. Much more information along these same lines is available from the executive summaries of the studies, and the researcher does not suggest that LabWorks purchase the full studies.

The potential market size (number of cell culture laboratories) does not seem to be readily available, but the 1997 study by PhorTech cites that "Over 60,000 U.S. life science researchers are currently involved with cell and tissue culture, spending approximately $100 million annually on instrumentation and media."[1] Providing a more global context, the Global Laboratory Product Usage study says that "the estimation of total population of life scientists is 356,600 worldwide, of whom 281,250 are working in the laboratory." Additional data in this study report that "61.14% of these life scientists are involved in cell culture." These numbers are provided to the client, and LabWorks determines that the numbers will suffice for current planning.

CONTRIBUTOR NAME: Jan Knight
AFFILIATION: Bancroft Information Services

---

1. 1997/98 US MSPPSA Series, "Cell and Tissue Culture Systems: An Analysis of Market Size and Growth, Market Share, Purchase Plans and Supplier Assessment for the U.S. Life Science Research Market" by PhorTech International, San Carlos, CA, July 3, 1998, <*http://www.phortech.com/97cell.htm*> (July 2, 2003).

USEFUL TIPS

- Reviewing what is available from large market research/survey companies is a good first step to determine the potential availability of information.
- Online buying guides are often a good place to find an initial list of competitors.
- The reverse look-up on a company Web site (*link:www. companyname.com*) helps to find strategic partnerships and potential advertising/marketing vehicles.

PROBLEM NUMBER 2: FINANCIAL SERVICES COMPETITIVE INTELLIGENCE: MAPPING THE COMPETITIVE LANDSCAPE FOR WEB-BASED CUSTOMER SERVICE

RESEARCH BACKGROUND: MaxMoney, a financial services company, is planning to roll out an extensive new Web-based service platform to provide customers with information, account access, new account applications, tax preparation, advice, and more. The financial services industry is a highly competitive, customer-oriented industry, and many companies in the industry are leaping into Web-based customer contact and services. To stake its claim in cyberspace, MaxMoney needs to know exactly what its competitors are doing—and planning to do—on the Web, as well as initiatives they may have abandoned. With this information, the company will be best able to position its own offerings and garner market share.

RESEARCH BUDGET: Many high-quality market research firms offer expensive reports detailing activity in the financial services sector. But MaxMoney is not willing to spend the $10,000 or more per report these firms charge. To minimize the costs of research, MaxMoney plans to identify and purchase discrete pieces of longer reports and to focus its strategy on free sources, including filings to the Securities and Exchange Commission (SEC), industry news journals, and the competitors' own Web sites. The company sets an overall budget of $3,000 for any information purchases it deems necessary and enlists the aid of a researcher in its market research department.

RESEARCH STRATEGY EMPLOYED: Each competitor has a Web site, so information gathering begins "at home," with these sites. The researcher conducts supplementary searches on the Wayback Machine (an archive of Web sites going back to 1996) to compare current strategy with past strategy. She also collects each competitor's most recent 10-Ks (annual reports) filed with the SEC. Trade magazines and journals are searched for relevant references to competitors, as well as references to proprietary research that might be available for review or purchase. Finally, she checks research-oriented portals for industry overviews and company-specific information; some relevant research reports are available on a "by-the-page" basis, and in some cases free summaries (abstracts, executive summaries, or even press releases) provide enough insight to fill in the picture. With this portfolio of information and the data in hand, MaxMoney will be able to improve its unique selling proposition in the Web-based marketplace.

RESEARCH RESULTS: Many overlapping research resources are employed for this project, all of which can be grouped into three categories:

Competitor Web Sites. Each competitor's Web site offers a wealth of information, including the following:

- Tag lines, images, colors, and other marketing/ communications cues indicating the marketing approach of the company.
- Customer service interfaces, showing which services and information customers can access via the Web.
- Press releases on initiatives, partnerships, structural changes, and earnings reports.
- A Contact Us page. Viewing this page offers unexpected rewards: new information on the competitor's marketing efforts. The form asks visitors, "How did you hear about us?" and provides a series of check boxes showing different places the competitor advertises or is otherwise visible.
- An About Us page. Careful review of the information on this page helps draw a more detailed picture of the way the competitor is positioning itself in the marketplace.

Because part of the research effort is to learn what has *changed* for competitors, the researcher also searches each competitor's files on the Wayback Machine (*http://www.archive.org*). Entering the competitor's URL into the Wayback Machine's search interface pulls up copies of the site as it appeared on any date going back to 1996. This search allows review and analysis of changes in product offerings, strategy, pricing, and target audience.

SEC Filings. Because all of the competitors under scrutiny are publicly traded companies, they all must file reports with the SEC. The most detailed and relevant report for MaxMoney's intelligence purposes is the 10-K, or the annual report. The 10-K includes sections that describe the business, market, competition, and strategy of the subject company and serves as an excellent source of detailed competitive information. Some companies make their SEC filings available directly from their Web sites, often in an Investor Relations section.

All SEC filings are easily retrieved directly from the SEC through the EDGAR database (*http://www.sec.gov/edgar/searchedgar/webusers.htm*), where a simple Web-based search form allows the user to search by a company name, index, state of incorporation, and SIC (Standard Industrial Classification) code. Because this project involves specific companies, the researcher enters the company names one by one in the search box and pulls up a complete list of filings for each. From this list, she selects and downloads 10-K. To simplify use of the 10-K, which is a lengthy document, she cuts and pastes the relevant sections into a word-processing document. This minimizes the size of the document and allows simple keyword searching through the word-processing program. Thus, each company's statements about Web-based customer service and the competitive marketplace are easily extracted from these filings.

Trade and Industry Publications. Next the researcher searches databases of business publications for articles dealing with Web-based offerings of financial services companies, as well as for overviews of market trends and proprietary research released in the past twelve months. Gale Group's Business & Industry Database, accessible through the public library, is a key source, as are ProQuest and InfoTrac. She conducts searches using combinations of terms, including competitor names and terms such as *Web services, electronic business, e-business, trends, research, competition,* and *outlook.* These searches yield a wide range of articles, including the following:

- Company profiles
- Articles comparing lead players in the industry
- Press releases and feature stories describing recent analysts' reports on the sector

- Reviews of Web-based service offerings
- Surveys of customer experiences on financial services Web sites
- Estimates of the size of the current and future market for Web-based services

Proprietary Reports. Several articles mention reports published by three different industry analyst groups—a professional association for financial services companies and two market research firms. A visit to the Web site of the professional association reveals that a PDF version of the research report is available simply by registering on the site. Although this report does not have the most recent or cutting-edge information, it does provide more depth than the news articles, as well as a helpful overview of factors affecting the market.

The two market research firms each have a large report on financial services trends in general, as well as shorter reports on e-commerce and e-business trends in the sector. The large reports cost between $8,000 and $10,000, and the shorter reports cost $5,000 each. The firms both indicate that the only way to get this information is to purchase the full report. However, a visit to a research portal proves otherwise: a search at MarketResearch.com (*http://www.marketresearch.com*) reveals that one firm's reports are available on a "by-the-slice" basis. The researcher identifies five relevant pages from the overall industry report and four chapters from the specific report on Web-based services and purchases them through the portal. The pages from the industry report cost $175 apiece, and each chapter from the Web-based services report costs $450, resulting in a cost of $2,675. The other firm's reports are not available anywhere on a per-page or per-chapter basis.

SUMMARY OF SOLUTION: Each competitor has been studied thoroughly for its current and proposed Web-based service offerings, abandoned initiatives, market standing, and outlook. MaxMoney has learned how its competitors are "slicing and dicing" the marketplace, where the market is stronger or weaker, and what specific factors affect consumer decisions about Web-based service and information offerings. Using a combination of competitor communications materials, SEC filings, historical Web site information, trade journal coverage, and proprietary research, MaxMoney has created a detailed map of the competitive landscape in Web-based financial service offerings. Because so much information was gleaned through publicly available sources, and because the researcher was strategic about where and when to purchase information, the budget of $3,000 was maintained. MaxMoney is now prepared to map out its own strategy for rolling out Web-based services.

CONTRIBUTOR NAME: Robin Neidorf
AFFILIATION: Electric Muse

USEFUL TIPS

- Competitive intelligence can start with the competitor. Visit a competitor's Web site and read public filings (if available); analyze the language you find there. How does the competitor present itself? What words and concepts appear frequently? How would you describe the competitor's market and unique selling proposition, based on the language the competitor uses?
- Obtaining data is rarely an "all or nothing" proposition. If a costly report has information you need, look for a source that might offer pieces of the report. Some research portals offer reports by the page or by the chapter. Additionally, news coverage announcing the publication of the report or quoting the authors of the report sometimes provides insight into the more detailed data. Just because you can't afford "all" doesn't mean you have to settle for "nothing."

PROBLEM NUMBER 3: ENTREPRENEURIAL RESEARCH: IF I OPEN A BICYCLE SHOP, WILL I BE ABLE TO MAKE A LIVING?

RESEARCH BACKGROUND: An avid bicyclist is interested in opening a retail bicycle shop in an affluent part of town. At this point the plan is conceptual, and he wants to know if such a business can be easily started on limited capital. He needs an industry overview on the profitability of bicycle shops.

RESEARCH BUDGET: The client is willing to pay the researcher for an hour of his time ($100) but wants to limit the search to free sources.

RESEARCH STRATEGY EMPLOYED: Industry overviews can often be found online through trade associations, association newsletters, magazines, or journals. These sites also often provide links to additional pertinent information. Government sites offer an abundance of statistical information, but lack of currency can sometimes limit its value.

The researcher begins with a search through Internet search engines in hopes of retrieving information from trade associations. If that does not prove fruitful, she will try Firstgov.gov for government information. She starts with Google (*http://www.google.com*), where she uses the search term *"industry overview" "bicycle shops."* On AltaVista, she employs the term *"industry overview" AND "bicycle shops."* (The default Boolean operator on most Internet search engines is AND, and AltaVista recently adopted that convention.)

RESEARCH RESULTS: Alta Vista returned four hits, the first of which is right on the mark: SIC 5941, Bicycle Stores (*http://www.valuationresources.com/Reports/SIC5941BicycleStores.htm*). The brief search description indicates that this industry overview is free of charge. Upon visiting the Valuationresources.com Web site, the researcher finds several more links to free or paid industry overviews.

This search identifies a trade association, the National Bicycle Dealers Association (NBDA), which offers a free industry overview (*http://nbda.com/site/page.cfm?PageID=34*). The site also has a relevant article titled "Want to Start a Bike Shop?" (*http://nbda.com/site/page.cfm?PageID=70*). This article lists the pros and cons of starting a shop, the growth and loss of dealers since the 1980s, the profit margin necessary to operate a store, and the average net profit of bicycle stores.

Among the several links provided at the NBDA site is Bicycle Retailer.com. This site provides a Reports and Analysis section (*http://www.bicycleretailer.com/bicycleretailer/reports_analysis*), which presents a number of articles on sales, distribution channels, and trends. One article from November 2001, titled "Managing Pays Retail Dividends, Survey Reports," clearly says that a person can make money selling bicycles.

These sites provided a sufficient overview of the industry, and no additional research was required at this time. The Valuationresources.com and the NBDA site gave the client enough information to decide that he should explore the concept further.

CONTRIBUTOR NAME: Kent A. Sutorius
AFFILIATION: Informed Solutions, Inc.

USEFUL TIPS

- For industry overviews, check trade associations and government statistic sites.
- Encapsulate your search terms with quote marks (e.g., *"industry overview"*).
- At each site visited, look for links to additional sources.

PROBLEM NUMBER 4: STATISTICAL RESEARCH: WHAT IS THE INCIDENCE AND PREVALENCE OF PROSTATE CANCER IN THE UNITED STATES?

RESEARCH BACKGROUND: The medical writing group of a biotechnology pharmaceutical company is working on a manuscript for publication in a medical journal, and the writer wants to verify statistics before including them in the paper. The company's market research department has been contacted to supply that information. The writers are interested in the answers to two questions: (1) How many men are diagnosed with prostate cancer each year? and (2) How many men currently have prostate cancer?

RESEARCH BUDGET: These statistics are publicly available, so the online costs should be minimal. The market researcher estimates that it will take an hour or so of search time to find and verify the information.

RESEARCH STRATEGY EMPLOYED: Statistical information of this nature is usually found at governmental agencies, specialized societies, or associations. A good starting place is association Web sites, and the researcher begins with the American Cancer Society (ACS) site (*http://www.cancer.org*), which includes a link for a report containing statistics from 1997 to 2002 (*http://www.cancer.org/downloads/STT/CAFF2003PWSecured.pdf*). The 2003 figures, which are estimates, state that 220,900 cases will be diagnosed, and 28,900 men will die of prostate cancer in 2003. The report does not say how many men currently have prostate cancer.

The report says that ACS gets its statistics from the National Center for Health Statistics (NCHS) at its Centers for Disease Control and Prevention (CDC) division (*http://www.cdc.gov/nchs/fastats/prostate.htm*). It also gets statistics from the Surveillance, Epidemiology and End Results (SEER) Program at the National Cancer Institute (NCI) (*http://seer.cancer.gov*). NCHS, NCI, and the SEER are three reputable sources for this type of statistic. The researcher will use these sources to verify the information found at the ACS Web site.

Another alternative is to perform a simple search using a search engine and the phrase *cancer statistics*. By reviewing the results, the researcher can identify key associations and government research sites to turn to for specifics, including ACS and SEER. One might wonder why the researcher does not use a more specific search to go straight to the statistics by using the search term *prostate cancer statistics*. The answer is that although this will retrieve results from many sites, they will be redundant—often portions from the same main source. In the long run this approach is time consuming, and it is best to go directly to the source. A search on *cancer statistics* brings up the ACS and SEER sites (see links above).

RESEARCH RESULTS: The researcher finds a cancer statistics section on the SEER home page. The relevant categories are Finding Cancer Statistics; Statistical Tables, Graphs, and Maps; and Using Fast Stats. There is also a Fast Stats pull-down menu on the upper right-hand side of the home page that allows one to designate a cancer site. For expediency's sake, the researcher decides to go with the Fast Stats pull-down menu and select Prostate. This takes him to the Incidence: Prostate Cancer page, where a sidebar on the left-hand side lists the categories of statistics: Incidence, Mortality, Prevalence, and Probability of Developing or Dying of Cancer. "Incidence" refers to the number of men who have been given a diagnosis of prostate cancer during a specific period. "Prevalence" refers to the total number of men who have been given the diagnosis and are still living.

Selecting Prevalence on the sidebar takes the researcher to a page that offers a number of selections. He clicks "View Complete Prevalence for a selected set of cancer sites." The figures on this chart, from January 2000, say that 1,637,208 men then had prostate cancer.

The researcher then views incidence and prevalence figures for 1973–1999 by returning to the SEER main page and selecting Statistical Tables, Graphs, and Maps under the Cancer Statistics heading. He then selects SEER Cancer Statistics Review (CSR). At the next page, SEER Cancer Statistics Review, 1975–2000, he selects Contents of the CSR, 1975–2000. On the following page, he selects Overview, which retrieves a PDF including incidence and mortality rates for 2003 on page 19. According to this table, there will be an estimated 220,900 new cases and 28,900 deaths in 2003.

Performing a search at NCHS/CDC (*http://www.cdc.gov/nchs*) also provides a few statistics; the researcher clicks FASTATS A to Z on the sidebar and then selects P on the following page to find statistics on prostate disease.

SUMMARY OF SOLUTION: For this type of problem, government sites or nonprofit associations are an excellent place to search for statistics. Performing a search on a search engine using *cancer statistics* will bring up the key associations and government sites. In this case, the SEER site had incidence and prevalence statistics for 1975 to 2000. There were also incidence figures for 2003.

For more challenging incidence and prevalence questions, one might also check the Incidence and Prevalence database from Timely Data (*http://www.tdrdata.com*) or via Dialog File 465.

CONTRIBUTOR NAME: Kent A. Sutorius
AFFILIATION: Informed Solutions, Inc.

USEFUL TIPS

- For free statistical information, search for appropriate government or association sites.
- Take time to view and understand the variety of ways statistics are presented at each site.
- If the subject is unfamiliar to you, overview information and definitions will help.

PROBLEM NUMBER 5: ESTIMATING MARKET SIZE: WHAT IS THE POTENTIAL MARKET SIZE FOR A SOFTWARE PROGRAM USED TO TEACH FOREIGN LANGUAGES AND ENGLISH AS A SECOND LANGUAGE?

RESEARCH BACKGROUND: CyberLingua, a start-up technology company, has created a software program for teaching foreign languages and English as a Second Language (ESL) to both adults and children. The marketing manager has identified specific markets for the product, namely academic, military/government, and corporate, and the company is in the process of looking for major funding to move into each of the identified markets. Research is needed to look only at the potential military/government market to determine the following: (1) Who are the key players in providing foreign language and ESL training to military and government employees? and (2) What is the potential size of this market segment? Additionally, CyberLingua has requested that any information supporting the assertion that there is a continual or increased need for this type of training in the military/government market be included in the report.

RESEARCH BUDGET: CyberLingua is still basically in start-up mode, and the budget for research of any kind is limited. However, the marketing manager understands how crucial this information is to the success of the business plan and subsequently for obtaining the funding that CyberLingua needs. She is not looking for an exhaustive list of current suppliers, nor is she looking for exact numbers, which would be difficult to quantify anyway. At this point she is looking only for key players in the industry and some general numbers. The plan is to commission more in-depth research as things move ahead. The marketing manager hires an independent researcher and approves a project fee based upon six to ten hours of labor at $75 per hour, with any database fees built into that project fee.

RESEARCH STRATEGY EMPLOYED: Given that the budget is small and the scope of the project fairly general, the researcher decides to use freely available Internet sources as the first step to determine who serves the markets mentioned and to obtain a general context for the remainder of the search. Another reason for starting with free Internet sources is that for this particular market segment, government/military, it seems likely that much of the information needed will be publicly available, or that public sources will at least provide a good, authoritative basis for additional research.

The research starts with a variety of general Internet searches using various combinations of the following keywords and phrases: *language learning; language training; foreign language learning; foreign language training; government; military; ESL;* and *English as a second language.* Later on, having reviewed the sources found, the researcher added the term *national security* to the search.

RESEARCH RESULTS: The initial results of a general Internet search on the Google (*http://www.google.com*) and Yahoo (*http://www.yahoo.com*) search engines using various permutations of the above terms provides information on the following five key providers of both English and foreign language training to the government and military market:

1. One of the first language training providers listed in the search results is the Defense Language Institute Foreign Language Center in Monterey, California. (*http://pom-www.army.mil/pages/dliflc.htm*). The Web site describes the institute as "the primary foreign language training institution within the Department of Defense (DoD) providing foreign language services to DoD, government agencies and foreign governments."

2. Another language training resource in the results from both searches is the Defense Language Institute English Language Center at Lackland AFB, Texas (*http://www.dlielc.org*). The Web site describes the center as the "Department of Defense (DoD) agency responsible for the management and operation of the Defense English Program (DELP) to train international military and civilian personnel to speak and teach English."

3. The Foreign Service Institute in Washington, D.C., also found within these searches (*http://www.state.gov/m/fsi*), has a main page describing the FSI as "providing training to enrollees from the State Department and more than 40 other government agencies and the military service branches."

4. Another resource is the Diplomatic Language Services (DLS) in Arlington, Virginia (*http://www.dls-inc.com/homepage/homepage1.htm*). The site explains that the DLS provides language training to "US Government personnel as well as corporate and private individuals in over 85 languages and dialects." It also indicates "DLS has provided nearly 1,000,000 hours of language instruction in these 85 languages in the past 15 years."

5. Finally, the initial Internet search identifies the National Foreign Language Center (NFLC) (*http://www.nflc.org/nflc_index*). Although the NFLC does not actually provide language training like those previously listed, its Web site does identify it as operating as a "think tank" that focuses on "language policy and U.S. needs for competencies in languages." The site includes a link to a helpful document, "National

Briefing on Language & National Security," from January 16, 2002 (*http://www.nflc.org/security/transcript.htm*). This transcript not only mentions many of the key players already identified above, but also provides support for CyberLingua's contention about the ongoing and growing need for this type of training.

The Internet search continues and the researcher determines that, although this is not an exhaustive search of all entities providing language training to the military/government market, the above sources do provide a picture of the key players along with some general numbers of people served. Further review within the Web sites of these suppliers provides more detailed information on the ways language courses are taught, by whom, and how. This information is also highlighted so that the marketing manager can refer to it later.

After reviewing the sources, the researcher decides to add the term *national security* to subsequent searches. As a result, transcripts and press releases are found identifying the growing need for language training in many branches of the government.

The following two NFLC sources provide additional support for CyberLingua's assertion that there is a growing demand for this type of training:

1. NFLC Testimony for Congressional Hearing, September 29, 2000 (*http://www.nflc.org/news/press_releases/congrtest.htm*)
2. "War on Terrorism: House Committee says, 'Language Is Single Greatest Limitation' in Intelligence," October 10, 2001 (*http://www.nflc.org/news/press_releases/languagelimitation.htm*)

There are no database costs associated with this search, and the time spent so far is within the budgeted amount. The additional time to organize and write the final report still keeps the project within budget but takes almost the maximum number of hours allotted. The report, referred to as the "deliverable," provides an introduction to the search strategy and presents the key findings, with lists of the key providers of language training in this sector. For each of the providers, a Web site address and contact information are provided, followed by a bulleted list highlighting data such as specific languages taught and the makeup of the student population, including the number of people served.

SUMMARY OF SOLUTION: According to the information collected from the Web sites of the main language training providers as well as from the transcripts and stories subsequently found, the researcher has determined that a handful of key sources provide either foreign language or ESL training to government departments.

The Defense Language Institute Foreign Language Center provides training to all four military services: army, air force, navy, and marines. Its Web site also says that three thousand enlisted and officer personnel receive language training each year. It breaks down the enrollment into the four services and provides much additional general information useful to the client.

The Defense Language Institute English Language Center Web site says that every year, the center provides language training to as many as five thousand military personnel. The Foreign Language Institute Web site says it serves more than thirty thousand enrollees a year and provides more than five hundred courses in sixty foreign languages.

The Web sites of these institutions, along with the others noted above, provide a good picture of the key government-centered players and the potential market size. The sites also provide details on how the training is offered, which is a nice information bonus for this project.

As to the question of ongoing or growing demand, a number of findings in the transcripts and the press releases are very useful to the client. These note that demand for language training for national security purposes has increased since the September 11, 2001, terrorist attacks; indeed, the NFLC press release says that "Language is the single greatest limitation in intelligence." U.S. troops are continually deployed abroad, and language proficiency is crucial to their ongoing integration. More domestically located agencies such as the Centers for Disease Control, the National Aeronautics and Space Administration, the Drug Enforcement Agency, and the FBI also provide language training to their staffs.

The final report suggests further in-depth review of the Web sites of the language providers to obtain even more detailed support for inclusion in CyberLingua's business plan.

CONTRIBUTOR NAME: Jan Knight
AFFILIATION: Bancroft Information Services

USEFUL TIPS

- As you are identifying search terms, be sure to try synonyms or alternative phrases. For example, you might try both *ESL* and *English as a Second Language*.
- When your budget is limited and you are looking for government information, start with free Internet sources. There is a wealth of authoritative government sources.

PROBLEM NUMBER 6: MARKETING AND STRATEGIC DIRECTION RESEARCH: REPOSITIONING COMPANY PRODUCTS TO MEET COMPETITIVE PRESSURE

RESEARCH BACKGROUND: Thermax, a manufacturer of industrial heating products, is seeking information on industry trends and current market positions in order to reposition its products and marketing strategies. Additional information and insight on marketing plans, international activity, and management or ownership changes of its main competitors is also requested.

RESEARCH BUDGET: This small company does not have extensive in-house resources to compile external information. Thermax does maintain company files on competitors of interest and has access to Dun & Bradstreet reports and similar financial information resources. There is a small outsourcing budget for hiring an independent researcher, and Thermax requests that she spend no more than $1,000 on online charges and research time for the first phase.

RESEARCH STRATEGY EMPLOYED: Given the budget and type of information requested, the researcher decides to spend as little time as possible online. The bulk of the research budget will be devoted to outsourcing telephone interviews to an associate and spending the time necessary to read, synthesize, and report results for a one-to-two-page brief. The following steps are taken by consulting the *Encyclopedia of Business Information Sources (EBIS)*, conducting a database and Internet search, requesting a special issue via postal mail, and then conducting telephone interviews:

- Because recent news events are key data sources for this project, a Dialog OneSearch on full-text newspapers (PAPERS) is conducted first to cull press stories on the industry and management changes.
- Research next focuses on Internet resources to explore associations and trade magazines referenced in the *EBIS*. Among these is the site for *Industrial Heating: The International Journal of*

Thermal Technology (*http://www.industrialheating.com*), which also provides contacts to additional sources.

- Using basic information from Thermax, the Internet, and the newspaper clippings, the researcher gleans names of trade journals and associations to include in the follow-up telephone interviews. Approximately a dozen sources to interview are identified through this initial research. They include technical experts, contributors to trade magazines, consultants, government agencies, and personnel at supplier and distributor companies. The sources are contacted and most, if not all, are able to either contribute information or refer the researcher to other sources that can.

- One of the industry's trade journals has recently published a special issue on a manufactured item that is of particular interest to Thermax, including a ranking of the top ten producers. The editor mails a copy of this issue to the researcher and supplies an educated opinion and referral.

- The researcher conducts an Internet search of regional newspapers at competitor locations. Although this does not yield a lot of useful information, it is an important step and retrieves some news tidbits that are useful in conducting the telephone interviews. I usually start with Bizjournals (*http://www. bizjournals.com*) and then use list sites for finding other regional newspapers not captured on this site.

SUMMARY OF SOLUTION: According to the information found in the telephone interviews, it has become apparent that the international industrial heating scene is becoming more important as offshore production picks up and domestic production falls off. A quick check with an expert reveals that there have been no changes in the regulations recently, and that none are foreseen. But it is important to verify this; before accepting it as fact the researcher would like to have it confirmed by other independent sources. An additional, unexpected benefit of the telephone interviews is the opportunity to hear comments about the client, both good and bad. These are an important "value add" that can be integrated into the executive brief.

The total cost of the data is negligible—less than $30. Conducting the telephone interviews and connecting the pieces took at least seven hours.

CONTRIBUTOR NAME: Margaret Metcalf Carr
AFFILIATION: Carr Research Group

USEFUL TIPS

- Don't overlook special issues that come as part of trade magazine subscriptions. Many magazines publish at least a few surveys a year. Even if the survey is not up to date, it will still provide a springboard for updating data during telephone interviews.
- Telephone interviews often involve some quid pro quo. Be ready to share something you've learned during your research that may be of interest to the interviewee.
- Work to verify any information you are given in at least three different sources.
- Regulations can be a major force in marketing plans—either helping or hindering the development of new products. Make sure you're up to date on the regulations or telephone a government organization, association, or trade expert who is.

PROBLEM NUMBER 7: RESEARCHING MARKET TRENDS IN THE GOVERNMENT SECTOR: THE PURCHASE OF SUBSTANCE ABUSE AND PREVENTION PUBLICATIONS AMID BUDGET CUTS

RESEARCH BACKGROUND: The world's largest nongovernment publisher of substance abuse treatment and prevention materials recognizes that dramatic budget cuts at the federal, state, and local level will have a negative effect on the ability of its institutional customers to purchase new materials. However, from budget numbers alone it is impossible to tell exactly how cuts may play out "on the ground," where purchasing decisions are made. To get beyond the numbers, the publisher recognizes that it needs to conduct research to learn how public agencies at the state level will actually cope with changing budgets. The executive team charges the marketing director with the task of collecting and reporting this information in time for a corporate strategy meeting, to be held in six weeks.

RESEARCH BUDGET: Learning the truth behind the numbers is extremely valuable to the publisher's marketing, editorial, and sales strategies. Without this information, the organization could be making extremely expensive mistakes. The publisher allocates staff time and resources equivalent to $10,000 to conduct research and compile a report that will be used to define the organization's strategy for the next several publishing seasons.

RESEARCH STRATEGY EMPLOYED: Because "on-the-ground" information is as critical as data about state budgets, the marketing director puts together a strategy that combines online research with phone interviews of key individuals within state agencies. The project is too big to take on in one wave, so she breaks it into two phases:

1. **Gather Background Data.** First, the research team will collect information from each state on budget allocations for substance abuse treatment and prevention in the schools, corrections facilities, and public health departments. To do this they will need to identify key agencies for the distribution of funds and collect any existing information on trends in funding for these areas and what drives those trends. Data sources will include state government Web sites and public information sites, online directories of state agencies, and searches in local newspapers (especially in capital cities). Some specific sources will be the federal agency Substance Abuse and Mental Health Services Administration (SAMHSA) (*http://www.samhsa.gov*); national nonprofits in drug treatment/prevention research such as Drug Strategies (*http://www.drugstrategies.com*), the Center for Substance Abuse Treatment (*http://www. treatment.org*), and Boston University School of Public Health (*http://www.jointogether.org*); ProQuest and InfoTrac, accessed through the local public library, for newspaper coverage; and Bizjournals for local news (*http://www.bizjournals.com*).

2. **Conduct Phone Interviews.** Next, the researchers will identify key individuals within agencies and conduct phone interviews. Questions to ask include, What portions of your budget come from public allocations? How are those allocations changing? How do you expect the changes, if any, to affect the way you deliver programs and services? and What internal and external factors will affect your budget and programs in the next three to five years?

RESEARCH RESULTS: The biggest expense associated with this project is the time required to perform the work. The research team is able to complete all research without paying for access to proprietary information. They devote approximately thirty-five staff hours to Step 1. In Step 2, interviews eat up an average of 3.5 staff hours *per state*, including time spent tracking down individuals, doing the phone interviews, and writing up results. Assembling the final report for the strategic planning group takes another ten hours.

Typical steps in the process are illustrated by the research for Wisconsin:

• Contact information for relevant agencies is researched at the state government Web site (*http://www.wisconsin.gov*). The agency index provides links to the appropriate agency home pages: Health and Family Services, Education, and Corrections.

- The researcher enters site-specific queries on agency sites, using the keywords *substance abuse; treatment; alcoholism; drug abuse; addiction;* and similar terms. Documents retrieved through these searches include agency reports, press releases, and contact information for public officers responsible for administering programs. These documents are saved in electronic format and annotated for easy search and retrieval.

- National clearinghouse sites, including Join Together Online (*http://www.jointogether.org*), SAMSHA, the Center for Substance Abuse Treatment, and Drug Strategies are accessed and searched with the terms *Wisconsin AND corrections OR treatment OR prevention.* Because these sites are subject-specific for drug and alcohol abuse, broad search terms are effective for retrieving relevant information. (In a general search engine such as Google, such broad terms would need to be qualified with a limiter such as *alcoholism; drug abuse;* or *substance abuse.*) Documents retrieved through these searches include program analyses, news articles, grant programs, and policy alerts. These documents are saved in electronic format and annotated for easy search and retrieval.

- Newspapers in Madison, Wisconsin, cover state government news in depth. The papers accessible through the city's Web site (*http://www.madison.com*) include *Wisconsin State Journal* and *The Capital Times.* The researcher searches public archives at this site, using the terms *funding; allocation; substance abuse; drug prevention; drug intervention;* and other relevant terms. They conduct separate searches that focus on federal funds and state funds by adding the limiters *federal* or *state* to the search terms. These searches retrieve numerous news articles identifying challenges at the state level, and the documents are saved in electronic format and annotated for easy search and retrieval.

The researcher reviews the electronic files with the following four questions in mind:

1. Are budget numbers for substance abuse treatment and prevention in public health, corrections, and education trending upward, downward, or staying the same?
2. What factors are affecting these trends?
3. Are funds other than those allocated by the state or federal government becoming available through other sources?

4. Who are the appropriate contacts at each agency to discuss the "on-the-ground" effects changing budgets may be having? If the appropriate contact has not yet been identified, what strategy can we employ to find the right person?

The researcher assembles a preliminary report, documenting findings to date. From this report, specific questions about changes in Wisconsin agencies are crafted, and contact with agencies is made. For each relevant agency, the individual or department responsible for substance abuse treatment and prevention is contacted and interviewed regarding the budget situation, creative methods they may be using to address budget shortfalls, the outlook for the next three to five years, and other factors affecting the way they deliver programs to individuals. In some cases, several calls are required to home in on the person who has the right answers and to complete the interview.

SUMMARY OF SOLUTION: The data gathered for each state paints a detailed picture of the complex interaction of public funds (both federal and state), politics, agency operations, and substance abuse treatment and prevention services. The publisher now has detailed information on the flow of funds to those who make material-purchasing decisions, and on how those individuals and departments may actually be making decisions.

Reduced funding for programs is indeed the trend, yet the publisher learns that some states and agencies are finding alternative funding sources or creative ways to maximize the funding they have so that they can continue to serve the needs of the public. Additionally, the publisher learns that not all states are facing the same kinds of budget shortfalls, and that some are actually experiencing increased budgets for a variety of political and/or legal reasons.

With this data, the publisher is able to make informed decisions about editorial direction, the kinds of materials that might be most welcome in the marketplace, where to focus the company's marketing and sales resources, and messages that will resonate with its audiences. An additional, unexpected benefit of this project is the creation of a robust database of information on state trends and issues; a maintenance program is designed so that the database can be updated on a quarterly basis.

CONTRIBUTOR NAME: Robin Neidorf
AFFILIATION: Electric Muse

USEFUL TIPS

- When searching subject-specific resources, use broader search terms than you would use in a general resource (e.g., *treatment* instead of *substance abuse treatment*).
- Published data doesn't always tell the whole story. For complex topics, ask an expert for assistance in interpreting the data. An "expert" can be anyone who is directly affected by the data.
- All state governments have Web portals that are, for the most part, well designed and easy to navigate. In searching for any state government information, the portal is the logical starting point and a good place to return to if you get stuck.

PROBLEM NUMBER 8: RESEARCHING TECHNOLOGY MARKET TRENDS: WHERE IS COMPUTER DISPLAY MONITOR TECHNOLOGY HEADED?

RESEARCH BACKGROUND: MonitorQuest, an industry leader in the production of computer display monitors for desktop and laptop computers, has an extensive understanding of the display market, but its marketing manager wants to be sure he's not missing something. To maintain the company's competitiveness, he wants to know what new technological developments are affecting the computer display industry. He also wants to know what innovations are in the works that might result in alternatives to the cathode ray tube (CRT) or the liquid crystal display (LCD). He assigns the project to an in-house researcher in MonitorQuest's market research group.

RESEARCH BUDGET: The marketing manager does not approve any budget ($0.00) for expenses and only about an hour of professional research time. Raw data with a summary will be adequate.

RESEARCH STRATEGY EMPLOYED: The researcher concludes that more current and extensive information on computer products and technology will be found via the Internet than through the more commonly used aggregators. With this type of search, a number of directions can be pursued; he decides that the best place to start is Webopedia (*http://www.webopedia.internet.com*) because it is important to identify the terminology used in the industry first so he can use it in the search language. The other benefit of Webopedia is that it provides access to a number of articles and links to relevant information.

The second direction would be to use a search engine to look up monitor display organizations. In the computer industry, standardization is critical to getting any product to the market. Monitor display organizations will provide information on technological advances and the feasibility of standardization.

The last place to check is market research reports, where information can be gleaned from the abstracts and table of contents of individual reports. Full-text market research reports are expensive, but sometimes single pages from the report can be purchased. These sites might also provide other linkable material.

RESEARCH RESULTS: A search using *"display screen" OR monitor* at Webopedia brings up a short description and a sidebar with related categories and terms. Selecting Monitors under Related Categories brings up a broader series of categories and terms: Parent Categories, Subcategories, and Terms. Selecting the subcategory Flat-Panel Displays leads to more defined terminology, listed by Parent Categories and Terms, and clicking Flat-Panel Displays again brings up a series of articles. One article, "Flat Panel Display Technology Overview" (*http://www.pctechguide.com/07panels.htm*), provides a very good overview on the technology.

If the researcher needs more information later, he will perform a search-engine search using *computer display organizations* or *computer display monitor organizations*, which would probably provide some interesting results. Display Search Links directs him to a list of organizations and industry resources. One of them is United States Display Consortium (USDC) (*http://www.usdc.org*). On the USDC site is a tab marked Industry Resources. Clicking one of the subtitles under that tab, Business and Market Info., brings him to a page of market forecasts, overviews, and statistics (*http://www.usdc.org/resources/GDN_business_market.htm*). Here there are a number of excellent reports, but the first one mentioned, "Analyst's Outlook: Boston, Display Search (pdf) (7/01)," is quite informative. Another subtitle under the Industry Resources tab is Tutorials, which offers more reports on forecasts and display technologies.

The researcher then looks at market research report material. The USDC has a link for such a report from its forecasts page to iSuppli/Stanford Resources, Inc. (*http://stanfordresources.isuppli.com/index.asp*). On the iSuppli/Stanford Resources site under Market Intelligence Products there is access to an excellent abstract and table of contents for "Emerging Displays Review." This information will complement and support previous research already accomplished. The researcher also uses a search engine to search for *display monitor reports*. This search retrieves the Display

Reports Web site (*http://www.displayreports.com*), where free information can be found by selecting Press Room on the sidebar. Here are a number of articles, including "Display Search's Annual *LCD Monitor Strategy Report* Projects LCD Monitors to Overtake CRT Monitors in 2004" (*http://www.displaysearch.com/press/2002/102302.htm*), which highlights trends and leading technological directions.

CONTRIBUTOR NAME: Kent A. Sutorius
AFFILIATION: Informed Solutions, Inc.

USEFUL TIPS

* Use a glossary or thesaurus to verify terminology, especially if it is unfamiliar.
* Look for market research report summaries and abstracts, which often provide useful information at no charge.
* Trade associations often have specialized information not available elsewhere.

PROBLEM NUMBER 9: FINDING INPUT COSTS TO DETERMINE COMPETITOR STRATEGIES: PRICING COSTS IN ELECTRONIC COMPONENT MANUFACTURING

RESEARCH BACKGROUND: Performance Electronics, a manufacturer of electronic components, wants to increase its market share. Because pricing is a key factor in winning bids in this industry segment, the company needs to know more about future cost trends to determine its pricing strategies.

RESEARCH BUDGET: Performance Electronics has a limited research budget and a limited amount of time to report research results. A not-to-exceed budget of $500 for the first phase, which includes some online research, is stipulated. Initial results are due back in one week. The company librarian, who will do the research, does not have access to any fee-based online research services but does have price lists from suppliers for commonly used raw materials. The project goes into phase two, where another $500–$600 is allocated to pay for additional research and retrieved documents. Additional time is allocated as well.

RESEARCH STRATEGY EMPLOYED: Given budget and time limitations, the librarian decides to retrieve as much information as possible from the Internet and follow up with phone calls. Because the research question deals largely with fixed costs, the core research strategy consists of determining the highest-cost items in the company's manufacturing process—utilities, labor, and raw materials—and then gathering the best information possible to compare these costs with market prices.

RESEARCH RESULTS: By consulting the *Encyclopedia of Business Information, U.S. Industry & Trade Outlook,* and the Internet, by conducting a database search to identify experts in the industry, and by making telephone calls to these experts, the librarian finds the following:

1. A quick read of the "Microelectronics" chapter of the *U.S. Industry & Trade Outlook* provides necessary background information, references, and Department of Commerce contacts. The librarian contacts the industry specialist, who provides further raw material production information, including faxed material that includes actual historical production data as well as a five-year forecast.

2. A quick database search on Dialog's Responsive Database Services' Business & Industry Database and a search on Factiva for company names reveals names of trade experts and a page from an investment report, which provides useful background information on sales and operating income trends for the competing companies.

3. An Internet and Dow Jones Interactive Publications Library Search provides clues on raw material trends, supply, and flow, and current pricing in trade tabloids (e.g., *Chemical Week*). This search also produces additional leads to industry experts and resources, including the USGS Bureau of Mines' *Minerals Yearbook,* now USGS Mineral Statistics Online (see Figure 3-1).

   By clicking on volume 1 of the *Minerals Yearbook* and then clicking on the latest PDF, the librarian is able to retrieve the chapter on aluminum. The last page of the chapter contains statistics and information.

4. The librarian then contacts major trade magazine editors and industry experts for their opinion on production and pricing trends. In some cases, the editors refer her to additional experts who have the inside scoop on who buys what from whom.

Figure 3-1. The Minerals Yearbook

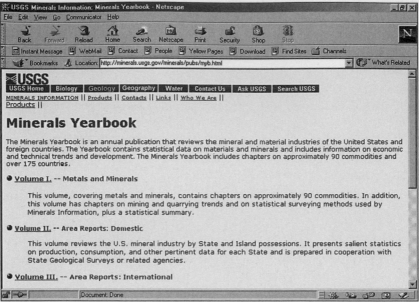

Reprinted courtesy of U.S. Geological Survey, U.S. Department of the Interior.

5. Because energy consumption is a large factor in electronic components manufacturing, the librarian then explores local utility or public service commission Web sites to check for contracts on file. Heavy energy users sometimes contract for their power, sometimes as much as five to eight years out. A document delivery provider is contacted to obtain the public filings necessary.

6. Because labor and wage data is also needed, the librarian uses a geographic dictionary to find out where manufacturers are. In addition to the broad information provided on the Internet by the Bureau of the Census, she collects the best wage and labor data using a concentric circle scenario, based upon the available statistics for the particular town/county/state in question.

7. Tax information is also desired, so local tax departments are contacted to obtain, if available, tax information for the past five years. Because tax information may be recorded "by parcel," some basic math functions come into play.

The total cost of the data is less than $400, which includes the costs of the online searching, printing a few articles, a research report page, and public record retrieval. The time to conduct the telephone interviews and to read, digest, and record the necessary information in a spreadsheet matrix consumes the most time, close to twelve hours.

SUMMARY OF SOLUTION: By collecting available utility, wage, tax, and material rates, the company is able to compare sensitive price points. This process is not without frustration. An exact apples-to-apples comparison cannot be done because there is unevenness in how data is collected from source to source and state to state. However, even when precise comparisons cannot be made, indications for the future are still evident, and these remain useful in the overall scenario. Chatter in the trade literature on the stability of the raw materials of interest adds to the overall picture.

CONTRIBUTOR NAME: Margaret Metcalf Carr

AFFILIATION: Carr Research Group

USEFUL TIPS

- Do your homework first. It is much easier to talk to an industry expert when you have a few specific questions based upon what you already know.
- Start with a government expert if you can. They often have several resources at their fingertips that are not easily found (or that cannot be found for free) elsewhere, and they will often fax you selected pages without charge. They can also suggest other experts or trade associations to contact.
- Don't be afraid to pick up the phone. Local chambers of commerce and local public libraries can often lead you to the best local public record sources.

PROBLEM NUMBER 10: DIGITAL PROJECTORS IN THEATERS: IS IT TIME TO MAKE THE SWITCH? THE DIALOG SOLUTION

RESEARCH BACKGROUND: The CEO of Edwards Cinema is considering when (or even whether) to move into digital projector mode. The cost of installation is extremely high. He needs to identify the trends in the motion picture industry and determine whether digital cinema is inevitable, or other options are in the pipeline.

RESEARCH BUDGET: The client has authorized up to $300 in search costs, and up to eight hours to retrieve the information, read it, and prepare a report summarizing the results. He contracts with an independent researcher to conduct the search.

RESEARCH STRATEGY EMPLOYED: The researcher will use Dialog-Classic; its set-building capability allows the user to add search terms sequentially and achieve a balance between broadness and specificity of results. She will take a three-step approach:

Step 1: Search DIALINDEX (File 411) to identify the most promising databases,

Step 2: Run a basic search in likely databases to identify keywords and concepts, and

Step 3: Run more specific searches using terms identified in Step 2.

RESEARCH RESULTS: Step 1—First the researcher searches DIALINDEX (File 411) to identify databases that contain items matching the search terms. She logs on to DialogClassic (*http://www.dialogclassic.com*) and opens DIALINDEX using "B 411"—"B" is an abbreviation for the Begin command to open a file, or database. In File 411 the first thing she must do is choose a set of files to search. She may choose individual files, OneSearch groups of files, or Supercategories. DIALINDEX OneSearch groups include Business Wire Files, Company Directories, and Medicine. Supercategories—such as ALLPAPER, which incorporates all newspaper databases—can be searched only in DIALINDEX.

The Bluesheets Web page (*http://www.library.dialog.com/bluesheets*) has links to descriptions of each Dialog file and group, and the Bluesheet for File 411 lists the Supercategories that can be used in this file. The researcher will search the ALLBUSINESS Supercategory using the command SF ALLBUSINESS NOT PAPERS (it doesn't matter whether you type your commands in caps or lowercase). She omits newspapers to shorten the processing time and eliminate the numerous repetitive short items the search would otherwise retrieve.

The research goal is trends in motion picture technology, so the researcher will include the search term *innovation* to pick up mention of new technologies. She adds the truncation symbol (a question mark in Dialog command language) for any word that might be either singular or plural, or have other alternative endings. For example, *technolog?* will find documents that include "technology," "technologies," and "technological." File 411 does not have set-building capability, so she constructs a broad search string: *s (movie? or motion()picture?) and technolog? and (trend? or innovat?).* Note that synonyms are grouped within parentheses, and that *s* is a shortcut for "Select," used in front of the words you wish to retrieve.

Once the search is complete, she uses the Rank File command (RF) to list the results in order of highest number of hits. (Note that you can't enter the next command before the system has finished processing the current command.) Figure 3-2 shows the top ten files for this search, ranked by the number of hits.

Figure 3-2. Search Results in DIALINDEX

```
Ref Items File
--- ----- ----
N1 16984 148: Gale Group Trade & Industry _1976-2003/Jan
28
N2 11846 20: Dialog Global Reporter_1997-2003/Jan 29
N3 11419 16: Gale Group PROMT(R)_1990-2003/Jan 28
N4 11265 727: Canadian Newspapers_1990-2003/Jan 29
N5 8121 484: Periodical Abs Plustext_1986-2003/Jan W3
N6 7685 781: ProQuest Newsstand_1998-2003/Jan 29
N7 6899 47: Gale Group Magazine DB(TM)_1959-2003/Jan 27
N8 5457 15: ABI/Inform(R)_1971-2003/Jan 28
N9 5270 9: Business & Industry(R)_Jul/1994-2003/Jan 28
N10 4919 570: Gale Group MARS(R)_1984-2003/Jan 28
191 files have one or more items; file list includes 308
files.
Enter P or PAGE for more -
```

Step 2—Next, the researcher runs a basic search in promising databases to identify keywords and important concepts. From the top-scoring files retrieved in Step 1, she selects Files 148, 47, and 16 (B 148, 47, 16). The same company produces them all, so the use of indexing terms should be consistent among them. The use of index terms helps limit the search to articles that are on target for a particular search, eliminating irrelevant articles that simply contain those words somewhere in the text. (Index terms used in a given file are listed on the Bluesheet for that file under the headings Basic Index and Additional Indexes.)

The researcher decides to start with a broad search and add specific terms until she obtains a manageable number of hits. She uses suffixes from the Basic Index to limit her search terms to appear in the title (TI) or descriptors (DE). Descriptors are index terms used to identify the main topics or themes of an article. She restricts the search to articles within the past four years or later by using the command PY=>1999, where "PY" specifies Publication

Year, the equals sign (=) specifies that articles be published in the year stated, and the greater-than sign (>) specifies that articles be published after the year stated. The complete search term is *s (movie? OR motion()picture? OR cinema?)/TI,DE AND PY=>1999.*

When the command has been processed, a results screen listing the outcome of the search appears (see Figure 3-3). The number of hits for each term is shown to the left of that term, and all of the terms are eventually combined into one set. In this case, Set Number 1 (S1) has 125,721 hits.

Figure 3-3. Results Screen for Search in Dialog Files 148, 47, and 16

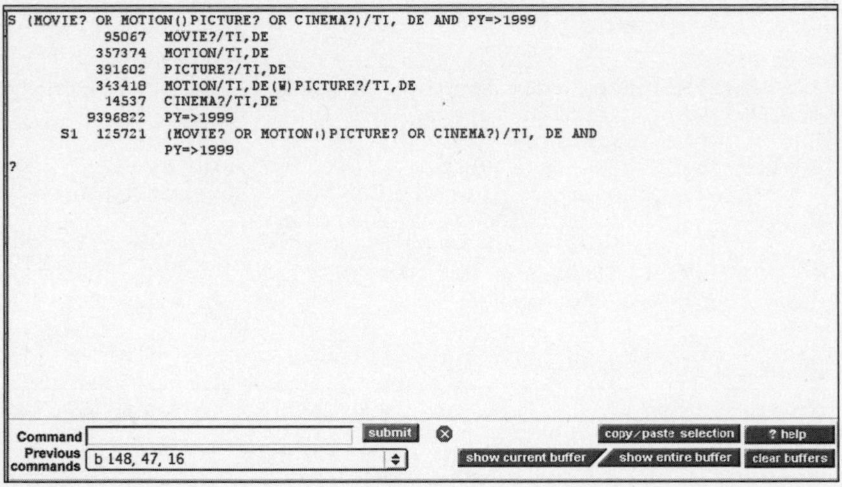
S (MOVIE? OR MOTION()PICTURE? OR CINEMA?)/TI, DE AND PY=>1999
95067 MOVIE?/TI,DE
357374 MOTION/TI,DE
391602 PICTURE?/TI,DE
343418 MOTION/TI,DE(W)PICTURE?/TI,DE
14537 CINEMA?/TI,DE
9396822 PY=>1999
S1 125721 (MOVIE? OR MOTION()PICTURE? OR CINEMA?)/TI, DE AND PY=>1999
?
Command
submit
copy/paste selection
? help
Previous commands
b 148, 47, 16
show current buffer
show entire buffer
clear buffers

2003® Dialog, a Thomson business, *http://www.dialog.com*. Reprinted with permission of the publisher.

Then the researcher adds terms to successively narrow the set. (Alternatively, she could type in a single long string incorporating all the terms. But this would give her less flexibility if she needed to try alternative strategies when a particular term turned out to be too limiting or not limiting enough.) Because she is searching multiple databases that may have some overlapping content, she ends with the RD (Remove Duplicates) command before retrieving her hits.

The Sort command displays the results in chronological order. The set to be sorted is indicated first, then the range of items to be sorted (all of them in this case), then the field to be sorted. The researcher specifies "pd,d," meaning that articles from all three databases will be integrated and sorted by publication date. If she didn't specify "d," then articles from each database would be kept together. The new search terms are *s S1 and technolog?/TI,DE; s S2 AND (trend? OR innovat? OR forecast?)/TI,DE; s s3 AND theater?/TI,DE; RD;* and *sort S5/all/pd,d.*

To see a summary of the searches, she uses the command DS (Display Sets). This gives her the results shown below:

```
Set    Items    Description
S1     125721   (MOVIE? OR MOTION()PICTURE? OR CINEMA?)TI,
                DE AND PY=>1999
S2     1494     S1 AND TECHNOLOG?/TI, DE
S3     132      S2 AND (TREND? OR INNOVAT? OR FORECAST?)
                /TI, DE
S4     17       S3 AND THEATER?/TI, DE
S5     16       RD (unique items)
S6     16       Sort S5/ALL/PD, d
?
```

The researcher has now created six sets, with successively decreasing numbers of items in each set. Set 6 (S6), containing sixteen items, reflects all of the search terms contained in the previous sets with duplicate items removed (RD—Remove Duplicates) and sorted by PD, or publication date.

The researcher now narrows Set S3 with the following search terms: *s S3 AND (projection OR projector?)/TI,DE; s S7 NOT S4; RD; sort S9/ALL/PD, d.* NOT is a Boolean operator, as are the more commonly used AND and OR. The NOT operator eliminates the items that she already found in the previous searches. As shown below, her new search on projectors yields a total of seventeen items, nine of which were not found previously and seven of which are unique.

```
Set    Items    Command that gave this set
S7     17       S3 AND (projection OR projector?)/TI,DE
S8     9        S7 NOT S4
S9     7        RD (unique items)
S10    7        Sort S9/ALL/PD,D
```

The researcher saves the search (SAVE TEMP MOVIE) so she can eliminate from subsequent searches the records she has already found. (You can choose any name for your search that is six characters or less.) She then sees the response "SAVE TEMP MOVIE, Temp SearchSave 'TDMOVIE' stored." Search sets are saved for twenty-four hours. (If the researcher loses the connection or has to log off, she can retrieve them by logging on and typing *exs tdmovie.*)

The researcher displays the hits from sets 6 and 10 in format 8 to be sure they're relevant. Format 8 is a low-cost way to view titles and then retrieve the citations and full-text versions of those that appear relevant. It also shows index terms, which can give the searcher ideas for ways to expand or focus subsequent searches. The researcher selects format 8 for these two sets with the term *T S6/8/all; T S10/8/all.*

"T" is the shortcut for "TYPE;" "S6" and "S10" are the search sets to be displayed; "8" defines the display format (available formats and their charges are listed in the Bluesheet for each file); and "all" displays the full set of titles. (If she had obtained a lot more results than she expected and wanted to see if the search was on target, she could display just the first ten results by entering *T S6/8/1-10.* This would tell her if she had inadvertently chosen a search term that pulled out lots of hits she didn't anticipate and didn't want.) The display for the first two articles retrieved is shown in Figure 3-4.

Figure 3-4. Citation list of Articles Retrieved in Format 8

```
6/8/1 (Item 1 from file: 148)
DIALOG(R)File 148:(c)2003 The Gale Group. All rts. reserv.

14976158 SUPPLIER NUMBER: 91579514
Imaxing Hollywood hits for a big, seat-shaking second
helping of thrills.(Imax creates technology to play 35 MM
films on its 70 MM projector)(Living Arts Pages)
Sept 16, 2002

 COMPANY NAMES: Imax Systems Corp.--Planning
 DESCRIPTORS: Motion picture theaters--Planning; Motion
picture projectors--Innovations
 GEOGRAPHIC CODES/NAMES: 1USA United States
 PRODUCT/INDUSTRY NAMES: 7830000 (Motion Picture
Theaters)
 SIC CODES: 7830 Motion Picture Theaters
 NAICS CODES: 51213 Motion Picture and Video Exhibition
 FILE SEGMENT: NNI File 111

6/8/2 (Item 2 from file: 148)
DIALOG(R)File 148:(c)2003 The Gale Group. All rts. reserv.

14692948 SUPPLIER NUMBER: 87522416 (USE FORMAT 7 OR 9 FOR
FULL TEXT)
Pop Beat; They're Rockin' at the Multiplex; Digital tech-
nology allows cinemas to beam in concerts, but the jury
is out on whether it will be just a fad.(Calendar)
```

```
June 15, 2002
WORD COUNT: 1151 LINE COUNT: 00087

DESCRIPTORS: Motion picture theaters--Innovations;
Concerts--Innovations; Digital video--Innovations
 GEOGRAPHIC CODES/NAMES: 1USA United States
 PRODUCT/INDUSTRY NAMES: 7830000 (Motion Picture
Theaters)
 SIC CODES: 7830 Motion Picture Theaters
 NAICS CODES: 51213 Motion Picture and Video Exhibition
 FILE SEGMENT: NNI File 111
```

The researcher notes which articles are available in full text and flags items of potential interest that are not available in full text (such as Item 1 in Figure 3-4). If she decides any others are important later, she can retrieve the citations and track down full-text versions in other databases or by a retrieval service. She can also copy and paste the results into a word-processing document that can be annotated, or she can simply use the Save As function of her browser. To include all of the search commands, she clicks on the Show Entire Buffer button at the bottom of the Dialog search screen. This will display everything she has seen in the search window since she began the search session.

The researcher retrieves the full-text articles that appear relevant with *T S6/9/1-3, 5, 7-12*. Format 7 retrieves the citation and full text but not the indexing. Format 9 retrieves citation, full text, and indexing. The articles retrieved fall into several categories: some discuss digital cinema; some discuss IMAX; others discuss special topics or the movie theater industry in general. She organizes the citations into categories and notes concepts and possible new descriptors to search in the second round.

From the articles that mention digital technology, the researcher finds the following sources:

1. Boucher, Geoff. "Pop Beat; They're Rockin' at the Multiplex: Digital Technology Allows Cinemas to Beam in Concerts, But the Jury Is Out on Whether It Will Be Just a Fad." *Los Angeles Times*, F-1, June 15, 2002. Reports the use of digital and satellite technology to exhibit live concerts in movie theaters. It suggests that the additional uses make the investment in digital projection more viable.

2. Crabtree, Sheigh, Nicole Sperling, Chris Marlowe. "Lucas Declares Cyber War: Web Site Urges Fans to Support Digital

Films." *Hollywood Reporter* 373, no. 24 (May 15, 2002): 1(2). Author points out that exhibitors and distributors are hesitant because the technology is not yet uniform, and that there is uncertainty over how cost will be shared by distributors and exhibitors.

3. Farthing, Nicolle. "Globalisation and Technology to Transform Cinema Industry." *Leisure & Hospitality Business* 3 (May 31, 2001). Reports a roundtable discussion hosted by the periodical. UCI Cinemas is digitally transmitting business conferences, live events, and games on a trial basis. The article predicts a global market within five years.

4. Doherty, Richard. "To Infinity and Beyond: Digital Cinema's Promise." *Electronic Engineering Times* 85 (December 1999). This article is enthusiastic about the future of digital cinema and mentions specific technologies used by LucasFilms.

5. Poor, Alfred. "Star Wars Goes Digital: The Digital Technology Used to Create and Present *Star Wars Episode I: The Phantom Menace.*" *PC Magazine* 35 (June 22, 1999). Reports that *Star Wars I* will be shown digitally in two cities, on two different projectors. Says the next *Star Wars* film will be shot completely with digital equipment.

6. Quan, Margaret. "Hollywood Eyes Digital Projectors, Compression, Encryption: Curtain Rises on E-cinema." *Electronic Engineering Times* 1, no. 1 (April 19, 1999). Raises technical issues, including the loss of image quality with compression for digital transmission; describes the technologies, strengths, and limitations of available digital projectors; points out that there is not yet a standardized technology for projection of digital cinema.

From other articles about IMAX Theater our researcher learns that IMAX is creating a technology to play 35 mm films on its 70 mm projectors (i.e., they will be able to display Hollywood hits on their giant screens). Another reference, lacking full text, mentions a technology introduced by Boeing Company, and two additional references, also lacking full text, mention the new "MaxiVision" projection technology developed by MaxiVision Cinema Technology to adapt 35 mm film for better projection quality.

In the first two steps of her research plan, the researcher has identified the following four key issues to pursue: (1) the standardization of digital video technology, (2) the current status of IMAX, (3) the nature of the Boeing technology, and (4) the current status of MaxiVision technology. She decides to perform another round of more specific searches to learn more about these issues.

Step 3—The researcher runs more specific searches using terms identified in Step 2. First, she calls up her old search: "B 148, 47, 16, EXS TDMOVIE."

To find out more about the standardization of digital cinema technology, she truncates "standard" to retrieve variations such as "standards" and "standardize" as follows:

```
Set    Items    Command that gave this set
S11    18       (DIGITAL()CINEMA AND STANDARD?)/TI, DE and
                PY=>1999
S12    18       S11 NOT (S4 OR S7)
S13    16       RD (unique items)
```

2003® Dialog, a Thomson business, *http://www.dialog.com*. Reprinted with permission of the publisher.

Among sixteen records found in this search, the following are of immediate interest:

1. "Working Kinks Out of D-Cinema: Dolby's Allen Shepherds Format's Standards, Sees Potential." *Hollywood Reporter* 375, no. 30 (October 11, 2002): 59(1). Names the consortium of seven studios (NewCo) that has formed to resolve commercial and technical issues in the establishment of digital cinema.

2. Bloom, David. "Debate Brews Over Special 'K' Standards." *Daily Variety* 277, no. 3 (October 9, 2002): A10(2). Notes that competing technologies are still in development. There are technical issues besides resolution: "much more complex issues, such as how subtly the technology can display differences in blacks, how many shades of colors can be stored, and more."

3. Crabtree, Sheigh. "Issues, Exec Defection Vex D-Cinema's Future." *Hollywood Reporter* 374, no. 38 (August 14, 2002): 5(1), August 14, 2002. Notes that multiple, incompatible digital projection systems exist.

4. "TI Dialed into D-Cinema Future: Company Set to Work with Studios on Standard for Technology." *Hollywood Reporter* 372, no. 45 (April 5, 2002): 16(1). In this interview, a Texas Instruments executive says that format and compression technology are the main issues. It also mentions that Boeing and Technicolor are pursuing solutions to distribution and financing.

5. "Majors Attempt to Push Digital Forward: Major Motion Picture Producers Jointly to Support Digital Cinema Standards and Equipment." *Screen Digest*, March 2002: 68. Item mentions that a consortium of seven major studios may form to expedite development and implementation of d-cinema, including the issue of financing.

6. Sperling, Nicole. "Digital Cinema Sneak Peek: Cost, Standards, Biz Plans—Panel Explores Ways to Make System Viable." *Hollywood Reporter* 372, no. 22 (March 5, 2002): 6(2). Reports that international theater owners express a conservative view on adopting digital cinema till issues of standards, cost structures, and business plans are resolved.

7. Yoshida, Junko, and Margaret Quan. "Compression Auditions for Digital Cinema Role." *Electronic Engineering Times* 1 (April 30, 2001). Reports on technologies demonstrated at the National Association of Broadcasters convention. There are many competing technologies for compression and the decoding of digital cinema.

8. Nelson, Lee J. "National Institute of Standards Takes Up Digital Cinema Image Handling and Security." *Advanced Imaging* 16, no. 2 (February 24, 2001). Details the issues of encryption, compression, and distribution/transmission, and concludes that digital cinema is inevitable, but does not predict how long it will take to achieve standardization.

To find out more about her second item of interest, IMAX, the researcher decides that it is important to take advantage of in-depth indexing to find articles that are primarily about IMAX, rather than those that make only a passing mention of it. In the files she is searching, the Company field is phrase indexed. That means that she wouldn't find all the relevant sources by simply entering the name as "IMAX" rather than "IMAX CORP." So she expands the company name to find all the variant names under which it is indexed—*E CO=imax*— obtaining the results listed below:

```
Ref     Items      Index term
E1      1          CO=IMAVI
E2      7          CO=IMAVOX CORP.
E3      140        *CO=IMAX
E4      1          CO=IMAX (CANADA)
E5      1          CO=IMAX (US)
E6      1          CO=IMAX ATTRACTIONS
E7      7          CO=IMAX CORP.
E8      1          CO=IMAX RIDEFILM
E9      3          CO=IMAX RIDEFILMS
E10     1          CO=IMAX SPACE
E11     2          CO=IMAX SPACE LTD.
E12     2          CO=IMAX SPACE TECHNOLOGY INC.
   Enter P or PAGE for more
Ref     Items      Index-term
E13     1027       CO=IMAX SYSTEMS CORP.
E14     1          CO=IMAX SYSTEMS LTD
E15     2          CO=IMAX THEATER
E16     6          CO=IMAX THEATER CORP.
```

```
E17    1        CO=IMAX 3-D
E18    2        CO=IMAXO INC.
E19    2        CO=IMAZING! CJRW
E20    2        CO=IMAZING!CJRW
```

2003® Dialog, a Thomson business, *http://www.dialog.com*. Reprinted with permission of the publisher.

As the figure below shows, IMAX is entered in the "CO=" field in fourteen different ways. To retrieve all of them in one search set, she selects all of them from E3 through E17: *S E3:E17:*

```
Set    Items    Command that gave this set
S14    1195     S E3:E17 (printout says CO='IMAX':CO='IMAX
                3-D')
```

2003® Dialog, a Thomson business, *http://www.dialog.com*. Reprinted with permission of the publisher.

She then runs successive searches to narrow the set of results: first to articles that mention Hollywood, then to items published since 2001. Then she eliminates articles retrieved in previous searches, and duplicated items, as shown below:

```
Set    Items    Command that gave this set
S15    183      S14 AND HOLLYWOOD
S16    46       S15 AND PY>2001
S17    45       S16 NOT (S4 OR S7 OR S11)
S18    28       RD (unique items)
S19    28       Sort S18/ALL/PD, D
```

2003® Dialog, a Thomson business, *http://www.dialog.com*. Reprinted with permission of the publisher.

From the twenty-eight unique hits retrieved, two full-text articles are of interest. Articles with earlier dates discussed essentially the same issues: plans to exhibit the remastered *Apollo 13* and the financial state of IMAX Corporation:

1. "A Really Big Show: Two Ex-Drexel Bankers Had an Interesting Idea for Expanding the Large-Screen Film Specialist: Eight Years Later They're About to See If It Works." *Institutional Investor International Edition* 27, no. 10 (October 2002): 18(2). Reports that IMAX hopes to expand into commercial theaters, exhibiting remastered Hollywood films.
2. "IMAX Signs Exclusive Agreement with Regal Entertainment Group to Install IMAX Theatre Systems in Five Locations: Significant Boost to IMAX Commercial Theatre Strategy." *PR Newswire*, NYW05230102002 (October 30, 2002). Announces that IMAX has contracted to install its systems in five commercial theaters, and so the technology appears to be a possibility to be watched.

Next the researcher needs to look further at the nature of the Boeing technology. First she expands CO=Boeing to identify the variant names, then she searches on the expanded set: *E CO=Boeing; S E4:E50* (see below):

```
Set Items  Command that gave this set
S20 22661  E4:E50 AND PY=>1999 (printout says
           CO='BOEING':CO='BOEING CO. AIRCRAFT MISSILE
           SYSTEMS DIV.' - AND PY=>1999)
S21 28S20  AND MOTION()PICTURE?/TI, DE
S22 26S22  NOT (S4 OR S7 OR S11 OR S16)
S23 18RD   (unique items)
S24 18Sort S23/ALL/PD, D
```

2003® Dialog, a Thomson business, *http://www.dialog.com*. Reprinted with permission of the publisher.

A scan of the titles retrieved tells her that the Boeing venture involves satellite transmission of digital films.

Finally, she investigates the status of MaxiVision using the search term *E CO=maxivision; S E3:E4* (see below):

```
Set    Items   Command that gave this set
S25    5       S E3:E4 (printout says CO='MAXIVISION':
               CO='MAXIVISION CINEMA TECHNOLOGY INC.')
S26    3       S25 NOT (S4 OR S6 OR S9 OR S14 OR S18)
S27    3       RD (unique items)
S28    3       Sort S27/ALL/PD, D
```

2003® Dialog, a Thomson business, *http://www.dialog.com*. Reprinted with permission of the publisher.

This yields only one hit—an article from the *Hollywood Reporter* that gives the background of two recently hired MaxiVision executives. Because there is so little about MaxiVision, the researcher decides to try searching without restricting to index terms, to see if the company is mentioned in other articles: *S maxivision* (see below):

```
Set    Items   Command that gave this set
S29    14      MAXIVISION
S30    12      S29 AND (MOVIE? OR MOTION()PICTURE? OR
               CINEMA?) (omitting this step yields
               citations about eye surgery.)
S31    7       S30 NOT (S4 OR S6 OR S9 OR S14 OR S18 or S26)
S32    6       RD (unique items)
S33    6       Sort S32/ALL/PD, D
```

2003® Dialog, a Thomson business, *http://www.dialog.com*. Reprinted with permission of the publisher.

Of the six hits retrieved, one yields useful information—an article that describes the MaxiVision technology, a retrofit to existing projectors that costs much less than the purchase of a digital projector. This retrofit improves image quality and reduces damage to the film. Proponents of MaxiVision argue that the resolution of film is not yet matched by digital cinema.

Both of the MaxiVision articles retrieved so far were published in 2000. To see if MaxiVision is still in active development, the researcher returns to DIALINDEX to look for current (early 2003) references in other databases. She uses the search term *S maxivision AND PY>2001.*

Because she is searching the full text in this case, she does not expand first. The search retrieves sixteen files that contain the term "maxivision" within the date range specified. She begins with those from the top ten that carry news items (four provide ownership and other basic company information, and one was searched already): *B 9, 15, 20, 727, 781*(see below):

```
Set    Items    Command that gave this set
S1     34       MAXIVISION and PY=>2002
S2     8        S1 AND (MOVIE? OR MOTION()PICTURE? OR
                CINEMA?)
S3     8        RD (unique items)
```

2003® Dialog, a Thomson business, *http://www.dialog.com.* Reprinted with permission of the publisher.

Of the eight hits, several are newspaper columns by Roger Ebert that discuss the virtues of MaxiVision:

1. "Final Frontier: Is the World Ready for Digital Cinema?" *Electronic Engineering Times* UK, October 07, 2002: 12. Provides some conservative views on the inevitability of digital cinema. It also mentions an investment analyst's report. It points out the advantages of MaxiVision.
2. Ebert, Roger. *National Post,* Toronto and Vancouver edition, P PM5, July 05, 2002.
3. ———. *National Post,* national edition, P PM9, June 21, 2002.
4. ———. *Chicago Sun-Times,* Sunday, July 28, 2002, p. 4.
5. ———. "ANSWER MAN: Projections on Future of Digital." *Chicago Sun-Times,* Sunday, June 30, 2002, p. 4.

List items 2 through 5 are excerpts from a question-and-answer/opinion column by Roger Ebert. He is enthusiastic about MaxiVision and also quotes the Credit Suisse First Boston analyst's report cited in the first article listed above. He details the advantages of MaxiVision over digital cinema, including better image quality and lower cost of projector, and argues that this data makes MaxiVision a viable possibility. He adds that investment analysts' reports might be a useful source for readers who want more information.

To extend the search further, the researcher checks the ALLPAPER Supercategory in File 411: *B411, SF ALLPAPER, S maxivision AND (movie? OR motion()picture? OR cinema?).*

She then saves her search, opens the files that contain articles, and executes the same search there (she doesn't have to type in the search name when executing a search just saved): *SAVE TEMP MAXI, BHITS, EXS.* "BHITS" opens all of the files that contain the search terms.

```
Set     Items     Command that gave this set
S1      17        MAXIVISION AND (MOVIE? OR MOTION()PICTURE?
                  OR CINEMA?)
S2      17        RD (unique items)
```

2003® Dialog, a Thomson business, *http://www.dialog.com*. Reprinted with permission of the publisher.

Many of these items are columns by or interviews of Roger Ebert. From them the researcher learns of a growing grassroots movement against digital and in favor of film. (The movement is apparently documented by Matthew Eggers and Mathew Jones on their Web site, *http://www.cinemanifesto.org*, but the researcher reaches a "server not found" message when she tries the URL.) Ebert also reports that because "some perceptual psychologists argue that film and video are perceived differently by the mind (film creates an alpha state, resembling reverie, while video produces a beta state, resembling hypnosis), digital video projection might in fact destroy the moviegoing experience as we know it."

An August 2002 article in *USA Today* reports that MaxiVision plans to retrofit projectors for free, then charge a monthly lease fee of $280. A visit to the MaxiVision Web site (*http://www. maxivisioncinema.com*) yields a twenty-seven-page PDF document, dated July 2002, that describes the technology and includes a pertinent excerpt of the Credit Suisse First Boston (CSFB) analyst's report. There is no mention of films in production, nor any indication that this would take place in the near future. The complete CSFB analysts' report can be found at *http://www. sabucat.com/digital.pdf*.

The total cost of the data from these searches was $221.90 for database fees and articles retrieved. Total time for searching was about two hours, plus several additional hours to read and organize the information retrieved and prepare the report.

SUMMARY OF SOLUTION: The researcher has found the following:

1. Digital transmission and projection technology will make some alternative revenue streams possible by digital transmission of live events such as business conferences, music concerts, and sports events. According to the articles she found, this has been implemented only on a demonstration basis so far; a general distribution system was not described.
2. Technical and business issues need to be resolved before digital cinema becomes widely accepted by filmmakers and theater owners. There are groups within the industry working to solve the problems, but it is not clear how long this will take.
3. Two alternative technologies, IMAX and MaxiVision, offer improvements in visual quality and are receiving some support in the industry. The cost of implementing IMAX is extremely high. The cost of MaxiVision projection equipment would be much less than that of digital projectors, and there are advantages in image quality. But there is no mention yet of the technology being accepted and implemented by the motion picture industry.

Overall, digital cinema appears to be the strongest contender, and it has been installed in a small number of theaters already. MaxiVision and IMAX are interesting contenders, however. The theater owner must choose whether to be prudent and wait till technical standards and financing structures are in place before installing the technology, or decide that the benefit of being the first in his market to offer digital cinema outweighs the risks of investing in technology that might become outdated relatively quickly.

CONTRIBUTOR NAME: Wendy S. Katz
AFFILIATION: Factscope LLC

USEFUL TIPS

- When running a series of Dialog searches with slight variations, use "NOT S#" to eliminate citations already found in previous searches.

- Expand a company name before searching on it (E CO=**name**) to find all the different ways it might be entered into phrase-indexed fields.

PROBLEM NUMBER 11: DIGITAL PROJECTORS IN THEATERS: IS IT TIME TO MAKE THE SWITCH? THE LEXISNEXIS SOLUTION

RESEARCH BACKGROUND: The CEO of Edwards Cinema is considering when (or even whether) to move into digital projector mode. The cost of installation is extremely high. He needs to identify the trends in the motion picture industry and determine whether digital cinema is inevitable, or other options are in the pipeline.

RESEARCH BUDGET: The client has authorized up to $300 in search costs, and up to eight hours to retrieve the information, read it, and prepare a report summarizing the results. He contracts with an independent researcher to conduct the search.

RESEARCH STRATEGY EMPLOYED: The researcher will search the RDS Business & Industry Database on Lexis (*http://www.lexis.com*), beginning with a broad search to identify technologies of interest and then examining each technology in more detail. She will search the News Group File to seek more information on a little-discussed subtopic, and then she will visit Web sites mentioned in the previous searches.

RESEARCH RESULTS: The researcher decides that it is most economical to make the first search somewhat broad, and then narrow within those search results using the Focus feature, unique to LexisNexis, which incurs no additional charge. The search can't be too broad, however, because the system will interrupt a search that finds more than three thousand hits.

Step 1. Run a general search on technology trends in the movie industry.

From the Lexis.com home page, the researcher clicks on the News and Business tab and then selects Market and Industry within that category. Then she selects the RDS Business and Industry database and specifies a time range to search the previous five years.

She does not search the news database to start because a single news item can be duplicated among many newspapers, requiring a search to be very specific to avoid an interruption of one that is yielding too many hits.

She begins by restricting the search with indexing: *Subject (Movie Industry)*. Because *Subject* is an index category, this search will retrieve articles in which the movie industry is a major focus, weeding out the many articles about home theater equipment and other nonpertinent items about the entertainment industry. The full search string is *Subject (Movie Industry) AND technology AND (trend OR innovation)*.

LexisNexis automatically searches for the plural form when you type in the singular form of a word, so there is no need to include both singular and plural in the search string. This search yields 206 hits.

Step 2. Use the Focus feature to narrow down the results to a manageable number of hits.

The researcher clicks Focus and enters *projector,* which yields seven hits. Viewing the full text of these articles, she learns the following:

1. "Up and Over: Box Office for 2002 Will Break Records, but Exhibitors Still Face Key Financial Security and Technology Issues (Showeast 2002)." *Hollywood Reporter* 375, no. 27 October 8, 2002): E-1(13). The movie studios have formed a consortium, originally called NewCo but now called Digital Cinema Initiatives. Its mission is to determine standards for digital cinema and organize distribution of digital technology. Some voices in the technology industry are concerned that too much time spent debating standards will cause the crucial manufacturers to turn their energies elsewhere. The CEO of Loews Cinema predicts that exhibitors will begin focusing on alternative revenue streams, citing digital advertising and digital transmission of sports events as examples.

2. "Sound Surrounded: Future D-Cinema Systems Might Offer Infinite New Options to Audio Experts, But First They Must Set Standards (Cinema Sound)." *Hollywood Reporter* 375, no. 27 (October 8, 2002): S-1(3). Discusses setting standards for sound on digital films.

3. "Will H'w'd Freak at Endless Tweaks? Last-Minute Digital Pic Fixes: Helmers Happy, Studios Stew (Film)." *Variety* 387, no. 9 (July 22, 2002): 9(1). Discusses the cost and contractual issues raised by George Lucas's last-minute modifications to *Star Wars: Episode II—Attack of the Clones.*

4. "Livin' Large: Could the Participation of Hollywood Heavyweights Mark the Turning Point for the Large-Format Film Business? (Large Format)." *Hollywood Reporter* 373, no. 20 (May 10, 2002): 9(2). Discusses the pros and cons of a recent

move by Disney and Universal to remaster existing features or create new features to be shown on IMAX or similar large-format systems. Cites the gross receipts of several large-format film releases.

5. "The Next Wave: Digital Cinema on the Rise." *Entertainment Design* 35, no. 9 (September 2001): S1(6). This article makes passing mention of concerns about standards and security, but overall it is very optimistic about the imminence of widespread digital cinema production and distribution. Describes in detail the equipment and technologies available at the time of writing.

6. "Cinemas Lack Vision to Fill Seats." *Crain's New York Business* 17 (February 26, 2001): 3. Discusses innovative marketing strategies in Manhattan theaters. No significant discussion of technology.

7. " INSIDE TRACK: Film Industry Cries 'Cut' Over E-Cinema: TECHNOLOGY MOVIE DISTRIBUTION: Digital Distribution Remains in the Can because of Cost Issues, Says Ashling O'Connor." *Financial Times,* London edition, June 7, 2000, p. 21. Discusses concerns about image quality and start-up cost for theater owners converting to digital technology.

In the first round of searching, the researcher has learned that standardization and cost are recurring concerns and that innovations by IMAX make it a possible contender for theaters looking into new technologies. Now she will run new searches to investigate these topics in more depth.

Step 3. Run new searches based on clues found in the first search.

The researcher runs new searches in the same database (RDS Business and Industry) and time range to find discussion of standards for digital cinema and to find discussions of IMAX. She uses the search term *(digital cinema) and standard!* The exclamation point is the LexisNexis truncation symbol, which allows the searcher to retrieve variants such as "standardize" and "standardization."

This search yields twenty hits, among them the following:

1. "Warner Bros., QuVis Link for High-Res Digital Output: Software Raises Standard for Postprod'n (News)." *Hollywood Reporter* 377, no. 13 (February 7, 2003): 6. Reports that Warner Brothers has entered a licensing agreement that commits to a standard known as 4K.

2. "Digital Cinema Initiatives Designates the USC Entertainment Technology Center the Test Site for Digital Cinema Technologies." *Hollywood Reporter* 376, no. 24 (December 11, 2002): 27.

3. "Video Encryption: Try, Try Again (Contributing Contrarian)" *Washington Techway*, September 16, 2002, p. 15(1). Discusses technologies for encryption and copy protection of digital cinema. Cites a Credit Suisse First Boston analysis that is essimistic about the near-term future of digital cinema. The researcher notes this as an item to explore further (see Step 4 below).

4. "TI Dialed into D-Cinema Future: Company Set to Work with Studios on Standard for Technology (Convergence)." *Hollywood Reporter* 372, no. 45 (April 5, 2002): 16(1). Reports that Texas Instruments has installed digital cinema in fifty movie theaters worldwide. Identifies the key issues in digital cinema development as agreement on technical standards for format and compression and financing the transition to digital projection.

5. "Studios Raising Curtain on Initiative for Digi Film." *Hollywood Reporter* 372, no. 43 (April 3, 2002): 8(2); "Hollywood 7 Unite to Push Digital." *Hollywood Reporter* 372, no. 30 (March 14, 2002): 1(2). These two articles describe the formation of a seven-studio consortium to decide on technical standards and evaluate strategies for financing the deployment of digital projection equipment. Cites the high cost of projection systems as a problem for exhibitors wishing to convert to digital.

6. "Leaner, Meaner Exhibs Celebrating in Las Vegas: Industry Enjoying an Economic Recovery." *Hollywood Reporter* 372, no. 21 (March 4, 2002): 1(2). Reports "confusion surrounding progress on the digital cinema front." One executive is quoted: "The technology is getting better, but the price point is too high and there are too many questions to be answered." Points out that Technicolor Digital Cinema and Qualcomm Technologies promised last year to install one thousand digital systems within the year—in fact, only ten had been installed.

7. "Studio Report Card." *Hollywood Reporter* 370, no. 34 (October 30, 2001): W-25. Reports that Hollywood studios have released a total of 26 films in Texas Instruments' DLP digital format since 1999. This compares with 478 films released in the United States in 2000. Three studios were most active; three had yet to release a digital feature. Mentions the concern that quality of theater experience outpace improvements in home theater technology.

8. "Until Studios and Exhibitors See Eye to Eye, the Future of Digital Cinema Remains Grainy." *Hollywood Reporter* 368, no. 39 (June 19, 2001): 12. Identifies the "4K standard" mentioned in an article above as equal to the resolution provided by conventional film. The first TI DLP projection systems offered much lower resolution.

The search *IMAX and Hollywood* yields 207 hits. The researcher clicks Focus and adds *projector or projection system*. This brings the number of hits down to a manageable 22. From these she learns the following:

1. "Omaha, Neb., Firm Makes Movie Projection Equipment Deal with Philadelphia Firm." *Knight-Ridder Tribune Business News,* December 6, 2002. IMAX has a competitor named Mega-Systems Inc. [The company] "has been in operation for about nineteen years and has motion picture equipment, sound systems, and other technology in more than two thousand theaters worldwide. Its projectors are in twenty theaters."

2. "Large Format Film Operator Recovering (Finance & Business)." *Screen Digest* No. 371 (August 2002): 231. IMAX intends to use digital remastering technology to offer Hollywood films in large format. *Space Station* grossed more than $21 million in sixteen weeks.

3. "Imax's Hopes for DMR Loom Large: Technology Could Help Boost Selection of Giant-Screen Films (Money)." *Hollywood Reporter* 373, no. 7 (April 23, 2002): 13(1). At the time of writing, there were 110 IMAX screens in the United States, 37 of which were in commercial theaters (as opposed to museums and other institutions). The company hopes the digital remastering project will entice more theater owners to install large-format technology and screens. Cinemark Theaters has five Imax theaters; they say they are taking a wait-and-see approach. A sidebar reports that there are 225 IMAX theaters operating worldwide.

4. "IMAX Enters Mainstream Sector." *Inland Valley Daily Bulletin* (Ontario, CA), April 8, 2002. Names some theaters that operate IMAX systems. This and information in previous articles could be targets for primary research to determine potential profitability. Reports that the Edwards chain has three non-IMAX large-format theaters in Southern California.

5. "An Overview of the Entertainment and Media Industry: Trends and Statistics." Chapter 2 of *Plunkett's Entertainment & Media Industry Almanac,* January 2002. Provides an Internet research tip: Log on to the Motion Picture Association of

America's site (*http://www.mpaa.org*) for information on many aspects of the industry, including industry news, statistics, legislation, and more.

6. "Imax, TI Agree on Digital Projection." *Hollywood Reporter* 363, no. 18 (June 6, 2000): 8. IMAX licensed Texas Instruments digital projection technology for use in 35 mm and large-format exhibition.

7. "Crossing Over." *Hollywood Reporter* 355, no. 27 (December 8, 1998): 16. Discusses the success of *Everest* and its significance for the growth of large-format exhibition, taking into account the costs of production and distribution.

Step 4. New avenues to explore: The Credit Suisse First Boston Report and the Motion Picture Association of America's site (*http://www.mpaa.org*).

Now the researcher would like to find more detailed mention of the Credit Suisse First Boston (CSFB) report on the future of digital cinema that was cited in the *Washington Techway* article. She uses the search string *<subject (movie industry) AND credit suisse first boston>*, obtaining twenty-four hits. Then she omits "digital cinema" from the search string to see if CSFB is cited regarding film technologies other than digital. This retrieves an October 2002 article from the *Electronic Engineering Times* that cites the Credit Suisse First Boston report in some detail:

1. "In their recent sector review, the aptly titled Digital Cinema: Episode II, they have pushed back their original projection of 5 percent penetration in the cinema market to a 2004–2006 timeframe."

2. "CSFB analysts Gibboney Huske and Rick Vallieres note: 'Two years ago, digital cinema proponents were predicting that there would be more than one thousand screens by now, with the cost of a digital projection system coming down to $50,000. In fact, there are fewer than one hundred screens with system costs still north of $100,000.'"

3. The article notes that the financial benefits of digital production go mainly to the studios and distributors, whereas the costs go mainly to the theater exhibitors. Schemes to balance this are confounded by anti-trust laws and conditions on subsidies.

4. The article mentions a competing technology called MaxiVision.

5. Maxivision uses a retrofit to existing projection equipment, at roughly 10 percent the cost of purchasing new digital equipment. MaxiVision provides better resolution than 35 mm, whereas digital does not yet equal 35 mm in resolution.

Other articles from this search discuss various financial ventures involving CSFB and the motion picture industry.

To find more information on MaxiVision, the researcher does a search on the company name. This retrieves five hits: three are about eye surgery, and one is the article described above. The other article, in the *Hollywood Reporter,* simply mentions that Mitchell Goldman served as a consultant to MaxiVision.

Turning to the News Group File, the researcher searches the file for articles published in the past two years. The search term *Subject (movie industry) AND maxivision* yields only two versions of the *Electronic Engineering Times* article, and one additional item that she will see also in her next search: *maxivision AND (movie OR motion picture).*

This search yields twenty-five hits. Many of them are duplicates of two installments of a syndicated column by Roger Ebert, dated June and August 2002. In them he mentions the advantages mentioned by CSFB, and points out that the MaxiVision projector can play either traditional 35 mm or films in the larger MaxiVision format. He says the MaxiVision projector is designed to be much less damaging to film, so that wear and scratching is less of a problem, and that the vibration-free motor allows the projected image to be more clear, even when showing 35 mm film. One column provides a link to a PDF file of the full CSFB report (*http://www.sabucat.com/digital.pdf*). These items tell the researcher that MaxiVision remains a viable possibility, and that investment analysts' reports might be a useful source if the client wants more information.

A visit to the MaxiVision Web site (*http://www.maxivisioncinema.com*) yields a twenty-seven-page PDF document, dated July 2002, that describes the technology and includes a pertinent excerpt of the CSFB analyst's report. There is no mention of films in production, nor any indication that this would take place in the near future.

The Motion Picture Association of America's site (*http://www.mpaa.org*) did not contain any pertinent information at the time the researcher examined it. It does have links to studios' Web sites.

The total cost of the data from these searches ranges from $75 for a single day of access to news and business databases, to hundreds of dollars per month for ongoing unlimited access. Total time for searching was about two and a half hours, plus several additional hours to read and organize the information retrieved.

SUMMARY OF SOLUTION: The research found the following:

1. Digital transmission and projection technology will make some alternative revenue streams possible by digital transmission of live events such as business conferences, music concerts, and sports events. According to the articles found, this has been implemented only on a demonstration basis so far; a general distribution system was not described.

2. Technical and business issues need to be resolved before digital cinema becomes widely accepted by filmmakers and theater owners. There are groups within the industry working to solve the problems, but it is not clear how long this will take.

3. Two alternative technologies, IMAX and MaxiVision, offer improvements in the projected images and are receiving some support in the industry. The cost of implementing IMAX is extremely high. The cost of MaxiVision projection equipment would be much less than that of digital projectors, but there is no mention yet of the technology being accepted and implemented by the motion picture industry.

Overall, digital cinema appears to be the strongest contender and has been installed in a small number of theaters already. MaxiVision and IMAX are interesting contenders, however. The owner of Edwards Cinema must decide whether to be prudent and wait till technical standards and financing structures are in place before installing the technology, or decide that the benefit of being the first in his market to offer digital cinema outweighs the risks of investing in technology that might become out of date relatively quickly.

CONTRIBUTOR NAME: Wendy S. Katz
AFFILIATION: Factscope LLC

USEFUL TIPS

- For economical searching of LexisNexis, run a fairly broad search and then use the Focus feature to pull out more specific subsets of articles.

PROBLEM NUMBER 12: AN INDUSTRY OVERVIEW: WHAT ARE THE MARKET TRENDS AND COMPETITOR MARKET POSITIONS IN THE TEST AND MEASUREMENT EQUIPMENT INDUSTRY?

RESEARCH BACKGROUND: QuantiMart, a manufacturer of test and measurement equipment, is reevaluating its product line, so the marketing department is interested in learning more about the market, including market trends, market size, market share, market positioning, and competitor strengths and weaknesses.

RESEARCH BUDGET: Only a $1,000–$1,500 budget can be allocated for research at this time. Realizing there is a trade-off in fast versus cheap, a member of the marketing staff familiar with online research is given as much as one month's time to collect company literature, perform telephone interviews, do background literature and market research literature searches, and summarize results.

RESEARCH STRATEGY EMPLOYED: Both the nature of the information required and the tight budget will require extensive primary research. As in most market and industry research exercises, the first step after planning the project is to collect background information, examine trends in the overall niche industry, identify major market players and technical experts, and follow general market trends by performing a literature search on both Factiva and LexisNexis. Once the background work is complete, the plan is to "fill in the blanks" by looking at financial databases such as Investext and market research reports from aggregators such as IMR Mall (now incorporated into the ECNext Knowledge Center).

RESEARCH RESULTS: The following results were obtained in a multistage, parallel research process to achieve the desired data within the time allocated:

1. First, the researcher performs a literature search on LexisNexis to cull background information and leads, using databases such as Trade & Industry Index, Newspapers, Newsletters, RDS, and PROMT. He also searches for market reports on market report systems such as Investext and IMR Mall.

2. Then he consults the Thomas Register of American Manufacturers on the Internet to aid in identifying key market players and obtaining telephone numbers. After he verifies six to eight key market players, both in the literature and with the client, marketing staff members telephone all the companies on the list and request product literature by mail.

Trade magazines often publish buyers' guides, and in this case, the *Test & Measurement World* Web site has a helpful one (*http:// www.e-insite.net/tmworld/index.asp?layout=buyersguide*). Typing a keyword in the search box and clicking on the Search button retrieves a list of suppliers. Likewise, with the Thomas Register, you can search for a product by simply entering the word(s) into the search box and then clicking on the Find It button.

3. Next the marketing staff phones appropriate trade associations, magazines, equipment distributors, and technical experts to verify trends and garner opinions on market trends and individual product producers.

4. As product literature arrives, the researcher plugs data into an EXCEL spreadsheet for comparing instrument data, features, and variety of models.

5. As opinions and rankings of the players are received, he records information in a table format.

SUMMARY OF SOLUTION: Although the literature has provided some very good background information as a springboard, the real treasure comes from speaking to the technical experts and trade literature editors. In addition to finding that many new and more sophisticated products are entering the market, the marketing team has discovered that sophistication comes at a hefty price tag, one that not all potential buyers in the target marketplace can afford. In speaking to several individuals, it has also become apparent that QuantiMart is considered to be "off the map"—the company has not been exhibiting at trade shows lately, and distributors are thinking it has simply gone out of business. Not only has the company become aware that it needs to step up its marketing efforts, but it has also discovered where its strengths lie vis-à-vis its competitors and how it can use that to its advantage.

CONTRIBUTOR NAME: Margaret Metcalf Carr

AFFILIATION: Carr Research Group

USEFUL TIPS

- Individual company Web sites often lead you to the associations and distributors with whom they are associated. They can also point you to key market trend articles where they are mentioned or included in a ranking.

- Don't be afraid to pick up the phone. Trade magazine editors are a treasure trove of knowledge: they have a finger on the pulse of the industry, can often refer you to others "in the know," and are often eager to share their opinions and insights.
- Annual surveys in trade journals can often be purchased for a low fee and are well worth the wait to get the hard copy by postal mail.
- Taking the time to plug data into tables or spreadsheets as you get it saves you time later on and keeps you focused on what you really need to know by helping you cut down on the "nice to know" but irrelevant information.

PROBLEM NUMBER 13: UNDERSTANDING THE REGULATORY ENVIRONMENT: HOW WILL THE REORGANIZATION OF FDA CENTERS AFFECT THE REVIEW OF THERAPEUTICS CURRENTLY UNDER REVIEW OR ABOUT TO BE SUBMITTED FOR APPROVAL?

RESEARCH BACKGROUND: Since its inception, the biotechnology industry has been regulated by the Center for Biologics Evaluation and Research (CBER) at the Food and Drug Administration (FDA). On September 6, 2002, the FDA announced its decision to move this responsibility to the Center for Drug Evaluation and Research (CDER).

BLA Biologics is a biotechnology company that is developing therapeutics using pure monoclonal antibodies. The regulatory affairs department head has seen the September 6 press release and wishes to know whether oversight of therapeutic monoclonal antibodies remains with CBER or will move to CDER. She needs to determine whether the company's products will be affected and when the changes are likely to take place, and she approves the hiring of an independent research consultant to find out. The search is conducted in early November 2002.

RESEARCH BUDGET: The department head knows that FDA approval is essential for the success of BLA Biologics' business. She has authorized up to $200 in database costs and eight hours for research, analysis, and preparation of a report.

RESEARCH STRATEGY EMPLOYED: The researcher will take a three-part approach:

1. Check the FDA Web site for announcements following the press release
2. Search periodicals databases for pertinent reporting and analysis
3. Return to the FDA Web site to obtain contact information by which the client can receive timely updates

RESEARCH RESULTS: The results can be summarized in three steps as follows:

Step 1. Check the FDA Web site for announcements following the press release.

To find the FDA Web site, the researcher types *FDA* into the search box of the Web search engine Google (*http://www.google.com*). He then clicks the link to the FDA home page (*http://www.fda.gov*). On the home page he clicks a link to press releases (*http://www.fda.gov/opacom/hpnews.html*).

On the press release page, the titles are listed in reverse chronological order. Scrolling down to early September, the researcher finds the September 6, 2002, press release and sees that there are no subsequent releases on this topic as of early November. Clicking on the title of the press release takes him to the text, where he finds that the agency expects to develop an action plan and timeline by January 2003. In the interim, companies are advised to continue in their relationships with CBER or CDER.

The researcher would like to find a specific statement regarding the review of monoclonal antibodies under the new system. The FDA site is complex, and there is not an obvious route to the answer by simply following links, so he will use the site's search capability. He selects the Advanced Search option to obtain as much precision as possible (see Figure 3-5). On the Advanced Search page he selects Search Tips to find the most effective way to structure his queries. The list of tips tells him the following:

1. *AND* is automatically entered between terms (i.e., all of the terms entered will be present in each search result, though they won't necessarily be adjacent or present in the order entered).
2. Common words such as "where" and "how" are automatically excluded unless they are included in a specific search phrase, described below.

3. The search is not case-sensitive, so it doesn't matter whether you enter *cder* or *CDER.*

4. Only the specific word is searched; there is no stemming or wild card search. So the researcher will have to search separately for similar terms, such as "antibody" and "antibodies."

5. There is no *OR* connector term, so the researcher will have to run separate searches for synonymous terms or phrases.

Figure 3-5. FDA Advanced Search Page

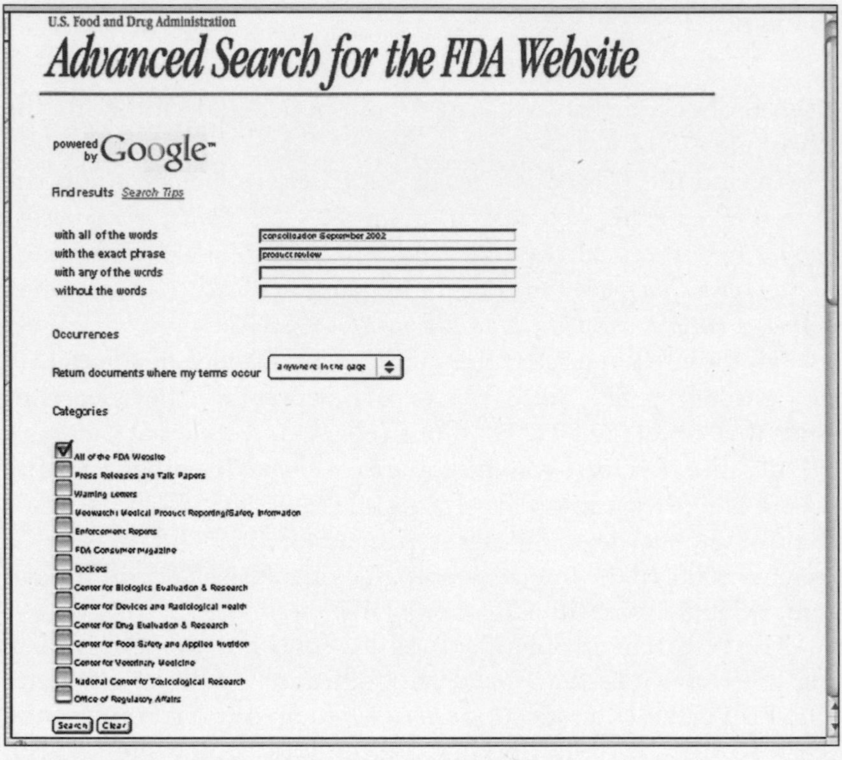

Reprinted courtesy of U.S. Food and Drug Administration.

The Advanced Search page contains three sections (see Figure 3-5). The first section, Find Results, is for entering the search terms and includes four search boxes. The researcher examines the press release and chooses keywords based on the terminology there. In the box for "with the exact phrase" he enters *product review.* In the box for "with all of the words" he enters *consolidation.* He also enters *September 2002* to exclude older items; he will try *October 2002* in a second search.

The second section of the advanced search page, labeled Occurrences, allows the user to specify where the search terms appear: anywhere in the document, in the title, or in the URL. The researcher indicates that the terms may appear anywhere in the document.

The third section, labeled Categories, allows the user to specify the type of page in which the search terms appear. The researcher selects "All of the FDA Website."

Among the first hits retrieved are the following two relevant items: (1) a presentation by the deputy commissioner of the FDA given at an FDA/PDA conference in September 2002 (*http://www.fda.gov/oc/speeches/2002/pda0924.html*) and (2) the October 2002 issue of *CDER News Along the Pike* (*http://www.fda.gov/cder/pike/septoct2002.htm*). The first does not include any substantive information that adds to the information given in the press release. The second item announces that monoclonal antibodies are among the products whose review will be transferred from the CBER to the CDER. Repeating the search using *October* in place of *September* does not produce any more useful items.

Step 2. Search the periodicals databases for pertinent reporting and analysis.

For investigative reporting and analysis, the researcher now turns to the periodicals databases offered by Dialog (*http://www.dialog.com*) and Factiva (*http://www.factiva.com*). He will compare (1) a cost-conservative approach using DialogWeb, (2) a more comprehensive search using DialogClassic, and (3) a search using Factiva.

The following search string is used in all three searches, with slight variations in syntax specific to each database provider: *fda AND consolidat? AND product( )review? AND PD=020906:021031.*

1. **A cost-conservative approach using DialogWeb.** Logging on to DialogWeb, the researcher clicks on Industries and Markets within the Medicine and Pharmaceuticals Supercategory. Within this category, he has several choices. Clicking on Pharmaceutical Regulation reveals that the category offers twelve databases; Regulatory News offers five databases; Industry News: Pharmaceutical offers thirty-three databases. Within this window the Targeted Search: Pharmaceutical News (eight databases) provides a cost-conservative approach.

He leaves the Company and Title boxes blank and enters the search string in the Text box. The search is case-insensitive. He truncates *consolidation,* using the wild card symbol (question mark) to find variants such as "consolidate" and "consolidated." To find the exact phrase *product review,* he uses empty parentheses, which is a shortcut for typing the WITH (w) connector. This means the two terms must be adjacent and in the order specified. He specifies date limits in the Year pull-down menus.

The researcher examines the titles found and selects those that appear relevant by clicking on the boxes to their left. Then he chooses a destination from the pull-down menu at the top of the window and clicks Display/Send. One article, dated September 16, says, "CDER emphasizes that it does not expect to be asked to redo any work already completed by CBER. The biotechnology sector, in particular, is concerned that the transfer yield minimal disruption in pending applications (see preceding story)." The same source names the key personnel involved in decision making. Another source, dated October 21, yields the following information: "Crawford said the FDA will have the transfer of therapeutic biologics from CBER to CDER effectuated by the end of the year, but maybe not much before then." It further says that the "FDA's working group on the CBER/CDER reorganization, chaired by Senior Associate Commissioner Murray Lumpkin, MD, met Oct. 17 and is expected to develop by January an implementation action plan and timeline for the consolidation, which will address logistical issues." The cost of this search was $27.76.

2. **A more comprehensive search using DialogClassic.** To compare these results with a more thorough search, the researcher will start with DIALINDEX (File 411) in DialogClassic, screening all files except newspapers for hits that match the search string. Explanations of the search commands and categories for DIALINDEX can be found on its Bluesheet (*http://library.dialog.com/bluesheets*). The sequence of commands is as follows:

- *BEGIN 411*(This opens DIALINDEX.)
- *SF ALL NOT PAPERS*(This tells DIALINDEX to search all files except the newspapers.)
- *S FDA AND consolidat? AND product()review? AND PD=020906:021031*(S is the abbreviation for "select." The convention for specifying dates is yymmdd.)
- *SAVE TEMP PHARM* (This saves the search string so the researcher doesn't have to type it again when he leaves File 411 to search other files.)

- *BEGIN HITS* (This opens all the files that contain "hits" or articles found by the search.)
- *EXS*(This runs the saved search in the files just opened.)
- *RD*(This is short for Remove Duplicates. Some of the databases searched have overlapping content, so some articles are found more than once.)

    After removing duplicates, this search yields the same four relevant articles, at a cost of $41.98.

    Subsequent monitoring of the print media can be done more economically as a targeted search of Pharmaceutical News, or even more economically by monitoring File 187 (F-D-C Reports), which gave the most useful articles.

    What happens if the researcher uses a broader search string? Returning to the press release, he sees that "reorganization" is sometimes used in place of "consolidation," and that "review" can appear with "product(s)" or "biologic(s)." Thus, he can search the expanded string: *s fda AND (consolidat? OR reorganiz?) AND ((product? OR biologic?)(n)review?).* This yields thirteen more hits, including some useful quotes analysis by leaders or former executives in the industry and the FDA.

    Among these, a September 30 article in the San Diego Business Journal quotes a trade group: "There is hope the move will speed up the review of drug applications, because the Center for Drug Evaluation and Research, or CDER, is more experienced and has a better track record in evaluating drugs." This article also lists a possible source of assistance outside the FDA, the Biotechnology Industry Organization. "The nation's largest trade group, [the BIO] has organized a CDER-CBER taskforce to help with the transition, according to BioCentury, a biotechnology newsletter." Other sources identify possible changes that may occur under the new system.

    Additional articles provide more commentary, but no new facts of practical use for the client. The cost of the expanded search: $59.20. All of the prices cited include the charges for full-text articles retrieved.

3. **Search using Factiva.** Turning to Factiva (*http://www.factiva.com*), the researcher runs the same search, obtaining eight hits, of which three appear relevant:
   - "FDA Restructures New Product Review Centers." *Nature Biotechnology* 1 (October 2002). On September 6, the FDA announced that it will consolidate its two new drug product review centers into a single center to be called the Center for Drug Evaluation and Research. The center will be based in Rockville, Maryland. One goal of . . .

- "FDA Deputy Commissioner Presentation at Parenteral Drug Association Conference Biomedical Market Newsletter," September 30, 2002. Lester M. Crawford, Jr., D.V.M., Ph.D. Deputy Commissioner U.S. Food & Drug Administration Washington DC Sept. 24, 2002. "As you just heard, I first joined the FDA 27 years ago. Now that I am back on my fourth tour with the agency, I find . . ."
- "US FDA Consolidates New Drug Review. (Brief Article)." *Marketletter* 16 September 2002. The US Food and Drug Administration's responsibility for reviewing new pharmaceuticals, currently conducted at both the Center for Drug Evaluation and Research and the Center for Biologics Evaluation and Research, is to be consolidated into . . .

The first item is a one-paragraph document that yields no useful information. The researcher recognizes the second item as the text of a speech that also is posted on the FDA Web site. The third item contains the statement that a timeline for consolidation is expected by January 2003. Overall, the concise Factiva search yielded less information, but at a cost of $2.95 per article retrieved with no search costs, it was worth checking. Running the broader search string on Factiva yields thirty-one hits, many of which are duplicate newswire items. Five of the hits offer substantive analyses. They provide some interesting political insights, but no information that addresses the client's primary questions.

Step 3. Return to the FDA Web site to obtain contact information by which the client can receive timely updates.

The researcher hopes that the FDA Web site will provide contact information for FDA staff who can provide the most current information on product submissions during the transition period. Following the links from the home page (from Contact FDA to Regulated Industry) he finds a page of links (*http://www.fda.gov/oc/industry/default.htm*), including What's New at FDA. From here he clicks the Subscribe to Email Lists link (*http://www.fda.gov/emaillist.html*). This takes him to a collection of links to e-mail lists that provide news from various FDA departments.

The following choices appear useful:

- FDA News Digest: Current FDA activities, with links to press releases, talk papers, and more

- Center for Drug Evaluation and Research: Daily or weekly notices of new additions to the CDER Web site
- Center for Biologics Evaluation and Research: Lists for blood product recalls and other CBER information

Under the heading Contact the FDA, the researcher follows the Ombudsman link (*http://www.fda.gov/oc/ombudsman/homepage.htm*). The Office of the Ombudsman lists as one of its roles "to determine the appropriate classification and regulatory pathway for combination products and for drug, device, and biological products when the jurisdiction of a product is unclear or in dispute." On this page, the link How to Contact the Ombudsman (*http://www.fda.gov/oc/ombudsman/howcon.htm*) provides postal and e-mail addresses, and telephone and fax numbers. Also under the Contact the FDA heading is an employee directory that is searchable by name or browsable by department.

SUMMARY OF SOLUTION: According to statements on the FDA Web site, the review of therapeutic monoclonal antibodies will be transferred from CBER to CDER, and until the logistics of transfer are worked out, companies are advised to continue in their relationships within CBER or CDER.

Turning to Dialog to examine articles from trade journals, the researcher has found the names of key decision-making personnel within the FDA and the prediction that the action plan for consolidation will be developed by January 2003. He has also found that opinions of industry insiders vary on whether the consolidation will speed or impede the review process. F-D-C Reports (File 187 on Dialog) has turned out to be a good source to monitor for reporting and analysis as consolidation of the centers progresses. The database plus document costs came to $59.20.

Returning to the FDA Web site, the researcher found the following:

- How to subscribe to FDA-produced e-mail lists that provide news about general FDA news and news specific to each center (*http://www.fda.gov/emaillist.html*)
- How to contact the Office of the Ombudsman (*http://www.fda.gov/oc/ombudsman/homepage.htm*)
- Links to an employee directory that is searchable by name, agency, or job title (*http://directory.psc.gov/employee.htm*) or browsable by department (*http://directory.psc.gov*)

The regulatory affairs department head concludes that the transfer will not affect the BLA Biologics products already in review; later submissions will be affected, but it is not clear when the transfer will take effect. She decides to monitor developments and consult FDA personnel to determine which center should receive submissions after the first of the year. The total cost of the data from this search came to $150.65 for a thorough search of two database services. Total time spent searching, reading, organizing information and preparing a report was about eight hours.

CONTRIBUTOR NAME: Wendy S. Katz
AFFILIATION: Factscope LLC

USEFUL TIPS

- When you are faced with a large and complex Web site, using the site's search tool can save you time.
- Many search forms provide a link to "search tips" that help you choose the most effective search syntax.
- For a simple, focused search, DialogWeb is easy to use. For a comprehensive search, start with DIALINDEX to find all available sources.

PROBLEM NUMBER 14: A MARKET OVERVIEW: WHAT ARE THE MARKET SHARE, MARKET PROJECTIONS, TECHNOLOGIES IN USE, AND TRENDS FOR THE ELECTRONIC/DIGITAL WHITEBOARD MARKET?

RESEARCH BACKGROUND: HitechTronics, a computer hardware company, holds patents on certain technologies that could be applied to improving existing whiteboard products. The company itself does not produce whiteboards, but it is considering the possibility of doing so, along with the concept of partnering with an existing whiteboard producer to create improved products. Before exploring these options any further, the management wants to understand the whiteboard market, including who the major players are, their market share, the technology in use, and trends in product development. The marketing department will gather this information and pass it along to the managers, who will decide how to proceed.

RESEARCH BUDGET: The information will be delivered within two weeks and will include an analysis and summary of the data found. Although the marketing department will absorb the cost for this research and no one will be "charged" for it, per se, the department does like to keep track of expenses such as this. The market researcher estimates that the cost will include about three to four hours of research time, another three to four hours to analyze and write up the findings, and less than $250 in online costs.

RESEARCH STRATEGY EMPLOYED: The researcher begins by working on a list of terms and synonyms related to electronic whiteboards. These include "electronic whiteboards," "interactive whiteboards," "digital whiteboards," and "virtual whiteboards." Because she has no specific knowledge of the key sources of information in whiteboards, a general business or market research source seems like a reasonable place to start. The next steps will depend upon the results of the first few sources explored.

Because this marketing department is in a fairly large company, a number of research options are available, including market research aggregators, business databases through aggregators, and the Internet. The researcher will start with market research reports, move to the business databases, and plan to fill in the blanks from other sources as needed. Market research costs have been accounted for in the department's budget, so there is no particular need to take a low-budget approach to this project. In fact, because the deadline is two weeks away and the researcher needs time to analyze and summarize the findings, it will be most cost-effective to use some of the proprietary databases available to the department.

RESEARCH RESULTS: The search begins in Profound because it offers broad coverage of market research reports. Accessing the ResearchLine Reports through Profound's WorldSearch and entering *whiteboards* as a title word returned 246 hits. Ordinarily 246 would be more hits than a researcher would want to look through, but on the first page of results there is a Frost & Sullivan report from October 2002 called *World Interactive Whiteboards Market.* Jackpot! The full report costs $1,092, but Profound allows subscribers to purchase by the page. A look at the table of contents for this report shows that Figure 1-6, "Company Market Share by Revenues," and Chart 1-4, "Percent of Unit Shipments by Product Type," can be purchased for a total of $60. The researcher selects and purchases these two pages.

These two charts answer the questions about the major players and what share they have in the marketplace. Although the researcher was prepared to search the business literature using the tried and true approach of a search string such as *whiteboard? (10n)(market(3n)share)*, this has not been necessary. (This search string, applied to the Dialog databases, would find any reference to the word "market" within three words on either side of the word "share," with that phrase within ten words of the words "white-board" or "whiteboards.")

The search for information on technologies being used begins with the Web sites of the companies identified as the major players in the Frost & Sullivan report. These sites reveal that the companies use their technologies for product differentiation and gear it to various potential customers. Major differences center on front versus rear projection; plasma displays with screen overlays versus the ceramic steel writing surface; wireless versus not wireless inter-action; and special optical styli versus standard whiteboard markers. The size of the screen is another variable that depends upon the technology in use.

So far the only indication of a trend is Chart 1-4 from the Frost & Sullivan report, which shows a slight movement away from rear projection and toward front projection systems. For additional trend information and insights into the marketplace, the market researcher moves to the Business & Industry databases on Dialog: Gale Group's PROMT File 16 and Gale Group's Trade & Industry File 148. These databases are available elsewhere, but the researcher prefers Dialog for this project because it offers some unique search options. The following search string permits a comprehensive search with a reasonable amount of precision:

1. To retrieve articles mentioning "whiteboards" enter *(electronic OR interactive OR digital OR virtual)(3N)whiteboard?)*.
2. Combine that with *(market(3N)size OR market(3N)share OR trend? OR forecast?)*.
3. For this search, the index term for the event code related to sales and consumption (EC=650) is added, but it did not improve the search results, so it is subsequently omitted.

Several good articles are retrieved from these two Gale business databases to fill in the blanks related to trends and technology. Indications are that the trend is toward rear projection, wireless technology, with larger and larger screen size.

SUMMARY OF SOLUTION: The research process outlined above has yielded all of the information the marketing department needs to prepare a useful report for the company decision makers. They are now able to determine how their intellectual property might enhance existing products and to determine which companies in the marketplace might make good candidates for collaboration.

The market researcher's strategy has worked well: moving from the general market research sources, through the relevant Web sites, and on to the business databases to fill in the blanks. Experience in completing searches like this one has resulted in an excellent estimate of time and online resources required, so the project is delivered on time and within budget. The summary fits on two pages, and the final report, including supporting articles and references, is forty-one pages long.

CONTRIBUTOR NAME: Cynthia L. Shamel

AFFILIATION: Shamel Information Services

USEFUL TIPS

- Start by compiling a list of as many search terms and synonyms as you can think of. Be prepared to add to the list as the search goes on.
- When you need product information, the company Web site can be a good place to look, especially for "sales" features.
- Searching for *market* within three words of *share* will retrieve the phrase *market share* and the phrase *share of the market*.

PROBLEM NUMBER 15: FINDING COMPENSATION SURVEYS: HOW DOES THE OWNER'S SALARY COMPARE TO INDUSTRY NORMS?

RESEARCH BACKGROUND: Rose and Associates, an accounting firm, is working on a valuation of a privately held mechanical engineering firm. The firm needs to determine if the engineering firm owner's salary is excessive compared with industry norms. A staff member is assigned to find compensation surveys for engineers. She is to focus her search on senior-level and/or executive-level mechanical engineers. Her manager wants her to gather what free information she can find and also compile a list of compensation surveys that are available for purchase.

RESEARCH STRATEGY EMPLOYED: As is often the case with research projects, the place to begin the search is not immediately obvious. The researcher would like to see if anyone has created a portal for the type of information she needs. In this case the ideal portal would be an Internet site providing links to compensation data. One of her favorite ways to find this kind of specialized portal is the Librarians' Index to the Internet(LII) (*http://www.lii.org*), which describes itself as a "searchable, annotated subject directory of more than 11,000 Internet resources selected and evaluated by librarians for their usefulness to users of public libraries." On the LII home page she can either do a keyword search or look through the list of subject headings.

The researcher starts by entering *compensation surveys* in the search box. This search retrieves two hits, one of which looks interesting: Valuation Resources (*http://www.valuationresources. com*), a portal of information of interest to business appraisers. She follows the link to the site, and after spending a minute looking over what it has to offer, finds the link Salary Surveys. She follows that link and finds a gold mine: links to eighteen different sources of salary data.

However, before following any of the links, she scrolls to the top of the page and begins reading. This is helpful, because she finds the following statement: "The 'Salary Surveys' section provides a comprehensive listing of compensation resources for a wide variety of industries. For resources specific to a particular industry, see 'Industry Resources Reports.'" She follows that link, which works well, because the site's owner, business appraiser Jerry Peters, has already gone through the eighteen sources of salary data listed and has pulled out those that contain salary data for engineers.

The Industry Resources Reports page is organized by Standard Industrial Classification (SIC) code. The researcher doesn't know the code for engineers, so she does a keyword search on *engineer* using her browser's Find function (Control F in Internet Explorer) and lands on SIC 8711 Engineering Services. The first paragraph on the page that follows has the link compensation surveys, where she finds links to seven sources of salary and compensation data for engineers from the Web sites of trade associations, consultants, information publishers, and the U.S. government. Many of these sites have useful information that she will include in her report to her manager. In addition to the sites specifically geared toward the engineering industry, one general site is listed: JobStar Central (*http://jobstar.org*). This portal is developed and maintained by librarians who have compiled links to more than three hundred general and subject-specific salary surveys.

The researcher wants to make sure she hasn't missed any good sites, so she goes back to LII and drills through the site's subject headings. She starts with Business, Finance, and Jobs, and then moves to Wages and Benefits. In this search she finds a few sites that she didn't find on the engineering industry list at Valuation Resources, including one from the *Wall Street Journal.*

The Web site for the *Wall Street Journal*'s CareerJournal (*http://www.careerjournal.com*) is touted as "The Premier Career Site for Executives, Managers and Professionals." From the home page the researcher follows the link Salary and Hiring Info and finds two search options listed in the center of the page: (1) Search Our Database of Salary Data and (2) Review Salary and Hiring Trends. The former is a salary database called Salaryexpert.com. (Note that there are other ways to get from the CareerJournal page to the Salary Expert database. One is to use the drop-down menu under Salary and Hiring Info to choose Salary by Title. Another is to click on the Salary and Hiring Info tab and choose Salary by Title from the menu bar on the left.)

She searches the database by job title. She has to narrow the search by geographic area, because there is no option to search the United States as a whole, so she adds a zip code or state as requested. However, when the report is generated, she finds U.S. national average data along with the regional data. She wants to find more information about the database, so she follows the link to find out that the database is created by Baker Thomsen Associates Insurance Services. The firm offers a more detailed "Executive Compensation Report" for $189.

Following the Review Salary and Hiring Trends link, from the center of the Salary and Hiring Info home page (*http://www. careerjournal.com/salaries/index.html*), the researcher selects Engineers from the list of Industry and Job Functions, which takes her to a page containing links to a few current articles and a list titled "More salary tables for engineers." This list contains links to some great data, including charts of salary data culled from trade journals and organizations' reports. The researcher finds two charts containing data from the Abbott, Langer & Associates' Compensation in Mechanical Engineering 2002 report, which she prints out for her report. She then follows the link provided to the Abbott, Langer & Associates site and finds even more free information from the report.

Finally, she does a search on Google using a variety of keywords, such as *mechanical engineers compensation survey*, and find links to sites that she had already found from LII and from Valuation Resources.

RESEARCH RESULTS: The researcher writes a memo to her manager and attaches the free compensation data she found on the Internet and a summary of surveys the company can purchase if more detailed data is needed (see Figure 3-6). Because her manager needs compensation data for senior- and executive-level engineers, she did not include data on entry-level positions.

Figure 3-6. Summary of Research Results: Compensation in the Engineering Field

Free Information
- From CareerJournal.com's Salary Expert database I found a chart containing low, high, and average compensation plus bonus and benefits figures for mechanical engineers in the United States.
- Also from CareerJournal.com I found three charts from an Abbott, Langer & Associates report. The charts are "Mechanical Engineers Median Annual Income," "Mechanical Engineers by Specialty Annual Median Income," "Mechanical-Engineering Independent Consultants Annual Median Income," and finally, the "Professional Engineers by Industry/Field, Registration Status and Responsibility" from the National Society of Professional Engineers' *Income and Salary Survey 2000*.
- On the Abbott, Langer & Associates Inc. home page, I found a "summary data" page from their *Compensation in Mechanical Engineering 2002* report.

Additional Reports Available for Purchase
- Baker Thomsen Associates' (*http://www.btabta.com*) *Executive Compensation Report* is compiled by SIC code, organization size (revenues), and by region (national, state, county). Cost: $189. The report is not generated on the Internet. Customers e-mail or call with their orders.
- Integra Information (*http://www.integrainfo.com*) provides a five-year benchmarking report that contains the one-line item "Officer compensation." Cost: $140. The report can be ordered online. Customers must specify report by SIC code and sales range.
- The National Society of Professional Engineers' *2002 Income and Salary Survey*(*http://www.nspe.org/em5-sal.asp*) is available in print and on CD-ROM. It provides salary data for "licensed vs. non-licensed engineers with similar experience, education, and level of responsibility. New income data also include size of firm, gender/origin, co-op level jobs and shared jobs, and overtime pay benefits offered to salaried engineers." Cost: $150 for members and $375 for nonmembers.
- PAS, Inc. (*http://www.pas1.com/surveys/engsal.html*) is a private, for-profit corporation that "specializes in wage, salary and benefit information primarily for the construction and engineering industry." The firm's *Consulting Engineering & Design Staff Salary Survey,* published every April, contains "the detailed analysis necessary for maintaining accurate wage information for electrical engineers, mechanical engineers, civil engineers and architects employed within the construction design industry." Cost: $330.
- PSMJ Resources (*http://www.psmj.com/website/index.asp*) is a consulting firm specializing in the architecture and engineering fields. Its *A/E Management Salary Survey* can be purchased for $299.99.
- Zweig White & Associates (*http://www.zwa.com/zwa/profile.htm*) publishes the *2002 Principals, Partners & Owners Survey of A/E/P & Environmental Consulting Firms,* which contains "comprehensive data on all major forms of compensation and perks for principals." Cost: $275.

SUMMARY OF SOLUTION: Starting with a directory site (Librarians' Index to the Internet), the researcher has found several portals dedicated to compensation data. One portal provides links to sources of compensation data (ValuationResources.com), and another portal (CareerJournal.com) provides a compensation database and abstracts of larger, fee-based reports. It is definitely worthwhile to find portals of compensation and salary data, because the portal owners have already done a lot of the research by gathering data from a variety of sites. The researcher was able to provide a handful of free charts that summarize the current compensation for engineers and a fairly lengthy list of more-detailed reports for a fee.

CONTRIBUTOR NAME: Jan Davis

AFFILIATION: JT Research LLC

USEFUL TIPS

- When using a directory site such as Librarians' Index to the Internet, use the keyword search *and* the subject directory search features. By doing so you may get different yet more relevant results.
- Take the time to review a Web page instead of immediately clicking on links. You may find that the site owner has put relevant, time-saving information on the page.
- Think of synonyms for your search words, such as "salary" and "wages" for "compensation."
- When you find pertinent data on the Internet, find the source of the data and go to *its* Web site. You may find even more information on your subject.

PROBLEM NUMBER 16: CONDUCTING PRODUCT "USES AND USERS" RESEARCH: HOW CAN I FIND NEW CUSTOMERS FOR MY PRODUCT?

RESEARCH BACKGROUND: An accounting consultant has mentioned to the CEO of IdealClamp, a C-clamp manufacturing company, that he has heard of a research method called product "uses and users" review. Through this method a company is able to refine what its product is being used for (uses) and determine who uses its type of product (users). The IdealClamp CEO is interested in having the same method of research applied to his company's market since their regular defense department/high-technology client base has been shrinking because of defense spending cutbacks. Half of the manufacturing plant's workers have been laid off because of reductions in contract cash flow, and the firm's management wants to revive the business to be able to rehire the workers. The company also wants to expand its client base, particularly in the private sector (e.g., individual hobbyists). But first management needs to know more clearly what uses there are for IdealClamp products in this market sector and who the users might be.

RESEARCH BUDGET: The CEO agrees to a do-not-exceed budget of $200 for all research, including labor and database costs. Database costs are estimated at $50–$70, with the remainder for labor. The CEO offers no deadline or time constraints but does note that raw data is not acceptable because the firm's management is unfamiliar with data analysis.

RESEARCH STRATEGY EMPLOYED: Given that the client has a limited budget, the researcher wants to concentrate mainly on free sources of information, performing a couple of quick fee-based searches to bring in the value provided by online databases. The client has little knowledge of the Internet and no knowledge of online databases, so these searches are structured, performed, and analyzed for them. To obtain the best coverage and yet remain within the budget, the researcher decides to begin with brief searches of free Internet sources and then, depending on the results, move toward fee-based databases. Thus Internet searches are done first through the Los Angeles Public Library and BullsEye Pro, followed by a progression of quick online searches using Dialog, ProQuest, and LexisNexis. The analysis is conducted using askSam and Microsoft Excel.

RESEARCH RESULTS: The research process and results are summarized below:

1. First the researcher logs in to the Los Angeles Public Library's free databases (*http://databases.lapl.org*). To get an idea of his client's market sector as a starting point for the research, he uses InfoUSA's Business database and looks up IdealClamp. He finds the company's size (revenues) and type (using the SIC [Standard Industrial Classification] codes). (Note: One might also use Hoover's Online to perform this step if the company is large enough to be reviewed/listed in the free part of the Hoover's database.) He also reviews IdealClamp's Web site and skims the information there for useable search terms for comparable companies' products, in addition to the terms he has obtained from discussing this with the CEO.

2. Now the researcher goes to Bullseye Pro, a fee-based search agent software program from InfoSeek that searches a number of Internet search engines at once. In Bullseye Pro, he searches

the Internet for a comprehensive view of the types of information available about the client's product (C-clamps). (Note: Infoseek's Profusion or Copernic could also be used, as they are similar in function to Bullseye Pro.)

3. Next he performs Bullseye Pro searches for discussion groups. This type of search can yield what people are saying to each other in a variety of discussion group forums and can often provide interesting results, especially in the "hobbyist" realm. (Note: One could also use several other search engine sites for discussion groups, including Google Groups [*http://www.google.com*] and Dogpile's Message Board [*http://www.dogpile.com*].)

    Any of the discussion groups with good hits could presumably be a consumer base for IdealClamp. For instance, according to a posting on the "rec.motorcycles.harley" newsgroups list, Harley Davidson recreational motorcycle enthusiasts use C-clamps to repair rear-wheel flat tires. The researcher decides to suggest that an IdealClamp employee monitor the discussions of the specific consumer groups found, perhaps posting C-clamp solutions to their problems and thus increasing the exposure of the company's products.

4. Next the researcher conducts the equivalent of a free information search on DialogWeb to get an idea of which Dialog files have information related to C-clamps, so that he can download some relatively inexpensive files/results. Judiciously choosing results from certain files from this search yields results in data with a scientific/technical perspective. (Because this might seem somewhat esoteric to those who have never seen Dialog results, I have included an example below of a Physics "Uses & Users" result in the Summary of Solution section below.)

5. The researcher now searches ProQuest abstracts to test his search strategy before going online to perform a LexisNexis literature search. ProQuest is similar to LexisNexis but more limited in the depth and breadth of coverage. (Note: Performing this step depends on the type of LexisNexis account your company has. If you have access to a flat-rate account, you can skip this step and go directly to LexisNexis. However, if you have a transactional account, then it sometimes makes sense to see if you are likely to get effective results before incurring the search charge of a LexisNexis search. Keep in mind that you may need an account with ProQuest; although you may be able to access this information via your public library's databases for general knowledge purposes, you could not sell this data to clients.) Because the researcher finds many intriguing results on ProQuest, he decides to perform a full LexisNexis search.

6. Because he is looking for current market uses and users for C-clamps and is trying to keep the cost down, the researcher performs a LexisNexis search of Current News (CURNWS file, last two years). This search yields results from newspapers, magazines, and trade journals (industry/professional journals), including information about how C-clamps are used to build gazebos, C-clamp use by "do-it-yourselfers," and so on.

7. Finally, the researcher analyzes the data using askSam's free-form database (*http://www.asksam.com*), the "uses and users" keyed into each search result (see example of Dialog data below), and Microsoft Excel's Pivot Tables. A description of this process is detailed in the accompanying article from the askSam Web site.

The researcher may have used Alacra (*http://www.alacra.com*) or Dialog Profound (*http://www.profound.com*) had he had access to them at the time. With either of these resources, market research reports can be accessed and just the applicable page of a professionally prepared market research report could be purchased very economically (for a few dollars, compared with the thousands of dollars that the report may cost if purchased in its entirety). Additionally, Alacra can be used for industry search terms and quick industry knowledge, if the industry in question is unfamiliar to the researcher.

SUMMARY OF SOLUTION: As a result of this work, the researcher was able to isolate specialty niche uses and users, including do-it-yourselfers, architects designing chandeliers out of lucite and C-clamps, and more. Altogether there were 3 Dialog articles, 46 LexisNexis stories, 38 ProQuest documents, with 42 Web results, with 129 data sources all told. The combined text from all of these sources would have come to 112 pages in Microsoft Word, which is why the researcher used a database/analysis software tool (askSam) to analyze the data (see the "Special Recommendation" section below).

SPECIAL RECOMMENDATION:

"askSam Used in Research Projects" by Karl Kasca

[This researcher has begun using "askSam," a data analysis and reporting tool with the following experience.] I use askSam, but still consider myself somewhat of a novice as I'm still learning about different uses of the product and I haven't had any formal training in it. So far I've just used the manuals that came with the CD. By the way, if anyone is apprehensive about beginning their first askSam project, here's my biggest tip: Just pull out the really thin "Getting Started Installation & Tutorial" pamphlet and zip through it and you'll be up and running in askSam in no time.

My bottom-line is that askSam is a very valuable tool/resource for handling large amounts of data. This is a tremendous value to information professionals/researchers because we encounter so many resources and data within our research that sometimes it's difficult to "pull it all together" and "make sense of it." With askSam this sometimes-formidable task is greatly facilitated.

Maybe the best way to illustrate this would be an example. I did a market research project for a clamp manufacturer. The clamp company had lost touch with its client base, e.g., who is currently using its clamps and for what purposes. (This was what I would call a "Uses and Users" project on clamps). For this project I did searches using Dialog, Lexis-Nexis, Proquest, the Internet (using BullsEye Pro, "free" Web searches, and specific Web searches, e.g., discussion groups).

First I "normalized" the data a bit in separate Microsoft Word documents using specifically phrased Find and Replace(s) and some manual (grunt) inserting/editing of words like "SOURCE:" "ARTICLE#:" "JOURNAL" etc. Sometimes I use MS Word macros to do this too, especially if there's a lot of consistent inserting/editing to be done. By the way, if anyone finds a Macro/text editor that's easier to use than MS Office's Visual Basic, please let me know since I'm not planning on becoming a VBA programmer anytime soon!

Also, I inserted some unique text at the start of each "article." This is so askSam can recognize the beginning of each article (or "document" in askSam). I like to use "~!@" (or, Shift and "`12", the first three keys in the upper left of your keyboard, without the quotation marks). In most cases I use Find and Replace to do this.

Then I copied all of the data/information into a single Word Text document and imported it into askSam Pro (Pro can index "large" databases more efficiently). Using the unique text at the start of each "article," I could then have askSam separate each "article" into a separate "document." Then I had askSam automatically (!) recognize all of the data fields, e.g., any text after a colon (for instance, any text after "SOURCE:") would be considered data.

From there I could search all of the "documents" for specific information of interest using Boolean (or other searches) and see particular results.

Also, I could create various askSam reports using *all* of the data from my research. These reports can also include askSam's version of what would be comparable to KWIC (Key Words in Context). For example, the partial result for one "document" from one report looked like:

```
SOURCE: DIALOG
ARTICLE#: 3
DATE: Feb. 28...
JOURNAL: Applied Physics...
TITLE: Photothermal spectroscopy using multilayer
cantilever...
BODY: The authors demonstrate photothermal spectroscopy
using a
high-aspect-ratio multilayer cantilever to measure...
A comparison...accounts for conduction loss through the
cantilever clamp and to air along the length of the
cantilever
surface is presented.
USE: Applied Physics research (cantilever clamp).
USER: Applied Physics researchers
```

(NOTE: I inserted the "USE" and "USER" description information manually.)

Then I exported certain fields of this report's delimited text (*.csv) into an MS Excel spreadsheet and created two (sorted) Pivot Tables based on the USES and USERS of the clamps, so the client could easily see the results of who is using clamps and what they are using them for. These were summarized to a higher level in the final report's conclusions, e.g., something like Physics, Researchers, or Scientists.

It was also easy to do an askSam report of all journals, listed alphabetically, with the sources and article numbers. The list of journals was to give the clamp company's CEO ideas of where they might consider placing advertisements for their clamps. The sources and article numbers were provided so that the company could look up the original article in the search results to see more about the Uses and Users if they wished.

Now, all of this might seem pretty easy for only 3 Dialog articles, 46 LexisNexis stories, 38 ProQuest documents, and 42 Web results, or 129 overall data sources. But the combined text from all of these sources was 112 pages in MS Word. That's a lot of data to "hold in your head" if you were just trying to analyze this data manually, so askSam is very helpful for seeing not only the trees in the forest, but in identifying groups of trees (which in this case represented the potential customer base for my client. Also keep in mind that in the terms of sheer data this was actually a small project, and askSam can be just as effective for large projects with many megabytes of data, which "ups the ante" in human processing/analysis terms.

In another project I used the Show command in an askSam Report to extract the sentences in the articles that had the words "results" or "conclusions" in them. This was very effective in highlighting the bottom line for each article (in addition to the other data provided, e.g., the articles' citations, etc.). This was value-added considering that the initial Dialog data was 158 pages (about 0.5 megabyte) in Word. Another part of this project involved using askSam reports to summarize 826 pages of LexisNexis data (about 2 megabytes) in Word using askSam reports. Clearly it's easy to see how helpful askSam's free-form database can be for analyzing large amounts of data.

Again, askSam is a very useful tool along with all of the other tools in our data analysis toolbox. I highly recommend it.

SOURCE: Kasca, Karl. "askSam Used in Research Projects." *askSam Surf Report* 18, June 24, 2002. <*http://www.asksam.com/four/surf18/userstory.asp*> (June 26, 2003). Reprinted with the permission of askSam Systems, *http://www.askSam.com*.

CONTRIBUTOR NAME: Karl Kasca
AFFILIATION: Kasca & Associates

USEFUL TIPS

- Try Profusion or Dogpile as low-cost Web-based search agent options until you can obtain Bullseye Pro.
- Public library e-databases can be used for subject background knowledge, but the results cannot be sold to clients.
- Use a freeform database, such as askSam, if you need to analyze large amount of data.

4

Market and Industry Research Data Source Evaluations and Reviews

Market and industry researchers generally require access to a broad range of sources. The twenty-first-century global economy encompasses hundreds of industries, each having its own experts, analysts, journalists, and publishers who follow that industry. The data points that are used to characterize a market can also seem limitless, including such details as products, prices, advertising media, market size, market share, customer base, product features, product benefits, and so on. Couple this with the need to verify and cross-check information from multiple sources, and the prospect of wading through the data source options can seem overwhelming.

This chapter looks at the strengths and weaknesses of some of the data sources most important to the market and industry researcher. These sources include online access to market research reports; databases of trade and industry magazine and journal articles; local, regional, and national news sources; and reports, data, and filings from government agencies. Because this material is often available through multiple outlets, aggregators, portals, or database developers, we will look at some of the various options and point out which sources work best in certain situations.

The thirty-one detailed, critical reviews of business data sources provided in this chapter will assist the reader in selecting which source or service to use for market and industry research. The sources included were carefully selected based upon this editor's research experience, acting in concert with the editorial board. Contributors also recommended key sources for inclusion.

Experienced researchers have prepared the detailed source reviews included here to describe the source's general content and value, as well as to look at costs, currency, comprehensiveness, and ease of use. Industry changes resulting from mergers, acquisitions, partnerships, and closures seem to occur with increasing frequency among information providers, and we've made the information in this volume as current as possible. However, readers are encouraged to suggest changes and additions. All reviews will eventually be made available online.

Given the large number of sources that are essential for market and industry research, it was impossible to include fully developed source evaluations for all of the most important sources. So, at the end of this chapter is a section containing annotations of additional key sources. These sources are no more or less important than those that received full reviews. But they have either been discussed and illustrated sufficiently in other chapters, or they are so straightforward in content and organization that a review simply seemed to restate the obvious. In a couple of cases the sources are complex and extremely rich in content, but the occasion for their use is infrequent. Still, the researcher should be aware of their existence and be prepared to explore and discover their value when the need arises.

Keeping track of the availability and content of online business databases is a monumental task. A database from one publisher may be available through three or four database portal services. The search interface for each portal will affect how the database is searched and which output format is used. Even the actual content of the database may differ from service to service.

Deciding which service and/or database will provide the needed information most effectively and economically is always a tremendous challenge. The value-rated data source reviews in this chapter are designed as a guide for that decision-making process. Although the sources evaluated represent only a small portion of the resources available, they are deemed essential for market and industry research and are the data sources anyone who performs such research should know about.

DATA SOURCE RATINGS

All of the data source reviewers were asked to rate each source on the basis of the following eight categories, using 10 as the highest rating and 1 as the lowest (80 being a perfect score):

1. Relative cost-to-value (a 10 would be very cost-effective)
2. Relative timeliness of data
3. Relative comprehensiveness of data
4. Ease of use
5. Search options available
6. Level of support services
7. Level of training offered
8. Amount/kinds of special services offered

The editors also provided the following general rating instructions to the reviewers: "Under this section we would like you to be critical but fair, bearing in mind that no source is perfect, complete, and free. It would be most useful if you always compare this source to similar sources when answering the following questions:

- How would you rate/describe the cost in terms of other sources? Do you feel the source is cost-effective for the applications/questions/data you are using it for?
- Describe the various cost schedules and/or options as you know and use them.
- How timely is the data? How often is it updated? Is the updating partial or complete?
- How comprehensive is the data? Consider such factors as breadth, depth, and completeness of coverage.
- How easy is the source to search? What do you like best about the user interface?
- What is the level and value of technical support offered? What is the cost for this?
- What type of training is offered, and how effective is it? What is the cost for this?
- Summarize and comment on a total rating you would apply to this data source, using the guidelines from the rating scale above.

Many of the initial source review ratings were double-checked by editors and other contributors, but, in the end, these opinions were expressed by individuals whose professional experience with the source under review was honestly stated. A different set of reviewers might very well arrive at different conclusions, and the reader is advised to use these ratings with some caution. A broad-based survey of one thousand users of the same source would be necessary to ensure reliable quantitative results, but that more elaborate process was not feasible for this series.

The rating results for the source reviews in this chapter are shown in Tables 1-1 through 1-10 below, with one table for each rating category and sources ranked from high to low. A summary table showing the comparative ranking of all sources is also provided (see Table 4-2). Ratings tables for *all* sources reviewed in *all* volumes of this series are provided in Appendix C, both alphabetically by publisher and as a total ranking for all eight rating categories, from high to low.

Table 4-1. Data Source Ratings: Alphabetical by Data Source

DATA SOURCE	1. RELATIVE COST-TO-VALUE	2. RELATIVE TIMELINESS OF DATA	3. RELATIVE COMPREHENSIVENESS OF DATA	4. EASE OF USE	5. SEARCH OPTIONS AVAILABLE	6. LEVEL OF SUPPORT SERVICES	7. LEVEL OF TRAINING OFFERED	8. AMOUNT / KINDS OF SPECIAL SERVICES OFFERED	TOTAL
10k Wizard	9	10	10	10	10	10	5	9	73
ABI/Inform	6	10	7	10	10	8	8	10	69
Adweek and Brandweek	7	10	10	5	3	5	5	3	48
Alacra	8	8	8	7	7	8	7	7	60
Bureau of Economic Analysis (BEA)	10	10	10	8	5	7	6	8	64
Bureau of Labor Statistics	10	10	10	6	8	8	7	8	67
Bureau of the Census	10	10	10	6	7	8	8	8	67
Business & Industry	7	6	8	8	8	7	8	6	58
Country Data	10	10	10	8	8	10	6	10	72
Datamonitor Market Research	7	6	9	8	6	6	5	5	52
Dialog	7	8	9	6	8	8	9	9	64
EIU ViewsWire	8	9	9	10	9	9	9	8	71
Encyclopedia of Associations (EA)	9	8	8	8	9	9	5	5	61
EventLine	7	8	7	7	10	10	10	5	64
Factiva	9	10	10	8	7	5	6	9	64
FreeEDGAR/ EDGAR Online/ EDGARpro	6	9	7	6	7	8	8	6	57

207

Table 4-1. Data Source Ratings: Alphabetical by Data Source (cont.)

DATA SOURCE	1. RELATIVE COST-TO-VALUE	2. RELATIVE TIMELINESS OF DATA	3. RELATIVE COMPREHENSIVENESS OF DATA	4. EASE OF USE	5. SEARCH OPTIONS AVAILABLE	6. LEVEL OF SUPPORT SERVICES	7. LEVEL OF TRAINING OFFERED	8. AMOUNT / KINDS OF SPECIAL SERVICES OFFERED	TOTAL
Gale Group New Product Announcements/Plus (NPA/Plus)	7	10	9	8	9	9	8	7	67
Gale Group Trade & Industry Database	8	9	6	8	9	4	5	5	54
Hoover's Online	9	8	7	8	6	7	6	9	60
Investext	7	7	8	6	8	7	6	7	56
LexisNexis	8	8	7	7	8	7	7	8	60
Market Share Reporter	10	5	10	10	10	10	8	10	73
MarketResearch.com	8	9	9	10	10	10	7	8	71
Markets and Industry Library on LexisNexis	8	10	10	7	8	10	10	10	73
MindBranch	9	8	9	9	7	10	2	7	61
OneSource	8	8	8	10	9	8	8	9	68
Profound	9	10	9	9	9	9	10	10	75
PROMT	8	10	7	7	7	6	6	7	58
Reuters Business Insight	7	6	7	8	5	9	9	7	58
Thomson Research	5	10	10	7	8	6	5	8	59
USADATA	10	8	9	10	3	8	8	9	65

Note: Reviewers were asked to rate each research data source on the basis of a 10 being the highest, most complimentary, rating and 1 being the lowest, or least complimentary. A perfect score would be 80.

Table 4-2. Data Source Ratings: Ranked by Overall Rating

DATA SOURCE	1. RELATIVE COST-TO-VALUE	2. RELATIVE TIMELINESS OF DATA	3. RELATIVE COMPREHENSIVENESS OF DATA	4. EASE OF USE	5. SEARCH OPTIONS AVAILABLE	6. LEVEL OF SUPPORT SERVICES	7. LEVEL OF TRAINING OFFERED	8. AMOUNT / KINDS OF SPECIAL SERVICES OFFERED	TOTAL
Profound	9	10	9	9	9	9	10	10	75
10k Wizard	9	10	10	10	10	10	5	9	73
Market Share Reporter	10	5	10	10	10	10	8	10	73
Markets and Industry Library on LexisNexis	8	10	10	7	8	10	10	10	73
Country Data	10	10	10	8	8	10	6	10	72
EIU ViewsWire	8	9	9	10	9	9	9	8	71
MarketResearch.com	8	9	9	10	10	10	7	8	71
ABI/Inform	6	10	7	10	10	8	8	10	69
OneSource	8	8	8	10	9	8	8	9	68
Bureau of Labor Statistics	10	10	10	6	8	8	7	8	67
Bureau of the Census	10	10	10	6	7	8	8	8	67
Gale Group New Product Announcements/Plus (NPA/Plus)	7	10	9	8	9	9	8	7	67
USADATA	10	8	9	10	3	8	8	9	65
Bureau of Economic Analysis (BEA)	10	10	10	8	5	7	6	8	64
Dialog	7	8	9	6	8	8	9	9	64
EventLine	7	8	7	7	10	10	10	5	64
Factiva	9	10	10	8	7	5	6	9	64

Table 4-2. Data Source Ratings: Ranked by Overall Rating (cont.)

DATA SOURCE	1. RELATIVE COST-TO-VALUE	2. RELATIVE TIMELINESS OF DATA	3. RELATIVE COMPRE-HENSIVE-NESS OF DATA	4. EASE OF USE	5. SEARCH OPTIONS AVAILABLE	6. LEVEL OF SUPPORT SERVICES	7. LEVEL OF TRAINING OFFERED	8. AMOUNT / KINDS OF SPECIAL SERVICES OFFERED	TOTAL
Encyclopedia of Associa-tions (EA)	9	8	8	8	9	9	5	5	61
MindBranch	9	8	9	9	7	10	2	7	61
Alacra	8	8	8	7	7	8	7	7	60
Hoover's Online	9	8	7	8	6	7	6	9	60
LexisNexis	8	8	7	7	8	7	7	8	60
Thomson Research	5	10	10	7	8	6	5	8	59
Business & Industry	7	6	8	8	8	7	8	6	58
PROMT	8	10	7	7	7	6	6	7	58
Reuters Business Insight	7	6	7	8	5	9	9	7	58
FreeEDGAR/ EDGAR Online/ EDGARpro	6	9	7	6	7	8	8	6	57
Investext	7	7	8	6	8	7	6	7	56
Gale Group Trade & Indus-try Database	8	9	6	8	9	4	5	5	54
Datamonitor Market Research	7	6	9	8	6	6	5	5	52
Adweek and Brandweek	7	10	10	5	3	5	5	3	48

Note: Reviewers were asked to rate each research data source on the basis of a 10 being the highest, most complimentary, rating and 1 being the lowest, or least complimentary. A perfect score would be 80.

DATA SOURCE RATINGS:
RANKED BY INDIVIDUAL CRITERIA

Table 4-3. Ranked by Relative Cost-to-Value

DATA SOURCE	I. RELATIVE COST-TO-VALUE	TOTAL
Market Share Reporter	10	73
Country Data	10	72
Bureau of Labor Statistics	10	67
Bureau of the Census	10	67
USADATA	10	65
Bureau of Economic Analysis (BEA)	10	64
Profound	9	75
10k Wizard	9	73
Factiva	9	64
Encyclopedia of Associations (EA)	9	61
MindBranch	9	61
Hoover's Online	9	60
Markets and Industry Library on LexisNexis	8	73
EIU ViewsWire	8	71
MarketResearch.com	8	71
OneSource	8	68
Alacra	8	60
LexisNexis	8	60
PROMT	8	58
Gale Group Trade & Industry Database	8	54
Gale Group New Product Announcements/Plus (NPA/Plus)	7	67
Dialog	7	64
EventLine	7	64
Business & Industry	7	58
Reuters Business Insight	7	58
Investext	7	56
Datamonitor Market Research	7	52
Adweek and Brandweek	7	48
ABI/Inform	6	69
FreeEDGAR/ EDGAR Online/ EDGARpro	6	57
Thomson Research	5	59

Note: Reviewers were asked to rate each research data source on the basis of a 10 being the highest, most complimentary, rating and 1 being the lowest, or least complimentary. A perfect score would be 80.

Table 4-4. Ranked by Relative Timeliness of Data

DATA SOURCE	2. RELATIVE TIMELINESS OF DATA	TOTAL
Profound	10	75
10k Wizard	10	73
Markets and Industry Library on LexisNexis	10	73
Country Data	10	72
ABI/Inform	10	69
Bureau of Labor Statistics	10	67
Bureau of the Census	10	67
Gale Group New Product Announcements/Plus (NPA/Plus)	10	67
Bureau of Economic Analysis (BEA)	10	64
Factiva	10	64
Thomson Research	10	59
PROMT	10	58
Adweek and Brandweek	10	48
EIU ViewsWire	9	71
MarketResearch.com	9	71
FreeEDGAR/ EDGAR Online/ EDGARpro	9	57
Gale Group Trade & Industry Database	9	54
OneSource	8	68
USADATA	8	65
Dialog	8	64
EventLine	8	64
Encyclopedia of Associations (EA)	8	61
MindBranch	8	61
Alacra	8	60
Hoover's Online	8	60
LexisNexis	8	60
Investext	7	56
Business & Industry	6	58
Reuters Business Insight	6	58
Datamonitor Market Research	6	52
Market Share Reporter	5	73

Note: Reviewers were asked to rate each research data source on the basis of a 10 being the highest, most complimentary, rating and 1 being the lowest, or least complimentary. A perfect score would be 80.

Table 4-5. Ranked by Relative Comprehensiveness of Data

DATA SOURCE	3. RELATIVE COMPREHENSIVENESS OF DATA	TOTAL
10k Wizard	10	73
Market Share Reporter	10	73
Markets and Industry Library on LexisNexis	10	73
Country Data	10	72
Bureau of Labor Statistics	10	67
Bureau of the Census	10	67
Bureau of Economic Analysis (BEA)	10	64
Factiva	10	64
Thomson Research	10	59
Adweek and Brandweek	10	48
Profound	9	75
EIU ViewsWire	9	71
MarketResearch.com	9	71
Gale Group New Product Announcements/Plus (NPA/Plus)	9	67
USADATA	9	65
Dialog	9	64
MindBranch	9	61
Datamonitor Market Research	9	52
OneSource	8	68
Encyclopedia of Associations (EA)	8	61
Alacra	8	60
Business & Industry	8	58
Investext	8	56
ABI/Inform	7	69
EventLine	7	64
Hoover's Online	7	60
LexisNexis	7	60
PROMT	7	58
Reuters Business Insight	7	58
FreeEDGAR/ EDGAR Online/ EDGARpro	7	57
Gale Group Trade & Industry Database	6	54

Note: Reviewers were asked to rate each research data source on the basis of a 10 being the highest, most complimentary, rating and 1 being the lowest, or least complimentary. A perfect score would be 80.

Table 4-6. Ranked by Ease of Use

DATA SOURCE	4. EASE OF USE	TOTAL
10k Wizard	10	73
Market Share Reporter	10	73
EIU ViewsWire	10	71
MarketResearch.com	10	71
ABI/Inform	10	69
OneSource	10	68
USADATA	10	65
Profound	9	75
MindBranch	9	61
Country Data	8	72
Gale Group New Product Announcements/Plus (NPA/Plus)	8	67
Bureau of Economic Analysis (BEA)	8	64
Factiva	8	64
Encyclopedia of Associations (EA)	8	61
Hoover's Online	8	60
Business & Industry	8	58
Reuters Business Insight	8	58
Gale Group Trade & Industry Database	8	54
Datamonitor Market Research	8	52
Markets and Industry Library on LexisNexis	7	73
EventLine	7	64
Alacra	7	60
LexisNexis	7	60
Thomson Research	7	59
PROMT	7	58
Bureau of Labor Statistics	6	67
Bureau of the Census	6	67
Dialog	6	64
FreeEDGAR/ EDGAR Online/ EDGARpro	6	57
Investext	6	56
Adweek and Brandweek	5	48

Note: Reviewers were asked to rate each research data source on the basis of a 10 being the highest, most complimentary, rating and 1 being the lowest or least complimentary. A perfect score would be 80.

Table 4-7. Ranked by Search Options Available

DATA SOURCE	5. SEARCH OPTIONS AVAILABLE	TOTAL
10k Wizard	10	73
Market Share Reporter	10	73
MarketResearch.com	10	71
ABI/Inform	10	69
EventLine	10	64
Profound	9	75
EIU ViewsWire	9	71
OneSource	9	68
Gale Group New Product Announcements/Plus (NPA/Plus)	9	67
Encyclopedia of Associations (EA)	9	61
Gale Group Trade & Industry Database	9	54
Markets and Industry Library on LexisNexis	8	73
Country Data	8	72
Bureau of Labor Statistics	8	67
Dialog	8	64
LexisNexis	8	60
Thomson Research	8	59
Business & Industry	8	58
Investext	8	56
Bureau of the Census	7	67
Factiva	7	64
MindBranch	7	61
Alacra	7	60
PROMT	7	58
FreeEDGAR/ EDGAR Online/ EDGARpro	7	57
Hoover's Online	6	60
Datamonitor Market Research	6	52
Bureau of Economic Analysis (BEA)	5	64
Reuters Business Insight	5	58
USADATA	3	65
Adweek and Brandweek	3	48

Note: Reviewers were asked to rate each research data source on the basis of a 10 being the highest, most complimentary, rating and 1 being the lowest, or least complimentary. A perfect score would be 80.

Table 4-8. Ranked by Level of Support Services

DATA SOURCE	6. LEVEL OF SUPPORT SERVICES	TOTAL
10k Wizard	10	73
Market Share Reporter	10	73
Markets and Industry Library on LexisNexis	10	73
Country Data	10	72
MarketResearch.com	10	71
EventLine	10	64
MindBranch	10	61
Profound	9	75
EIU ViewsWire	9	71
Gale Group New Product Announcements/Plus (NPA/Plus)	9	67
Encyclopedia of Associations (EA)	9	61
Reuters Business Insight	9	58
ABI/Inform	8	69
OneSource	8	68
Bureau of Labor Statistics	8	67
Bureau of the Census	8	67
USADATA	8	65
Dialog	8	64
Alacra	8	60
FreeEDGAR/ EDGAR Online/ EDGARpro	8	57
Bureau of Economic Analysis (BEA)	7	64
Hoover's Online	7	60
LexisNexis	7	60
Business & Industry	7	58
Investext	7	56
Thomson Research	6	59
PROMT	6	58
Datamonitor Market Research	6	52
Factiva	5	64
Adweek and Brandweek	5	48
Gale Group Trade & Industry Database	4	54

Note: Reviewers were asked to rate each research data source on the basis of a 10 being the highest, most complimentary, rating and 1 being the lowest or least complimentary. A perfect score would be 80.

Table 4-9. Ranked by Level of Training Offered

DATA SOURCE	7. LEVEL OF TRAINING OFFERED	TOTAL
Profound	10	75
Markets and Industry Library on LexisNexis	10	73
EventLine	10	64
EIU ViewsWire	9	71
Dialog	9	64
Reuters Business Insight	9	58
Market Share Reporter	8	73
ABI/Inform	8	69
OneSource	8	68
Bureau of the Census	8	67
Gale Group New Product Announcements/Plus (NPA/Plus)	8	67
USADATA	8	65
Business & Industry	8	58
FreeEDGAR/ EDGAR Online/ EDGARpro	8	57
MarketResearch.com	7	71
Bureau of Labor Statistics	7	67
Alacra	7	60
LexisNexis	7	60
Country Data	6	72
Bureau of Economic Analysis (BEA)	6	64
Factiva	6	64
Hoover's Online	6	60
PROMT	6	58
Investext	6	56
10k Wizard	5	73
Encyclopedia of Associations (EA)	5	61
Thomson Research	5	59
Gale Group Trade & Industry Database	5	54
Datamonitor Market Research	5	52
Adweek and Brandweek	5	48
MindBranch	2	61

Note: Reviewers were asked to rate each research data source on the basis of a 10 being the highest, most complimentary, rating and 1 being the lowest, or least complimentary. A perfect score would be 80.

Table 4-10. Ranked by Amount/Kinds of Special Services Offered

DATA SOURCE	8. AMOUNT / KINDS OF SPECIAL SERVICES OFFERED	TOTAL
Profound	10	75
Market Share Reporter	10	73
Markets and Industry Library on LexisNexis	10	73
Country Data	10	72
ABI/Inform	10	69
10k Wizard	9	73
OneSource	9	68
USADATA	9	65
Dialog	9	64
Factiva	9	64
Hoover's Online	9	60
EIU ViewsWire	8	71
MarketResearch.com	8	71
Bureau of Labor Statistics	8	67
Bureau of the Census	8	67
Bureau of Economic Analysis (BEA)	8	64
LexisNexis	8	60
Thomson Research	8	59
Gale Group New Product Announcements/Plus (NPA/Plus)	7	67
MindBranch	7	61
Alacra	7	60
PROMT	7	58
Reuters Business Insight	7	58
Investext	7	56
Business & Industry	6	58
FreeEDGAR/ EDGAR Online/ EDGARpro	6	57
EventLine	5	64
Encyclopedia of Associations (EA)	5	61
Gale Group Trade & Industry Database	5	54
Datamonitor Market Research	5	52
Adweek and Brandweek	3	48

Note: Reviewers were asked to rate each research data source on the basis of a 10 being the highest, most complimentary, rating and 1 being the lowest or least complimentary. A perfect score would be 80.

DEVELOPMENT OF THE REVIEWS

The review process was undertaken in full cooperation with the data source publishers. All the publishers were invited to participate in the project, and each one that accepted the invitation provided a password so that a reviewer could access the source. A few publishers did not respond, and hence there are some obvious and regrettable omissions. All publishers were asked to read and comment on the review of their data source, so the responsibility for any errors or misstatements is shared by both sides of the review process.

All of the market and industry data source reviews were prepared by experienced database searchers, many of whom are business school librarians and/or professional information researchers. (Contributors' biographies appear in Appendix D.) Each review follows a standard format that includes a description of the source, an overview of the source content, and an evaluation of the content and its use. Most of the reviews conclude with search tips helpful for researching that particular source. Although you will need to evaluate the reviews in terms of your own needs and capabilities, these business data source evaluations should help as you sort through the most important information resources available to market and industry researchers.

ARRANGEMENT OF THE REVIEWS

The business data source reviews within this chapter have been divided into five categories. Some of the sources could fit into several of these groups; to find a particular source, consult the source review listing in the table of contents.

The Big Three Database Aggregators

The three most important online information research services and database aggregators are, without question, Dialog, Factiva, and LexisNexis. They are the supercenters of online research, and it would be difficult to conduct real secondary research without resorting to one of these three excellent services at some point.

Each of the "Big Three" has a few sources the others lack. All include a variety of interfaces to satisfy the needs of the novice as well as the experienced researcher. They all carry thousands of full-text sources and are deeply indexed so that they can be searched efficiently with training.

In terms of business content, Dialog, Factiva, and LexisNexis are somewhat comparable, although Factiva may have a slight edge when it comes to company and industry research. Table 4-11 presents a quick summary comparison of the three services that was prepared by contributor Hal P. Kirkwood, Jr.:

Table 4-11. Comparison A of Dialog, Factiva, and LexisNexis

DATABASE FEATURES	DATABASE NAMES		
	DIALOG	FACTIVA	LEXISNEXIS
General Content	Breadth of coverage across humanities, sciences, and social sciences	General news and newswires (national and international) and business information	Accounting, tax, and case law information and general news
Business Content Strength	Market research reports, country reports, full-text business publications, and company financials	Current and historic market data, full-text *Wall Street Journal*, and international business coverage	Accounting resources and publications, tax law, and company financials
Pricing	Subscription with search charges or pay per view	Standard fee based on usage and an fee based on number of users	Subscription and pay per view
URL	*http://www. dialogweb.com*	*http://www.factiva.com*	*http://www.nexis.com*

Another contributor, Meryl Brodsky, provided a different comparison of the "Big Three" as follows:

Table 4-12. Comparison B of Dialog, Factiva, and LexisNexis

DATABASE FEATURES	DATABASE NAMES		
	DIALOG	FACTIVA	LEXISNEXIS
Content	Excellent	Very good	Very good
Searchability	Good	Excellent	Good
Support	Excellent	Good	Excellent
Price	Good	Very good	Very good
Unique Features	Amazing breadth and depth of content	Excellent search interface, very customizable	Legal, accounting, tax content
Unique Problems	Myriad of products and pricing models is mystifying.	Online help, phone help, and classes could all be better.	Search screens look similar, and there is so much content, selecting sources is difficult.

Pricing and cost comparisons between the three are more difficult to construct; all three have a number of pricing options, each of which differs from any known standard. Meryl Brodsky provided the following price comparison summaries:

DIALOG. In addition to DialogClassic, which is expensive, other Dialog products include DialogSelect (with two pricing options, DialogSelect and Open Access) and DialogWeb. Dialog also offers DialogPRO and Dialog1. For people who need only occasional access to Dialog, the Open Access program is best. You don't have to subscribe, and the interface is menu driven, so it's not hard to use. As with many menu-driven systems, the interface is a little chunky. This means that if you know what you're looking for, it can be difficult to make the menus find what you want, in the database you want to search in. For those searchers used to using more sophisticated search techniques, going to a menu-driven system is almost like trying to speak English in a foreign country. English can be understood, but you're not sure it's going to work, and it is inelegant at best. Charges are based on output and there are no connect-time costs. The per-record price is about 25 percent higher in Open Access than in DialogSelect (for subscribers). That means articles cost roughly $4 for most industry publications, and $3.40 for newspaper articles.

FACTIVA. Factiva offers several pricing models, including a subscription for up to five users at $1,000 per month. There is no pay-per-article plan for Factiva right now. Factiva has recently rolled out a plan where, for an annual subscription fee of $69, you will be able to search Factiva.com for free, and pay $2.95 per article. Other content, such as company profiles, investment and analysts' reports, and corporate credit reports, will likely cost between $5 and $15.

LEXISNEXIS. LexisNexis offers pricing models ranging from the all-you-can-eat variety (annual subscription or $250/week for news, business, and financial information or less for just one of the three) to document fees, which range from $3 for news articles to $12 for legal documents.

All three sources provide options to serve the needs of small businesses or the occasional business researcher. The source chosen may have more to do with content needs and frequency of use than with price. Dialog (DialogClassic) covers the most subject areas and offers the greatest variety of search options, from forms-based research to sophisticated search software capabilities not available in the other online services. Dialog also includes science and technology and academic journal databases that do not appear elsewhere.

For obtaining a few specific articles, the best choice may be Factiva, because it offers a low-priced per-article fee and free searching through a simple search interface, with more advanced search tools when needed.

LexisNexis would be the most appropriate source for an occasional need for in-depth research or legal materials. The daily and weekly passes offer good value, particularly if several research projects are batched and run at once. There are a couple of sources in LexisNexis not readily available elsewhere, including the Market Share Reporter, which would have significant value to a market and industry researcher.

Government Information

Government sources truly shine when it comes to statistics and company filings at the Securities and Exchange Commission. The Bureau of Economic Analysis publishes statistics that help explain U.S. and international economic activity. The Bureau of Labor Statistics is the place to go for information on employment, the consumer price index, wages and salaries, and productivity. The Bureau of the Census provides demographic information in such detail, both in terms of content and geographic specificity, that primary research of a target market is often not required. The Economic Census provides data on all industry sectors down to the county level. EDGAR is a searchable database of SEC filings available through the SEC Web site. A number of entrepreneurs have taken these electronic SEC filings and enhanced their content and searchability for value-added business searching. Some, such as the 10k Wizard product, are fully searchable by keyword, facilitating powerful research of executive names, market share data, market size, and product-specific information.

Aggregators and Portals

A number of enterprising businesses have concluded that there are certain types of information that will be of value to a large segment of business researchers. These companies have bundled representative sources of information together in one place or through one interface to create a "one-stop shop." Alacra, OneSource, Reuters Business Insight, and Thomson Research serve this purpose. Note that Thomson Research includes the Trade Association Research database, which is not generally available elsewhere. In addition, Investext is the place to go for analysts' reports collected from more than 950 firms. MindBranch, Marketresearch.com, and Profound all collect market research information, but each offers unique content , pricing, and search capabilities. The comprehensive market researcher will want access to all three.

Individual Databases Covering Multiple Industries and Markets

ABI/Inform, Business & Industry, Datamonitor, Gale Group New Product Announcements/Plus, Gale Group Trade & Industry, and PROMT are available through a variety of database services. Markets and Industry Library is a collection of databases, including PROMT, available through LexisNexis. (The slice of PROMT available on LexisNexis can vary from the slice available on Dialog, so it is important to keep that in mind if dates are important.) ABI/Inform is known for its deep archive, going back to 1971, and for content related to management techniques, finance, and corporate strategies. Business & Industry and Trade & Industry are complementary databases. Whereas Trade & Industry covers primarily North America, Business & Industry covers more than thirty countries. Together they index more than one thousand trade, business, and industry publications. Both have powerful indexing that allows the searcher to find market share, consumer behavior, and forecast or trend information. PROMT is a good place to start when searching for events, trends, corporate activities, facilities, and product information. When searching on Dialog, Business & Industry, Trade & Industry, and PROMT can be searched simultaneously. LexisNexis offers similar capability in its Markets and Industry Library. Simultaneous searching of these powerful business databases offers thoroughness and the opportunity to eliminate duplicate hits. Datamonitor provides a unique look at markets and industry, since its reports are based on primary research and generated internally by industry experts. If all you need is market share, then Market Share Reporter separates these statistics from the surrounding content and offers just the facts.

Subject-Specific Special Sources

The sources discussed in this section provide the details often necessary to round out a market or industry profile. Go to *Adweek* and *Brandweek* for product and advertising information. Country Data and EIU ViewsWire provide the global insights necessary to understand the political and economic environment of suppliers and partners. The Encyclopedia of Associations and EventLine can lead the researcher to just the right organization or trade show that might provide the needed answers. Hoover's is an excellent source, providing just enough free company and industry information to point the way, and in many cases to make you want to subscribe to the premium content also available. USADATA is an example of a mailing list service. These services are important to the market researcher who has determined that the secondary sources are not going to provide the necessary information, and that a survey or some primary research is required.

Key Additional Sources

This section of Chapter Four stands on its own as a directory of additional sources for specialized market and industry information. They are important complementary and supplementary sources to those evaluated at length, and no less important. Be sure to review the annotations in this section to round out your market and industry research toolbox.

DIALOG

ALTERNATE/PREVIOUS DATA SOURCE NAMES: DialogClassic, DialogWeb, Dialog1, DialogPRO, DialogSelect, Dialog Open Access

SERVICE/PORTAL NAME: *http://www.dialog.com*

SOURCE DESCRIPTION: Dialog is a leading worldwide provider of online information services that contain an impressive amount of information on an extensive variety of subjects. Dialog users can precisely retrieve data from more than 1.4 billion unique records, via the Internet or through delivery to enterprise intranets. Searchable content includes articles and reports from thousands of real-time news feeds, newspapers, broadcast transcripts, and trade publications, plus research reports and analyst notes providing support for financial decision making. Content also includes in-depth repositories of scientific and technical data, patents, trademarks, and other intellectual property data. Information professionals and end users at business, professional, andgovernment organizations in more than one hundred countries prize Dialog services for their depth and breadth of content, precision searching, and speed. This online information is offered through five product lines: Dialog, Dialog Profound, Dialog DataStar, NewsEdge, and Intelligence Data. The interfaces discussed in this review fall under the Dialog brand of services.

Dialog was formed as a commercial venture in 1972, originating from a project at Lockheed Corporation that dates back to the early 1960s. Today, Dialog is considered to be "the pioneer of online information services." It has developed and evolved through numerous iterations and owners, including Knight Ridder, MAID plc, and currently The Thomson Corporation. Web-based options include Dialog1, DialogClassic, DialogPRO, DialogSelect, and DialogWeb. Other interfaces include Dialog Company Profiles, Dialog NewsRoom, DialogLink for Windows, Dialog OnDisc, and Dialog thru Telnet. Dialog is also available in a selection of intranet options, including Dialog@Site and Dialog for Lotus Notes. Detailed information on these products can be found at *http://www.dialog.com/products/productline/dialog.shtml.*

Following is a detailed look at the five Dialog content options: DialogClassic, DialogWeb, DialogSelect, Dialog1, and DialogPRO.

1. **DialogClassic** is a Web interface to the command-line version of Dialog. Command-line access provides the most flexibility and control during a search. DialogClassic is text based for fast access, and images are available from the patent and trademark databases. DialogClassic requires the most user knowledge of the search options and format types of Dialog, and the sparse interface makes it necessary to also have a fairly thorough knowledge of the content of the Dialog databases. It is necessary to use the command language and the indexes specific to the selected database to create carefully crafted searches in the DialogClassic interface. This method of access is geared for the knowledgeable information professional who desires speed and precise control of the search to retrieve information.

2. **DialogWeb** provides a straightforward, graphical Web-based interface accessing the entire content of the Dialog service. It provides both a Guided Search and a Command Search option.

The Guided Search option allows the user to select from a menu of categories and subcategories until arriving at the Dynamic Search screen. The Dynamic Search screen presents the user with the option of searching simultaneously all of the relevant databases attached to that subcategory, or of selecting an individual database for information retrieval (see Figures 4-1–4-3).

Figure 4-1. DialogWeb Guided Search Interface, First Screen

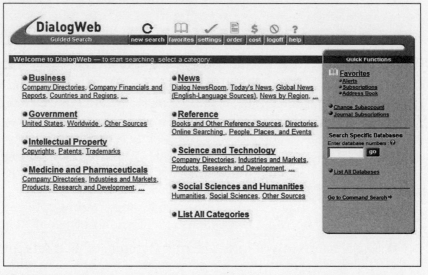

2003® Dialog, a Thomson business, *http://www.dialog.com*. Reprinted with permission of the publisher.

The Command Search option in DialogWeb provides the same flexibility and control as the DialogClassic version. Knowledge of the Dialog command language is necessary for effective searching, and database selection is facilitated by a browsable list of databases (see Figure 4-4).

DialogWeb serves both the experienced searcher and the novice/intermediate searcher by providing the two search options. The browsable category menus facilitate database selection for expert and novice alike. Command Language searching is another option. This interface will serve a varied user population.

Figure 4-2. DialogWeb Guided Search Interface, Second Screen

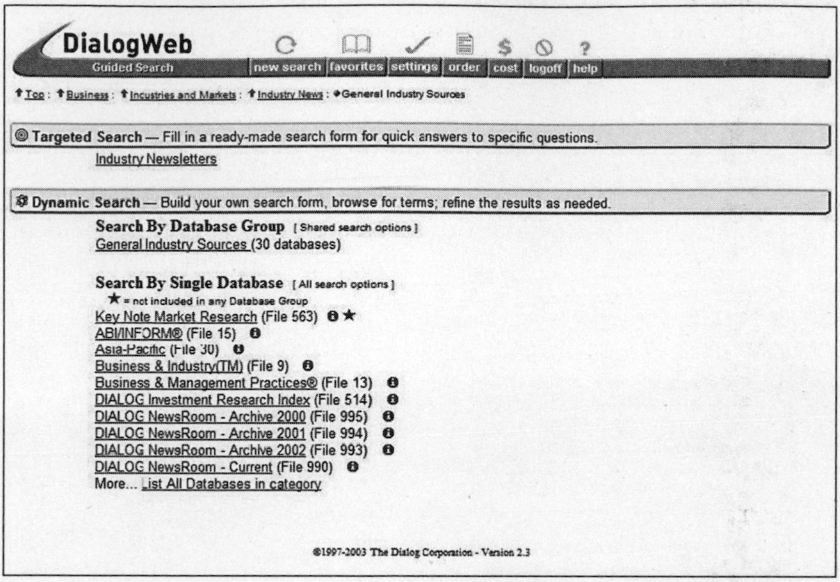

DialogWeb
Guided Search   new search | favorites | settings | order | cost | logoff | help

↑ Top : ↑ Business : ↑ Industries and Markets : ↑ Industry News : ◆ General Industry Sources

◎ **Targeted Search** — Fill in a ready-made search form for quick answers to specific questions.
        Industry Newsletters

❀ **Dynamic Search** — Build your own search form; browse for terms; refine the results as needed.
        Search By Database Group [Shared search options]
        General Industry Sources (30 databases)

        Search By Single Database [All search options]
            ★ = not included in any Database Group
        Key Note Market Research (File 563) ❸ ★
        ABI/INFORM® (File 15) ❸
        Asia-Pacific (File 30) ❶
        Business & Industry(TM) (File 9) ❸
        Business & Management Practices® (File 13) ❸
        DIALOG Investment Research Index (File 514) ❸
        DIALOG NewsRoom - Archive 2000 (File 995) ❸
        DIALOG NewsRoom - Archive 2001 (File 994) ❸
        DIALOG NewsRoom - Archive 2002 (File 993) ❸
        DIALOG NewsRoom - Current (File 990) ❸
        More... List All Databases in category

©1997-2003 The Dialog Corporation - Version 2.3

2003® Dialog, a Thomson business, *http://www.dialog.com*. Reprinted with permission of the publisher.

Figure 4-3. DialogWeb Guided Search Interface, Dynamic Search Screen

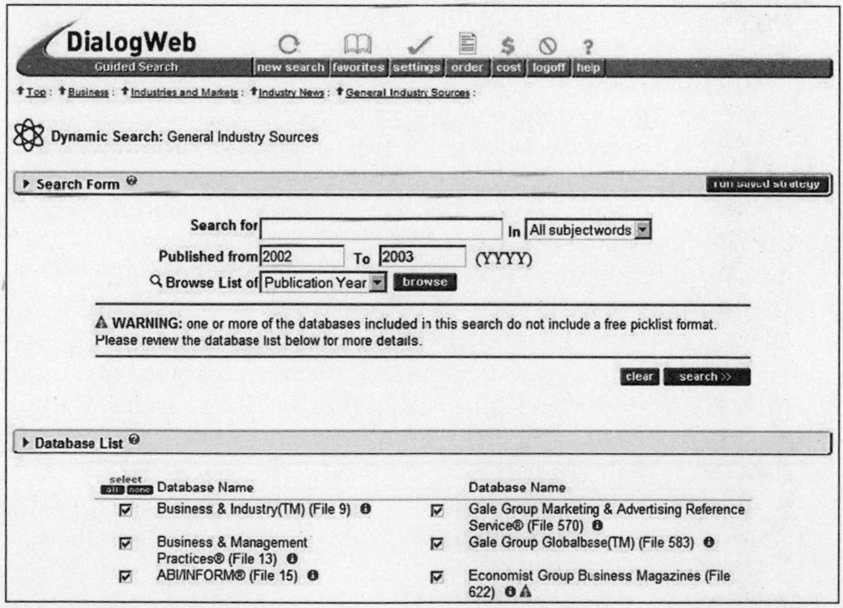

DialogWeb
Guided Search   new search | favorites | settings | order | cost | logoff | help

↑ Top : ↑ Business : ↑ Industries and Markets : ↑ Industry News : ↑ General Industry Sources :

✺ Dynamic Search: General Industry Sources

▶ Search Form ⊕   run saved strategy

            Search for [   ] In [All subjectwords ▼]
        Published from [2002] To [2003]   (YYYY)
        ⚲ Browse List of [Publication Year ▼] [browse]

        ⚠ WARNING: one or more of the databases included in this search do not include a free picklist format.
        Please review the database list below for more details.

                                                    [clear] [search »]

▶ Database List ⊕

    select
    all none Database Name   Database Name
        ☑   Business & Industry(TM) (File 9) ❸   ☑ Gale Group Marketing & Advertising Reference
                                                        Service® (File 570) ❸
        ☑   Business & Management   ☑ Gale Group Globalbase(TM) (File 583) ❸
            Practices® (File 13) ❸
        ☑   ABI/INFORM® (File 15) ❸   ☑ Economist Group Business Magazines (File
                                                        622) ❸⚠

2003® Dialog, a Thomson business, *http://www.dialog.com*. Reprinted with permission of the publisher.

Figure 4-4. DialogWeb Command Search Interface

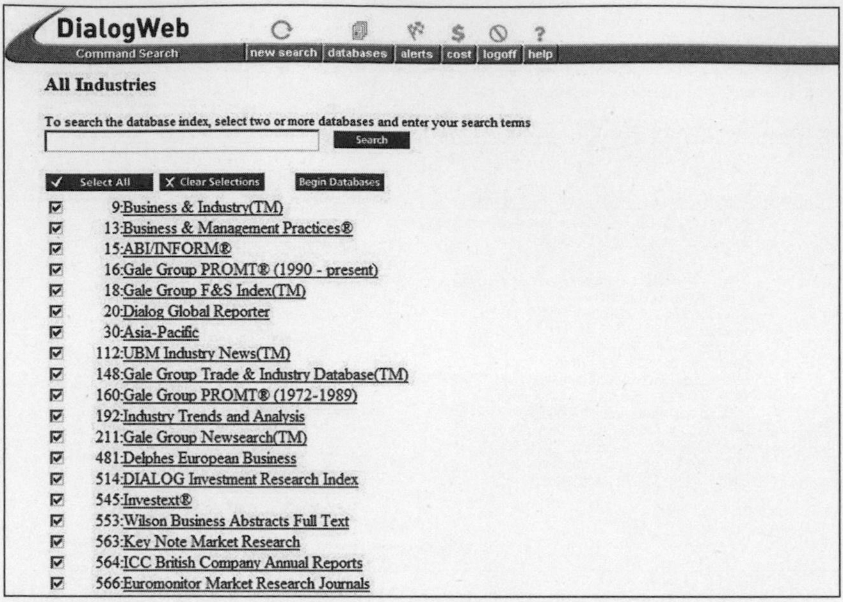

2003® Dialog, a Thomson business, *http://www.dialog.com*. Reprinted with permission of the publisher.

3. **DialogSelect** is a cross between DialogWeb and Dialog1, providing a Web-accessible interface to approximately three hundred databases from the main Dialog list. The information is organized into vertical categories to direct the user toward the desired content. Knowledge of the command language is not necessary, but searching is not as easy as in Dialog1. However, there is a fair amount of flexibility in creating a search, including proximity and Boolean (AND, OR, NOT) operators. There are a number of accessible fields that can be searched as well.

4. **Dialog1** is a simple interface to approximately 150 databases of Dialog content. The information is presented in Channels (see Figure 4-5) in a question-based format, leading the user through several menus and submenus until a search screen is provided that offers a clear search function, with preselected databases and appropriate content (see Figure 4-6). The search page often contains internal or hidden search parameters, created by information professionals, to facilitate the delivery of better results.

Dialog1 removes the agony of determining which of the nine hundred files should be searched to fill an information need. It provides access to a select subset and is geared for novice and infrequent users. It lacks flexibility in its search capabilities, but this is to be expected with a beginner audience as the target market.

Figure 4-5. Dialog1 Interface, Channels screen

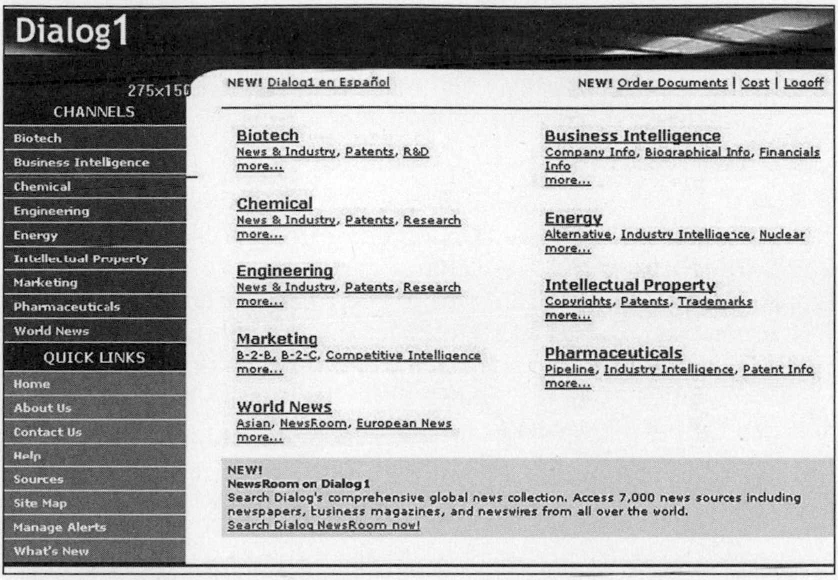

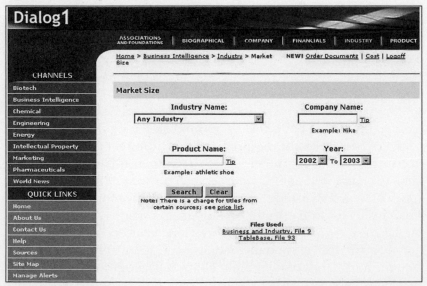

2003® Dialog, a Thomson business, *http://www.dialog.com*. Reprinted with permission of the publisher.

Figure 4-6. Dialog1 Interface, Search Screen

2003® Dialog, a Thomson business, *http://www.dialog.com*. Reprinted with permission of the publisher.

5. **DialogPRO** is similar to Dialog1 in that it provides access to a subset of the Dialog databases divided into Channels. This option is geared for small business owners (the "PRO" in "DialogPRO" stands for "Predictable Research Online"). Subscribers can select which channels are most relevant to their situation and pay a tiered flat fee for access. The whole content of Dialog is available on a transactional, as-needed basis. This option is particularly useful for infrequent users interested in controlling costs and in need of access to only a portion of the Dialog databases.

PRICING: The most complicated aspect of Dialog is the many pricing issues and options. Dialog charges both by connect time and by file format, and these charges are different across all of the databases. The charges range from $30 an hour for PsycInfo, with full abstracts costing $0.80 each, to $300 an hour for PharmaProjects, with full reports costing $13.40 each. Pricing for most databases falls between $80 and $300 an hour. Charges are also accrued for each User ID at the following rates:

United States and United Kingdom	1–5 User IDs	U.S.$14.00/month/User ID
Rest of the world	1–5 User IDs	U.S.$20.00/month/User ID

Dialog also offers a DialUnit charge rate, where the user is charged for the amount of system resources used during a given search session. With this option, searches that are more complex cost more money. The user can choose which method of charging is used within an account. The DialUnit charges span from $1.00 to $28.50 (for example, the DialUnit rate for PsycInfo is $3.50, and the rate for PharmaProjects is $28.50). These charges apply to DialogClassic, DialogWeb, and DialogSelect.

DialogSelect access is also available through Dialog Open Access, which is a pay-per-view option using a credit card. Dialog Open Access does not require a subscription fee, and it does not accrue any connect time or DialUnit charges. It is strictly pay-per-view for each document. Charges per document are 20 percent more than what is listed on the standard price list for the databases. Its interface is similar to the DialogSelect version.

Dialog1 is geared for less experienced users, so it does not accrue any connect time or DialUnit charges. There is a subscription fee and standard document charges. DialogPRO has a flat-fee pricing structure, with Primary, Plus, and Premier levels that provide increasing levels of access. The price points depend on the topic area and range from $60 a month to $500 a month. Several excellent articles have been written on this topic; see the "Source Reviews" section below.

SOURCE CONTENT: The information available through Dialog products and services consists of over nine hundred databases of content. These databases contain information on business, government, intellectual property, medicine and pharmaceuticals, news, science and technology, social sciences and humanities, and reference information. The information comes from journal and news articles, chemical abstracts, company financials, trade and country data, demographic information, government information, reference materials, intellectual property documents, and science, social science, and humanities data.

Among the Dialog databases are the following:

- Adis Clinical Trials Insight
- Brands and Their Companies
- Datamonitor Market Research
- EIU Country Analysis
- M&A Filings
- *Polymer Online*
- *San Francisco Chronicle*
- World Textiles
- Xinhua News

Some insight into the scope of the content can be obtained by viewing the subject menu for the Bluesheets:

- Business—Business & Industry
- Business—Business Statistics
- Business—International Directories & Company Financials
- Business—Product Information
- Business—U.S. Directories & Company Financials
- Social Science & Humanities
- Law & Government
- Multidisciplinary—Books
- Multidisciplinary—General
- Multidisciplinary—Reference
- News—U.S. Newspapers Fulltext
- News—Worldwide News
- Patents, Trademarks, Copyrights
- Science—Agriculture & Nutrition
- Science—Chemistry
- Science—Computer Technology
- Science—Energy & Environment
- Science—Medicine & Biosciences
- Science—Pharmaceuticals
- Science—Science & Technology

As this list illustrates, the depth and breadth of content offered in Dialog is unparalleled. Other resources that come close in size and scope within certain subjects would be LexisNexis and Factiva. However, neither of these can match the Dialog holdings across the humanities, sciences, and social sciences.

Help and Supporting Information. Dialog provides access to a substantial amount of supporting documentation for its massive quantity of information. Specifically, each of the nine hundred databases has a unique Bluesheet that provides detailed information on the database's content, date coverage, update frequency, and source of information (See Figure 4-7). In addition to this descriptive data, the Bluesheet provides possible search tips, a sample record, and a list of the basic and additional indexes for each database. These Bluesheets are available at no cost online through the Dialog Web site (*http://library.dialog.com/bluesheets*).

Figure 4-7. Sample Dialog Bluesheet

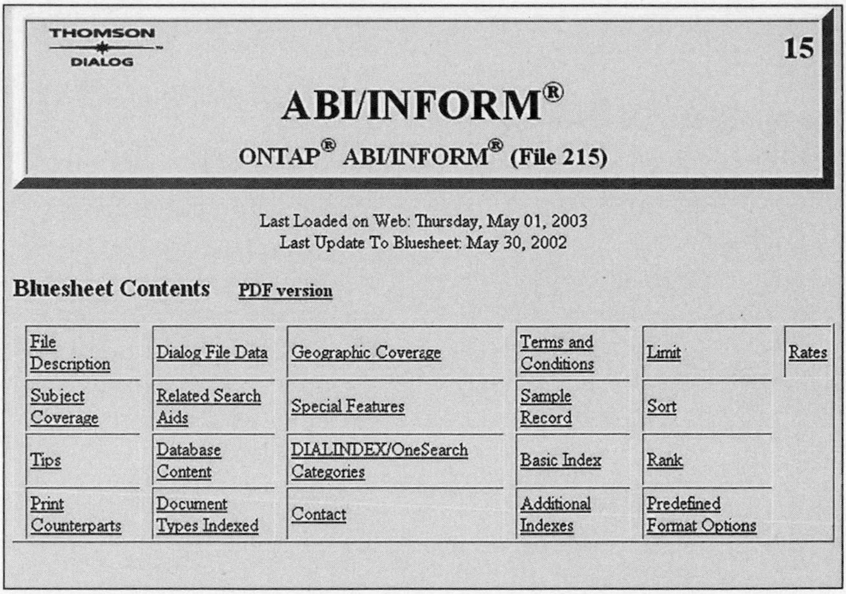

THOMSON
DIALOG
15

ABI/INFORM®

ONTAP® ABI/INFORM® (File 215)

Last Loaded on Web: Thursday, May 01, 2003
Last Update To Bluesheet: May 30, 2002

Bluesheet Contents   **PDF version**

File Description	Dialog File Data	Geographic Coverage	Terms and Conditions	Limit	Rates
Subject Coverage	Related Search Aids	Special Features	Sample Record	Sort	
Tips	Database Content	DIALINDEX/OneSearch Categories	Basic Index	Rank	
Print Counterparts	Document Types Indexed	Contact	Additional Indexes	Predefined Format Options	

Each Bluesheet includes specific information on the available retrieval format types. Each database has this menu of formats, with its own pricing structure. 2003® Dialog, a Thomson business, *http://www.dialog.com*. Reprinted with permission of the publisher.

Search Aids. In addition to the Bluesheets, Dialog provides other search aids and documentation to assist users. These aids include general information on the Dialog service, details on search support, a manual that details how to effectively search Dialog, and several other comparison tools and quick reference resources. Also available are several database-specific search aids that provide greater detail on the indexing and classification systems of many databases. Examples include Business & Industry Concept Terms, Definitions Used in Dun & Bradstreet, and GEOREF Geographic Coordinates Fields. These specific search aids can be found online at the Dialog Web site (*http://support.dialog.com/ searchaids/dialog/#aids*).

DIALINDEX and ONTAP Files. Two additional features within Dialog designed to help users learn and use the database are the DIALINDEX and the ONTAP files. DIALINDEX (*http:// support.dialog.com/searchaids/dialog/pocketguide/finding_tools.shtml*) allows the searcher to send a query across multiple databases. The results returned are a total number of potentially relevant hits found within each database. Thus, the searcher can rank the databases to determine which have the most content for their search. A list of Supercategories is available so that similar databases can be searched simultaneously.

The ONTAP files are small-sized versions of a select group of major database files. These versions do not accrue any connect time or file format charges and can be used to practice searching with the command language. There are thirty-eight ONTAP database files. This tool is highly recommended for beginners wishing to become more accustomed to using Dialog.

SOURCE EVALUATION: Dialog contains a tremendous amount of content, spanning every major subject category. It provides access to hundreds of databases through a variety of interfaces with a variety of pricing formats. Its scope, breadth, and depth are unmatched by any other database aggregator or portal service.

I recommend looking carefully at the content and pricing structure before you subscribe to Dialog, to determine if it meets your organization's needs. Although its breadth may make it an obvious choice for most any situation, it may be excessive (and costly) for some information needs. Also, carefully evaluate the interfaces to determine how much power you and other researchers in your organization need and are capable of handling.

I would recommend Dialog for researchers interested in having a broad array of sources at their disposal. Because there is connect-time charging for several of the Dialog interfaces, it may be important to carefully consider who the primary users will be and how experienced they are in information seeking. Keep in mind that a benefit of this clear pricing is that it makes it very easy to track costs and bill clients.

The Dialog Web site contains a large amount of useful information about the databases, pricing options, and support tools and should be perused before you make any final decision on acquiring this database.

SOURCE VALUE RATING: All of the data source reviewers were asked to rate each source on the basis of the following eight categories, using "10" as the highest rating and "1" as the lowest ("80" being a perfect score):

1. Relative cost-to-value:	8
2. Relative timeliness of data:	9
3. Relative comprehensiveness of data:	9
4. Ease of use:	7
5. Search options available:	10
6. Level of support services:	10
7. Level of training offered:	9
8. Amount/kinds of special services offered:	8
Total Rating:	70

SOURCE REVIEWS: This is only a selection of the articles available on Dialog and its services and pricing schemes:

Bates, M. E. "Dialog Pricing Redux: Deja Vu All Over Again." *Searcher* 10, no. 3 (March 2002): 36–49.

———. "Dialog's Connect Time Pricing." *Online* 26, no. 2 (March/April 2002): 88.

———. "Dialog One." *EContent* 23, no. 5 (October/November 2000): 96.

———. "Dialog's Dialunits: There Is a Great Disturbance in the Force." *Searcher* 7, no. 7 (July/August 1999): 52–57.

Hurst, J. A. "DialogWeb under the Microscope: Facts & Stats." *EContent* 23, no. 3 (June/July 2000): 35–38.

O'Leary, M. Dialog keeps end-user-searching edge. *Information Today* Vol.18:8 p 15-6 (September 2001).

———. "DialogSelect Opens Access to Premium Business Content." *Link-Up* 18, no. 3 (May/June 2001): 9–10.

Quint, B. E. "DialogPRO Brings Flat-Fee Subscriptions to Low-End Small-Business Market." *Information Today* 19, no. 4 (April 2002): 78, 80.

CONTRIBUTOR NAME: Hal P. Kirkwood, Jr./Meryl Brodsky
AFFILIATION: Purdue University/Consultant

USEFUL TIPS

- Read the Bluesheet prior to using any database.
- Use DialIndex to help determine which databases will be useful.
- Utilize both in-house and Dialog-supplied training options for your users to ensure effective and cost-conscious use of the databases.

FACTIVA

ALTERNATE/PREVIOUS DATA SOURCE NAMES: Dow Jones Interactive, Reuters Business Briefing, Dow Jones News/Retrieval

SERVICE/PORTAL NAME: *http://www.factiva.com*

SOURCE DESCRIPTION: Factiva is a joint venture, formed in 1999 by Dow Jones & Co. and The Reuters Group. Its flagship product, Factiva.com, is the successor online service to Dow Jones Interactive (formerly Dow Jones News/Retrieval) and Reuters Business Briefing, both of which were known for their focus on international information sources. Factiva.com now includes almost all of the content of both of its predecessors, along with capabilities and services not previously available.

Factiva contains four basic tabs: Search, Track, News Pages, and Companies/Markets, each of which is described in the Source Content section below. The heart of Factiva is its collection of nearly eight thousand publications in twenty-two languages from 118 countries, and its emphasis on acquiring content directly from publishers whenever possible. This enables the company to ensure that the updates are added as soon as they are available, and that the coverage of individual publications is as comprehensive as is feasible. Factiva data includes current news, archived articles, company data, investment analyst reports, market data, historical stock price performance, and company financials.

Factiva content includes ten basic categories of business information:

1. Local and regional newspapers, including exclusive access to the *Wall Street Journal*
2. Trade publications
3. Business newswires, including exclusive access to the Dow Jones & Reuters newswires

4. Press release wires
5. Media transcripts
6. Selected news photos
7. Investment analyst reports
8. Country and regional profiles
9. Company profiles
10. Historical and intraday market data

The Search function includes expanded content from eleven thousand Web sites in twenty-two languages, all judged to be of particular interest to business searchers. These sites pertain primarily to companies, newspapers, industry publications, government agencies, and trade associations. Areas within these sites are crawled at least daily, if appropriate, to retrieve and index content that is not otherwise available on Factiva ("crawling" is the process employed to find and index Web sites). The Search function also includes pictures from Reuters and Knight Ridder, with over four thousand images added weekly. Selected content is available in PDF format, and articles can be displayed and saved in rich text format (RTF) as well as in HTML and plain text.

Factiva has recently developed an indexing process called Factiva Intelligent Indexing, which assigns company, industry, regional, and subject codes consistently across all content in its Search and Track areas. These codes are based on international indexing standards, such as NAICS (North American Industry Classification System) and ISO (International Organization for Standardization), and include up to five levels of hierarchy. For example, a search on the industry term *Computers* would automatically include all the more granular terms within the Computer industry hierarchy.

The advantages of Intelligent Indexing are that you can search non-English content by using the Intelligent Indexing terms in the language you wish to use. Indexing terms are consistently applied across all content providers, and you can limit your search to a specific geographic region, to articles about a particular company—even if the name is misspelled (for example, it will find "DuPont" or " Du Pont"), or even to type of document (editorial, interview, or an overview of industry trends).

PRICING: Factiva offers several basic pricing structures, including flat-fee access and pay-as-you-go, transaction-based pricing. Since flat-fee subscriptions start at $1,000 a month, low-volume searchers will probably want to use the Individual Subscription option, which offers articles at $2.95 each with an annual fee of $69. Note that individual subscribers do not have access to the News Pages or Companies/Markets areas of Factiva.

SOURCE CONTENT: Factiva offers four basic navigational tabs: Search, Track, News Pages, and Companies/Markets. (Note that News Page and Companies/Markets tabs are not available to Individual Subscription users.) Below is a detailed commentary on the content of each tab.

1. **Search** provides access to eight thousand publications and content from eleven thousand business-related Web sites. Factiva supports both free-text searching and searches with the Factiva Intelligent Indexing codes.

   Although most researchers will use the free-text search box to construct their search, Factiva supports full Boolean logic, including the following terms:

   - AND
   - OR
   - NOT
   - ADJ**n**—Two terms in this order, within **n** words of each other
   - NEAR**n**—Two terms within **n** words of each other, in either order
   - SAME—Two words in the same paragraph
   - ATLEAST**n**—Frequency operator used to specify the minimum number of times (**n**) the search word(s) must appear in the text

   There are a relatively small number of words that cannot be routinely searched for in Factiva. These include *and, or, not, same, near,* and *date.* However, even these words can be searched for if enclosed in quotation marks. The search phrase *"to be or not to be"*—consisting entirely of words that are unsearchable in most online services—is a valid search in Factiva.

   Researchers can also limit the search by field; these include Headline, Lead Paragraph, Author, Word Count, Date, Publication Title, Language, and Intelligent Indexing term. Most of the field restrictions can be indicated through pull-down boxes, with an option to add a custom list of fields from a collection of thirty specialized indexing fields. The Factiva Intelligent Indexing terms are searchable through the links at the top of the Advanced Search page. Clicking on Company, Industry, Region, or Subject opens a new window to display the options available, as illustrated in Figure 4-8.

Figure 4-8. Factiva Search Option, Intelligent Indexing Search by Industry

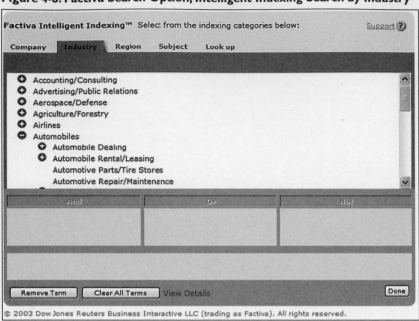

Each of the hierarchical categories that appears can be expanded by clicking the **Plus icon**. The default selection of sources to search is All Content, but sources can be specified by clicking the **Source Browser** link on the main search page, which allows the user to build a custom source list by selecting publications organized by title, industry, region, type, or language. Source lists can be saved for later use or selected for one-time searching. See Figure 4-9 for an example of the Publication Type Source Browser.

After a search has been executed, the default search results screen displays the complete citation, word count, and lead sentence. Articles can then be displayed in full or in one of several other formats, and the researcher can also create customized display formats. The results can be viewed and saved in rich text format as well as plain text, they can be e-mailed to the researcher or a third party, or they can be placed in the "Briefcase," which stores up to one hundred documents for thirty days.

Figure 4-9. Publication Type Source Browser in Factiva

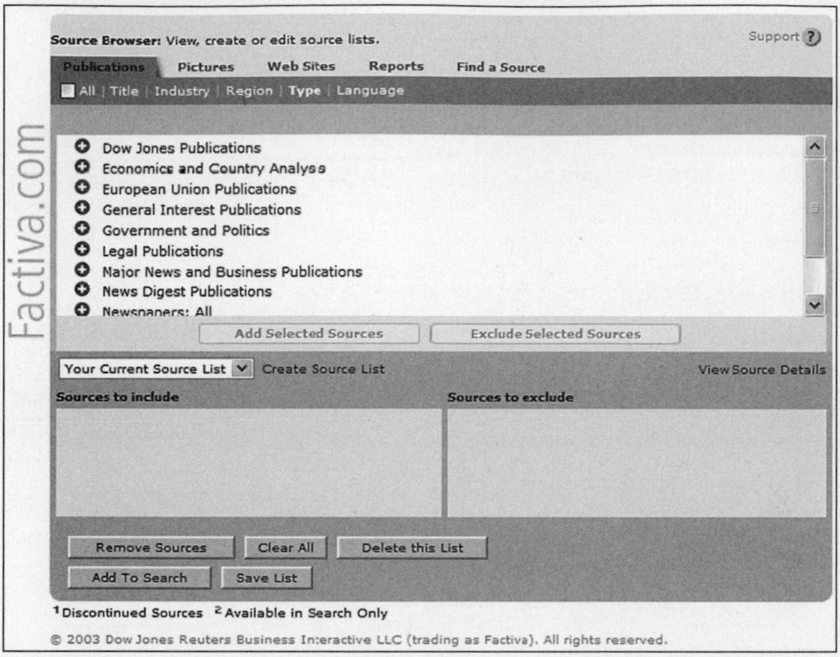

2. **Track** is an alerting tool that monitors news from close to six thousand publications and 750 Web sites. Track works continuously; the results can be viewed in the Track Folders, or they can be sent to an e-mail address, either throughout the day as articles are added or aggregated into a single e-mail once or twice a day. The search logic is similar to that of Search; both free-text searching and queries using Intelligent Indexing are supported. An interesting feature of the Track option is the ability to set the relevance level of the retrieved items to high, medium, or any degree of relevance. The relevance level score is based on the number of terms in the search query and how many of the terms appear in a document. The score also reflects the number of times a specific term appears in a document and the word count of the document. Searchers can use the relevance level setting to restrict the Track Folder to only articles that are directly about a particular topic or to expand the Folder to any articles that mention a topic or company, even just in passing.

3. **News Page** provides access to several content areas of Factiva from a single screen. The default Factiva Pages include the top news from up to ten major news sources, based on the subscriber's region; key stock market indices; and Editor's Links to Web sites of topical interest (see Figure 4-10). Note that with the pull-down menu at the upper left of the screen, the Factiva Pages can be customized by geographic region and by industry category.

Figure 4-10. Factiva's News Page Option

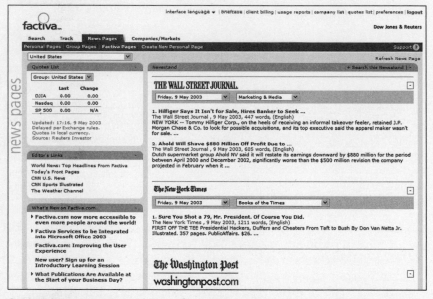

Other types of News Pages include Group News, set up by an organization's administrator to provide customized current news for selected groups of users with the organization, and Personal News, which subscribers can set up individually to display the sources and sections from publications they want to monitor.

4. **Companies/Markets** provides access to detailed information on companies in seventy-two countries. The Companies/ Markets area consists of five categories of content:

1. Financial data for 42,500 companies worldwide
2. 36.5 million Dun & Bradstreet records, with links to full Dun & Bradstreet reports
3. 30,000 investment analyst reports in PDF format

4. Stock quotes, often going back twenty-five years, on publicly traded securities

5. Company profiles, snapshots, and news

Subscribers can use the Companies/Markets area to build a list of companies that meet specific criteria, create charts of stocks, funds, and market indices, view investment reports on companies or industries of interest, and build customized company profiles. The Company Quick Search feature, shown below for Johnson & Johnson (see Figure 4-11), is particularly useful when one needs to pull together content from a number of sources and areas within Factiva.

Figure 4-11. Factiva's Company Quick Search Feature

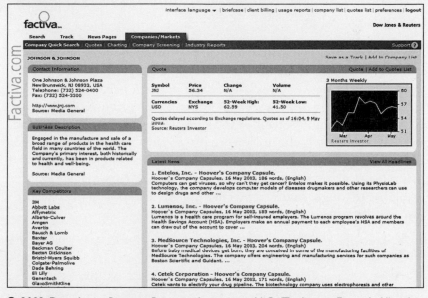

SOURCE EVALUATION: Factiva's strength lies in its focus on business and industry information sources and in its global content. It offers a powerful and flexible search interface, advanced search features, deep archives of content, and intuitive tools for pulling information together from a variety of sources. Keep in mind that because of its focus on business information, Factiva is *not* a one-stop source for researchers who also need access to scientific-technical, medical, or legal information.

Factiva has recently made some significant improvements to its service. One such improvement is the box on the Search screen that allows users to exclude republished news (which is so common in newswire data sources) and other types of articles. Intelligent Indexing is also an improvement over what Dow Jones had before, but it can be frustrating for professional researchers. Another limitation is that when one is using the More Like This function, it is not clear which indexing terms the system is keying on. The Help functionality could also be beefed up. When clicking on the question mark in the upper-right corner, you go to a very generalized Help menu and must scroll through to find what you need. Often you must go to the more detailed written guides on the Factiva site.

Through its partnership with Reuters and SunGard (Tradeline), Factiva has taken the integration of market data and business news to a new level, allowing users to see the direct effect of company news and announcements on stock price. Factiva subscribers can drag a mouse over the performance line or bars in a company's historical stock chart to see headlines that link to stories describing the cause in the rise or fall in stock price.

Factiva's user interfaces are both feature rich and intuitive. Many of the default settings can be customized through the Preferences screen, which further enhances the usability of the interfaces. The user interfaces are available in nine languages. Factiva offers several technical support and customer service options, available through Factiva's by clicking the Support icon. Support and service options include:

- A knowledge base of frequently asked questions, under the Find Answers tab
- Ask-A-Question via e-mail, with responses within one hour, during business hours
- Call-Me 24x7, through which a customer service representative calls the subscriber with an answer within ten minutes of an e-mail request, Monday through Friday, or within one hour during weekends and holidays. (This is not available to Knowledge Tier customers.)

Flat-fee subscribers can also call a toll-free number for live customer service and technical support. User documentation, case studies, reports, and white papers are also available online (*http://www.factiva.com/collateral*). Some of these documents are available in multiple languages, including French, German, Italian, Spanish, and Japanese. In addition, Factiva offers free self-directed lessons and product tours, and online and face-to-face training sessions throughout the world. The schedules for these sessions are listed online (*http://www.factiva.com/learning*).

SOURCE VALUE RATING: All of the data source reviewers were asked to rate each source on the basis of the following eight categories, using "10" as the highest rating and "1" as the lowest ("80" being a perfect score):

1. Relative cost-to-value:	8
2. Relative timeliness of data:	10
3. Relative comprehensiveness of data:	10
4. Ease of use:	8
5. Search options available:	7
6. Level of support services:	6
7. Level of training offered:	6
8. Amount/kinds of special services offered:	9
Total Rating:	65

SOURCE REVIEWS: Factiva is one of *KM World Magazine's* "Top 100 Companies in Knowledge Management" and part of *EContent* Magazine's "Top 100 content companies to watch." Factiva is also recognized as a winner of the 2002 Software & Information Industry Association's Codie Awards in the Best Online Business, Corporate or Professional Information category. Other reviews include:

> Hane, Paula. "Serious About Customer Service." *Information Today* 20, no. 3 (March 1, 2003). Interview with Clare Hart, CEO of Factiva.com, in which she discusses the company's products and plans, as well as trends in the information industry.
>
> O'Leary, Mick. "Factiva.com: The New Dow Jones/Reuters Synthesis." *EContent* 24, no. 5 (July 2001). This in-depth article discusses the formation of Factiva.com and introduces the major Factiva.com modules.
>
> Wood, Anthony. "Factiva: The Way We Search Now." *Business Information Searcher* 11, no. 3/4 (February 2002). Extensive review of Factiva's search module, its standard and advanced user interfaces, and output options.

CONTRIBUTOR NAME: Mary Ellen Bates/Meryl Brodsky

AFFILIATION: Bates Information Services, Inc./ Consultant

USEFUL TIPS

* You can save frequently run searches by clicking the Save Search icon at the bottom of the Search screen.
* How-to-use guides are available from the Factiva Web site (*http://www.factiva.com/collateral/download_brchr.asp?node=learning2*). You must have Acrobat Reader software to access them.
* In the Search area, there is a pull-down menu that allows you to sort results by date (either chronological or reverse chronological) or by relevance. Another pull-down menu allows you to select the format of the results. Using these display functions can save time.
* Factiva.com offers a number of preferences that can be set by the user, including the default search interface and date and language restrictions, and the format of search results. The Preferences link is in the top-right corner of the main Factiva.com screen.

LEXISNEXIS

ALTERNATE/PREVIOUS DATA SOURCE NAMES: LexisNexis at lexis.com, LexisNexis at nexis.com, LexisNexis by Credit Card, LN Academic, Anti-Money Laundering Solutions, Authority On Demand, Automated Forms, BNA Mergers & Acquisitions, Collection Solutions, LN Company Analyzer, LN Congressional, Corporate Legal, Courtlink eAccess, Courtlink eFile, LN Document Solutions, LN Environmental, LN Europe Web Product, Get & Print, Gov Periodicals Index, Primary Sources in U.S. History, Insurance Solutions, Intranet Solutions, LN for Law Schools, Law Enforcement Solutions, lexisONE, Mealey's Online, PeopleWise.net, Pranywhere, PowerInvoice, requester, Risk Management Solutions, Scholastic Edition, LN State Capital, LN Statistical, LN Development Pro, Web Publisher, Butterworths LexisNexis Direct, LexisNexis Martindale-Hubbell

SERVICE/PORTAL NAME: *http://www.lexisnexis.com,*
http://www. lexisone.com

SOURCE DESCRIPTION: LexisNexis serves a broad spectrum of the legal, business, government, financial, and academic communities, providing access to current and historic materials in the areas of law, science/medicine, finance, news, international news, and public records from more than thirty-one thousand database sources. The majority of the material in LexisNexis is full text, even in the older files.

LexisNexis is best known as one of the two great sources of legal information; Westlaw is the other. It's practically a given that LexisNexis and/or Westlaw can be found in almost every law office in the country. Lawyers and others who need to research and prepare legal materials use LexisNexis, in part, because it allows users to "Shepardize" legal articles—that is, to research cases and the cases that are cited in those cases. Shepardizing is citation research that leads back to the original case in which the legal matter was first reported. This process is invaluable for gaining perspective, and lawyers depend on it to understand the legal ground they are covering. As a legal research tool, LexisNexis is excellent. Because it serves as a one-stop shop for lawyers, it has also evolved into an excellent news, tax, and accounting source.

The Lexis side of the service, begun in 1973 in Dayton, Ohio, by Mead Data Central, is one of the two major sources of case law, statutes, and administrative and regulatory information at the state and federal levels. International law also is covered. The material is organized into libraries, allowing for either geographic or subject-oriented lists of possible sources to be viewed. At about the same time, Mead Data Central began offering the National Automated Accounting Research Service (NAARS), a tax database from the American Institute of Certified Public Accountants. This file has been superceded by a number of other tax materials available from a variety of sources.

Over the years, Lexis has added many new features and options. A number of purchases and alliances have added many titles previously available only in print editions to the list of offerings available on Lexis. In a departure from the traditional Lexis subscription-based approach, a more flexible option is now available, the lexisONE service (*http://www.lexisone.com*), which is priced by the day, week, or month for the individual or small firm. Also, the acquisition of CourtLink Corporation allows customers to electronically file legal documents and access and monitor court records. This option is of use to the business community, as well as to attorneys, as will be seen in the discussion of public records below.

Nexis was introduced in 1980, offering several magazines and newspapers as well as the Reuters and Associated Press newswires. Several years later the New York Times Information Service and its INFOBANK library were added to Nexis, which remains the only place to search the full-text of the *New York Times* back to 1980. Also added during this period was the LEXPAT service, with more than

650,000 patents issued since January 1, 1975. Over the years, a software package made patent drawing sheets available in the first and largest commercial online database of image files—5 million in number.

In the two decades since its inception, Nexis has evolved into a comprehensive collection of and international business information sources in several languages that includes current and archived news, newspapers, broadcast transcripts from major networks, wire services, magazines, and trade journals. In 1994, Mead Data Central was acquired by Reed Elsevier plc, an Anglo-Dutch Company, which changed the company's name to LexisNexis. The LexisNexis Group is now the global legal and information division of Reed Elsevier. New alliances have since been made that add both depth and breadth to the LexisNexis list of offerings.

For example, a real-time, dial-up service for Securities and Exchange Commission electronic EDGAR filings was made available through the new EDGAR Interactive Service. Also in the nineties, LexisNexis formed a strategic alliance with the National Fraud Center (NFC) to collaborate in the development and delivery of fraud prevention, investigation, and recovery solutions worldwide. This approach has continued, as specialized applications have been developed for a number of segments of the business world. Taking advantage of technological advances, LexisNexis released its full-blown Web product for business professionals, LexisNexis Universe, in 1998. This product combined the functionality found in traditional dial-up access with some of the new bells and whistles that have since become the norm for Internet users.

With the new millenium, LexisNexis announced "a family of knowledge solutions to help customers transform information into business-critical knowledge to drive better decisions." LexisNexis Web Publisher, LexisNexis Intranet Publisher, LexisNexis Custom User Interface, and LexisNexis Portal Integration allow corporations and government agencies to combine local content with relevant services that are part of their LexisNexis subscription.

As part of its global branding initiative, LexisNexis introduced the new corporate Web site at *http://www.LexisNexis.com.* The new site gives customers a view of all the company's products and services offered for sale in the United States, with drop-down menus for browsing by industry, occupation, task, or featured products.

LexisNexis offers two different types of searching: "term and connector" and "natural language." The term and connector method employs keyword searching separated by the Boolean connectors AND, OR, and WITHIN. In natural language searching, searches are entered in plain English without using Boolean connectors. The natural language search in LexisNexis ranks the search results according to relevance, something that really sets the source apart from its peers. To add synonyms, word variations, and other terms or phrases to the search statement, you simply click Suggest Words and Concepts for Entered Terms on the natural language search screen.

No matter which search method you choose, conducting a search on LexisNexis requires first selecting a source, and then entering the search statement. The source selection menu and the search interface look similar, so this part can be confusing. As an alternative, you can use the Guided Search Forms, in which sources are preidentified. Or you can use Command Searching, which is designed for people familiar with the database structure. Command Searching is covered in the LexisNexis training.

After signing on to either Lexis or Nexis, the user is taken to a screen that can be customized or personalized in a number of ways, either by the user or with the assistance of the company's local representative. In addition, a number of standardized home pages have been developed for particular types of users.

To meet the needs of different types of users or search requests, several approaches are presented for searching under the following categories:

- *Quick Search*. Allows simple searches across a combination of file types simultaneously and presents results.
- *Subject Directory*. Searches on one of thirty-four categories of subject headings for current articles on more than twelve hundred topics.
- *Power Search*. Searches the full text of 3 billion documents in more than thirty-one thousand individual publications or large groups of sources. Allows more sophisticated search strategy construction using Boolean logic, date limitations, and so on.
- *Personal News and Shared News*. Provides regular updates about specific topics of interest to your organization, delivered via e-mail or published on your intranet.

The example shown in Figure 4-12 is customized for use by a business power searcher. The **Personal News** link on the left side of the page leads to search results for search strategies created by the user to monitor topics of choice. These can be created using either keywords or phrases, or an actual search strategy such as *john w/3 jones*. The latter would return hot-linked citations to articles than mention "john" within three words of "jones"—in any order. If this strategy retrieves too many irrelevant articles, narrower construction of search phrases is possible. **Real Time News** functions in the same way. This link uses search terms or strategies created by the user to retrieve articles from the newswires, which are updated at least hourly.

The center section of the power search page is where the actual search is constructed. The Source to Search box for this searcher's page offers two options: All Services/Less Investext, as shown in the figure, and Public Records. The next box contains a drop-down list of the user's favorite sources, to be searched in the typical search request. As shown, the list may be expanded or changed easily by clicking on one of the two buttons provided for this purpose, Find More Sources and Edit My Sources. Examples and hints are provided underneath the next box, where the actual search strategy is entered.

Experienced searchers or those with a complex research problem will probably take advantage of one or more of the various options available for this purpose. But Nexis has added another invaluable tool to this page—the index tool. When one enters a search term, such as *derivatives,* four broad categories and six company names using the word appear in the index box, with buttons that will add them to the search strategy constructed previously. When the user clicks on the categories returned, definitions and possible broader search terms are displayed. This tool may not be needed for every search, but it is bound to be helpful when dealing with unfamiliar terms or when too few articles are retrieved using other search strategies.

The Search Forms box on the right side of the screen provides search forms for individual items in the list of sources chosen by the researcher. This approach is useful when the search should be limited to a specific source.

Figure 4-12. Power Search Page on LexisNexis

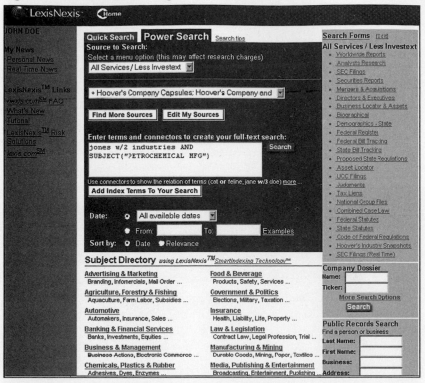

LexisNexis is a trademark of Reed Elsevier Properties, Inc. Reprinted with the permission of LexisNexis.

The remaining areas of the business research power search page include Company Dossier, Public Records Search, Market Information, and Subject Directory. The Company Dossier tool locates companies by name or ticker symbol. Additional search options will identify companies by location, industry, size, or financial status. The amount of information retrieved will vary depending on whether the company is publicly or privately held. A sample search on a major corporation, for example, yields a lengthy report consisting of information from Hoover's Company Capsules, a summary of yearly financials and detailed financials from Disclosure, stock quotations and charts, a listing of officers and directors, parent-subsidiary information, key competitors, and recent news articles mentioning the company.

Another useful link accessible in the Company Dossier section offers a Company Compare option. Up to four additional companies may be compared to the company being searched. Balance sheet, income statement, and ratio information will be reported for companies that are listed on one of the U.S. stock exchanges in the currency that the company reports to the SEC.

For company research outside of the United States, Nexis offers group files, such as All International Company Reports, All Europe Company Information, and All Asia & Pacific Rim Company Information. Additional possibilities for locating foreign companies include a long list of country-specific or international directory files.

Examining industries is another common business research application. A link on the home page points to a group file called INDNWS, which retrieves industry-oriented articles from among the publications in the Nexis collection. Nexis also offers Responsive Database Service's TableBase, a database specializing exclusively in tabular data. TableBase includes data on companies, industries, products, and demographics from over one thousand sources, including RDS's Business & Industry database, privately published statistical annuals, trade associations, government agencies, nonprofit research groups, and industry reports prepared by investment research groups. Figure 4-13 shows a table retrieved with TableBase from a detailed article on packaging strategies.

TableBase is used for researching topics such as market share, company and brand rankings, industry and product forecasts, production and consumption statistics, imports and exports, usage and capacity, number of users/outlets, trends, and much more.

LexisNexis also offers a large quantity of non-U.S. data. Country reports are available from several highly respected sources, and searching for non-U.S. news and information may be expedited by using categories such as (Non-U.S.), Asia & Pacific Rim, Europe, and Middle East & Africa.

Public records provide a wealth of information for the business researcher looking for information about companies or individuals. Real and personal property records, business and person locators, civil and criminal court filings, secretary of state records (including corporate charters), liens, judgments, UCC filings, jury verdicts and settlements, professional licenses, and bankruptcy filings are included among the record types found in LexisNexis, representing counties and states from across the United States. Information found within these documents can be used to locate a company or person's current address, uncover hidden assets or associations, discover legal entanglements, and more.

Figure 4-13. Sample of the TableBaseFeature on LexisNexis

LexisNexis Home   Customize · Sign Off · Help

RDS TableBase Results for: nanotubes   Track in Personal News

FOCUS™   Search Within Results   Edit Search ↻ New Search ↻

Tag for display and delivery Display Tagged Items >>   Print | Email | Download

CLEAR   List | Expanded List | KWC™ | Full | **Custom**

More Like This   Change Custom View   ◄ prev Document 5 of 9 next ►

TABLE-TITLE: US market size forecast for nanocomposite packaging materials as consumption in pounds for 2006 and 2011, with breakdown for each of eight application categories

TABLE:
Market Projections for Nanocomposites in Packaging

```
                                    Million lb
                                           Nanocomposite Usage
                          Total
                          Potential
    Application           Market      2006       2011
Carbonated soft drinks    250 - 3,000  0.5       50.0
Beer bottles              100 - 1,100  3.0       20.0
Meats                     600          0.6       10.0
Packaged food & condiments 100 - 200   0.2       10.0
Cheese                    70           0.2        3.0
Juice packaging           10           0.1        1.0
Pet food                  10           0.2        1.0
Pharmaceutical products   10          <0.1        0.2
Total                     1,150 - 5,000 4.8       95.2
Source: Packaging Strategies/BRG Townsend, Inc. estimates
```

Figure 4-14. LexisNexis Supports Public Record Searching with Numerous Options

Public Records Search Results for: jones industries   Track in Personal News

FOCUS™   Search Within Results   Edit Search ↻ New Search ↻

Tag for display and delivery Display Tagged Items >>   Print | Email | Download

CLEAR   List | **Expanded List** | KWC™ | Full | Custom

Sort by: ⊙ Date ○ Relevance   Documents 1 - 61 of 61

17. JONES' INDUSTRIES, 2/3/1995, TEXAS FICTITIOUS BUSINESS NAMES

18. JONES IMP., TRADE NAME, ACTIVE, 10017484, NESOS
    JONES INDUSTRIES, INC. OWNER APPLICANT ...

19. JONES INDUSTRIES, INCORPORATED, CORPORATION, 5/9/1978, 5/9/1978, CONNECTICUT SECRETARY OF STATE

20. JONES INDUSTRIES, L.L.C., OTHER (DOMESTIC LIMITED LIABILITY CO), 7/14/1995, L07536789, ARIZONA CORPORATION COMMISSION, CORPORATIONS DIVISION

21. JONES INDUSTRIES, INC., CORPORATION (PROFIT), 1/2/1959, 1/2/1959, C0030451, IDAHO SECRETARY OF STATE

22. JONES INDUSTRIES, NEW FILING, 10/1/1998, 1998-08918, SAN BERNARDINO COUNTY, CALIFORNIA, FICTITIOUS BUSINESS NAMES

23. JONES INDUSTRIES, ASSUMED NAME, 1/30/1991, 91012390, DALLAS COUNTY, TEXAS, ASSUMED BUSINESS NAMES

24. JONES INDUSTRIES, ASSUMED NAME, 3/9/1994, 94028722, DALLAS COUNTY, TEXAS, ASSUMED BUSINESS NAMES

25. JONES INDUSTRIES, INC., DOMESTIC FOR PROFIT, 11/18/1965, 298865, FLORIDA DEPARTMENT OF STATE

26. JONES INDUSTRIES SCREEN ENCLOSURES, INC., DOMESTIC FOR PROFIT, 1/6/1968, 324910, FLORIDA DEPARTMENT OF STATE

27. JONES INDUSTRIES, ARTICLES OF INCORPORATION (DOMESTIC), 2/4/1987, 1578478, CALIFORNIA SECRETARY OF STATE

28. JONES INDUSTRIES, INC., ARTICLES OF INCORPORATION (DOMESTIC), 4/27/1998, 2107385, CALIFORNIA SECRETARY OF STATE

29. JONES INDUSTRIES, ASSUMED NAME, 2/3/1995, 0892414, HARRIS COUNTY, TEXAS, ASSUMED BUSINESS NAMES

30. JONES INDUSTRIES, INC., DOMESTIC PROFIT, 2/2/1968, A800567, GEORGIA SECRETARY OF STATE

31. JONES INDUSTRIES INC, FOR-PROFIT DOMESTIC CORPORATION, 1/3/1983, INDIANA SECRETARY OF STATE

32. JONES INDUSTRIES, INC., FOR-PROFIT DOMESTIC CORPORATION, 11/7/1996, INDIANA SECRETARY OF STATE

33. JONES INDUSTRIES, 3/21/1994, TEXAS FICTITIOUS BUSINESS NAMES

34. JONES INDUSTRIES, 4/1/1997, 2456759446, TEXAS FICTITIOUS BUSINESS NAMES

35. JONES INDUSTRIES RAINBOW, 3/24/1993, CALIFORNIA FICTITIOUS BUSINESS NAMES

In Figure 4-14, a search for *Jones Industries* was entered in the Public Records search box of the Power Search page. The search turned up companies with this name, or variations thereof, in eight U.S. states. It revealed that incorporation records for Jones Industries exist in Connecticut, Arizona, Idaho, Florida, California, Georgia, and Indiana. By examining one of these records and noting the Corporate Charter ID number, your company could contact the secretary of state to order a copy of that charter and gain valuable information not available publicly elsewhere. Assumed or fictitious name filings also appear for several states. In Texas, Jones Industries is apparently not incorporated with the secretary of state, but the assumed name record provides the name and address of the party registered to use that business name.

The handy Public Records Search feature lets you perform a quick Public Records search in the LexisNexis EZFIND combined person-location file and the ALLBIZ file, which provides business and corporation information. Several other public record types are included in the list of links on the right side of the business searcher home page. Figure 4-15 shows the search screen available for Commercial Code (UCC) filings, which provide evidence of debt in the form of loans or leases.

Additional links provide access to similar search forms for the Asset Locator, Uniform Judgments, and Tax Liens.

Figure 4-15. UCC Filings Are Searchable on LexisNexis

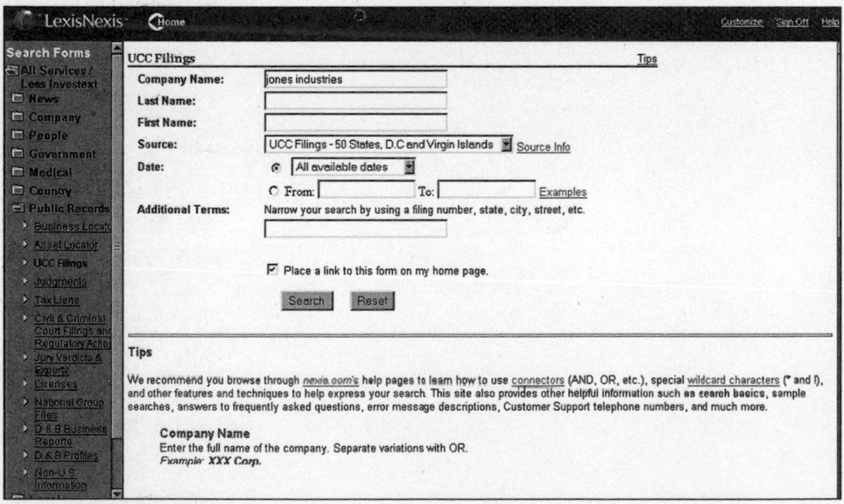

LexisNexis is a trademark of Reed Elsevier Properties, Inc. Reprinted with the permission of LexisNexis.

Most large companies find that it is important to keep up with new federal legislation or in the state(s) where they do business. New laws that may affect taxation, environmental issues, and many other matters can have a significant impact on a company's ability to do business profitably. LexisNexis offers both Federal Bill Tracking and State Bill Tracking databases for this purpose. Additional links on the business researcher's home page provide access to the full text of federal or state bills and to the *Federal Register* and Proposed State Bills.

PRICING: Cost is an important factor to consider when performing online research. LexisNexis has supplemented its original monthly subscription-based approach by adding a number of new purchasing options. Large companies, law firms, or academic institutions would likely prefer the flat-rate subscription that is negotiated based on the number of users, typical amount of searching per month, and other factors. Small firms or individual users may purchase short-term packages, say for one day or one week, and download as much as they want during the lifetime of the package. For $75 per day or $250 per week, a searcher could plan a concentrated period of search activity. This could be a very cost-effective way to use LexisNexis when needed.

Another approach provides "pay-as-you-go" access. In this case prices can vary from $1 for a public record to $12 per document for company or financial information. Certain files may not be included in these package deals, but if these files are required, it may be possible to make special arrangements through Customer Service. Spokespeople for LexisNexis stress the flexibility in their purchase plans. Complete descriptions of these nonsubscription pricing plans and lists of files or titles available under either of the plans can be viewed by clicking on the link entitled **Nonsubscribers: Pay as you go!** which is found in the upper-left corner of the main LexisNexis home page (*http://www.lexisnexis.com*).

SOURCE EVALUATION: The fact that LexisNexis offers many business-related databases in full text has facilitated the development of the new products described previously. When combined with the wide range of subject matter available, the availability of full text may mean that the user can complete a major business research project with one-stop shopping at *http://www. lexisnexis.com.*

Customer Support via telephone has always been both friendly and high quality in this reviewer's experience. Support personnel, divided into Lexis and Nexis categories, are obviously knowledgeable about their databases. On more than one occasion a support person has tried various searches for the caller, discussed what was found, and then provided the exact search strategy that was successful. Free training may be arranged telephonically through a link at *http://www.lexisnexis.com.* The session lasts for about one hour and can be customized according to interests and level of expertise.

SOURCE VALUE RATING: All of the data source reviewers were asked to rate each source on the basis of the following eight categories, using "10" as the highest rating and "1" as the lowest ("80" being a perfect score):

1. Relative cost-to-value:	8
2. Relative timeliness of data:	9
3. Relative comprehensiveness of data:	8
4. Ease of use:	7
5. Search options available:	8
6. Level of support services:	8
7. Level of training offered:	7
8. Amount/kinds of special services offered:	7
Total Rating:	62

SOURCE REVIEWS:

Bates, Mary Ellen. "Can Small Businesses Go Online?" *Searcher* (January 2003): 16. Dialog, LexisNexis, Factiva, and Northern Light are compared, mostly in terms of "by-the-drink" prices.

"Choosing a Journal Database Provider: Current Options for Searching Journal Databases Online." *The Information Advisor* 15, no. 4 (April 2003). Reviews current vendor options for searching key databases of trade and journal articles.

Christiani, Linnea. "Meeting the New Challenges at West and LexisNexis." *Searcher* 10, no. 5 (May 1, 2002): 68. Interviews with the chief technology officers at West and LexisNexis.

Gordon, Stacey L. "What's New on Westlaw, LexisNexis, Versus-Law, and Loislaw." *Legal Information Alert* 21, no. 10

(November 1, 2002): 1. Updates, including content and technological enhancements to the user interface.

Hurst, Jill Ann, and David M. Oldenkamp. "LexisNexis Statistical Universe, Web Wise Ways." *Searcher* 6, no. 10 (June 1, 2002): 18. Detailed review of what is now called LexisNexis Statistical.

Lawrence, Stephanie. "Natural Selection Is the Key to Software Evolution, Consult on All Proposed Changes and a Successful Program Can Be Updated to Appeal to Less Sophisticated New Users Without Alienating Savvy Old Hands." *Information World Review* (December 1, 2002): 26. Discussion of the evolution of software at LexisNexis. The author is a product manager at LexisNexis Butterworths Tolley.

Matesic, Maura. "International News Sources." *Toronto Chapter SLA Courier,* Summer 2001 <*http://www.sla.org/chapter/ctor/courier/v38/v38n4a4.htm*>. Discusses international news searching on Factiva's Dow Jones Interactive, LexisNexis, and free Internet news Web sites in terms of search engine, content, and delivery method.

Russell, Roger. "LexisNexis Targets Small to Midsized CPA Firms." *Accounting Today* 16, no. 4 (February 25, 2002): 22. Discusses how small and medium-sized accounting firms can use LexisNexis.

CONTRIBUTOR NAME: Helen P. Burwell/Meryl Brodsky
AFFILIATION: Burwell Enterprises/Consultant

USEFUL TIPS

- Look for group files that cover all sources on LexisNexis that cover your topic.
- Add links to your LexisNexis home page for sources that you use frequently. Watch for a box on the search screen that says "Place a link to this form on my home page."
- Try customizing your LexisNexis home page. This saves time in the long run.
- The pay-as-you-go option allows you to conduct a search or view headlines for no charge. Users pay only for the complete text of articles that they view.
- The pay-by-the-day (or week) option allows unlimited access to specific subsets of the LexisNexis database (and its documents) at a set price.

BUREAU OF ECONOMIC ANALYSIS (BEA)

SERVICE/PORTAL NAME: *http://www.bea.doc.gov*

SOURCE DESCRIPTION: The Bureau of Economic Analysis (BEA), a division of the U.S. Department of Commerce, provides economic statistics in support of government, business, and individual decision making. The cornerstone of the BEA is the national income and products account (NIPA), whose key element is the gross domestic product (GDP).

As stated on the Web site, "the BEA prepares national, regional, industry, and international accounts that present essential information on such key issues as economic growth, regional economic development, inter-industry relationships, and the Nation's position in the world economy." As an example of the wide variety of information available on the BEA Web site, Table 4-13 presents a portion of a table reporting personal income statistics.

Table 4-13. Sample BEA Table: Personal Income Statistics

SA05 Personal income by major source and earnings by industry -- United States (thousands of dollars)		
Code	**Item** *Income by place of residence ($000)*	**2001**
0010	Personal income	8,678,255,000
0011	Nonfarm personal income	8,638,185,000
0012	Farm income 2/	40,070,000
0020	Population (persons) 3/	284,796,887
0030	Per capita personal income (dollars) 4/	30,472

Reprinted courtesy of U.S. Bureau of Economic Analysis.

PRICING: Access to the Web site is free, and the majority of the tables are available at no cost. The comprehensive files that must be purchased cost $35 or less.

SOURCE CONTENT: This site is divided into the four sections listed below:

* **National Economic Accounts** provides an overview of how the U.S. economy is performing.
* **Industry Economic Accounts** analyzes the input of private industry and the government to the GDP.
* **Regional Economic Accounts** contains reports showing estimates and analysis of personal income, population, employment, and gross state product.

- **International Economic Accounts** includes a number of charts providing breakdowns of U.S. direct investment abroad, foreign direct investment in the U.S., and the balance of payment.

The charts are available in a variety of formats, including HTML, PDF, text, XLS, and CSV. Large tables providing historical data are presented in zip or self-extracting .exe formats. There are also many technical notes and articles explaining how the data is analyzed. These documents, generally hyperlinked to the table or chart they explain, include descriptions of the data sources and the assumptions made in the compilation of the table or chart. Additionally, the researcher will find links (under Publications) to the monthly *Survey of Current Business*, which provides articles and tables related to the four main areas of statistical data provided by the BEA. Links are included for issues from 1994 to the present.

SOURCE EVALUATION: This site provides a wealth of information for the researcher charged with tracking the economic health of the United States. For the most part, the site is clearly organized and labeled. That said, the sheer number of tables available might overwhelm the first-time user, as the assumption is that the user is familiar with the various tables offered. For example, a new user may not know what data will be retrieved when the link to "Current period estimates for tables 1 through 10 in the International Transactions Accounts" is clicked. For help with the International Economic Accounts portion of the site, you can click on the Interactive Access link for a list of the table names. The other option is to go to the Methodologies section of the Web site to find descriptions of the available economic indicators provided in each of the major sections.

The tables are updated on varying schedules. Some come out monthly, others are published quarterly or annually. Annual and five-year compilations are provided for most tables. Tables covering larger time spans can be downloaded or purchased on disk or CD. Not all historical tables are provided free of charge.

The BEA site does not include a search engine. The Help file suggests that the user go to the FirstGov Web site (*http://www.firstgov.gov*) if a search function is needed. To test this, I used FirstGov to execute a search for a BEA table showing the depreciation of consumer durable goods. I found what I was looking for by using the advanced search feature. Using FirstGov is a good idea if you aren't sure if the data you are looking for exists, or which agency publishes it. However, I don't recommend this approach for searching for specific items that you know are on the BEA site; I found the table more quickly by simply browsing the BEA Web site itself.

Instead of a search engine, this site provides an Index to the NIPA Tables (*http://www.bea.doc.gov/bea/dn/nipaweb/ NIPATableIndex.htm*). This is useful for finding specific tables, but it is slow. The page is very large and takes a while to load, even using a high-speed connection. The index is another example of the need for previous experience with the tables to retrieve the needed data. Under the index term *Amusements* is a list for "Personal consumption expenditures 2.4, 2.5, 2.6, 2.7, 7.5, 7.20." Each number is a link to a table. There are instructions for deciphering the numbering system at the bottom of the index, but the explanation is incomplete. The user either needs to know what table is needed, or must consult the list of NIPA tables.

All of the sections provide some degree of interactive access to the data. In the regional section, the user can select specific datasets, specify geographic areas (states), and select the needed dates. Once all selections are complete, a table is created. The national, industry, and international sections allow the user to change certain aspects of a table (e.g., years covered, annual versus quarterly data) once a table has been selected.

Technical support is available only via e-mail. There is no charge for requesting assistance. E-mail addresses are listed for questions pertaining to each of the four sections of the site. In addition, there is a list of names and phone numbers to contact with specific questions about the statistics provided. The Using Our Site link is meant as the training area. This document deals primarily with the file formats used, as well as printing, privacy, and so on, but it provides little assistance with actually using the site. It does provide a link to A Tour of BEA's Web Site. This file is very dated and some of the information is no longer valid, but an updated version is due out soon.

As of this writing, the BEA is offering a preview of a newly redesigned Web site that describes the nature of the changes (see *http://www.bea.doc.gov/bea/delete/bea/redesign/index.htm*). The look of the site will change, and it will also offer improved navigation, an A–Z index, and "fingertip" access to economic indicators. It looks like the site will be even easier to use after this redesign.

Despite the shortcomings of this site, it is an invaluable resource for the business researcher. With just a little experience, the user can find a vast amount of data with only a few clicks. The monthly updates make the information very timely. The site is easy to use once the user is accustomed to the layout. It would be even easier if the developers were more consistent with design (e.g., making all interactive access the same). Although I don't find the lack of a search engine a problem, my one suggestion is that the Index to NIPA Tables be divided into smaller parts so it loads more quickly. Since I didn't ask for technical support, I don't know how quick the response time is. I do like the idea of having names and phone numbers available for dealing with questions about the data.

SOURCE VALUE RATING: All of the data source reviewers were asked to rate each source on the basis of the following eight categories, using "10" as the highest rating and "1" as the lowest ("80" being a perfect score):

1. Relative cost-to-value:	10
2. Relative timeliness of data:	10
3. Relative comprehensiveness of data:	10
4. Ease of use:	8
5. Search options available:	5
6. Level of support services:	7
7. Level of training offered:	6
8. Amount/kinds of special services offered:	8
Total Rating:	64

CONTRIBUTOR NAME: James Harrington
AFFILIATION: Fujitsu Network Communications

USEFUL TIPS

* Give yourself time to explore the BEA site.
* View the list of NIPA tables first. Don't waste time looking for a report that doesn't exist.

BUREAU OF LABOR STATISTICS

ALTERNATE/PREVIOUS DATA SOURCE NAMES: Department of Labor, Bureau of Labor Statistics

SERVICE/PORTAL NAME: *http://www.bls.gov*

SOURCE DESCRIPTION: According to its Web page, "The Bureau of Labor Statistics (BLS) is the principal fact-finding agency for the (United States) Federal Government in the broad field of labor economics and statistics. The BLS is an independent national statistical agency that collects, processes, analyzes, and disseminates essential statistical data to the American public, the U.S. Congress, other Federal agencies, State and local governments, business, and labor. The BLS also serves as a statistical resource to the Department of Labor."

Bureau of Labor Statistics data satisfy a number of criteria, including relevance to current social and economic issues, timeliness, accuracy, and impartiality in both subject matter and presentation. The indicators provided by the BLS, including the Consumer Price Index (CPI) and the Producer Price Index (PPI) are among the major measurements of inflation.

PRICING: No cost; free Web site.

SOURCE CONTENT: As is usual with government Web sites, the BLS site includes an almost overwhelming amount of information. This summary will deal with the main areas displayed and the information contained within these areas.

- **Inflation and Consumer Spending.** The main information sources in this area are the CPI, a CPI calculator, the consumer expenditure survey, the PPI, and Import/Export Price Indexes. All data is available in table format, and customized tables can be formed. Large files can be transferred using file transfer protocol (FTP). But for most users the customized tables supply the needed information.
- **Wages, Earnings, and Benefits.** Includes information on wages by area and occupation, earnings by industry, employee benefits, and costs, state and county wages, national compensation data, and statistics on the collective bargaining area. As in all areas of the site, users can customize tables by using the Detailed Statistics section.
- **Productivity.** Includes productivity and costs and international wage comparisons.
- **International.** Includes Import/Export Price Indexes and imports and exports searchable by Harmonized Classification systems and SITC (Standard International Trade Classifications) number.
- **Employment and Unemployment.** Lists occupational and demographic characteristics of the labor force as well as injury and fatalities data by national, state, and local geography.

- **At a Glance Tables.** Includes data for the past six months, in table format, for the main indicators: Unemployment Rate, Change in Payroll Employment, Average Hourly Earnings, Consumer Price Index, Producer Price Index, U.S. Import Price Index, Employment Cost Index, and the Productivity Index. A link is provided to annual data for ten years in table or graph format. The data is also available at the region or state level.

- **Publications and Research Papers.** Includes occupation and career guides, but perhaps most useful, it links to the online full-text edition of the *Monthly Labor Review.*

- **BLS Information Offices & Other Statistical Sites.** These sections provide links to regional offices that provide contact information, as well as links to other federal statistical sites.

- **Other Sections.** Other sections include statistical information on Industries, Business Costs, Geography, Safety and Health, Occupations, and Demographics. The latest index numbers are displayed in the center of the page, as are questions from users of the site.

SOURCE EVALUATION: Although the sheer amount of information on this site can be overwhelming, the information is presented in a logical manner. Some information, such as the CPI, is available in more than one section and so is easily found. The At a Glance Tables section satisfies most information needs, and the ability to customize other tables is invaluable. There is also a search box, an excellent A–Z index, and a glossary. Maneuverability within the sections is not impossible, but it is much easier to return to the BLS home page (a link is available on each screen) to begin a new search.

SOURCE VALUE RATING: All of the data source reviewers were asked to rate each source on the basis of the following eight categories, using "10" as the highest rating and "1" as the lowest ("80" being a perfect score):

1. Relative cost-to-value:	10
2. Relative timeliness of data:	10
3. Relative comprehensiveness of data:	10
4. Ease of use:	6
5. Search options available:	8
6. Level of support services:	8
7. Level of training offered:	7
8. Amount/kinds of special services offered:	8
Total Rating:	67

SOURCE REVIEWS:

"Webwatch" [column]. *Library Journal* 123, no. 18 (November 1, 1998): 28. "Data tables download quickly and print easily. Labor demographic data with links to the full reports will be found at Economy at a Glance, Surveys and Programs, and Publications and Research Papers. Bottom Line: This site offers timely information on labor and financial demographics—a narrower mandate than the Census site."

CONTRIBUTOR NAME: Rita W. Moss/Patricia A. Watkins

AFFILIATION: University of North Carolina–Chapel Hill/Thunderbird School of of International Management

USEFUL TIPS

- Spend time clicking on all the data and tools.
- Make use of the e-mail alerting service for new statistical releases.
- By clicking on the Detailed Statistics area in each section, one can easily customize tables.

BUREAU OF THE CENSUS

SERVICE/PORTAL NAME: *http://www.census.gov*

SOURCE DESCRIPTION: The Bureau of the Census (or the Census Bureau) was established as a permanent office by an act of Congress on March 6, 1902, but the major functions are authorized by the U.S. Constitution, which provides that "a census of population shall be taken every ten years."

The Census Bureau is the preeminent collector and provider of timely, relevant, and high-quality data about both the people and economy of the United States. The Census Bureau home page is the gateway to all the information gathered by the bureau to fulfill its official purpose of providing a population count. Included are statistics relating to business ownership, labor, education, health, age, income, expenditures, and industry. This site provides access to both data and tools necessary for its analysis and distribution.

For the latest developments at the site, check out the New on the Site section (*http://www.census.gov/newonsite*) or the News Releases section (*http://www.census.gov/Press-Release/www*). Alternatively, subscribe to the mailing list (*http://www.census.gov/mp/ www/subscribe.html*).

PRICING: No cost; free Web site.

SOURCE CONTENT: This summary provides information on the key areas of the Web site that are especially useful to business. Each section links not only to statistics but also to publications and reports, mostly available in PDF format:

1. **People.** This section provides links to demographic information, including the latest federal and state projections, and to income data. It also provides in-depth information on housing, including property characteristics, housing completions, and residential segregation. Also included are international population data tables and a link to the International Data Base, which is a computerized data bank containing statistical tables of demographic and socioeconomic data for all countries of the world.

2. **Business.** The economic census is the major source of facts about the structure and functioning of the economy. The economic census has been taken at five-year intervals since 1967, but only the information from 1992 and 1997 is available electronically from this Web site. The census provides data on all industry sectors, down to the county or place level, and includes establishment, revenue, and payroll information.

3. **Geography.** This is the section that links to the Geographical Information Systems (GIS) maps, products, and data sections. Included are Census 2000 Maps and Boundary Files, Glossaries, Relationship Files, 2000 Tabulation Tallies (number of geographic entities for Census 2000), and the Census 2000 TIGER (Topically Integrated Geographic Encoding and Referencing system) Line. These tools are useful for creating specialized maps demonstrating certain factors such as population, major roads, or nearby water resources.

4. **American FactFinder.** This service lets you search, browse, retrieve, view, map, print, and download census data. One can create custom tables and maps to compare data for different geographic areas or use the Data Sets feature to access all available tables for the 2000 and 1990 Decennial Census, as well as the 1997 Economic Census and American Community Survey data. Tables can be downloaded either as rich text or in a comma-delimited or Microsoft Excel format.

5. **Subjects A to Z.** This alphabetical subject index is for those who are not sure where to look for the needed information. Linked topics range from "Accommodation and Foodservices Sector" to "Zip Code Statistics."

SOURCE EVALUATION: The Census Bureau is the major collector and provider of demographic and economic data. Commercial publishers use this data to compile subject or age-specific reports and then sell this information. Using American FactFinder, the user can now compile the most recent information into tables and maps specific to individual needs.

Figure 4-16. Census Bureau Home Page

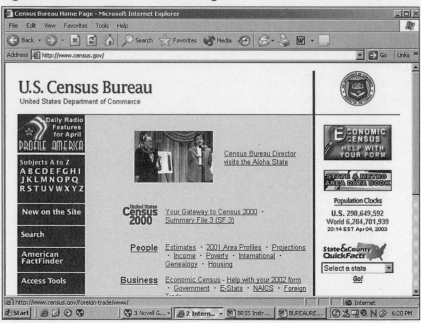

Reprinted courtesy of Public Information Office, U.S. Census Bureau.

Figure 4-16 shows the basic components of the Census Bureau Web site, which also provides a subject index and a search feature. Navigation within the various levels of the page are more challenging, although one click on the U.S. Census logo returns the user to the home page. After descending through several levels of reports this may be the only way to regain some focus. In the Data Sets section of American FactFinder, tabs at the top of the page enable the user to move within sections. The layout is not ideal, but both access and data are free and the amount of information available is impressive. The links to access tools and other sources of information are invaluable.

SOURCE VALUE RATING: All of the data source reviewers were asked to rate each source on the basis of the following eight categories, using "10" as the highest rating and "1" as the lowest ("80" being a perfect score):

1. Relative cost-to-value:	10
2. Relative timeliness of data:	10
3. Relative comprehensiveness of data:	10
4. Ease of use:	6
5. Search options available:	7
6. Level of support services:	8
7. Level of training offered:	8
8. Amount/kinds of special services offered:	8
Total Rating:	67

SOURCE REVIEWS:

"Webwatch" [column]. *Library Journal* 123, no. 18 (November 1, 1998): 28. "Bottom Line: The Census site is the treasure trove of demographic data. But because it may be intimidating to use, other sites in this column (BLS.com, fedstats.com) may link faster to certain information."

Neuhaus, Paul. "U.S. Bureau of the Census."*Electronic Resources Review* 2, no. 2 (1998): 10–11. "The Bureau designed this site 'to be intuitive, concise, and quick loading' with the user not needing to know the internal Census Bureau structure to access the information. The agency has successfully met these goals. Most information can be accessed by following logical links, often with links to the same page from different starting points. . . . This Web site is an excellent place to begin a search for statistical data. The information available provides insights into many facets of American life. It is accessible to Web users from many different backgrounds and with a wide variety of information needs."

CONTRIBUTOR NAME: Rita W. Moss/Patricia A. Watkins
AFFILIATION: University of North Carolina–Chapel Hill/Thunderbird School of International Management

USEFUL TIPS

- The amount of information on the Census Bureau Web site can be overwhelming at first, so check out the site a few times before you need to use it just to become familiar with the type of information and its limitations.
- For the latest information, begin with American FactFinder and then move on to the full census reports if more is needed. Help is always available from depository libraries and Census Bureau offices.

FREEEDGAR / EDGAR ONLINE / EDGARPRO

SERVICE/PORTAL NAME: FreeEDGAR (*http://www.freeedgar.com*), EDGAR Online (*http://www.edgar-online.com/start.asp*), and EDGARpro (*http://www.edgarpro.com*) are related Web sites from the same parent company. All contain public company filing information from the Securities and Exchange Commission (SEC).

SOURCE DESCRIPTION: Public companies in the United States and foreign companies trading on U.S. stock exchanges are required to file various types of disclosure documents with the SEC. Beginning in 1996, these filings were required to be made electronically. EDGAR is an acronym for Electronic Data Gathering, Analysis, and Retrieval, the term the SEC uses for the electronic gathering and storing of these company filings. The term has also enjoyed widespread use as a generic term for an electronic archive or repository of company filings made with the SEC.

EDGAR Online, Inc. produces three resources to give users access to SEC filings. These resources vary in content and functionality. The free resource, FreeEDGAR, requires users to register before they can access information on the site. EDGAR Online is a fee subscription site that builds on FreeEDGAR's functionality, resulting in more advanced searching and other capabilities. EDGARpro is a fee subscription site aimed at professionals. It contains the same functionality as EDGAR Online, but with some additional features. These three services will be examined in the following section.

SOURCE CONTENT: This summary provides information on the three EDGAR resources: FreeEDGAR, EDGAR Online, and EDGARpro.

FreeEDGAR. This resource provides access to thousands of SEC filings, updated as the filings are received. You can search for filings for a specific date or by form type (i.e., 10-K), or you can perform a quick search by company name or ticker symbol. A Watchlist feature allows users to track the filings for companies they select.

You can search for companies by name, ticker symbol, or SIC (Standard Industrial Classification) code by clicking on the Search Filings link. Enter as many as ten ticker symbols per search.

A search by ticker symbol will bring up a Search Results page, which offers two options: View Filings or Add to Your Watchlist. The page also includes a More Info box with links to EDGAR Online and other options; some of these options and the Watchlist require a subscription to EDGAR Online to use.

Figure 4-17. FreeEDGAR Ticker Symbol Search Results Page

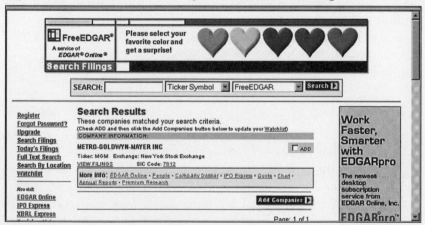

Reprinted with the permission of EDGAR Online, Inc.

Filings appear in a frames format, which can be changed to no frames if desired. The filings can be navigated via a table of contents.

Although you will note a link to a filing when using the frames version of FreeEDGAR , you cannot download filings in Rich Text Format (RTF) from the link. You can print the filing from your browser screen and you can also change the font size, but any downloading requires a subscription to EDGAR Online. This is an example of the minimal functionality that exists within FreeEDGAR.

EDGAR Online. This resource functions almost identically to FreeEDGAR. A quick search feature allows searches by either company name or ticker symbol, and you can also view today's filings. The added value that comes with the subscription is that you can now download your filings in RTF format, create a Watchlist, and search the full text of filings. In EDGAR Online, you can search full-text filings by company name, ticker symbol, CIK (the Central Index Key is a unique identifier assigned by the SEC to each filing company), industry, sector, city, state, and form type, and you can limit by date range or target by a specific date. Full-text searches will go back to 1994.

Users can order hard copies of a company's annual report or obtain further information, such as a Company Dossier, financial information, stock quotes and charts, free analyst research, initial public offering (IPO) information, or a list of executives and directors. With the Premium Research tool, users can link to other, fee resources, such as Dun & Bradstreet and Multex. EDGAR Online also provides a link to Global Information, a section that covers some non-U.S. companies. These can be browsed by company name, country, index, or exchange or accessed via a quick or advanced search.

EDGARpro. This resource is a subscription site with EDGAR Online's functionality, as well as additional features. It allows users to enter "tracker" numbers that appear in usage reports, allowing for the charging back of research costs to clients.

The full-text search template automatically appears on the EDGARpro home page, and the ubiquitous Quick Search option appears at the top of the page as well. The full-text search functions identically to that in EDGAR Online. For example, a search of 10-Ks for disclosure about "exploitation costs," which include the marketing and advertising of feature films, retrieves the results shown in Figure 4-18.

EDGARpro allows users to access company profiles from the results list (see the *P* icon in Figure 4-18), as well as download filings in RTF or Excel format. You can also track which filings you have viewed via the check mark in the Viewed column. Searches can be saved using the Save or Save As links. You can administer your saved searches by clicking on the Monitor tab. Filings in EDGARpro are more professional in appearance than those in FreeEDGAR, and the results also print well without any need for formatting by the user. EDGAR Online filings also print well.

Figure 4-18. Sample EDGARpro Search Results List

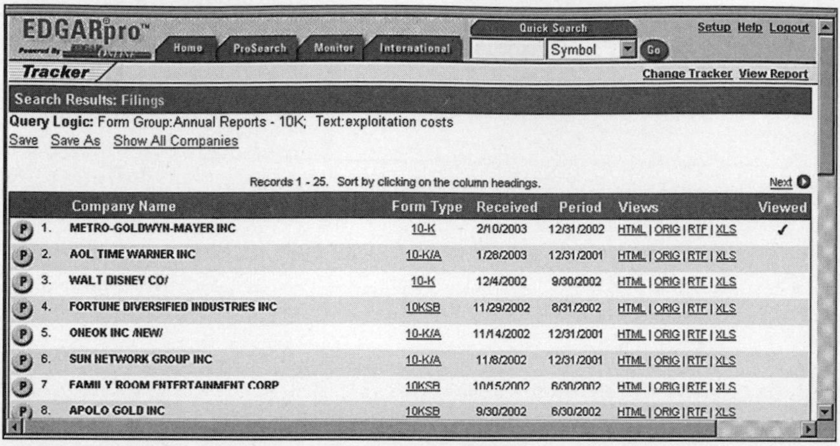

Reprinted with the permission of EDGAR Online, Inc.

EDGARpro's ProSearch feature allows for full-text searching of filings, with the option to include or exclude paper filings.

Figure 4-19. EDGARpro's ProSearch Screen

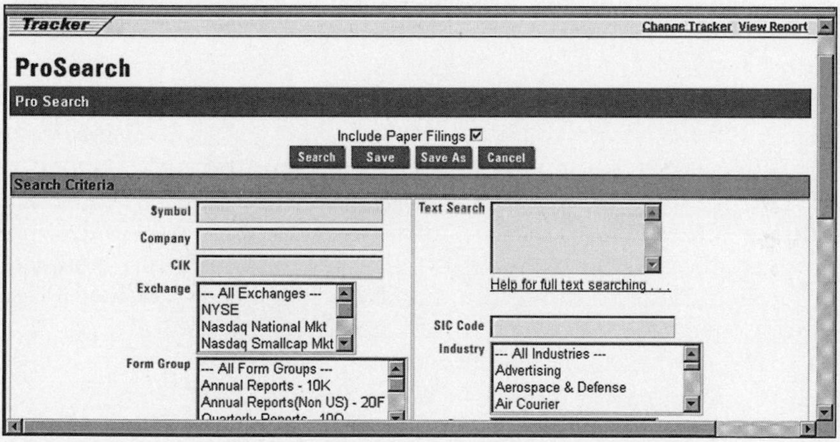

Reprinted with the permission of EDGAR Online, Inc.

As previously noted, EDGARpro enables users to charge back their usage or to track it through its Tracker feature. Information entered into the Tracker appears on usage reports you can download from the EDGARpro site.

Figure 4-20. EDGARpro Usage Reports Generator

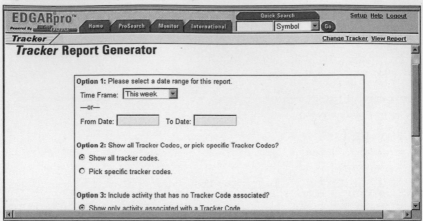

Reprinted with the permission of EDGAR Online, Inc.

SOURCE EVALUATION: FreeEDGAR is aimed at the layperson and has limited functionality. Even though links to such features as full-text search appear on the FreeEDGAR home page, those features require a subscription to EDGAR Online. FreeEDGAR is very basic in its offerings and can be a quick, free resource to use when simply trying to find company filings by SIC code and when it does not matter whether the filings "look pretty." It can also be a quick resource for finding company filings in general, but the EDGAR database at the Securities & Exchange Commission Web site is just as quick and easy to use, with about the same functionality. In fact, the filings from the SEC Web site look better when printed. FreeEDGARalso contains *lots* of advertising, including pop-up ads, which distract from its usability and can make it difficult to find information. Finally, every time you log in to FreeEDGAR, you receive an "offer" page; you must scroll down the page and then accept or decline the offer before you can proceed to using FreeEDGAR itself. This is very annoying and keeps appearing no matter how often you decline.

EDGAR Online is designed for the savvy layperson. Its increased functionality over FreeEDGAR, especially the full-text search and download capabilities, makes it worth the subscription price. In the subscription format there is also a sharp decrease in the number of ads on the site, which reduces clutter and confusion and increases usability. The search results are difficult to browse, however, because of the way they appear on the screen. With much of the emphasis on promoting EDGARpro and other areas of the site, the remaining screen area is "stuffed" with too much information for the limited space. Similar data sources, such as

10k Wizard, are easier to use and browse. (In EDGARpro, however, you are able to view your search terms in context within the filings by clicking on the HTML link next to the filing name in the search results list, and then using the First Hit/Next Hit/Last Hit buttons.)

EDGARpro is aimed at professional researchers and would be the best option for librarians and information professionals. Its search functionality and results lists are the best of the three related products. Ads are minimal, and download capability is extended to Excel format, which is important for the financial information in SEC filings. The Tracker feature allows for usage tracking and reporting—another vital feature of any subscription service used in a business research setting. The company summaries and profiles include financial ratio information, institutional ownership, newswire stories, and other information missing from both FreeEDGAR and EDGAR Online. One drawback is that you cannot see your search terms in context when viewing filings. Also, international content is accessed via Global Reports or Perfect Information, and not in the general search features.

SOURCE VALUE RATING: All of the data source reviewers were asked to rate each source on the basis of the following eight categories, using "10" as the highest rating and "1" as the lowest ("80" being a perfect score):

1. Relative cost-to-value:	6
2. Relative timeliness of data:	9
3. Relative comprehensiveness of data:	7
4. Ease of use:	6
5. Search options available:	7
6. Level of support services:	8
7. Level of training offered:	8
8. Amount/kinds of special services offered:	6
Total Rating:	57

CONTRIBUTOR NAME: Jan Rivers/Patricia A. Watkins

AFFILIATION: Dorsey & Whitney LLP/Thunderbird School of International Management

USEFUL TIPS

---

* It is best to use FreeEDGAR solely for finding known entities, such as a specific company's 10-K filing.
* Full-text searching of any kind with these three products can be done only in EDGAR Online or EDGARpro.
* For obtaining copies of filings, use EDGAR Online or EDGARpro . If you wish to print free copies of filings without using a subscription resource, use the SEC's Web site (*http://www.sec.gov*).
* EDGARpro has the most functionality and value-add of the three resources.

10K WIZARD

SERVICE/PORTAL NAME: *http://www.10kwizard.com*

SOURCE DESCRIPTION: 10k Wizard was formed in April 1999 by Martin Zacarias, a graduate and financial analyst, and Kee Kimbrell, a game software developer. Recognizing the need for expanded coverage of and advanced search capabilities for the Securities and Exchange Commission (SEC) database, together the two developed proprietary software to search through the vast amount of information available to the public via the SEC's EDGAR (Electronic Data Gathering, Analysis, and Retrieval) system. Not only can the user search by company name or ticker with 10k Wizard, but the Power Search feature also allows one to search the whole document for individual words or word phrases and to use Boolean operators (AND, OR, NOT). Search returns display complete company files or specified sections. There are several additional modules, including Alert Streaming, Portfolio Wizard, IR Wizard, and Global Reports, as well as Fundamental Financials, which offers 140 data points taken from the income statement, balance sheet, and cash flow statement and then displayed in annual, quarterly, and trailing twelve-month views.

PRICING: Base price is $150 per year, $25 per month, or $50 per quarter. For pricing information on additional modules contact 10k Wizard at *http://www.10kwizard.com*.

SOURCE CONTENT: 10k Wizard is the name given to the basic package offered on this Web site. Tabs along the top of the page link the user to seven different search mechanisms or search areas: Basic, Advanced, Exhibits, Corporate Actions, Profiles, Annual Reports, and Financials (this is an optional upgrade). Basic searching is free and open to all. Any of the other search options, including financials, requires a subscription. One can search free in the Basic mode, but document retrieval requires a subscription. All the other search areas require a subscription before access.

In the Basic mode one can search by company name, ticker, CIK, words, and industry and limit by type of form group and dates. The advanced search adds the ability to drill down as far as ZIP code or area code in searching and to limit by specific form and fiscal year end. The Exhibits section allows one to search by the entire group or within specific exhibits. This is particularly helpful when you need to quickly find information not included in the forms, such as agreements with other groups. Corporate Action is the section for tracking resignations, acquisitions, changes in control, and bankruptcies. The Profile section will provide some descriptive material, a list of the latest filings, and links to filings by companies in the same industry group—here 10k Wizard is linking to a company's competitors. The Annual Report section supports searching, at this time, for fifty-six countries. Although annual reports are searchable, there is an added cost to purchase them.

There are five add-on modules or sections:

1. **Insider Trading.** In this section one can search either EDGAR or non-EDGAR filings. Searching is available by company name, ticker, word, or search form number. One can limit by date range. It is simple to choose a date and form type and retrieve names of the people who bought, sold, or exercised an option on those days.

2. **Fundamental Financials.** This is an added optional module that enables comparisons across companies. Comparisons can be obtained for seven years of annual data, sixteen quarters, or a trailing twelve months. Ratios are provided annually and quarterly. Data is taken from income statements, balance sheets, and cash flow information in the various SEC documents. Coverage is provided for companies listed on the NYSE, AMEX, NASDAQ, and OTC.

3. **Alert Service.** An added module, this provides streaming service, to the desktop, for an alert list set up by the user. Each alert is linked to the full-text filing.

4. **Portfolio Wizard.** This service tracks large listings of financial and news resources and is most suited to analysts, brokers, and institutions with large holdings. It is integrated into a company's Web site, and the interface can be customized. This is an added module.

5. **IR Wizard.** This tool enables a company to integrate its SEC filings onto the company Web site, where they can be accessed by customers and investors. This is an added module.

SOURCE EVALUATION: Overall, 10k Wizard is a solid corporate resource that enables the user to save time in finding needed company financial information. The range of search features makes it easy for even the novice to quickly find the needed material. Even the basic search feature is a big improvement on the EDGAR database, which allows a search for information in the headers only. The added modules give the option of amalgamating more features, but the basic database is by itself a reliable and useful resource.

SOURCE VALUE RATING: All of the data source reviewers were asked to rate each source on the basis of the following eight categories, using "10" as the highest rating and "1" as the lowest ("80" being a perfect score):

1. Relative cost-to-value:	9
2. Relative timeliness of data:	10
3. Relative comprehensiveness of data:	10
4. Ease of use:	10
5. Search options available:	10
6. Level of support services:	10
7. Level of training offered:	5
8. Amount/kinds of special services offered:	9
Total Rating:	73

SOURCE REVIEWS: This Web site was nominated for a Webby Award in 2002 (*http://www.webbyawards.com/main/webby_awards/nominees. html#finance*).

Hoover's Company Capsules, via Factiva database search. "M10K Wizard Technology, LLC–Hoover's Company Capsule." May 10, 2002. "Need a little magic to sort through SEC filings? 10K Wizard Technology provides free online access to Securities and Exchange Commission filings (more than 70 types of documents), as well as powerful searching and parsing tools to sort through the information. Users can search by company name, ticker, SIC code, industry type, or keyword, and registered users can receive e-mail alerts of new filings. 10K Wizard also uses its technology to power the SEC portions of Web sites, including Hoover's [publisher of this profile]."

CONTRIBUTOR NAME: Rita W. Moss/Patricia A. Watkins
AFFILIATION: University of North Carolina–Chapel Hill/Thunderbird School of International Management

ALACRA

ALTERNATE/PREVIOUS DATA SOURCE NAMES: Originally founded as Data Downlink Corporation (1996), renamed Alacra in 2001. Product releases: .xls (1997), compbook (1999), privatesuite (2000), Portal B (2000), Alacra Book (2001), Alacra Model (2002, Excel add-in capability).

SERVICE/PORTAL NAME: *http://www.alacra.com*

SOURCE DESCRIPTION: Alacra provides a total business information resource targeted exclusively to business users. The various components of the service help users search for information and then use online tools to find, analyze, package, and present business information. The specially selected Web sites and premium database sources at Alacra provide worldwide data on economics, market and investment research, news, shareholding and bond-holding, company financials, corporate deals, business directories, and earnings estimates. Alacra offers the ability to conduct business searches across more than one hundred Premium Databases and the Alacra Business Web a specialized database of forty-five thousand content-rich business-information-only Web sites aggregated by Alacra. "Build a Book" is an Alacra tool that allows the user to build a PDF file containing data from various premium sources, including Web sites as well as proprietary content.

There are several ways to search for information at Alacra. The home page presents a clean look with an easy-to-read menu (see Figure 4-21). At the top of the home page are links to the various sections: Databases, Build a Book, and Apps and Help. The Alacra Build a Book feature is clearly visible as a stand-alone link in the middle of the menu bar, encouraging immediate access.

Figure 4-22 shows Alacra search results for *General Motors*. Results are returned with tabs indicating the data available from the Alacra Premium databases and the Alacra Business Web, as well as shortcuts to Company snapshots and News and Market Research content.

Figure 4-21. Alacra Home Page

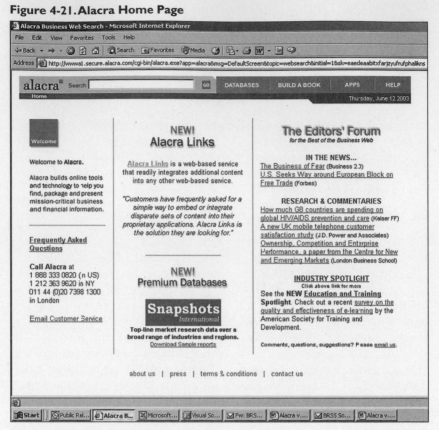

Reprinted with the permission of Alacra, Inc.

The following search and select options can be found in the Databases menu tab:

- **Databases.** This section provides (1) a shortcut list to the user's selection of most frequently used premium databases, (2) Sources List: a listing of all 100+ Premium databases in Alacra, each Web-enabled directly to the database, allowing for direct searches within that database, and (3) access to Alacra Directories specialized lists of all sites available in the Alacra Business Web. Users can also select from 12 various organization types, 18 business topics, 95 industries, 28 specialty directories, 11 geographic regions, or 204 countries.

- **Apps.** Containing more advanced search capabilities, this section includes the following options: Advanced Web Search, Advanced Database Search, Public Company Search, Private Company Search—based on descriptive and financial data that the user selects, and Search Library—an archive of a user's saved searches.

Figure 4-22. Alacra Search on General Motors

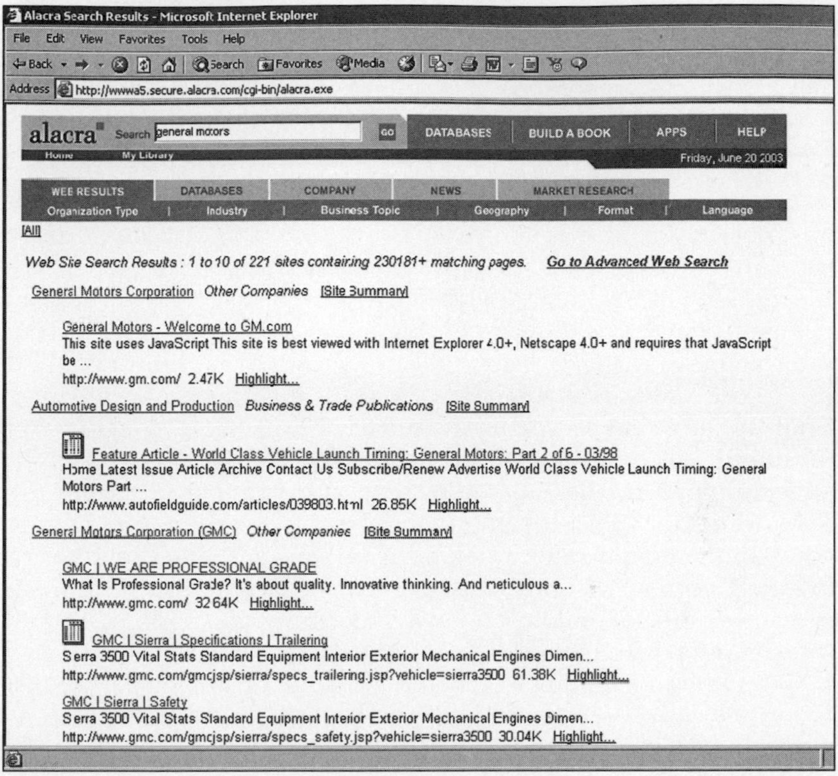

Reprinted with the permission of Alacra, Inc.

PRICING: The basic $150 monthly access fee gives a single user access to all Alacra features and Premium content on a pay-per-view basis. The pricing for access to Alacra is scalable; the more user IDs a firm subscribes to, the lower the cost per user. Additional charges are incurred as data is downloaded, on a per-article or -report basis from the Premium databases. Article and report download fees can be viewed during search sessions, allowing the user to track spending for individual projects. The forty-five thousand Web sites indexed in Alacra Directories provide a lot of excellent, free, Internet-based information that is easily accessible before the researcher begins tapping into the Premium databases.

The fee for an article or report section depends on the database. For example, a single article from Business & Industry might cost $3.50 to download, whereas a single section of a Datamonitor report might be $100. Users have the option of purchasing as little or as much text as they wish from the various databases to suit their research budget.

Most premium database providers inAlacra offer subscription access to their databases, where the user or firm pays a fixed rate (monthly or annual fee) for the content and is not charged per download. Alacra does a considerable amount of custom development and applications for large customers, and in those cases, there are also development and custom site fees.

SOURCE CONTENT: A user can search within Alacra in a variety of ways: (1) enter keywords (Web syntax only) on the home page to search across all Alacra premium content and the Alacra Business Web simultaneously, (2) search the one hundred Premium databases individually via a custom search screen from the Databases menu *or* search all or a subset of Premium content using the Advanced Database Search in Apps, (3) perform Boolean searches across the Alacra Business Web (forty-five thousand business-information-only Web sites specially chosen and evaluated for business relevance and reputation) using the Advanced Web Search, and (4) search for public and private companies and any relevant content using the Public Company or Private Company Search in Apps. The Web sites and databases provide a mix of public and private companies, and U.S. and international resources.

The Premium database menu is available in an alphabetical list as well as a category list. Alacra content categories are Company Profiles and Financials, Deal Information, Earnings Estimates, Economic Data & Analysis, Executives, Filings and Documents, Investment Research, Investment Risk Models, Market Research, Mutual Fund Research, News, and Share Ownership. The categories capture information relevant to a broad mix of business applications: finance, marketing, strategic planning, research, and competitive intelligence.

The Premium database sources present a broad range of content, representative of those used by business and research professionals. Some of the Premium databases available for searching include the following:

- **Company Profiles and Fundamentals.** Barra Beta Books, Datamonitor, Dun & Bradstreet, EDGAR Online, Gale Company Profiles, Hoover's Company Profiles, Mergent, Multex, ICC Information Limited, Nikkei, Thomson Financial Disclosure, ValueLine, Graham and Whiteside, Harris Infosource, idExec, Corptech *DealInformation*: Mergerstat, TF Joint Ventures, TF Mergers and Acquisitions, TF New Issues, TF Venture Economics (Firms and Funds), M&A Monitor

- **Earnings Estimates.** Multex Global Estimates, Nelson Consensus Estimates, I/B/E/S First Call
- **Economic Data.** Economist Intelligence Unit (EIU), Datamonitor Country Profiles, Quest Economics
- **Market and Investment Research.** Datamonitor Industry Profiles, Economist Intelligence Unit Country Analysis, Freedonia Market Research, Gale Market Share Reporter, Harris Industry Reports, TableBase, Moody's Global Credit Research
- **Mutual Fund Research.** Weisenberger
- **News.** ABI/Inform, Business & Industry, Business and Management Practices, EBSCO, Factiva (by subscription only), NewsEdge, Reed Business Information, Nexis (by subscription only)
- **Share Ownership.** TF Ownership Data (institutions), TF Ownership (securities), TF/Carson (funds/institutions and securities), Vickers Stock Research (funds/institutions and securities)

Those familiar with Factiva will likely find the Alacra Premium database search interface nearly identical to the stand-alone product. Here, too, searchers are able to preselect language, industry, date, region, and news subject from convenient pull-down menus. Figure 4-23 shows search results for General Motors within Factiva. Note how article titles, dates, and sources make it easy for users to get the data they need.

Figure 4-23. Results for General Motors Search within Factiva at Alacra Premium Database

Date	Headline	Source	Word Count
☐ MARCH 17, 2003	GAINING ON THE LOCALS In Russia, foreign carmakers can't produce fast enough	BusinessWeek	814
☐ MARCH 17, 2003	MUSICAL CHAIRS WITH MEDIA ASSETS	BusinessWeek	187
☐ MARCH 17, 2003	AN `AMERICAN BMW'? DON'T HOLD YOUR BREATH Bob Lutz's plan to revamp Pontiac is still in first gear	BusinessWeek	856
☐ MARCH 17, 2003	This truck's wheels go round and round	U.S. News & World Report	154
☐ MARCH 17, 2003	Brawl at the mall	U.S. News & World Report	791
☐ MARCH 17, 2003	Bye-Bye Pension ; Soon hundreds of corporations may slash pensions by as much as half.	Fortune Magazine	4219

Done | Internet

Start | Novell GroupWise ... | Alacra - Microso... | 2 Microsoft Word | 2:52 PM

Similarly, the Alacra Premium Business & Industry database search page interface is nearly identical to the stand-alone version (see Figure 4-24). In Business & Industry, searchers may choose keywords, company, concept terms, industry, SIC codes, and sources to narrow the scope of a search.

Figure 4-24. Basic Search Screen for Business & Industry Premium Database

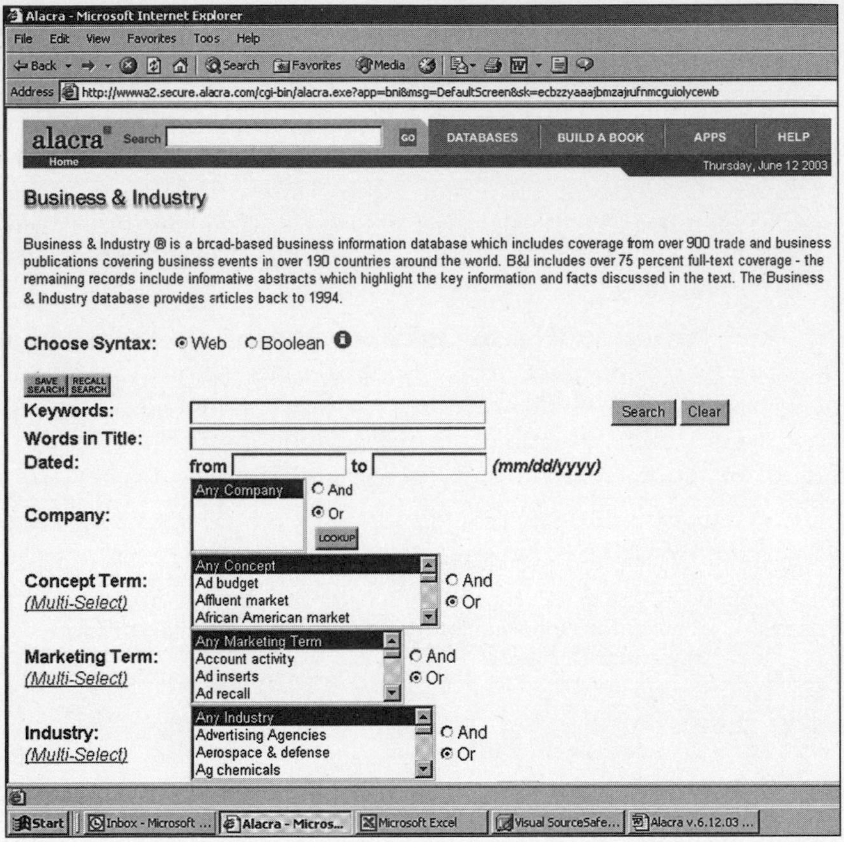

Reprinted with the permission of Alacra, Inc. Reprinted with the permission of Gale Group.

Figures 4-25 and 4-26 show examples of a search in the Alacra Premium database Nikkei, Japan's leading financial data vendor. The searcher sees the cost for an individual financial report and the option to download the data in Excel. Note the general format for a search in Nikkei for manufacturer (in this case, Toyota), as well as the data options available, costs for each, and the Excel data retrieval format page.

Figure 4-25. Initial Alacra Search Screen in Nikkei Premium Database

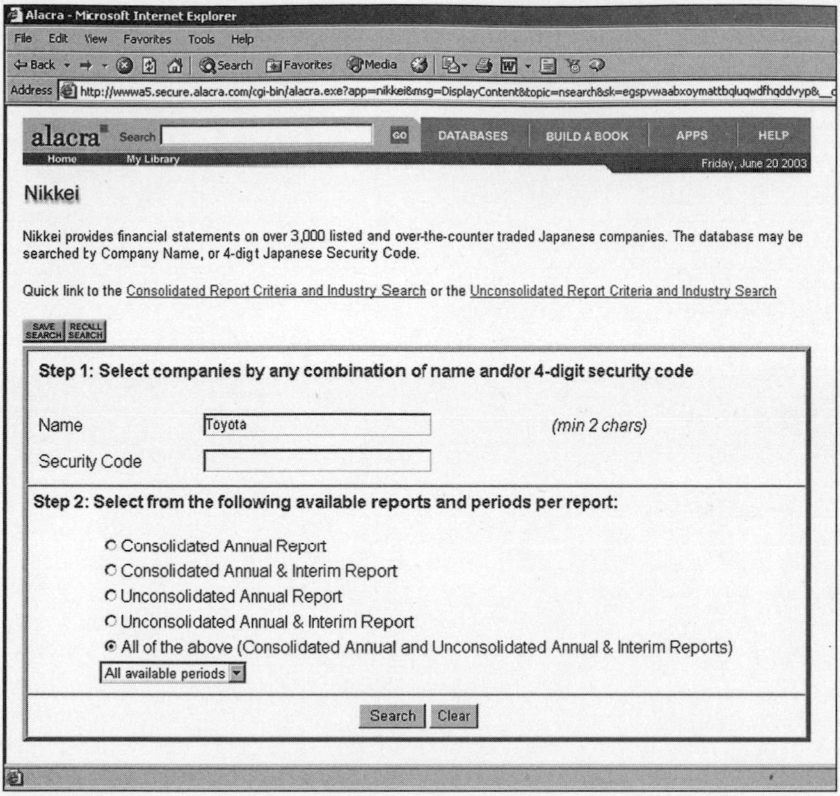

Reprinted with the permission of Alacra, Inc. Reprinted with the permission of Nihon Keizai Shimbun, Inc.

SOURCE EVALUATION: Overall, Alacra is an excellent source of one-stop shopping for the business-intelligence researcher. It provides a broad range of excellent premium databases and Internet resources and the ability to track and control search costs. Alacra contains fairly simple search tools suitable for everyone from the generalist to the seasoned researcher. The Alacra Build a Book is a great tool for quickly compiling data resources into an easy downloadable business package, allowing the searcher to include Web site data or the user's own resources.

The menu selections for Databases, Build a Book, and Apps are intuitive to use. Alacra will require some time and practice, particularly for the novice researcher unfamiliar with the power of the Premium databases. The Build a Book feature requires some back-and-forth usage before creating a book becomes second nature, and the service seems a bit slow when loading documents

Figure 4-26. Results of Excel Spreadsheet Download for Toyota Motor Corporation from Alacra Nikkei Premium Database

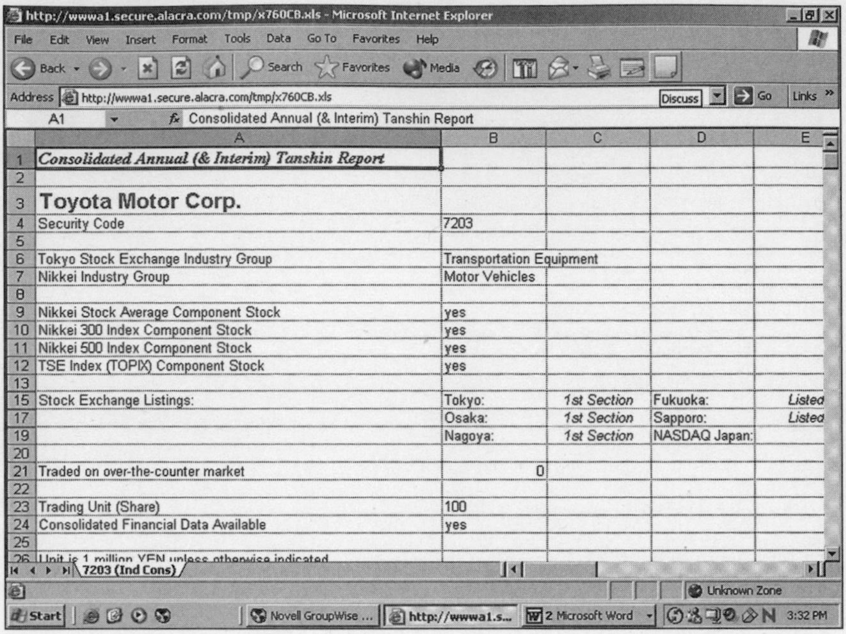

Reprinted with the permission of Alacra, Inc. Reprinted with the permission of Nihon Keizai Shimbun, Inc.

during the book-building phase. However, the final PDF document is e-mailed to the user fairly quickly and proves to be an excellent basic business-briefing package for updated news and financial information, particularly for public companies.

According to an Alacra representative, most Premium databases are updated independently of one another through direct feeds/data files delivered to Alacra by the content providers. Frequency of updates might vary from daily to annually; details about frequency of updates for each premium provider are available from the Help link. Clicking on Help for the current page from any search screen will display the help for that particular page. Each Alacra customer account is assigned an account manager who is responsible for training all new users, informing users of enhancements and changes to the service, and providing ongoing training and technical support throughout the terms of the contract. Customer service desks in New York and London are available seven days a week, Monday through Friday, from 8:00 a.m. to 8:00 p.m., and Saturday and Sunday from 9:00 a.m. to 5:00 p.m. (EST and GMT). There are no fees associated with customer or technical support.

SOURCE VALUE RATING: All of the data source reviewers were asked to rate each source on the basis of the following eight categories, using "10" as the highest rating and "1" as the lowest ("80" being a perfect score):

1. Relative cost-to-value:	8
2. Relative timeliness of data:	8
3. Relative comprehensiveness of data:	8
4. Ease of use:	7
5. Search options available:	7
6. Level of support services:	8
7. Level of training offered:	7
8. Amount/kinds of special services offered:	7
Total Rating:	60

SOURCE REVIEWS:

"Alacra: Snazzy, Upscale and a Feature-Filled Model." *The Information Advisor: A Monthly Newsletter.* Find/SVP 14, no. 5 (May 2002). "We really liked this product—it is both very powerful, because of its excellent content, and incredibly simple to use. It's also a good example of how an automated system can be used to improve the search process. . . . Our only complaint is that Alacra was sometimes slow to construct our book. And, while not really a complaint as much as a caution, it can be tempting to think that using Alacra means you are covering all your business research bases. . . . But if you want news and financials for public firms, Alacra is an excellent product."

Kassel, Amelia. "Tales of a Searchers' Life: A Comedy of Errors or a Test of Patience?" *Searcher,* September 1, 2002. "I was pleased to locate information about venture capital firms financing the company in question in the Thomson Database. . . . Only this source carried dollar amounts and dates of each round's funding. To access this database, I used Alacra (formerly. xls, formerly PortalB), which may constitute the only pay-as-you-go avenue available for this database, although Alacra itself is a subscription aggregator requiring an active account. I recommend Alacra because of its unique sources such as this one (Thomson Financial

Securities Data/Venture Economics' Venture Capital Financing), not available from other transaction-based vendors."

Tudor, Jan Davis. "Alacra: Cheerful Willingness, Readiness or Promptness?" *Searcher,* January 1, 2003. "One reason why I've become a fan of the service is because it was developed for the Internet, making it not only a dependable system, but also a breeze to use technically. I appreciate the broad range of databases available, the ability to download much of the information directly into spreadsheets (hence the former name, .xls), and finally—it has one of the best customer support teams around. . . . [T]he new Alacra has done a good job of balancing the needs of the researchers of various levels by developing a streamlined interface that users can navigate in a number of different ways."

CONTRIBUTOR NAME: Patricia A. Watkins

AFFILIATION: Thunderbird School of International Management

USEFUL TIPS

- Become familiar with the thousands of organizational, business type, and specialty Web sites in the Directories tab for business-related information free of charge.
- Go through the Sources List link in the Databases tab and learn about the various Premium databases in Alacra and the most suitable search application for each.
- Experiment with building a book to learn how this tool works (i.e., cost, various database sources, etc.) before working on a project deadline.

INVESTEXT

SERVICE/PORTAL NAME: Thomson Research (*http://research.thomsonib.com*)

SOURCE DESCRIPTION: Since the early 1980s, Investext has been the largest database of company and industry analysis available. Collected from many of the world's leading investment, consulting, and market research firms, Investext provides an exceptional source for detailed company, industry, and geographic data, in-depth analysis, and forecasts.

The product is considered a basic resource for business and investment research. Though often used to access equity research information for its detailed company analysis and forecasts, Investext provides ready entry to industry analysis that can often deliver a depth and breadth of information unavailable elsewhere. Investext on Thomson Research is a combination of four major research resources: Investext, MarkIntel, Industry Insider, and a new Morning Meeting Notes database.

PRICING: Pricing for Investext through Thomson Research is variable, but costs as much as $2,000 can occur for multiple company/industry searches. Dialog pricing, too, is variable, and depends on the amount of time spent searching, the articles and format for reports and articles, and the Dialog interface chosen (i.e., DialogClassic, DialogWeb).

SOURCE CONTENT: This summary will review the key offerings of Investext on Thomson Research (*http://research.thomsonib.com*) in four content collections: Investment Research, Market Research, Trade Research Association, and Morning Meeting Notes as follows:

1. **Investment Research.** The main and traditional Investext database is a collection of millions of reports from more than six hundred leading investment and brokerage firms. Written by many of the financial services industry's leading analysts, reports found onInvestext provide company, industry, geographic current data, and financial forecasts for more than sixty thousand domestic and international companies. Although high priced, Investext is often a solid starting point for gathering primary and secondary company research and analysis.

2. **Market Research.** Also known separately as MarkIntel, Market Research provides access to primary research and statistics from more than 145 of the leading independent market research organizations, such as the Yankee Group, Datamonitor, IDC, and the Gartner Group. Although similar to investment research reports in format, market research reports are almost exclusively market- or industry-focused, and often provide current and forecast statistics in greater depth than other research resources.

3. **Trade Research Association.** Also known as Industry Insider, Trade Research Association is a smaller compilation of research from a variety of key professional and trade associations that generally track their industries for the benefit of their members. Research provided is usually from a collection

of sources, both primary and secondary, and often contains industry insights not found in other publications.

4. **Morning Meeting Notes.** A collection of research notes released from the major brokerage houses, Morning Meeting Notes are excellent sources to track a company or industry that is undergoing rapid change. Updated daily, these briefings also track macroeconomic changes and commentary from many of the leading equity and fixed income analysts on global and American markets.

SOURCE EVALUATION: Investext is an invaluable business research resource. Although costly, it provides an unsurpassed collection of millions of research reports from more than a thousand research-driven investment, consulting, and market research firms. Often a mandatory resource in the financial community, Investext is an excellent "first source" for large industry and market studies and is an exceptional point of access to leading analysts. The key limitation of Investext is the lack of "real-time" updating of reports. Most reports can take weeks to become available because of limitations imposed by their providers. Additionally, although the cost per page is reasonable given its value, the cost of whole reports is still too high, especially given the lower-cost options available elsewhere.

The arrangement of Investext's full search screen on Thomson Research follows a standard pattern: Company or Ticker, Industry (by name, SIC, or NAICS codes), Region (geographic), Title & Free-Text Searching (FT search available only since 1999), Date, Contributor (corporate), Author, Collection, Report Number, and Date (see Figure 4-27). This organization is fairly straightforward and intuitive for the beginning searcher. Additionally, the look-up functions provide solid search-refinement tools. Help windows are available and fairly solid, although the help function lacks true interactivity with a user's level in search and retrieval. Additionally, the Show Criteria window on the initial search page and on the results page is exceptionally useful for editing searches on the fly. The best feature about the database, however, is the ability to customize almost all search and display settings, which allows each user to deliver a highly tailored research product.

The only real flaw I found is that the static Support tab available on the upper right-hand corner of every page lists only the phone numbers and e-mails of regional technical support. This link would be more useful if it were to refer the user to the available Help files.

Figure 4-27.Thomson Research Full Search Screen

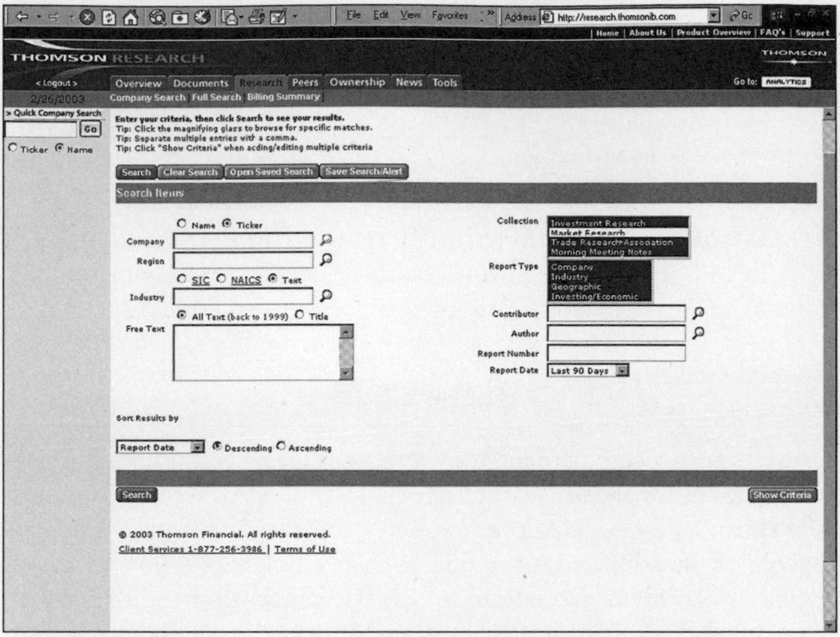

Reprinted with the permission of Thomson Financial Networks.

For first-time users, Thomson Research offers a simple Company search page that allows for searches by Company Name, Ticker, and Industry (by Industry name, SIC, or NAICS codes). This is a fine initial search engine for pulling industry and company reports. However, it lacks the ability to limit a search by anything other than the above indexing and is not recommended for anyone other than the most inexperienced researcher.

SOURCE VALUE RATING: All of the data source reviewers were asked to rate each source on the basis of the following eight categories, using "10" as the highest rating and "1" as the lowest ("80" being a perfect score):

1. Relative cost-to-value:	7
2. Relative timeliness of data:	7
3. Relative comprehensiveness of data:	8
4. Ease of use:	6

5. Search options available:	8
6. Level of support services:	7
7. Level of training offered:	6
8. Amount/kinds of special services offered:	7
Total Rating:	56

CONTRIBUTOR NAME: William S. Marriott/Patricia A. Watkins

AFFILIATION: Marriott Research and Recruitment/ Thunderbird School of International Management

USEFUL TIPS

- Always try to complement your Investext usage with Multex, which provides full analyst research reports for hundreds if not thousands less than Investext. However, keep in mind that Investext provides superior indexing and is the only resource that allows you to view tables of contents and purchase only the pages you need of analyst reports. Additionally, both Multex and Investext have significant overlap, but each does offer its own exclusive sources.
- Unless you are looking for specific research notes, ignore any report fewer than five pages long (>5), especially during earnings report season. These are often only a regurgitation of a company's press release, which can be found for free or for little cost.
- Excellent industry and company reports are often available when an analyst initiates coverage. Try to look for these, as they often provide incredibly detailed studies of, and methods for, evaluating companies, industries, and geographies.
- Stay away from Corporate Technology Information reports and older reports from Market Guide. They provide no original forecasts, just a restatement of earnings reports with basic financial ratios and other information available from alternative, less expensive sources.

MARKETRESEARCH.COM

ALTERNATE/PREVIOUS DATA SOURCE NAMES: Formerly Kalorama Information

SERVICE/PORTAL NAME: *http://www.MarketResearch.com*

SOURCE DESCRIPTION: MarketResearch.com is a Web-based aggregator of market research reports from a variety of publishers and providers. Market research reports, including investment analyst reports, provide an in-depth look into a particular company or industry and can vary in length from just a few pages to several hundred pages or more. Based on primary research and analysis, these reports are generated by a variety of entities such as market consulting and research firms, boutique investment analyst firms specializing in specific industries, or large multi-industry firms. Market research reports are frequently used to gauge the market potential of a product under development, or to help determine the long-term prospects or outlook for a specific industry or business.

PRICING: Market research reports available through MarketResearch.com can vary significantly in price, from less than $100 to several thousand dollars per report, depending on the content and publisher. Consequently, researchers frequently prefer to purchase reports by the page or section. MarketResearch.com can be searched for free, but with an account you will have enhanced search privileges, including permission to access the tables of contents and the ability to see search terms within the text of the report and additional listing information to help you better access the available reports. There is no cost to set up an account (which can be done online), and there are no subscription fees. A credit card account allows transactional access to the actual reports available through Marketresearch.com. A corporate account offers a little more flexibility in payment and ordering and would be set up through an account representative.

SOURCE CONTENT: MarketResearch.com contains more than fifty thousand analyst reports from more than 350 publishers, including Mintel, Datamonitor, Euromonitor, Economist Intelligence Unit, Packaged Facts, Kalorama Information, Global Industry Analyst, Freedonia Group, Gale, TowerGroup, and Yankee Group. The site's home page includes a subject directory of report categories.

You can search for reports by keyword or browse subject categories. The main subject categories are Consumer Goods, Food and Beverage, Life Sciences, Technology & Media, Marketing & Market Research, Service Industries, Heavy Industry, Public Sector, and Company Reports. Subject categorization is extensive and includes more subtopics than those appearing on the site's home page (see Figure 4-28). You can also use the Browse by Popular Publisher feature found at the bottom of the home page to access publications by specific publishers in specific topic areas (see Figure 4-29).

Figure 4-28. Example of MarketResearch.com's Subject Category Subtopics

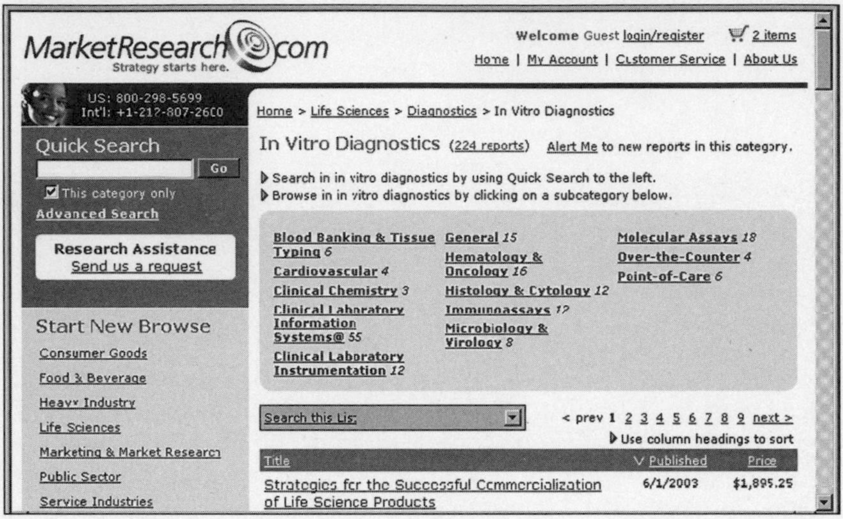

Reprinted with the permission of MarketResearch.com, Inc.

Figure 4-29. Browse by Popular Publisher Feature, MarketResearch.com Home Page

Reprinted with the permission of MarketResearch.com, Inc.

MarketResearch.com has also added a Matching Categories feature, which classifies search results into relevant industry groups. These functions allow users to perform searches within specific topic categories and gives them the ability to refine their searchers using keywords, publisher name, date published, price, and geographic region. Browsing by publisher, for example, results in a list of reports available via MarketResearch.com from a specific publisher. You can further refine the results list by restricting the search to a certain subject category or geographic area, for example, and you can sort the results list by date, title, or price.

Figure 4-30. MarketResearch.com's Advanced Search Page

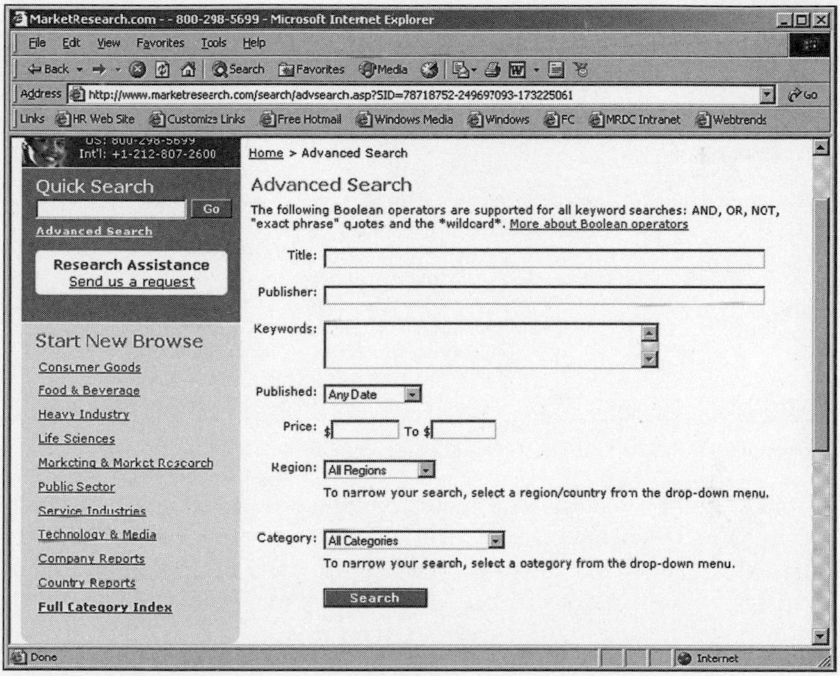

Reprinted with the permission of MarketResearch.com, Inc.

The site's Advanced Search feature (see Figure 4-30) allows you to tailor your search using cost parameters and other criteria. For each report in MarketResearch.com, you will receive citation information (publisher, date, number of pages), cost information, and an abstract, as well as the report's coverage (i.e., global) and subject categorization. You can also use the site's free registration to access the table of contents and abstract for each report, and you can view your search terms within the context of the report using the Search Inside this Report feature.

Some reports can be purchased by section; these are marked with a "Buy By The Slice" icon, as shown in Figure 4-31.

Figure 4-31. "Buy By TheSlice" Option in MarketResearch.com

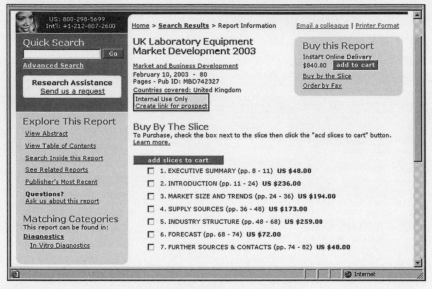

Reprinted with the permission of MarketResearch.com, Inc.

SOURCE EVALUATION: MarketResearch.com is a good source for market research information. Free searching on this site is especially useful for getting a sense of availability on a topic, industry, or company without incurring online costs. The product is easy to use and intuitive to navigate. Virtually all the information a researcher may need is available within three clicks. The site map provides a list of all categories and subcategories, as well as all 350-plus content providers. Coverage is international and includes highly specialized reports costing more than $10,000, as well as smaller, general reports costing less than $100. Some reports in MarketResearch.com are available for purchase by section. Availability of this "Buy By The Slice" option depends upon the report's publisher and does not reflect on MarketResearch.com as a resource.

SOURCE VALUE RATING: All of the data source reviewers were asked to rate each source on the basis of the following eight categories, using "10" as the highest rating and "1" as the lowest ("80" being a perfect score):

1. Relative cost-to-value:	8
2. Relative timeliness of data:	9
3. Relative comprehensiveness of data:	9
4. Ease of use:	10
5. Search options available:	10
6. Level of support services:	10
7. Level of training offered:	7
8. Amount/kinds of special services offered:	8
Total Rating:	71

SOURCE REVIEWS:

Fulton, Marsha. "Market Research Aggregators." *Searcher* 11, no. 2 (February 2003): 10 <*http://www.infotoday.com/searcher/feb03/searcher.htm*> (June 30, 2003).

CONTRIBUTOR NAME: Jan Rivers/Cynthia L. Shamel/ Patricia A. Watkins

AFFILIATION: Dorsey & Whitney LLP/Shamel Information Services/Thunderbird School of International Management

USEFUL TIPS

* You can submit search queries via e-mail from the site to Market-Research.com's "super searchers."
* The Reading Room allows you to access, read, and print any reports you ordered for Instant Online Delivery. Everything you purchase from MarketResearch.com remains in the Reading Room forever, so it becomes your individual library.
* To see a list of available reports similar to one that fits your needs, click on the subject category links in the report's synopsis.
* With an enterprise account, the account administrator can view everything housed in all individuals' Reading Rooms on that account. This enables users to share what has been purchased, resulting in cost savings for the company.

- The Search Inside This Report option, which allows you to view your search terms within the text of the report, is a vital tool in determining the relevance of a publication or sections of a publication before making a purchasing decision.

MINDBRANCH

ALTERNATE/PREVIOUS DATA SOURCE NAMES: Publications Resource Group, Inc. (PRG)

SERVICE/PORTAL NAME: MindBranch.com

SOURCE DESCRIPTION: MindBranch.com is a market research distributor and technology company whose services are designed to centralize, streamline, and manage market research purchases. The resource covers more than 130 global industry segments in the areas of Business/Finance, Computers/IT, Health Care, Internet, Communications, Consumer Products, Industrial Markets, and Manufacturing. MindBranch carries more than forty thousand research reports, newsletters, directories, databases, country reports, subscription services, and company profiles. In addition, it offers nearly thirty-five thousand stock reports and other information for the investment community.

Individual visitors to the site can register for free and personalize their profile to receive updates on new research, plus information on specific industries, sectors, keywords, and competitors. Report descriptions and tables of contents may be searched and viewed without subscribing, and there is no charge to access any of the information on the site. In addition, MindBranch offers a desktop tool, QuickLink, which allows companies to centralize research and avoid redundant purchasing. Corporate clients may also qualify for other cost savings accrued through a loyalty program, which offers credits toward future spending. There is no subscription fee for QuickLink.

MindBranch's Web site can be beneficial to individuals or businesses looking for extensive, targeted market research across a range of industries and segments. In addition to offering prepublished research, MindBranch acts as a broker to help clients who need custom research to "choose the right analyst." MindBranch will take time to learn about your information need, write your Request for Proposals, and submit it to the appropriate analysts. To use this service, submit a request to MindBranch and they will select a publisher to complete the work. Clients can choose to remain anonymous throughout the bidding process.

PRICING: Prices range from $50 to $10,000, and reports can be purchased in segments so you can purchase just the chapter needed, at considerable cost savings.

SOURCE CONTENT: MindBranch distributes market and investment research publications, in addition to brokering custom research. MindBranch represents more than three hundred publishers, analysts, and consultants who produce the content; some of the publishers are well-known suppliers such as Datamonitor Publications, Freedonia Group, Yankee Group, Reuters Business Insight, Decision Resources, Kline & Company, ValuEngine, and Ovum.

Users can browse for market research publications by drilling down through eight major categories: Business/Finance, Health Care, Computer/IT, Internet, Communications, Consumer Products, Industrial Markets, and Manufacturing. Clicking Health Care, for example, creates further subdivisions, such as Biotechnology/Immunology. The alternative to browsing is to find reports by entering a keyword or words in the Find search box, at the top left of every page. An advanced search feature lets you filter keyword searches by date, geographic region, product type, industry area, and price and sort by title, price, publication date, and relevance (see Figure 4-32).

You can find general descriptions for individual publishers from the Research Partners tab on the top navigation bar. The Market Research Partners pages allow you to search or browse through studies by an individual publisher. Results produce a list of publications available from MindBranch that are limited to a particular publisher. Further refining the results provides information limited to specific topics and/or industry areas.

For independent equity research on public companies and stocks, users can choose ticker symbols to track and review publications. Tickers may be changed or edited at any time, and purchases can be made either individually or through "soft dollar" brokers, a popular way for professional investors to make transactions.

For all market research publications listed on MindBranch. com, you can view citation information (publisher, publication date, price, geographic coverage), a full description, and a table of contents for free. Newsletters may include sample issues, and some reports may contain sample pages. Some studies also provide a list of countries or geographic regions available for individual purchase, and choosing from the drop-down menus allows you to specify a country with your order (see Figure 4-34). Depending on

Figure 4-32. Example of MindBranch.com's Advanced Find Feature

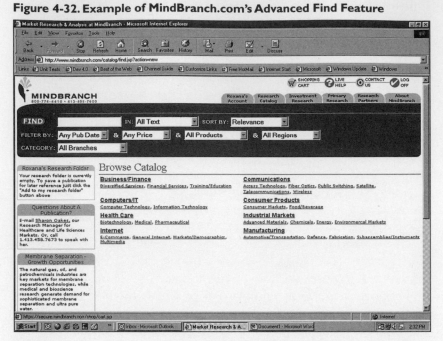

This feature allows you to filter using multiple criteria. Reprinted with the permission of MindBranch, Inc.

Figure 4-33. Sample Results List for Independent Equity Research Tracking (GlaxoSmithKline and Abbott Laboratories)

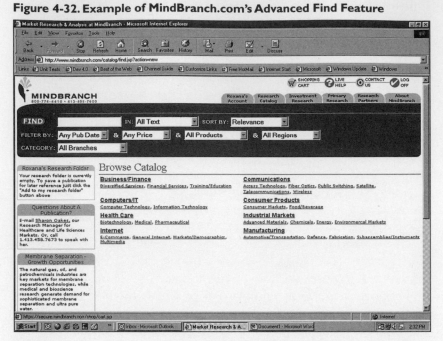

Reprinted with the permission of MindBranch, Inc.

individual publisher requirements, some studies may be purchased by the piece either directly via the Web site or by calling for pricing information and other details.

Figure 4-34. Example of a Publication Page at MindBranch.com, Including the Option of Purchasing by Region or Country

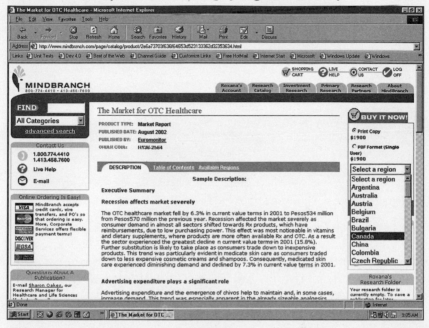

Reprinted with the permission of MindBranch, Inc.

Upon ordering, publications may be downloaded instantly, sent via e-mail in PDF format, or mailed in print form in five to eight days or sooner, depending on the customer's location. Corporate clients that have signed up for QuickLink have additional secured Web site features and functionality. The entire organization can view a list of all publications that have been purchased, and users can sort the list by date purchased, title, or publisher (see Figure 4-35). Links to the Research Forum allow users to share information between locations and business units. In addition, designated employees can manage acquisitions and track purchases with daily Web-based summaries that include detailed information about every purchase, including the buyer, license information, and order status. Compiled data by business unit, publisher, and research subject is also available.

Figure 4-35. Sample of a Limited-Access Feature: Account Summary Information

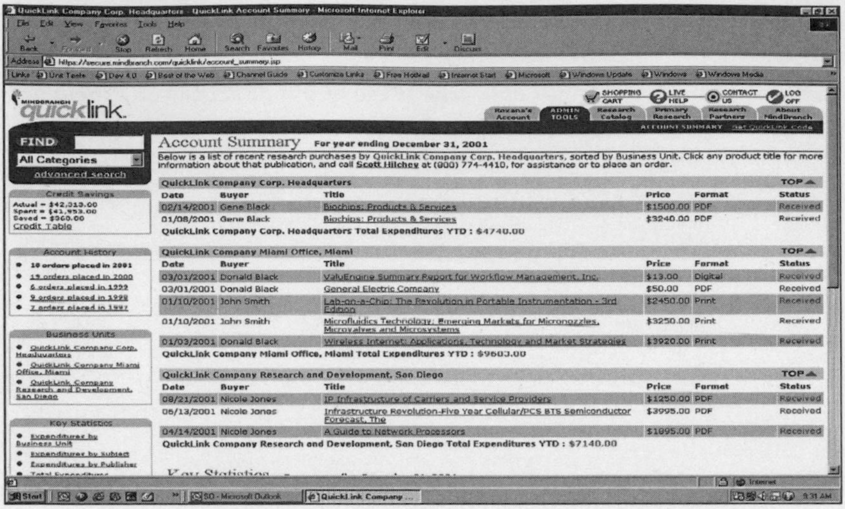

Reprinted with the permission of MindBranch, Inc.

SOURCE EVALUATION: The quality of the content and the Web site's ease of use make MindBranch a viable option for market research. Most of the respected marketing research firms are represented. The primary benefits of MindBranch are convenience for ordering and the custom research services. MindBranch coordinates the purchases and provides a centralized means for tracking each purchase.

MindBranch's chief Web site competitor, MarketResearch.com, also serves as a clearinghouse for about 350 market research publishers. MarketResearch.com content overlaps about 50 percent with MindBranch, and navigation and results presentation are also similar. MarketResearch.com offers more opportunities to purchase sections of reports electronically, but ads on the Mind-Branch site advise clients to call for more information, as many publishers sell sections on a per-request basis. Market Research.com also charges a fee to review tables of contents, whereas Mind-Branch does not. Obviously, a researcher might shop directly with most of the publishers who partner with MindBranch or Market-Research.com. Keep in mind that MindBranch offers all research at the same price as its publisher partners.

If in-depth research and analyst time is needed in a targeted market, the user might consider taking time to develop a direct relationship with one or two market research firms. A valued, repeat customer of a market research firm might be provided with extra discounts or benefit from more personalized service. Mind-Branch offers industry studies from $50 and up, and many publishers provide $100–$500 industry overviews for good, basic background information. Customers of these reports are probably either already active in the markets or seriously considering a first entry.

MindBranch markets "newsletters" to those who register at the site. "Newsletter" can often be a buzzword in market research circles to signal content in a report about a hot trend. MindBranch uses its newsletter as a sales flier announcing new reports available for purchase. No original market content is included in the newsletter itself. Registered users may elect to receive a personalized weekly e-mail newsletter from MindBranch, *The MindBranch Monitor*. The newsletter highlights a featured report, other similar recommended reading, a featured publisher, links to new reports in the user's chosen industries, plus alerts to new studies associated with keywords that the user has added to his or her profile.

SOURCE VALUE RATING: All of the data source reviewers were asked to rate each source on the basis of the following eight categories, using "10" as the highest rating and "1" as the lowest ("80" being a perfect score):

1. Relative cost-to-value:	9
2. Relative timeliness of data:	8
3. Relative comprehensiveness of data:	9
4. Ease of use:	9
5. Search options available:	7
6. Level of support services:	10
7. Level of training offered:	2
8. Amount/kinds of special services offered:	7
Total Rating:	61

SOURCE REVIEWS:

> Fulton, Marsha. "Market Research Aggregators." *Searcher* 11, no. 2 (February 2003): 10 <*http://www.infotoday.com/ searcher/feb03/searcher.htm*> (June 30, 2003).

CONTRIBUTOR NAME: Brenda Reeb/Patricia A. Watkins

AFFILIATION: University of Rochester/Thunderbird School of International Management

USEFUL TIPS

- Take advantage of MindBranch's free desktop tool, QuickLink. It helps centralize procurement and management of multiple report purchases, and you can avoid redundant purchases.
- Take advantage of the free help you can receive from MindBranch's research managers, and call them to learn more about research publications before you purchase.
- Carefully peruse the content of each report you want to purchase. If sections of it would meet your needs, purchase just those sections and avoid the higher cost of the entire report.
- When choosing between two services similar in content, base your decision on the customer service model that best suits your company.

ONESOURCE

ALTERNATE/PREVIOUS DATA SOURCE NAMES: OneSource Business Browser

SERVICE/PORTAL NAME: *http://www.onesource.com*

SOURCE DESCRIPTION: OneSource is just what the name implies: a one-stop shop for profile and background information on over 1.5 million large and midsized companies worldwide. This aggregation of different information sources is provided by OneSource Information Services, a publicly traded company on NASDAQ [ONES]. The company was actually started as a division of Lotus, the software company now owned by IBM, after Lotus bought Isys and Datext, two developers of CD-ROM information products. Lotus spun off the company in 1993, and it began the transition to online services in the mid- to late 1990s. In 1999 the company went public, purchased CorpTech, a popular directory of technology companies, and released the European version of its Business Browser. For the purposes of this review, I will focus on the edition of the Global Business Browser.

The OneSource Business Browser products are only available through the Web, but the company's CorpTech product is available as a stand-alone CD-ROM. In a move being widely adopted throughout the information provider industry, OneSource also makes the Business Browser available as an application programming interface (API) so that companies can incorporate OneSource content directly into their intranet and other enterprise applications.

OneSource is targeted toward business customers, especially those who need a quick way to obtain company profile information, such as sales and marketing executives. OneSource provides some industry information and some in-depth financial material, but it is primarily used to either obtain data on one specific company or to create a list of companies meeting certain criteria.

PRICING: OneSource is priced per user for unlimited usage—a subscription that includes all content with no additional charges. The cost is $5,800 for one user per quarter, or $21,000 for one year for one user. For ten users, the cost is $8,800 per quarter and $32,000 for one year.

SOURCE CONTENT: OneSource utilizes over thirty separate information partners, representing over twenty-five hundred content sources, to provide a comprehensive picture of and global businesses. The content includes financial filings, company profiles, trade publication articles, investment analyst reports, market research, biographies, stock quotes, and more. For the material it provides, OneSource does a good job of covering most of the major industries.

To obtain a more precise understanding of the scope of this resource, it helps to identify some of the data providers. Some of the more well-known information providers available through OneSource include Market Guide, Thomson Worldscope, Gale Publications, Dun & Bradstreet, Harris InfoSource, Investext, the *Financial Times,* COMTEX News Network, ProQuest, Freedonia, Euromonitor International, Marquis Who's Who, and EDGAR Online.

The fact that the content comes from all of these different information providers is primarily hidden from the end user, who need only be familiar with the OneSource Business Browser interface. All of the searching is done through a simple interface that allows the user to search for a specific company or industry profile and to find lists of companies, articles, or executives. This product also has an alert service and built-in tracking.

OneSource presents the content in a flexible way, and the user has many different options for using the product and for viewing and downloading information. The basic options include searching for company or industry profiles, finding lists of companies, articles, and executives that meet search criteria, and tracking specific information via e-mail.

Searching for company profiles by company name produces a list of all matching choices, which the user can choose from. Company searches can provide a plethora of information, including recent articles, analyst reports, market research, brief or in-depth profiles, financial filings, and much more. The industry profile search screen brings you to a page presenting overall industry categories and then to further breakdowns, grouped by SIC codes. The material might include market research, market share, analyst reports, and articles on industry trends. Choosing a specific company or industry brings up more detailed information, allowing the researcher to look for the exact kind of material required.

The other main section of the beginning search screen, besides the Tracking service, is the Find section. The Find All Companies and Find Public Companies functions allow the user to create lists of companies by specific search criteria, such as SIC code, geographical location, sales, and employee numbers (see Figure 4-36). The user can also search for topics and can narrow the search by News, Articles and Tables, Analyst Reports, or SEC Filings. This material can also be sorted by date. Finally, one can create a list of executives or directors using a combination of sources included in OneSource.

Reviewing the results of all of these various search options can be a bit daunting, but this is all the more reason to take the time to explore this product. Tables and graphs can be exported in Excel format, analysts' reports can be immediately saved or printed out in PDF format, and company profiles can easily be saved as HTML files or copied into a word-processing program or other desktop application. There are literally dozens of different ways to slice the information available through OneSource, and the researcher would be well advised to experiment with the different options to get the best results.

SOURCE EVALUATION: OneSource is an expensive product, but if used often and properly it could be worth the price. The trade publications and company profiles alone do not necessarily justify the price, but with the inclusion of investment analyst research, market research reports, financial filings, and other advanced content, the product provides high value for the price. Because it is a flat-rate, fixed-price source, the user does not have to worry about incurring costs while learning to use OneSource and can experiment with different search strategies to find the most effective way of using it.

Figure 4-36. OneSource/Global Business Browser Search Criteria for Creating Lists of Companies

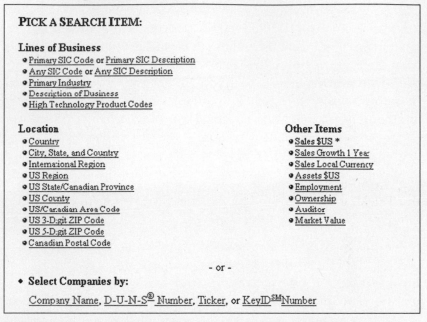

PICK A SEARCH ITEM:

Lines of Business
- Primary SIC Code or Primary SIC Description
- Any SIC Code or Any SIC Description
- Primary Industry
- Description of Business
- High Technology Product Codes

Location
- Country
- City, State, and Country
- International Region
- US Region
- US State/Canadian Province
- US County
- US/Canadian Area Code
- US 3-Digit ZIP Code
- US 5-Digit ZIP Code
- Canadian Postal Code

Other Items
- Sales $US *
- Sales Growth 1 Year
- Sales Local Currency
- Assets $US
- Employment
- Ownership
- Auditor
- Market Value

- or -

- **Select Companies by:**

  Company Name, D-U-N-S® Number, Ticker, or KeyID℠Number

Reprinted with the permission of OneSource Information Services, Inc.

Most of the data included in OneSource is very current, with the articles, financial filings, and other material updated daily. The user should be aware, however, that the investment analyst material is on a two-week delay and that, aside from the most recent three multipage reports, all of the investment analyst material consists of one- and two-page analyst reports. These brief reports often do not provide the depth of analysis needed for sound investment decisions, and for researchers in the venture capital community or other areas where timely investment analyst opinion is critical, the material provided in OneSource will not be sufficient. These researchers will still want to have a subscription to Investext, Multex Fundamentals (recently purchased by Reuters), or some other provider of current investment analyst research.

The excellent company coverage provided by OneSource includes the most comprehensive listing of U.S. technology companies on the market, the CorpTech Directory of Technology Companies. As a heavy user of CorpTech as a stand-alone product, I find it very useful to be able to search it alongside the company listings provided by the other vendors bundled into OneSource. The industry coverage in OneSource is also very thorough, and any researcher should be able to do a fair amount of competitive analysis using both the industry and company profiles.

The news, articles, and tables provided in OneSource are current and comprehensive, though certainly not as exhaustive as what the user might find in Factiva, LexisNexis, or Dialog. But this product is more than sufficient for current awareness and general literature searches. As OneSource continually adds new features and content partners, the coverage will only expand and we can expect to see OneSource eventually give the other "Big Three" aggregators a run for their money.

Compared broadly to similar aggregators of business information content, OneSource definitely is in the top rank of these products. It is difficult to make a straight comparison with other products because OneSource aggregates so many types of information sources that are not usually offered together. It may not include all of the trade publications available through Factiva, but the inclusion of analysts' reports and market research make it unique. OneSource does not have the depth of database selection available in Dialog or LexisNexis, but it offers the ability to search all of the included content at once rather than having to switch between databases. The inclusion of investment analyst reports from Investext and market research from Freedonia is a unique feature not available in many information aggregator products, and this is certainly one of the things that make OneSource stand out. It is also what makes this product a bit costly, and potential users should carefully evaluate their specific need for this type of material, as the news articles and company profiles may be available in other less-expensive sources.

The search functionality of this product seems very easy to understand, and new users should not have difficulty navigating through the product. The greatest challenge may lie in becoming familiar with all of the various types of content available through OneSource and understanding the best way to get at each type. The simple entry search page, with all of the options laid out clearly, is a pleasant change from the more complicated database interface in which the user has to know the names or numbers of the specific files desired.

The OneSource staff is available to help should the need arise, and the built-in **Help** link on each page takes the user to specific information for that section and appears to answer most, if not all, of the questions one might have.

Overall, I would recommend this product to researchers who do not need a great amount of specialized material in any specific industry but need to have a quick and efficient way to get background information on companies or industries. The price, while a bit steep, is justified if the product is used heavily and the researcher is fully aware of all of the available content.

SOURCE VALUE RATING: All of the data source reviewers were asked to rate each source on the basis of the following eight categories, using "10" as the highest rating and "1" as the lowest ("80" being a perfect score):

1. Relative cost-to-value:	8
2. Relative timeliness of data:	8
3. Relative comprehensiveness of data:	8
4. Ease of use:	10
5. Search options available:	9
6. Level of support services:	8
7. Level of training offered:	8
8. Amount/kinds of special services offered:	9
Total Rating:	68

SOURCE REVIEWS:

"OneSource—The Name Tells It Like It Is" [review]. *The Information Advisor* 13, no. 5 (May 2001). At the time the reviewers found that the product "covers many more companies, has more information providers, and is superior in its topic searching and its news and journal coverage" than other news aggregators in its category.

CONTRIBUTOR NAME: Samuel Werberg/Patricia A. Watkins
AFFILIATION: FIND/SVP, Inc./Thunderbird School of International Management

USEFUL TIPS

- Go through the source list and familiarize yourself with all of the different resources available through OneSource, especially sources that might be particularly relevant to your industry area or research needs.
- Use the Top Participants feature to create comprehensive lists of competitors based on sales, employees, or assets.

- Take advantage of the Market Share, Industry Norms, and Market Research features to get the most bang for your buck from OneSource.

PROFOUND

ALTERNATE/PREVIOUS DATA SOURCE NAMES: Dialog Profound

SERVICE/PORTAL NAME: Profound, also known as Dialog Profound, is a service of Dialog, a Thomson business. It can be accessed on the Web at *http://www.profound.com* or via the product listings on the Dialog Corporate Web site at *http://www.dialog.com*, and the UK version can be found at *http://www.profound.co.uk*. This discussion and evaluation was completed via the Web interface of *http://www.profound.com*.

SOURCE DESCRIPTION: Dialog is known as "the worldwide leader in providing online-based information services to organizations seeking competitive advantages in such fields as business, science, engineering, finance, and law." Dialog's Profound allows business professionals to track companies, regions, industries, products, and people worldwide. It allows users to analyze markets, track competitors, monitor product activities, identify emerging markets, and gather in-depth financial and investment data. Profound also offers a wide range of international market research reports.

PRICING: Profound may be especially well suited to nonprofessional searchers, as there are no searching or browsing fees. This means that you do not have the stress of watching your "connect time" while you search. When you find an article or report that you think is pertinent to your search, you are able to review the price before purchasing it. For market research reports, the table of contents for each report is available for viewing before purchasing, and the sections that contain your search terms are highlighted. This feature makes it easy to identify which sections are most relevant to your search and saves you money by allowing you to purchase them separately. Many sections are available at very reasonable prices. This is a great feature and is not always available in other database products. Newspaper and magazine articles, for example, are often available for purchase at $2.95 each. This is comparable to other online information providers such as Factiva, which also charges $2.95 per article.

SOURCE CONTENT: Although the evaluation section of this summary of Profound will focus primarily on the WorldSearch feature, I will also review all content areas available through the service.

Profound represents more than 750 industries in its diverse set of databases. Content is divided into three primary sections: World-Search, QuickSearch, and Briefings, with this latter section being further broken down into Market, Company, Investment, and Country Briefings. For easier access, the main page identifies these as six separate links.

- **WorldSearch.** Drilling down further into each of these sections, we find that WorldSearch contains (1) ResearchLine, with more than 130,000 market research reports from such companies as Frost & Sullivan, Datamonitor, EIU, and Euromonitor, (2) Dialog NewsRoom, with more than 7,500 sources of international news, trade, consumer, and scholarly publications, and (3) CountryLine, with information on overseas markets using economic, political, and social indicators.
- **QuickSearch.** The second major section, QuickSearch, contains (1) Company Information, with financial, product, and investment data on companies, searchable by region, industry, company, and numerous other factors, (2) Intellectual Property, offering international patent and trademark information, (3) Research & Development, with in-depth technical and scientific research covering a range of industries: Aerospace, Biosciences & Biotechnology, Chemical, Energy & Environment, Engineering, Food Science & Agriculture, Materials Science, Medical & Pharmaceutical, Medical Journals, Pharmaceutical Newsletters, and Scientific Articles, (4) North American Newspapers, with full-text U.S. and Canadian newspapers, searchable by region, and (5) TableBase, providing tabular data about businesses and markets around the world.
- **Briefings.** The third major section, Briefings, is further broken down into (1) Company Briefings, offering more than twelve thousand briefings and snapshots on companies, (2) Market Briefings, with more than six hundred briefings and snapshots from a multitude of industries, (3) Country Briefings, with more than one hundred briefings and snapshots on countries around the world, and (4) Investment Briefings, providing more than twelve thousand investment briefings from Market Guide.

SOURCE EVALUATION: A subscriber to Dialog Profound is provided full access to all of the content available through the service. In this section I will evaluate the product by four categories: content, searching, training and support, and administrative issues. This analysis will be followed by a more in-depth review of the World-Search section of the service.

- **Content.** Profound offers a wide range of business research, ranging from its market research reports to newspaper articles, and the sources of content are clearly identified. Also, when the timeliness of the content is a key issue, Profound describes how often the information is updated. For example, in the area of stock quotes, Profound provides details of how many minutes the information is delayed from sources such as the New York Stock Exchange. More in-depth information on sources and content can be found at the Web site *http://www.dialog.com/sources/sourcebook/additionalsources* and *http://www.dialog.com/sources.*

- **Searching.** The search interfaces within the various sections of Profound are easy to learn and use. The screens are intuitive and provide a number of search options. Novice searchers can use keywords or simply enter information into various well-labeled search boxes. Expert searchers can also choose to use more advanced Boolean search techniques.

  Searching is aided by a "behind the scenes" taxonomy called InfoSort. This indexing system, an integral part of Profound, helps direct searchers to either the preferred terms to use for improved retrieval or to broader, narrower, and other related terms that might prove useful in their search. A small magnifying-glass icon can be found next to the areas where the InfoSort thesaurus is available. For example, if a user enters the term *US* within the Locations search field of WorldSearch, then clicks on the magnifying glass icon to browse and then on Preferred Term, *USA* will be suggested as the indexing term to use for a more precise search.

- **Training and Support.** Profound offers an online demo (*http://www.dialog.com/products/profound/demo/movie.html*) that is an easy-to-follow tutorial and can be scrolled through at the user's own pace. It provides clear information on what the various sections can be used for and what information is included in each, and offers tips on how to search efficiently. *Fast Start for Dialog Profound,* a downloadable thirty-six-page PDF file (*http://training.dialog.com/sem_info/courses/pdf_sem/ fast_start_profound.pdf*), is designed to familiarize the new user with the basic features and content of Dialog Profound. Customer support is available by e-mail, online via the Web interface, and by telephone. Dialog also includes in-person training for Profound (among its many workshops held in various locations throughout the United States and around the world). In addition to these classes, a user may also be assigned a personal account manager for more customized support.

- **Administrative Issues.** In addition to being able to track searches via sub-accounts so that different projects can be tracked separately if necessary, users can also review a twenty-eight-day history of searches that have taken place. For example, one can review all reports and files accessed on any one day by simply using the Dossier feature and clicking on a specific day. It is also possible to review statements online so that you can see a record of daily and monthly expenses. These two features, Dossier and Statement, are great examples of good, customer-friendly product design. There are no extra charges for the use of these features.

Users also have the opportunity to edit preferences for many of these administrative functions. For example, if you do not want to see the price of a report or an article unless it exceeds a certain dollar value, you can select "Notify when price exceeds $ x"—then you will not be shown prices or asked to confirm when the dollar value is less than specified. Additional preferences available for editing include displays, default databases to search, and setting up customer sub-accounts. You can also create Alerts in Profound. The Alert feature allows you to set up automatic searches for a particular subject, to run either daily, weekly, or monthly. The resulting Alerts are then delivered via e-mail. The Alert Manager is the administrative function that allows a user to create, edit, or delete these Alerts.

WORLDSEARCH. The WorldSearch section of Profound provides a different set of information than that described in the Source Content section above. An example will help explain this feature. Let's say that a nonexpert searcher, a business professional, wants to gain some general information on the publishing industry, along with some potential details on trends or key players.

Figure 4-37 shows the main search screen for WorldSearch. Note that the Market Sector chosen is Publishing, the Database chosen is All, the Location chosen is USA, and under Free Text, the terms *trends* or *key players* have been entered. Although it is also possible for a user to be more specific and include more keywords, this example will illustrate how diverse the findings can be.

When the search button is pressed, the results are shown, categorized by the various databases selected (e.g., ResearchLine and NewsLine). If a database is found not to include any content for a particular search, this is noted by the phrase "No Titles Found." After reviewing the findings in this example, it is determined that there are many reports that might be of value for this research question. The user sees one report under ResearchLine that looks like a good source and clicks on the title link. The item

Figure 4-37. WorldSearch Search Screen (Publishing)

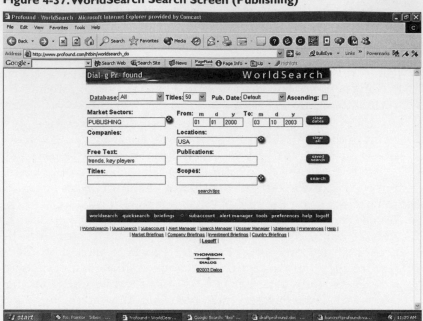

2003® Dialog, a Thomson business, *http://www.dialog.com*. Reprinted with permission of the publisher.

is titled "Book Publishers in the U.S.," the vendor is IBIS, and the date is November 2002. Clicking on the hyperlink reveals the table of contents screen shown in Figure 4-38. The screen continues down in this same manner, showing the table of contents in detailed categories with a price listed next to each section. The user can then elect to purchase an entire report or a subset of the report by clicking on the section. The title and price are shown again, and the user is asked to click on the "I accept" button. This feature is a wonderful double-check for the timid or beginning searcher and often comes in handy for an experienced searcher working at 1:00 a.m. with bleary eyes!

The entire report might be a bit expensive at $916, but sections of it are more reasonable. And there are likely to be many sections within this report that will be of use to our user, especially those under Industry Conditions, Industry Participants, and Industry Outlook, the latter of which is priced at $70.

Although some of the sources within Profound are available via other database aggregators, such as Factiva or LexisNexis, or even via their own Web site subscription (PR Newswire for example), this somewhat intuitive interface, along with the additional support of the downloadable manual and the online tutorial, provides good value for the price. It is especially nice to search without learning complicated search syntax, to have the prices so clearly identified, and to search without concern about connect time.

Figure 4-38. WorldSearch Table of Contents Screen

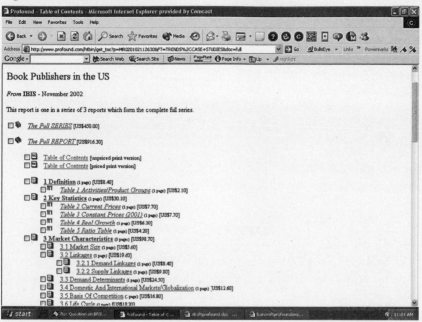

2003® Dialog, a Thomson business, *http://www.dialog.com.* Reprinted with permission of the publisher.

Client testimonials on Profound can be found in the About Profound section of the Web site. Among the positive features cited are "depth and breadth of information," "easy to use screens and search facilities," and "ability to narrow focus and not pay for entire reports." The fact that Profound has the Dialog name behind it also lends the product immediate credibility in the areas of authoritativeness, accuracy, and timeliness of sources.

SOURCE VALUE RATING: All of the data source reviewers were asked to rate each source on the basis of the following eight categories, using "10" as the highest rating and "1" as the lowest ("80" being a perfect score):

1. Relative cost-to-value:	9
2. Relative timeliness of data:	10
3. Relative comprehensiveness of data:	9
4. Ease of use:	9
5. Search options available:	9
6. Level of support services:	9
7. Level of training offered:	10
8. Amount/kinds of special services offered:	10
Total Rating:	75

CONTRIBUTOR NAME: Jan Knight
AFFILIATION: Bancroft Information Services

USEFUL TIPS

- Use the InfoSort Thesaurus to obtain additional potential search terms and to learn new terms used in an industry with which you are unfamiliar.
- Because searching is free, you should make good use of duplicate searches with varying keywords.
- Profound is a good starting point for industry, company, and market information.

REUTERS BUSINESS INSIGHT

SERVICE/PORTAL NAME: *http://www.reutersbusinessinsight.com*

SOURCE DESCRIPTION: Reuters Business Insight (RBI) is a joint project of the global news and financial services company Reuters and the market research firm Datamonitor. The service provides market research on consumer goods, health care, finance, and technology. RBI is targeted toward company executives, marketing professionals, business researchers, human resource managers, investors—basically anyone who needs a concise research report on an industry or trend in the four areas covered.

PRICING: Searching the RBI Web site is free; individual reports cost between \$1,140 and \$1,219. Subscriptions to the service may be purchased for specific industries, and costs vary with numbers of users, including global, enterprise-wide access. Subscriptions cost approximately \$3,000. Contact the company for more information and pricing levels.

SOURCE CONTENT: RBI is a source of market analysis with an emphasis on European, and especially, markets. The content of the reports is primary research by Datamonitor. The service sells reports both individually and by subscription (varying levels of access are available) from its Web site. Reports are delivered in electronic format instantly upon purchase, in the user's choice of HTML or PDF.

RBI provides a free-text search box; results can then be sorted by relevance or publication date. When a search is done on a major industry—banking, for example—RBI first searches titles and summaries and then offers the option of searching full text. At other times, RBI immediately performs a full-text search of the entire database. At present, there is no advanced search capability that would allow the user to specify search parameters manually. The site can be browsed by industry, and RBI says this capability will soon be enhanced to allow browsing by other criteria such as industry sub-sectors. The RBI home page features Recommended Reports, which makes suggestions based on the customer's subscription, stated interests, and past purchases. Reports in Reuters Business Insight are laid out in a clean, clear format that makes it easy to zero in on needed information. Important facts are highlighted in graphs and charts that present the essential information without overwhelming the user with overly detailed background data. The reports are comprehensive in scope and extensive—often two hundred pages or more in length. The content varies from topic to topic but is generally based upon some mixture of the following five features: (1) Introduction to the Industry and Key Issues, (2) Market Overview (market size, share, forecasts), (3) Distribution Channels, (4) Competitive Landscape, often including case studies or SWOT (strengths, weaknesses, opportunities, and threats) analyses of key players, and (5) Strategy. RBI reports usually contain some guidance on how to take advantage of emerging industry trends.

RBI is divided into five broad industries:

1. **Consumer Goods.** This category is concerned primarily with food and beverages but also includes cosmetics, electronic commerce, and retailing in general.

2. **Energy.** This category covers the traditional utilities of gas, oil, water, and electricity, but it also includes emerging technologies such as fuel cells and renewable resources ("green energy").

3. **Finance.** Financial services such as banking, investment management, and insurance are included here. This section is especially strong in the areas of e-banking and issues surrounding the euro.

4. **Health Care.** This category mainly covers pharmaceuticals, with special emphasis on cancer, cardiovascular, and central nervous system drugs.

5. **Technology.** This category includes reports on telecommunications, networks, call centers, electronic commerce (including financial services), and customer relationship management (CRM) systems.

SOURCE EVALUATION: RBI provides clear, current reports that are simultaneously comprehensive and concise. It is an especially valuable resource for firms that need market information on the UK and Europe; those firms would do well to consider subscriptions to industries of interest. Other users will find individual purchases to be sufficient. Several dozen new reports are published in RBI each year.

Quality market analysis is expensive to produce, a fact that is always reflected in the price of market research reports, regardless of producer. However, a search of an aggregator such as MarketResearch.com reveals that Reuters Business Insight reports are priced competitively.

Searching is an area where the database could be improved. The ability to perform Boolean searches (using AND, OR, NOT) or to limit searches to specific sections of documents would be a valuable enhancement. On the other hand, many customers will be interested in one specific industry or even an industry subsector, and so will not need sophisticated searching; browsing will work just as well for those researchers. Technical support and training are provided free of charge, from 9:00 a.m. to 5:00 p.m., Monday through Friday, Eastern time.

SOURCE VALUE RATING: All of the data source reviewers were asked to rate each source on the basis of the following eight categories, sing "10" as the highest rating and "1" as the lowest ("80" being a perfect score):

1. Relative cost-to-value:	7
2. Relative timeliness of data:	6
3. Relative comprehensiveness of data:	7
4. Ease of use:	8
5. Search options available:	5
6. Level of support services:	9
7. Level of training offered:	9
8. Amount/kinds of special services offered:	7
Total Rating:	58

SOURCE REVIEWS:

Hurst, Susan. "Reuters Business Insight." *Library Journal* 126, no. 13 (August 2001): 178.

CONTRIBUTOR NAME: Wes Edens/Patricia A. Watkins

AFFILIATION: Thunderbird School of International Management

USEFUL TIPS

- Try both British and American spelling; for example, try separate searches for *centre* and *center*.
- Enclose phrases in quotes when searching. For example: *"call centres"* will retrieve documents containing the entire phrase.
- Download a free table of contents, brochure, and press release before buying a report.

THOMSON RESEARCH

ALTERNATE/PREVIOUS DATA SOURCE NAMES: Disclosure Global Access, G.A Pro, Disclosure's Compact D/SEC, Worldscope, Laser D, Piranha, Investext, Research Bank Web, Industry Insider, I/B/E/S, Business & Industry, Business & Management Practices, TableBase, Extel Cards, MarkIntel, First Call Meeting Notes, and UK Regulatory News Service

SERVICE/PORTAL NAME: *http://research.thomsonib.com*

SOURCE DESCRIPTION: Thomson Research provides access to financial data from and foreign exchange filings, news/periodical articles on companies and industries, and investment and marketing reports. Marketing research reports are listed and available only on a pay-as-you-use basis; all the other data and reports are available in full-text format.

The major strength of this huge dataset of over 6 million documents, including 3.2 million research reports from twelve different databases, is its coverage of full-text financial filings (SEC filings and equivalent foreign filings) and its reports built from the data in these filings. In addition, it integrates information from Investext, MarkIntel, I/B/E/S, and periodical articles to provide more comprehensive information on companies and industries.

Much of the data is presented in image format including color annual reports, prospectuses, and circulars. Thomson Extel cards are presented in both HTML and PDF formats. SEC EDGAR filings are in HTML. This database is designed for research professionals and analysts at investment banks and at law, accounting, and consulting firms. It is used in corporations and university libraries. Researchers familiar with corporate research will recognize Thomson Research as the newest reiteration of Global Access.

The product available to academic libraries differs somewhat from that available to commercial/corporate libraries. Academic subscribers will see little difference between Global Access and Thomson Research except that the latter offers color and faster downloading of Adobe files. Commercial subscribers benefit from the integration of the research reports and periodical articles into the product. The periodical indexing/abstracting/full-text databases are also omitted from the academic version.

The history of this database goes back to the 1970s, when Disclosure produced microfiche copies of annual reports and SEC filings (10-Ks, 10-Qs, proxies, prospectuses) for U.S. publicly owned companies. Many corporate and academic business libraries stopped building print collections of these reports and began relying on Disclosure's microfiche at that time. About 1986 Disclosure designed a PC-based product that dramatically changed corporate research by extracting the most important financial and text data in the filings and placing it in a searchable database called Compact Disclosure (later named Compact D/SEC and Compact D/Worldscope). This product was so innovative that it was actually introduced before most librarians had access to departmental PCs, let alone desktop PCs; users were still using dumb terminals to do online searches. Compact Disclosure revolutionized corporate research, and every major business library quickly adopted it as a basic database subscription.

In 1988 Disclosure introduced Laser D, a CD-ROM product with full-text filings that caused another major change in corporation research. Soon after Disclosure was purchased by Primark, which took another step in the development of computer-based corporate research when it launched Piranha, integrating financial databases into a single delivery platform. Searchers could screen for specific companies and produce tables of the results. In addition they could integrate their own data into the tables or use any of the portfolios of predesigned reports available. All this could then be analyzed in spreadsheet software such as Microsoft Excel.

In mid-2000 Thomson acquired Primark Corporation and then rolled out Piranha Web, a Web-based program that allowed searching and screening across Primark's financial databases. Thomson Research was the natural next step in the development of corporate research products. Thomson Analytics is the replacement for Piranha. Subscribers can purchase either or both files. (This review is focused on Thomson Research, not Thomson Analytics.)

PRICING: Thomson Research is a high-priced research tool. Pricing is based on which database subfiles the customer chooses to buy, and commercial/corporate subscribers will pay between $55,000 and $60,000 annually. If the price seems high compared to expected usage, there is an option to pay as you go. To subscribe this way, a corporation would pay $2,500 for access and then pay for each report as needed. A 20 percent discount on reports is included with the access fee. Academic library subscription prices are between $30,000 and $42,000 annually, depending on the number of simultaneous users and full-time enrollment figures for the school. IP filtering is available for academic subscriptions. There is an additional subscription fee for Thomson Analytics.

SOURCE CONTENT: For each company the following seven types of data are available: Content Profile, Filings, Overview Reports, Research, News, Ownership, Financials, and Stock Graph, and these are described below:

1. **Content Profile** provides an outline and extensive list of documents available on the company, with hotlinks to each report. As soon as users log into Thomson Research, they are dropped

into the Content Profile of Thomson Corp. as a sample company and to show the type of the data available. To change the company listed, one can do a Quick Company Search via a window on the far left. From there searchers can link to Filings, Insider Analytics, Price and Earnings Data, Overview Reports, Research Reports, Spreadsheet Financials, and News.

Figure 4-39. Sample Thomson Research Content Profile Page

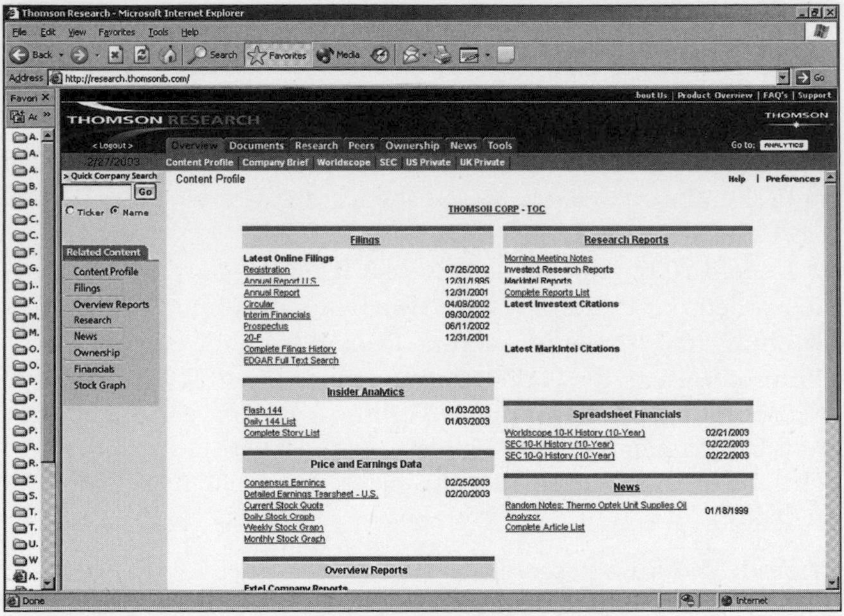

Reprinted with the permission of Thomson Financial Networks.

2. **Filings** includes hotlinks to Registrations, Annual Reports, 10-Ks, 10-Qs, Circulars, Interim Financials, Prospectuses, 20-F filings, and so on as well as an indexing of paper reports back to 1968. These documents are the source for financial data for investors. The annual report, the company's report sent to investors, is written for the nonprofessional. It can be used to see the style or corporate culture of a company, but it also has detailed and audited financial data.

3. **Overview Reports** in Thomson Research are Extel, Worldscope, SEC Reports, Price and Earnings Data, and Dun & Bradstreet Reports. These are all reports generated from the data in the financial filings, or I/B/I/S, with data in each report selected to target specific information needs. For example, the Worldscope Reports provide financial tear sheets, peer analysis, and industry reports. The SEC Reports provide annual or quarterly financials, ratios, and lists of direc-

Figure 4-40. The Overview Reports Option in Thomson Research

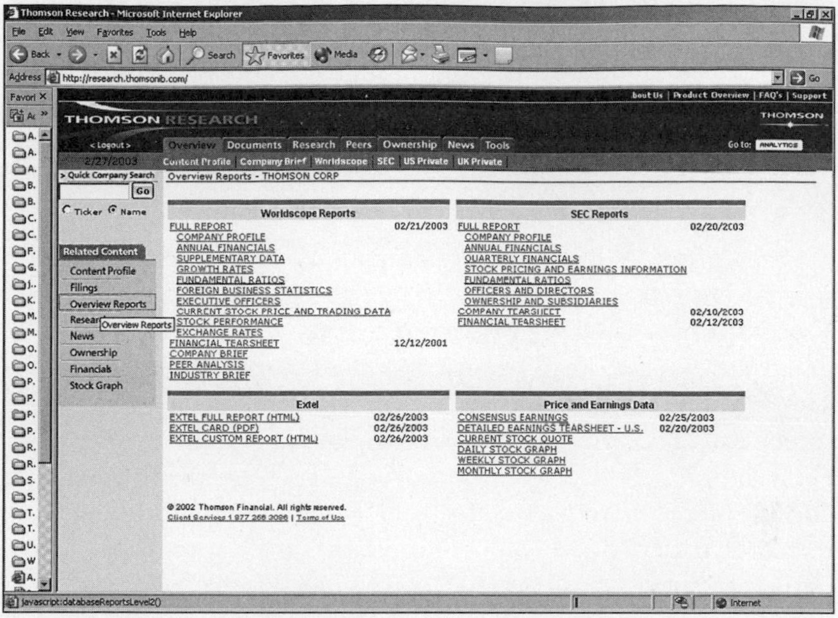

Reprinted with the permission of Thomson Financial Networks.

tors and subsidiaries. Price and Earnings Data give consensus earnings, a tear sheet of detailed earnings, current stock quotes, and daily, weekly, and monthly stock graphs.

4. **News** links users to the articles indexed in Business & Industry, Business and Management Practices, and TableBase. The first two databases are standard periodical index/abstracting/full-text tools. TableBase is somewhat unique in that it indexes and provides full text of the tables and charts inside of articles, making it easy to locate such things as market shares and rankings of companies.

5. **Research** reports include the Morning Meeting Notes, Investext Research Reports, Industry Insider, and MarkIntel Reports. Investext reports are from brokerage analysts and give lengthy advisory reports for investors on companies and industries. The Industry Insider database provides trade association reports, which are available on a pay-as-you-go basis (the full text is not included without charge with a basic subscription). MarkIntel reports are from investment banks, brokerage houses, market research firms, and trade associations and can be used for market research and topics such as company market share, industry trends, forecasts, and new product/new service markets.

6. **Ownership** provides access to information in newswires and the 3, 4, 5, or 144 filings on insider ownership (these are filings that 10 percent owners and others with inside information such as members of the board, relatives, and so on must make with the SEC every time they offer to sell, sell, or buy shares).

7. **Financials** provide preformatted tables of financial data from the current or historic 10-Ks, 10-Qs, or proxy filings.

8. **Stock Graph** provides graphs of a stock's activity.

Searching the databases is done via the tabs at the top of the screen: Overview, Documents, Research, Peers, Ownership, and News. These tabs expand out into further choices; for example, Overview expands into Company Brief, Worldscope, Peers, Private, and UK Private. Each of these brings up a different search screen with a custom-built search template to match that database. For example, the Company Brief search screen provides search choices by company name, ticker or CUSIP (Committee for Uniform Securities Identification Procedures) code, and SIC (Standard Industrial Classification) code. The Worldscope and SEC search screens provide additional search parameters such as fiscal year, net income, total assets, net sales, market capitalization, and P/E (price over earnings) ratio. Results of searches can be sorted by company name, ticker, exchange, state, and country.

The other search buttons also provide extended search options. Of note is the EDGAR Free Text option, which allows searching for any word within EDGAR documents. By searching within the Ownership tab, you can retrieve ownership information from newswires or 3, 4, 5, or 144 filings. The Holdings Common search button will retrieve a table of insiders with the position, transaction date, direct holdings, indirect holdings, total common holdings, and the holding source. Searching in the Peer section brings up a "Price Performance – 36 months" chart and a "1 Yr Sales Growth" chart for the major competitors of a company. It also retrieves a table of peer companies, including sales, net income, total assets, total liabilities, and various key ratios for competitors. Searches can also retrieve Industry Briefs with similar information.

Search functions are one of the strengths of the Thomson Research database. Simple and quick searches by company names and advanced searches are both available, and searches can be saved. Printing and downloading capacities are available, in image format, HTML, and page prints. Preformatted reports, full-text filings, and templates for selected data make printing and downloading easy. Adobe files download three times faster than they did in Global Access. ARS reports and other reports and graphs can be printed in color. Charts can be easily downloaded into Microsoft spreadsheets. Currently the downloading function for charts works best in Netscape. (See Useful Tips below.)

SOURCE EVALUATION: Overall, Thomson Research is a welcome expansion of Global Access, which has been recognized as a major research tool for finance and investment professionals. The data is very timely and updated daily. It covers all companies filing with the SEC (about twelve thousand) and a large number of international companies (about sixteen thousand), and it allows researchers to search for companies and analyze the data in spreadsheet form. For the commercial/corporate subscriber, Thomson Research integrates additional research reports and articles into the company research process. For the academic subscriber, it provides one major enhancement: faster downloading of image files. It is an essential database for anyone doing corporate research.

Mergent Online is a major, but less expensive, competitor to Thomson Research. Like Thomson Research, it provides full-text ARSs and SEC filings. Other competitors are Factiva and Hoover's. Mergent is the only competitor that approaches the screening features of Thomson Research. Even though we have all these choices in our library, our researchers still demand Thomson Research.

The arrangement of the databases in Thomson Research is generally logical and useful. However, I find that first-time users are confused by the fact that the program opens with a sample company. This seems to be the only database we have that does this when users are expecting a blank search template. It is also confusing that the names on the search tabs that run across the top of the screen seem to parallel some, but not all, of the Related Content buttons in the left window, which bring up a list of the documents available for the specific company. The response time is irritatingly slow, and the help screens do not tell you anything you could not have figured out from the screen. Expanded help is available under Help – View More Help, but this is hard to find.

SOURCE VALUE RATING: All of the data source reviewers were asked to rate each source on the basis of the following eight categories, using "10" as the highest rating and "1" as the lowest ("80" being a perfect score):

1. Relative cost-to-value:	5
2. Relative timeliness of data:	10
3. Relative comprehensiveness of data:	10
4. Ease of use:	7
5. Search options available:	8
6. Level of support services:	6
7. Level of training offered:	5
8. Amount/kinds of special services offered:	8
Total Rating:	59

SOURCE REVIEWS:

Quint, Barbara. "Thomson Financial Launches Thomson Research Web. *Information Today* 19, no. 9 (October 2002): 1, 30.

CONTRIBUTOR NAME: Judith M. Nixon/Patricia A. Watkins

AFFILIATION: Purdue University/Thunderbird School of International Management

USEFUL TIPS

- Thomson Research works best with Internet Explorer.
- Image comprehension software, which speeds up the downloading of image files, needs to be set up. To do this, log on as Administrator and set preferences for Image Compression Software.
- Downloading of spreadsheets in Thomson Research works best with Netscape. IE users will need to set their browser to open separate windows. To do this open Windows Explorer and go to Tools/Folder Options/File Types. Then choose Microsoft Excel Worksheet, click on the Advance button, and uncheck Browser in Same Window.

ABI/INFORM

SERVICE/PORTAL NAME: *http://www.proquest.com*; *http://www.il. proquest.com*

SOURCE DESCRIPTION: ABI/Inform began in 1971 when three graduate students at Portland State University were charged with designing a system that would improve corporate access to business literature. Inspired by the information service developed at a local power company and with contributions from a University of Wisconsin database project called Inform, the students succeeded in developing their system. After graduation they founded a small company that merged their new brand, ABI (Abstracted Business Information) with the Wisconsin database name, Inform, and ABI/Inform was born. The product generated minimal interest and profits until a Kentucky newspaper owner purchased it in 1973 and made the file available in Dialog. Initially, documents were in abstract-only form. But full-text records were added in 1991, making the product a forerunner among document delivery services for full-text information. After a bitter family argument, the Kentucky media giants sold ABI/Inform to UMI (University Microfilms) in 1986.

ABI/Inform supplies journal articles and abstracts of articles that contain business and management content. The database covers 1,116 periodicals (including a small number of business newspapers such as *Barron's*), of which 65 percent provide their articles in full text. ABI is known for providing more extensive archival information than its competitors; some retrospective articles date back to 1971. The average date span covers the past ten years.

ABI/Inform targets all environments that depend on business information—academic, corporate, and public. Because the service provides prolific amounts of business literature and can be expensive (depending on the institution size, number of users, and subscription details), most subscribers are larger, research-oriented organizations. Broad topical coverage includes business conditions and trends, management techniques, corporate strategies, and industry information on both a domestic and global level.

Aside from the ProQuest portal, ABI/Inform content may be accessed through any of the following products: Dialog (*http://www.dialog.com*), Ovid/Silverplatter (*http://www.ovid.com*), OCLC/FirstSearch (*http://www.oclc.org*), and the corporate version of LexisNexis (*http://www.lexis-nexis.com*).

PRICING: An annual subscription to ABI/Inform ranges from $6,000 to approximately $75,000.

Source Content: This section describes the content and related features of ABI/Inform under the following five categories:

1. **Origin of Information.** ABI/Inform does not create its content; rather, it gathers content created by others and provides the search engine and indexing that allows the information to be searchable. Journal aggregators such as ABI/Inform are evaluated on both the volume and quality of the incorporated publications and the effectiveness of the search engine.

2. **Navigation.** Six features are presented on the top horizontal navigation bar: Collections, Search Methods, Topic Finder, Browse Lists, Results & Marked List, and Search Guide. The key to searching ABI/Inform lies in understanding how to successfully use the search tools. The Search Methods button is the researcher's primary instrument. From Search Methods, the researcher has five different options, allowing for a range of searching styles—from "quick and dirty" searching in the Basic module to precision level in the Guided module.

3. **Search Methods.** The Basic search contains four drop boxes and three check-box options for fine-tuning a search. The search box allows for keyword searching of an article. The user is guided to fill in the box with a word, words, or specific phrase. The user next specifies a date range by choosing Current (1999–Present), Backfile (1986–1998), or Deep Backfile (Prior to 1986); the default is Current. For Publication Type, the user is prompted to choose All, Periodicals, or Newspapers; the default is All. Identifying whether the keywords should search just the citations and abstracts or the entire article text is the next step; the default is Citations and Abstracts. The searcher can further limit the results by clicking on a check box to turn on three different options: show results with full-text availability only, show articles from peer-reviewed publications only, and a more unusual limiter, or show total number of articles. Most journal aggregators automatically provide the total number of hits somewhere on the results pages. It is unusual that ABI/Inform does not. The searcher may turn on this feature by clicking a box.

   For the researcher requiring more defined searching options, there are advantages to using the other four search tools. The Guided search is geared toward precision searching. Whereas the basic engine is useful for "free searching"—looking for general research ideas—Guided search is best for the user with a citation in–hand: someone who already knows the article title or author. This tool allows for limiting by Article Type. For example, it is possible to narrow a search to editorials, cover stories, or interviews. Customizing the search to a specific company or geographic area is also possible.

The Advanced Word search page is arranged with the basic search interfaces on the top half and the Search Guide as the bottom half. It presents a method of searching various codes, a thesaurus, a hierarchical map of terms, and other tools that will encourage the user to choose search terms based on the way the indexing has been set up. The idea is to show how the categories and subcategories of subjects are arranged, so that the user will understand the logic and make better keyword and subject choices and hence receive better search results. Two features show how to search ABI/Inform using code numbers instead of words. Guides that offer information on connection operators (AND, NOT, etc.), stop words (ignored words such as "a," "the," etc.), and truncation techniques are also included.

Natural Language allows the user to search ABI/Inform in a conversational style. That is, you can ask the database a question, much as in the Internet-based search engine Ask Jeeves (*http://www.askjeeves.com*). The results list shows red graphic "stars" next to each article to indicate relevance.

With the Publication search tool, the researcher types the title of the desired journal into a search box. If the journal is part of the ABI/Inform database, a page of links appears, each link representing a volume/issue. When the user clicks on a link, the table of contents and list of articles for that particular volume are displayed. The user cannot perform a keyword search of a particular volume in this search module, but such a keyword search for a particular journal can be done in the Guided Search mode.

4. **Highlights of Other Web Features.**The Topic Finder offers an alternative to the "keywords-and-search-box" style of article searching. With Topic Finder, a hierarchy of hyperlinked business-related topics and subtopics are presented. The interface initially shows six main topic areas: Business & Industry, Computers & Internet, Economics & Trade, Environment, Government & Law, and Social Issues & Policy . When the user clicks on one of these, another group of hyperlinked subtopics appear. After clicking on a subtopic, the user gets a selection of article links to choose from.

Browse Lists offers a straight list of A–Z terms that are a combination of subjects, people, places, and companies. Under each term is a link prompting the user to use the View Articles link. Many of the terms also have a Narrow by Related Terms link. The user may either click hyperlinked alphabetical letters or enter a word in the search box to navigate through the list of terms.

The Results and Marked List button offers three features: Marked List & Durable Links, Results List, and Recent Searches. Marked List & Durable Links is a tool for managing saved articles. This section presents the user with the check-marked "favorite" articles that were selected. The user has the option of saving the durable link to the article by clicking the Export button. The user may then cut and paste the link as a URL into a browser and the article will be available for perusal for one month. Printing the article is also an option. Whether an article contains the abstract or full text of an article is indicated by icons of a camera or a sheet of paper, respectively. The words "abstract" and "full text" do not appear. This might be confusing to a researcher who doesn't understand the icons.

Also of note is a new tool called ProQuest SiteBuilder. This tool makes ABI/Inform articles available on third-party Web sites. Results List and Recent Searches are the article list result page of the latest search and a list of all the current session's executed search strings.

5. **Special Services and Competitor Comparison.** In addition to offering ProQuest SiteBuilder, ABI/Inform has other changes in the works. ABI/Inform's Archive Database is a recent addition, offering historical back-file content of twenty-fivebusiness periodicals, with coverage dates beginning in the early twentieth century. The back file includes image access, which allows viewing of advertisements from decades past. One of the newer features is the integration of Hoover's company profiles, although I was unable to access these from my portal.

A simple search of ABI and its main competitor, Business Source Premier, indicates a significant difference in the number and relevance of article results. Using the basic-level search option in Business Source Premier and ABI/Inform, I executed a search for the phrase *small business* among all articles published in 2002. I received 35 results using ABI/Inform and 116 using Business Source Premier. ABI/Inform results are more exact, according to the company's literature, because the articles are indexed with a high level of detail. This style of indexing, combined with an effective controlled vocabulary, culminates in what ABI brands "relevance bias." ABI/Inform indexes some unique fields such as article type, geographic name, classification code, personal name, headnote, and document column head.

SOURCE EVALUATION: If your organization is interested in purchasing the "Rolls Royce" of business journal databases, ABI/Inform is the database for you. ABI/Inform offers precision searching, daily data updates, superior technical service, useful archival content, and tools, such as the ProQuest SiteBuilder, that respond to the changing technological needs of its customers. The tools are arranged logically under main buttons, allowing the user to quickly identify the location of features.

Depending upon the type of institution and needs of its users, all environments may not need the high-powered features of ABI/Inform. ABI offers superior indexing and a search engine with more options than its competitors, but it comes at a price. A general cost analysis for a mid-to-large-sized academic institution suggests that an annual subscription price of ABI/Inform costs 35–45 percent more than a similar contract with EBSCO's Business Source Premier. Aside from being more economical, Business Source Premier offers a less complicated interface and easier-to-use, albeit less effective, search tools. In addition, it provides access to more full-text journals: 2,800 compared with ABI/Inform's 1,116. Keep in mind that "more" might not always mean "better." Looking through a specific crop of the best business journals could make for a better search pool than choosing from a larger unrefined group of irrelevant journals.

SOURCE VALUE RATING: All of the data source reviewers were asked to rate each source on the basis of the following eight categories, sing "10" as the highest rating and "1" as the lowest ("80" being a perfect score):

I. Relative cost-to-value:	6
2. Relative timeliness of data:	10
3. Relative comprehensiveness of data:	7
4. Ease of use:	10
5. Search options available:	10
6. Level of support services:	8
7. Level of training offered:	8
8. Amount/kinds of special services offered:	10
Total Rating:	69

SOURCE REVIEWS:

Chapman, K. "Full-Text Database Support for Scholarly Research in Finance." *Journal of Business & Finance Librarianship* 7 (2002): 35–44. Compares three business journal databases—ABI/Inform, Business Source Premier, and General BusinessFile—to determine the quality of finance coverage in the content. ABI/Inform is the writer's pick, providing the most comprehensive coverage with 76 percent of the articles, 35.9 percent of which are full text.

O'Leary, Mick. "Big Databases Pose Big Questions." *Online* May 25, 2001: 82–86. Comparison and review of "mega databases" created by Gale Group, ProQuest, EBSCO, and LexisNexis. This article argues that quantity does not guarantee quality. The author writes about "jumbo-sized" databases that are too big and costly. The source mentions ABI's focus on archived information.

CONTRIBUTOR NAME: Jen Venable/Patricia A. Watkins
AFFILIATION: Purdue University/Thunderbird School of International Management

USEFUL TIPS

- Use the Basic search module when executing keyword and subject searches.
- Use the Guided search module when you know the publication title, author, or article title.
- Use the Publication search module when you are interested in browsing a particular journal volume.

BUSINESS & INDUSTRY

ALTERNATE/PREVIOUS DATA SOURCE NAMES: Business & Industry News

SERVICE/PORTAL NAME: *http://rdsweb1.rdsinc.com/*

SOURCE DESCRIPTION: Business & Industry was originally produced by Responsive Data Services, Inc., as Business & Industry News and is now owned by Gale Group. Business & Industry is a full-text article database with multi-industry and international coverage. Content consists of over one thousand trade and business journals, industry newsletters, and regional, national, and international publications. The database has strong coverage of companies, industries, products, and demographic markets, ranging from July 1994 to the present.

As shown in Table 4-14, Business & Industry is available from a variety of sources:

Table 4-14. Business & Industry Access and Pricing

SOURCE*	PRICING INFORMATION
Gale Group, through the RDS Web interface	Single user: $6,300 Simultaneous users: Contact Gale Group for more information.
Dialog, File 9 (*http://www.dialog.com*)	Cost per DialUnit: $5.40 Cost per minute: $1.33 Format 2: $1.40 Format 9: $3.40
Alacra (*http://www.alacra.com*)	Access fee of $350 for up to five users provides access to the premium databases. Fee varies based on number of users. Cost per article: $3.50
ChemWeb (*http://www.chemweb.com*)	Pay per view: $5.00 One-month subscription: $400.00

* Business & Industry is also available through OCLC FirstSearch and LexisNexis.

SOURCE CONTENT: The Business & Industry database includes articles from over one thousand national and international sources, including business magazines, trade journals, international newspapers, and industry newsletters. Business & Industry claims that over 75 percent of the articles are available in full-text format, and that 50 percent of the articles cover global issues and events. The Business & Industry publication list includes many industry-specific trade publications and regional and international business publications that track and analyze the activities of markets and companies.

Available companion databases to Business & Industry are Business & Management Practices (featuring management practices articles) and TableBase (featuring data and statistical tables).

There is no choice between advanced and beginner search modes in the Gale interface. Instead, the search screen provides access to all of the search options for simple or complicated searches, including a wide variety of search options. Of particular note is the "Must Contain Table" check box near the Document Type window, which allows for filtering to articles with tables, thus facilitating access to statistical data that would otherwise be difficult to track down (see Figure 4-41). Also available is a separate text box for searching company names.

The drop-down menus provide browsing access to the index terms used to classify each article. Sample terms in the drop-down menus include:

- *Concept Terms.* African American Market, Corporate Strategy, Industry Overview, Trends
- *Marketing Terms.* Brand Equity, Corporate Advertising, Loyalty, Premium-Luxury Products
- *Industry Terms.* Apparel, Fast Foods, Industrial Industry, Trucking

Here is a sample of how this information is presented for a given article on market information:

Concept Terms: All market information; Sales

Geographic Area: North America(NOAX); United States (USA)

Industry Names: Food

Marketing Terms: All product marketing; Distribution channels

Product Names: Food and kindred products(200000); Beverages (208000)

These standard classifications can be found at the bottom of every article. Searching is greatly enhanced with this clear information on how the article was classified, which can lead a searcher to other related topics or terms. Together, the strong international content and the convenient drop-down menus provide a powerful search capacity that best serves marketing, advertising, and product research. In addition, the citation in a Business & Industry results page consists of an "enhanced" title at the top of the citation, written by Gale staff, that provides a brief summary of the article. The enhanced title is much more informative than the actual title.

Figure 4-41. Business & Industry Interface and Search Menu

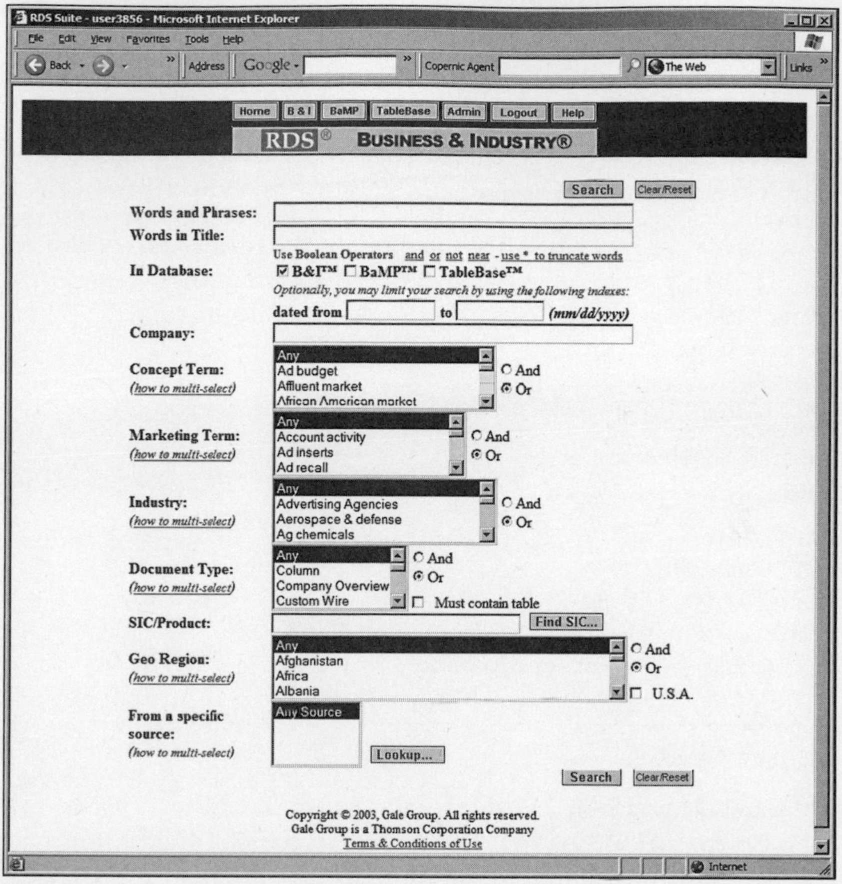

Reprinted with the permission of Gale Group.

SOURCE EVALUATION: Business & Industry's is a valuable article database. Its greatest value lies in its ability to provide data related to products, market information, and company/industry activities. The search interface provides a variety of search options. The content is strong across products, industries, and countries. This makes it an effective database for market share information, rankings, and international coverage of companies and products.

Some issues to be concerned with Business & Industry include the timeliness of articles. Also, the results screens tend to be a bit cluttered, with tightly packed table cells. It would help to have more specific information on the coverage of each journal within the database; source list information is available from the Gale Group site.

Even so, Business & Industry is a solid article database that does not hide layers of access behind beginner or advanced search options. Succinct and visual help is available to improve your ability to search the database, and hands-on training is available from a Gale Group representative. Business & Industry supplies researchers with a powerful and easy-to-use article database with solid coverage of markets and companies.

SOURCE VALUE RATING: All of the data source reviewers were asked to rate each source on the basis of the following eight categories, using "10" as the highest rating and "1" as the lowest ("80" being a perfect score):

1. Relative cost-to-value:	7
2. Relative timeliness of data:	6
3. Relative comprehensiveness of data:	8
4. Ease of use:	8
5. Search options available:	8
6. Level of support services:	7
7. Level of training offered:	8
8. Amount/kinds of special services offered:	6
Total Rating:	58

SOURCE REVIEWS:

Bates, Mary Ellen. "Business & Industry Database." *Database* 19 (Feb/March 1996): 112.

"Responsive Data Services Launches Business & Industry on the Web." *Information*Today 14, no. 9 (Oct. 1997): 43.

CONTRIBUTOR NAME: Hal P. Kirkwood, Jr./Patricia A. Watkins
AFFILIATION: Purdue University/Thunderbird School of International Management

USEFUL TIPS

- Before starting a search on Business & Industry, skim through the Concept and Market Term menus to determine if there are any relevant terms to include in your search.
- Use the many search options to create a more targeted search.
- If you are looking for numbers/statistics, select the "Must Have Table" option.

DATAMONITOR MARKET RESEARCH

SERVICE/PORTAL NAME: *http://www.dialogweb.com* (File 761)

SOURCE DESCRIPTION: Datamonitor is a collection of full-text reports from a specialized team of industry experts. The reports are based on primary research, including exclusive surveys, consumer panels, and in-depth trade interviews. The reports cover products, pricing, market share, competitors, and other relevant industry issues. The scope of coverage is international.

PRICING: Datamonitor Market Research is available on DialogWeb. The cost per DialUnit is $5.80, and the cost per minute is $1.67. For Format 2 the price is $2.70 and Format 5 is $26.65/section. The cost per report is $201–$300 (DialogWeb estimates).

SOURCE CONTENT: Datamonitor reports fall into these eleven general categories:

- Automotive and Transport
- Chemicals
- Consumer
- Energy and Utilities
- Financial Services
- General Business
- Health Care
- Media
- Packaging
- Retail
- Technology

The information is based on analysis by a group of industry experts. Primary research is conducted to write the research report, involving surveys, competitive analysis, and in-depth interviews. Datamonitor charges thousands of dollars for the complete reports. With user registration (which is free), the Datamonitor Web site provides access to an overview and a detailed product brochure of each report. These summary reports provide more than adequate information for determining whether or not to purchase the report.

The reports contain specific information on issues driving the industry as well as trends to watch for. A segmentation of the industry is provided, covering the unique aspects of the relevant market. DialogWeb displays each section separately, as well as the whole report. In-depth company profiles are also included within the report. Numerous tables and datasets are included to support the analysis. Many of the reports include three-year forecasts for the industry.

The DialogWeb interface allows searches by keyword, country name, industry description, publication date, section name, and several other fields. It is also possible to limit to U.S. or non-U.S. focus within the reports. DialogWeb also allows a browsing feature for the above-listed search fields.

SOURCE EVALUATION: Datamonitor reports appear to be rich resources for market, product, and company information. The information is especially useful because it is unique and based on primary research. This warrants the high cost, which is for this type of market research report. Because of the high cost of these reports, using the preliminary and summary information available on the Datamonitor site is strongly recommended to ensure you are purchasing a useful report.

SOURCE VALUE RATING: All of the data source reviewers were asked to rate each source on the basis of the following eight categories, sing "10" as the highest rating and "1" as the lowest ("80" being a perfect score):

1. Relative cost-to-value:	7
2. Relative timeliness of data:	6
3. Relative comprehensiveness of data:	9
4. Ease of use:	8
5. Search options available:	6
6. Level of support services:	6
7. Level of training offered:	5
8. Amount/kinds of special services offered:	5
Total Rating:	52

SOURCE REVIEWS:

Bates, Mary Ellen. "Finding Full-Text Market Research." *Database* 16, no. 4 (August 1993): 30 (7 pages).

CONTRIBUTOR NAME: Hal P. Kirkwood, Jr./Patricia A. Watkins
AFFILIATION: Purdue University/Thunderbird School of International Management

USEFUL TIPS

- Use the abstract format types in DialogWeb or the summaries on the Datamonitor Web site to review the content of the report before paying for it.
- Search on very narrow topics or industries to efficiently limit your results.
- Add specific countries when appropriate to focus your results.

GALE GROUP NEW PRODUCT ANNOUNCEMENTS/PLUS (NPA/PLUS)

ALTERNATE/PREVIOUS DATA SOURCE NAMES: Gale Group New Products Announcements/Plus (NPA/Plus)

SERVICE/PORTAL NAME: NPA/Plus, File 621 in Dialog Classic on the Web (*http://www.dialogclassic.com*), and also available through Dialog's proprietary software service. Available through some industry channels on Dialog1 on the Web.

SOURCE DESCRIPTION: Gale Group New Product Announcements/Plus (NPA/Plus) is more than just new product announcements (thus the "Plus"). Anyone who has spent time weeding through article database results chock-full of press releases knows how prolific some companies can be with this type of material. Although an annoyance in some circumstances, press releases can also be valuable when you are tracking the release of new products and a company's publicly stated strategies and directions. NPA/Plus serves this purpose to a tee.

The NPA/Plus database is available through all of the iterations of Dialog, through the Web, and through the Dialog software. For the purposes of this review I evaluated the product by using Dialog Classic on the Web (*http://www.dialogclassic.com*) and the Dialog 1 News and Industry Channels, also on the Web (*http://www.dialog1.com*). An understanding of basic Dialog search syntax will be useful to make the most of this product, but the database can be searched with ease, using a few simple commands.

PRICING: $3.45 per full-text press release, plus connection costs. The database is priced through Dialog, based on the amount of material actually retrieved and viewed, so regular users will want to familiarize themselves with the overall pricing structure of Dialog.

SOURCE CONTENT: The press releases included in the NPA/Plus database go back through 1985 and are updated daily with current content. Now numbering more than one million separate releases, they come from the PR Newswire, Business Wire, and other press release wires. The material included covers just about every industry, business, and geographical area, with no particular emphasis. It is important to note that, unlike coverage of a company or subject in business publications, press release coverage depends entirely on the company itself, and the depth of information available in the NPA/Plus database will be determined by their public relations efforts.

The full text of the press releases as put out on the wires by the issuing company is presented, indexed by Gale with a handful of searchable fields. These include company name, trade or brand name, and product category name (see Figure 4-42).

Note in Figure 4-42 the use of the question mark (?) for truncating the terms to pick up both singular and plural. Also note the combination of sets and the limiting by publication year (PY=2002:2003) to narrow down the search results to the most recent material. The data can be exported as full text or just headlines (see Figure 4-43), though advanced users of Dialog may want to try other search result options, such as keywords-in-context. Keep in mind that most companies append a bit of

Figure 4-42. Sample Search in NPA/Plus Using Product Name (PN) and Company Name (CO) Fields

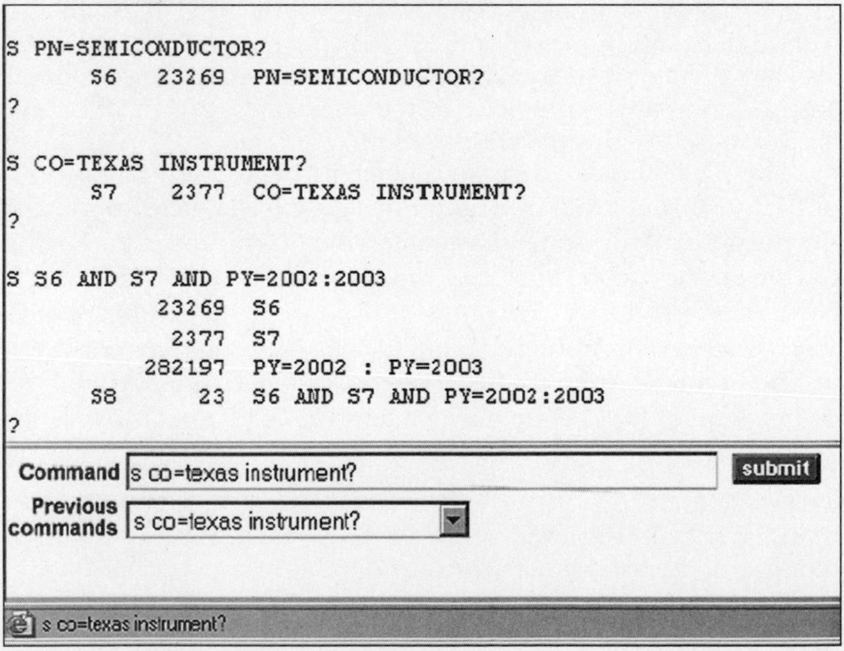

```
S PN=SEMICONDUCTOR?
       S6    23269  PN=SEMICONDUCTOR?
?


S CO=TEXAS INSTRUMENT?
       S7     2377  CO=TEXAS INSTRUMENT?
?


S S6 AND S7 AND PY=2002:2003
            23269  S6
             2377  S7
           282197  PY=2002 : PY=2003
       S8      23  S6 AND S7 AND PY=2002:2003
?
```

Command	s co=texas instrument?	submit
Previous commands	s co=texas instrument? ▼	

🥚 s co=texas instrument?

Reprinted with the permission of Gale Group.

self-hyping material at the end of their press releases, so if you are passing this material on to others, you may want to remove this material from all but the first press release on the same company.

The Dialog search syntax used to get this list, "T 8/6/20-23," basically says "Type out the results for Search Set 8 in Format 6 (brief citations) for the 20th to 23rd articles in the search results."

NPA/Plus provides only press releases and not any proprietary material from trade publications and business journals, so the researcher might be tempted to ask why one would pay for what is essentially free content. Certainly, one alternative would be to track down the Web site of the company or organization you are interested in and then search for press releases on that one site. Both PR Newswire and Business Wire also provide a limited amount of free current material on their Web sites, with archival material available for a fee. But none of the free sources of press releases provide the full search functionality of NPA/Plus, or the depth of coverage.

Figure 4-43. NPA/Plus Search Results Showing Citations Only

```
Address 🔁 https://www.dialogclassic.com/

T 8/6/20-23

 8/6/20
03093331    Supplier Number: 81969400  (USE FORMAT 7 FOR FULLTEXT)
National Semiconductor, Texas Instruments Develop Industry's First
Multipoint LVDS Devices Compliant With New Standard TIA/EIA-899; Market
Leaders Collaborate to Speed Adoption and Availability of M-LVDS
Technology.
Jan 21, 2002
Word Count:    779


 8/6/21
03091742    Supplier Number: 81850778  (USE FORMAT 7 FOR FULLTEXT)
Novellus' Speed(TM) Fluorinated Silicate Glass (FSG) Film Enables
High-Performance 300-Mm Copper Dual Damascene Production.
Jan 17, 2002
Word Count:    751


 8/6/22
03084837    Supplier Number: 81478895  (USE FORMAT 7 FOR FULLTEXT)
StockPickReport.Com Announces Investment Opinion; New Ratings for Disney,
Applied Materials, RF Micro, Broadcom, and Texas Instruments.
Jan 8, 2002
Word Count:    163
```

Reprinted with the permission of Gale Group.

Source Evaluation: Keeping in mind that this resource is providing only an easier way to search and retrieve what is essentially free material—company press releases—you would be hard-pressed to find another source as comprehensive and as easily searchable as Gale's New Product Announcements/Plus. Given its limited content, it might be easy to dismiss NPA/Plus as unnecessary. However, it remains a critical resource for looking at a competitor or an industry over time or trying to track new product announcements in a given space. It is also a valuable source for legal work involving identifying "prior art" and other historical material.

Back files of historical press releases are available through other sources for a fee, but with the NPA/Plus file you get a comprehensiveness that other products simply do not provide. A savvy searcher who does not necessarily need to see the full text of each press release but just wants to see the titles and dates can get a lot out of this product without incurring too much cost.

The data in NPA/Plus is extremely timely, up to the current date, and goes back through 1985. There are no limitations on older records, so finding a company's press releases from 1985 is just as easy as finding those from 2003. Again, knowledge of general Dialog search syntax is useful here, especially whenlimiting by date. The coverage is only as extensive as what is provided by the companies issuing press releases, and can be representative only of what companies actually take the trouble to put out. Not finding something mentioned in the NPA/Plus database is no indication that it doesn't exist, nor should a plethora of press releases on a product be taken as an indication of the product's actual popularity.

In general, it is quite easy to search this resource, using either free text terms or the company name, trade name, and product-type fields. If I had not been familiar with the Dialog interface from previous research, I would probably have found the product a bit harder to use. An important tool is the Bluesheet for the product, which can be downloaded from the main Dialog site (*http:// library.dialog.com/bluesheets/html/bl0621.html*) and is well worth consulting before beginning any research. (Bluesheets are available for all Dialog databases.) The NPA/Plus Bluesheet includes all of the searchable fields in this database, a list of charges for the product, and a thorough product description.

It is unlikely that any researcher will have access to only this one file and not to other material in Dialog, so the technical support would include both general Dialog support and support from Gale for this specific product. Either way, both Dialog and Gale offer plenty of support for their products, and the folks at Dialog are generally more than willing to walk the researcher through any search process to get the necessary results. Although contract prices for Dialog can differ greatly, I am not aware of any additional support costs, and it is in the company's interest to train users to use their products effectively.

Overall, I would rate this as an excellent product for exactly the purpose it is meant to serve: to provide a comprehensive database of press releases going back over time and across all industries. The one complaint I have with the product is that the "Plus" means that the database now includes financial statements, executive changes, and just about any other press release issued by companies. It is no longer focused on new product announcements, and that can be a bit frustrating at times when trying to home in on that type of material. But by using good search vocabulary, even a beginner researcher should have no problem pulling out relevant material.

SOURCE VALUE RATING: All of the data source reviewers were asked to rate each source on the basis of the following eight categories, using "10" as the highest rating and "1" as the lowest ("80" being a perfect score):

1. Relative cost-to-value:	7
2. Relative timeliness of data:	10
3. Relative comprehensiveness of data:	9
4. Ease of use:	8
5. Search options available:	9
6. Level of support services:	9
7. Level of training offered:	8
8. Amount/kinds of special services offered:	7
Total Rating:	67

CONTRIBUTOR NAME: Samuel Werberg/Patricia A. Watkins

AFFILIATION: FIND/SVP, Inc./Thunderbird School of International Management

USEFUL TIPS

* Use company, trade name, and product-type codes to obtain the most relevant search results.
* Remove duplicate material in numerous releases from the same company.
* Keep in mind that all material is self-generated and does not necessarily represent any type of third-party verification or objective validation of the information in the release.

GALE GROUP TRADE & INDUSTRY DATABASE

ALTERNATE/PREVIOUS DATA SOURCE NAMES: Information Access

SERVICE/PORTAL NAME: DialogWeb (*http://www.dialogweb.com*)

SOURCE DESCRIPTION: Gale Group Trade & Industry Databaseis a periodical indexing/abstracting/full-text database containing nearly 9 million records. It contains an index, and its abstract coverage ranges from 1981 to date, plus selective full-text coverage from 1983 to 1990 and cover-to-cover coverage from 1991 to the present. The database specializes in industry and company articles, including new product information, stock performance, and management news. Gale considers Trade & Industry a companion database to PROMT, which specializes in product and marketing information. Gale Group Trade & Industry Databaseincludes cover-to-cover indexing of periodicals, whereas PROMT uses article selection.

The articles in Trade & Industry are drawn from Gale Group's periodicals database—the same database that is used for General Business File ASAP (GBF) and Gale's Business & Company Resource Center (BCRC). Trade & Industry differs from GBF in that it is limited to periodical articles, whereas GBF includes directory information and Investext reports as well articles. BCRC is a much larger database and is considered a "resource center," a one-stop source for business information. It includes a whole host of other sources, such as industry essays from the Gale business encyclopedias, directory information, Investext reports, company histories, and market share statistics.

The Trade & Industry database was originally developed by Information Access Company as a periodicals index called Business Index. Gale Group merged with Information Access Company in 1998, and in 1999, Gale began development of the concept of fully integrated resource centers.

PRICING: Searching on Trade & Industry costs about $1.30 per minute. Article citations cost about $3.00 each and full text articles about $3.50 each—reasonable prices for online searching. Experienced Dialog searchers can retrieve five articles on specific companies or industries for about $25.00.

SOURCE CONTENT: This source indexes and abstracts over one thousand periodical sources such as business, professional, and trade journals, regional business publications, newswires, and newspaper articles focusing on business since 1981. Full text is available for over 75 percent of the periodical records. New records are loaded daily.

Records include title, author, source, word and line count, language, abstract, and full text (if available). To this data is added extensive indexing on special features such as illustrations or photographs, companies discussed, industry codes, subject headings/descriptors, SIC (Standard Industrial Classification) or NAIC (North American Industry Classification System) codes and ticker symbols, and other codes for product or industry. The records are constructed to facilitate access to company and industry information.

The Dialog search engine provides access to the file through one of the most robust search engines available, allowing users to drill down into the file and search for very specific information. Searches can be done by keywords using Boolean or proximity operators (AND, OR, NOT) in the bibliographic record or in the full text. As in all Dialog files, searches of specific fields are available, and multiple field searching is possible. For example, a user could search for a keyword in the lead paragraph or the Brand Name field. Or, one might specify English-language articles in the banking industry, published since 2000, that mention David Aaron. There are about twenty-five searchable fields. Results can be limited to full-text, English, or long articles (over one thousand words) or short articles (fewer than one thousand words). Results can be sorted by author, company, journal, date, or title.

SOURCE EVALUATION: The Gale Group Trade & Industry Database is a useful periodical database for industry and company information for regular users of Dialog, such as corporate librarians. It is also a file of first choice for any researcher looking for industry and company information.

Libraries with access to General Business File ASAP will *not* need to use Trade & Industry, because it contains virtually the same data. The content of Trade & Industry is available as part of the

News Library on LexisNexis and in Factiva, but Dialog offers more powerful searching of the file than is possible in LexisNexis or Factiva. Proquest's ABI/Inform, Wilson's Business Abstracts, and EBSCO's Business Source Premier are competitive products, similar in scope and coverage to Trade & Industry. One difference is that Trade & Industry does not contain as many theoretical or scholarly articles. Librarians who have searched any of these files would need to search Trade & Industry only if doing an exhaustive search.

SOURCE VALUE RATING: All of the data source reviewers were asked to rate each source on the basis of the following eight categories, using "10" as the highest rating and "1" as the lowest ("80" being a perfect score):

1. Relative cost-to-value:	8
2. Relative timeliness of data:	9
3. Relative comprehensiveness of data:	6
4. Ease of use:	8
5. Search options available:	9
6. Level of support services:	4
7. Level of training offered:	5
8. Amount/kinds of special services offered:	5
Total Rating:	54

CONTRIBUTOR NAME: Judith M. Nixon/Patricia A. Watkins
AFFILIATION: Purdue University/Thunderbird School of International Management

USEFUL TIPS

- To search Trade & Industry for a specific company, use co=**company name** or **company name/co**.
- To search for a specific industry by SIC code, use sc=**industry name**.
- To limit the search to full-text sources, use /full text.

MARKET SHARE REPORTER

SERVICE/PORTAL NAME: *http://www.nexis.com* (the news and business source) or *http://www.lexisnexis.com/research* (which includes legal sources)

SOURCE DESCRIPTION: Market Share Reporter is published by Gale and made available online through the LexisNexis information source (*http://www.nexis.com* or *http://www.lexisnexis.com/research*). The print version, often available in libraries, is a source database in Business & Company Resource Center. The data is gathered from 1,133 sources. According to the Gale Print Catalog, Market Share Reporter presents "comparative business statistics in a clear, straightforward manner." It "affords an immediate overview of companies, products and services and cites original sources. Each entry features a descriptive title; data and market description; a list of producers/products along with their market share; and more." Market Share Reporter often contains otherwise hard-to-find market share data for individual companies or products. Nexis.com is one of the search services that permits credit card or transactional searching, so for the occasional search this is an excellent source. This option also makes the Market Share Reporter available to any online searcher.

PRICING: According to a July 2003 price list, Market Share Reporter costs $6 to search and $2.75 per hit to print. A transactional/credit card option is available on Nexis.com.

SOURCE CONTENT: Market Share Reporter is a compilation of statistics from the business literature that contain information on products and producers and what share of the market they hold. This online version goes back to January 1991, so researchers can gather information to understand trends and changes over a number of years. The LexisNexis Searchable Directory of Online Sources describes the content this way: "Market Share Reporter provides information on over 2,000 national and international companies. A unique resource for competitive analysis and economic research featuring coverage of public and private sector activities. Provides extensive coverage in the areas most frequently in the news, such as the automotive industry and electronics and oil industries. Many of the analyses provided are relevant due to product recalls, new product introductions, mergers and acquisitions and other high profile events."

The content of this database is updated every fall, within two months of publication of the new print edition. To access Market Share Reporter, log on to *http://www.nexis.com* or *http://www. lexisnexis.com/research*. Choose the Market Share Reporter from the database list or enter the command BUSREF;MKTSHR. Then simply enter the keyword of interest and review the results. This interface allows the searcher to view the keyword in context to verify relevancy. The results are presented in plain text as excerpted from the original source.

SOURCE EVALUATION: Market Share Reporter, accessed through either *http://www.nexis.com* or *http://www.lexisnexis.com/research* , is an important tool in the online market researcher's toolbox. Market share information can sometimes be elusive, and this source makes it easy and relatively inexpensive to find. The content is not untimely, but because it is updated according to the publication schedule of the print version, it could seem a bit dated if searched just before the annual update. A researcher who needs to obtain information that might be a bit more current than what is found in Market Share Reporter can always search the online version, identify useful sources, then go to those sources directly to see if they have published any updates.

LexisNexis and Nexis.com on the Web are extremely easy to search. Once you are logged in, the search screens are intuitive and contain both simple and advanced search options. They provide extensive online training material, and the customer service call center is staffed twenty-four hours a day, seven days a week. Training and customer service assistance are available at no cost. Market Share Reporter via LexisNexis offers a unique online resource that might not otherwise be available. When it provides the information you need, it is invaluable. It is cost-effective to search and available on a transactional, credit card basis.

SOURCE VALUE RATING: All of the data source reviewers were asked to rate each source on the basis of the following eight categories, using "10" as the highest rating and "1" as the lowest ("80" being a perfect score):

1. Relative cost-to-value:	10
2. Relative timeliness of data:	5
3. Relative comprehensiveness of data:	10
4. Ease of use:	10
5. Search options available:	10
6. Level of support services:	10
7. Level of training offered:	8
8. Amount/kinds of special services offered:	10
Total Rating:	73

SOURCE REVIEWS:

O'Leary, Mike. "Business Site-Seeing: Nexis.com Shines in Web Research." *Link-Up* 18, no. 4 (July/August 2001). O'Leary likes the interface on Nexis.com, which "encases command-system search power in a user friendly shell, and packages it with a familiar Web-like look and feel."

CONTRIBUTOR NAME: Cynthia L. Shamel
AFFILIATION: Shamel Information Services

USEFUL TIPS

- Search using a keyword or a company name.
- If you have any doubts or reservations, call customer service. They will often try your search strategy and let you know generally how it works. They will also suggest alternatives searches.
- With LexisNexis it is a good idea to keep your initial search broad, then narrow as needed. Use the Focus feature to increase precision at no additional search charge.

MARKETS AND INDUSTRY LIBRARY ON LEXISNEXIS

ALTERNATE/PREVIOUS DATA SOURCE NAMES: MARKET

SERVICE/PORTAL NAME: LexisNexis (*http://www.lexisnexis.com/research* or *http://nexis.com*)

SOURCE DESCRIPTION: Markets and Industry Library on LexisNexis is a compilation of thousands of sources that together contain an extremely wide and industry research. Searchers will find company information, demographics, marketing and advertising resources, overviews of markets and technology, market research reports, full-text news stories, news by industry, and selected reference materials. For a complete listing of sources included in this Lexis-Nexis library, go to *http://www.lexisnexis.com*, click on the Customer Service Center link at the top, and go to the *Searchable Directory of Online Sources.*

PRICING: A number of pricing models are available to LexisNexis subscribers. Some researchers will choose a flat-fee account, diminishing the importance of individual search costs. For transactional searchers, a search in the PROMT or Marketing & Advertising Reference Service (MARS) sections of the MARKET library costs $15, with viewed documents costing $4 each. The News

(ALLNWS) section costs \$36 to search, with viewed documents priced at \$2.75 each.

SOURCE CONTENT: The Market and Industry Library contains the full text of information previously published in the business, news, trade, and market research literature. The content is grouped in databases within the library, with familiar sources such as Gale's PROMT, IAC's Marketing & Advertising Reference Service (MARS), Investext Reports, the Encyclopedia of Associations, and a multitude of newspapers. There are, among other things, business directories; Hoover's company profiles; and directories of advertisers, banks, information centers, and governmental advisory organizations. These sources can be searched individually, in customized groups, or in total.

To access the content of the Markets and Industry Library on *http://www.lexisnexis.com,* use the library group file name MARKET. On *http://nexis.com,* use the Power Search tab, click on Find More Sources, and choose Market & Industry. The Nexis.com portal contains a few more databases in the Market & Industry category than the MARKET group file does. For exact differences, contact customer service.

The content is presented in plain-text documents as taken from the original source. In some instances tables or graphs have been omitted. Documents can be downloaded to a file or e-mailed to the researcher. Figure 4-44 shows results of a search for *wd-40 and lava* in MARKET;MARS (MARKET=Markets and Industry Library; MARS=Marketing & Advertising Reference Service).

Figure 4-44. Sample Markets and Industry Library Research (WD-40 and Lava)

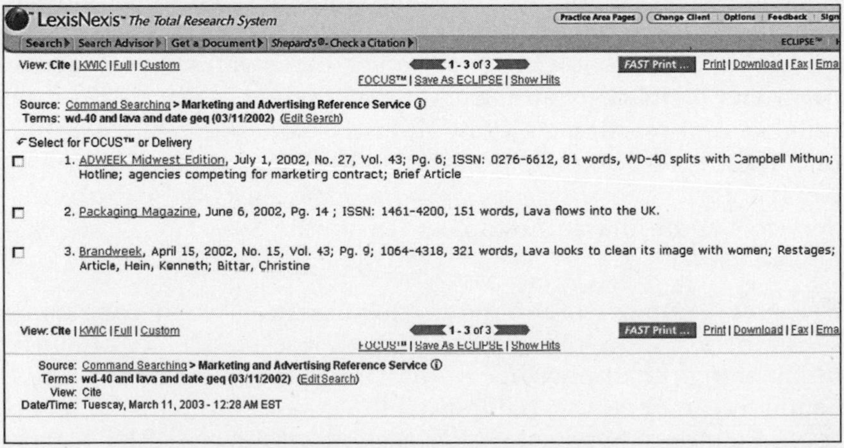

Figure 4-45 illustrates how the article from *Brandweek* (number 3) looked once it was e-mailed:

Figure 4-45. Sample Citation from Markets and Industry Library Search

```
                   Copyright 2002 Gale Group, Inc.
                   IAC (SM) MARS
               Copyright 2002 VNU Business Media
                   Brandweek
                   April 15, 2002
SECTION: No. 15, Vol. 43; Pg. 9; 1064-4318
IAC-ACC-NO: 84902478
LENGTH: 321 words
HEADLINE: Lava looks to clean its image with women;
Restages; Brief Article
BYLINE: Hein, Kenneth; Bittar, Christine
AUTHOR-ABSTRACT:
THIS IS THE FULL TEXT: COPYRIGHT 2002 VNU Business Media
Subscription: $ 105.00 per year. Published weekly.
BODY:
```

Hoping to ditch its reputation as a harsh, man's man soap, Lava will launch its first TV ad campaign in seven years featuring five spots that accentuate the fact that it's a heavy-duty hand cleaner for both sexes.

The $ 3 million-plus campaign, per Campbell Mithun, San Diego, targets both male and female do-it-yourselfers ages 18-54. Two 15-second and three 10-second spots feature vignettes: a boy fishing with a handful of worms; a gardener with her hands covered in berry stains; an urbanite painting his apartment; a man fixing his car; and, an industrial laborer hard at work.

The ads break nationally April 22 on network and cable TV. Tagline: "Whatever you're into, Lava gets it out." The 10-second versions will run as part of a series of 30-second spots that highlight other WD-40-owned brands, namely 2000 Flushes, X-14 and Carpet Fresh.

"The do-it-yourself market has exploded," said Tom Barman, brand manager for Lava Soap. "In the past, Lava [ads] had been positioned toward male users and were heavily industrial in focus. We're trying to branch out and be mainstream. People are doing more work around the house and on the car. They're taking matters into their own hands."

For the past decade, however, the Lava brand has virtually disappeared with advertising nearly non-existent. "The brand has more relevance [now] than it did 10 years ago," said Barman. "It's time to revitalize the brand and really get it into [the] hands of both men and women, and into the hands of their families." FSIs, dropping in May and August, also support. A May 12 FSI will feature Daytona 500 winner Ward Burton, who also serves as WD-40's overall company spokesperson.

The San Diego-based WD-40 purchased Lava from the now

```
dissolved Block Drug in 1999. Since then, unit sales have
fallen steadily For the 52 weeks ended Feb. 24, Lava
posted $ 4 million in revenue, down 6%, per IRI.
IAC-CREATE-DATE: April 19, 2002 LOAD-DATE: April 20, 2002
```

There are similar sources for the type of information found in the LexisNexis Markets and Industry Library. The Gale Group of business databases overlap MARKET, as do the business and news databases on Dialog and the news files on Factiva. All of these sources have value and should be part of a researcher's arsenal of resources. Keep in mind that no single source has everything, and that each source has some things not available elsewhere. It is a good strategy to search multiple sources when a comprehensive search is needed.

The opportunity to pay by credit card makes Nexis.com a more workable alternative for some searchers (note that DialogSelect also has a pay-by-credit-card option called Open Access). Another feature recently added to the LexisNexis search service is the ability to customize source selection. Searchers can create tabs leading to frequently used sources. Click on the tab to jump directly to the desired source.

SOURCE EVALUATION: Market and industry researchers have an ongoing and consistent need for information, ranging from the broadest industry overview to the smallest statistic or data point. To find that information in a timely and cost-effective way, researchers need to be able to search broadly across the published literature as well as to drill down with a precise search strategy. The Markets and Industry Library meets this need.

The various pricing models available to LexisNexis subscribers are competitive with similar sources. It is hard to say whether any one of these models presents a good value, since research budgets and needs vary so widely. Suffice it to say that if the Market and Industry Library provides just what you need to answer the question at hand, especially if the answer is not available in other sources, then it offers tremendous value.

LexisNexis keeps its databases as current as possible, uploading information as it becomes available. Depth is often a more important factor, one that researchers often consider when choosing which source to search for a given project. For instance, on Lexis-

Nexis, the PROMT database goes back to 1985, whereas on Dialog that database goes back to 1972. For the majority of searches, such differences probably will not matter; however, for those projects where it does matter, it is important to be aware of the relative depth of the various research sources.

Historically the database aggregators such as LexisNexis, Dialog, and DataStar have offered powerful search capabilities to subscribers. The trade-off for these search capabilities is the fact that they can be a little intimidating to search. A bit of training and practice is generally required. But that should not keep the beginning researcher from exploring these resources.

LexisNexis offers a fairly user-friendly interface through the Nexis.com portal, and the LexisNexis Web site provides comprehensive FAQs and search tips. Also, trainers are available for free telephone training and will spend as much as an hour at a time instructing the new searcher. Customer service is top-notch and available at no cost twenty-four hours a day, seven days a week. This level of customer service coverage is not universal. For instance, Dialog's Knowledge Center operates only Monday through Friday, 8:00 a.m. to 10:00 p.m. Eastern time, and it is closed on major U.S. holidays.

The Markets and Industry Library compiled and offered through LexisNexis is an important tool to the market and industry researcher. The costs may seem high compared with some of the business databases available through libraries, but the transactional pricing and powerful search capabilities make it a worthy addition to the researcher's toolbox.

SOURCE VALUE RATING: All of the data source reviewers were asked to rate each source on the basis of the following eight categories, using "10" as the highest rating and "1" as the lowest ("80" being a perfect score):

1. Relative cost-to-value:	8
2. Relative timeliness of data:	10
3. Relative comprehensiveness of data:	10
4. Ease of use:	7
5. Search options available:	8
6. Level of support services:	10
7. Level of training offered:	10
8. Amount/kinds of special services offered:	10
Total Rating:	73

SOURCE REVIEWS:

Bates, Mary Ellen. "Can Small Businesses Go Online? The Professional Online Services Flirt with Mom and Pop." *Searcher* 11, no. 1 (January 2003): 16–25.

CONTRIBUTOR NAME: Cynthia L. Shamel
AFFILIATION: Shamel Information Services

USEFUL TIPS

- Take advantage of LexisNexis training. They are good at it.
- Call customer service and ask them to suggest search terms or syntax. Ask them to try your search for you to see how it works before you run it.
- Use the *Online Directory of Sources* to see if the source you need is available and what dates are covered.

PROMT

ALTERNATE/PREVIOUS DATA SOURCE NAMES: Predicast's Overview of Markets and Technology, InfoTrac PROMT, Gale PROMT

SERVICE/PORTAL NAME: Accessed through InfoTrac on the Web for review (*http://infotrac.galegroup.com*) but also available through Dialog dial-up and Web versions (*http://www.dialog.com*)

SOURCE DESCRIPTION: PROMT is a full-text database of international trade and business journals, industry newsletters, and newspapers, plus summaries from investment and brokerage firm reports. This resource is owned by the Gale Group, which is in turn owned by the Thomson Corporation. Using PROMT through Dialog requires knowledge of search expressions and should not pose a problem for experienced Dialog searchers. If you are not experienced in using Dialog, I recommend accessing PROMT through InfoTrac instead.

PROMT is best used for general research when you need to gather articles on a company, industry, or topic. Although a researcher with advanced knowledge of search terminology will be able to use this resource most effectively, beginning researchers with a minimum of training can also find data fairly easily.

PRICING: $3.45 per full-text article retrieved from the database, plus connection fees.

SOURCE CONTENT: The full PROMT database includes roughly 3.5 million full-text articles, updated daily, from over 850 separate sources. The InfoTrac Web version provides data for the current year plus a rolling three-year backfile, and the Dialog version goes back a number of years, depending on the specific publication.

The majority of the sources in PROMT are business and trade publications, and there are also quite a number of local newspapers and business journals. Most of the content consists of full-text articles or abstracts formatted for online viewing or downloading. In some cases, the full-text article can be downloaded as a PDF file. From a list of search results, the full text of a number of marked articles can be printed, saved as a complete file, or e-mailed.

The best use of this resource will be for general information research on a company, industry, or topic and in cases where the researcher wants to see a good overview of recent press coverage on a topic. For historical coverage beyond the past three years, the researcher will want to use PROMT through Dialog, as the InfoTrac version only includes the current and previous three years. The sources are not limited tocoverage, so this resource can also be used to find international news.

Sources similar to PROMT include both ProQuest and Factiva, but each has some unique content and search abilities. Whereas Factiva provides more complex search strategies through the browser interface, PROMT requires an understanding of the search terminology and codes in order to get the most use out of the product. The coverage in PROMT is deeper than that available in ProQuest, and the search functionality is also more robust.

In the PROMT search interface, there are four basic choices for the type of search that can be conducted. The Subject Guide, Relevance Search, and Keyword Search options are all fairly basic and offer the simplest search mechanism. Researchers who want to take full advantage of the search functionality of PROMT through InfoTrac Web will want to familiarize themselves with the Advanced Search interface (see Figure 4-46). The advanced options include the ability to use the built-in PROMT search codes familiar to users of the product through Dialog. A few of the more interesting functions include the ability to search by journal name, product or event code, or subject list. A full list of the searchable fields and codes would be useful to have handy when you first start using the product.

The search results in PROMT are provided in a basic citation list, which includes the article title, source name, date of publication, and word count. There does not appear to be an option for presenting more information in the result list. The title of each article is linked to the full text, and you can mark each desired article in the result list or from the full text of the article itself. The exporting options (called "retrieval options") include printing from the Web browser in HTML or as a PDF, or e-mailing the articles to yourself.

Figure 4-46. The PROMT Advanced Search Screen: The Pull Down Menu Shows the Available Fields

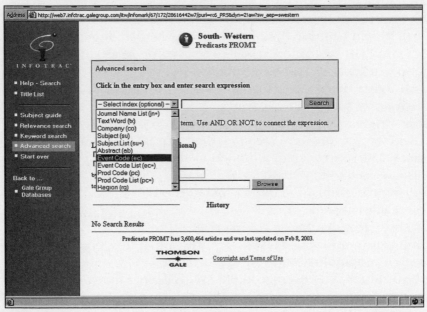

Reprinted with the permission of Gale Group.

SOURCE EVALUATION: Many researchers find PROMT to be a useful resource through Dialog. Taking advantage of the full search functionality available through the InfoTrac Web version involves a bit of a learning curve. If your research needs are primarily in the area of current awareness using trade publication coverage, then PROMT is a great source to use. The coverage is excellent and quite thorough, with hundreds of the top publications in dozens of industry areas. Although primarily focused on U.S. news, PROMT can also be used for international news, as it includes a number of key sources.

Researchers looking for very specific industry-related material may be less likely to use PROMT, not for any shortcoming of this resource but because there are other, more appropriate databases to use. In PROMT, for example, I cannot specify that I want to search only in health-care-related publications or trade journals covering the technology industry. I can certainly use Subject or Product codes, and I can search on one or more specific publications, but I may choose to use a different industry-specific database for material other than general business coverage. For example, health-care researchers may opt for the Adis newsletters or clinical trial databases, and technology researchers may need the details available through IEEE publications, neither of which is included in PROMT. For general business information and top-line current awareness coverage, however, PROMT is a good source and can be used by both beginner and advanced researchers alike.

PROMT is updated daily, and its source lists, downloadable in HTML, PDF, Word, or Excel format, do a good job of describing when each specific source begins full-text coverage. If you need to find results from any one specific trade publication or business journal, be sure to check the title list to find out when coverage starts in that source.

I found actual searching in PROMT to be a little frustrating at times, and I had to refer to the help files numerous times to check my search syntax. Although there is a clear link to the Help file from the left-side menu and there is an index to the Help section, there does not appear to be any downloadable Help file or guide, and the Help section itself could be a bit more organized and could use more examples. A concise printable guide would be helpful, as I found myself having to click through to the Help files numerous times throughout the search process.

I found the support staff at Gale to be very helpful in answering any questions I had about the product, and they quickly responded to any requests I had for additional information. They are more than happy to walk you through the product over the phone, and depending on your organization's specific needs, an in-house training session can also be arranged.

SOURCE VALUE RATING: All of the data source reviewers were asked to rate each source on the basis of the following eight categories, using "10" as the highest rating and "1" as the lowest ("80" being a perfect score):

1. Relative cost-to-value:	8
2. Relative timeliness of data:	10
3. Relative comprehensiveness of data:	7
4. Ease of use:	7
5. Search options available:	7
6. Level of support services:	6
7. Level of training offered:	6
8. Amount/kinds of special services offered:	7
Total Rating:	58

SOURCE REVIEWS: There have been no reviews in the past two years. Most reviews cover Dialog as a whole and do not deal specifically with PROMT.

CONTRIBUTOR NAME: Samuel Werberg/Patricia A. Watkins
AFFILIATION: FIND/SVP, Inc./Thunderbird School of International Management

USEFUL TIPS

- Use Event Codes to find articles about specific business topics, such as Mergers & Acquisitions.
- Use the Advanced Search screen to create a more precise search strategy.
- Check the title list to make sure the publications of interest to you are included.

ADWEEK AND BRANDWEEK

ALTERNATE/PREVIOUS DATA SOURCE NAMES: *Brandweek* was known as *Adweek*'s *Marketing Week* until 1992 and until 1986 as *Adweek* (National Marketing Edition), which superseded *Ad Forum* in 1985. Since the mid-1970s *Adweek* has published a series of regional titles, including East, Southeast, Midwest, Southwest, New England, and West. In early 2003 the six regional titles were combined into one national edition.

SERVICE/PORTAL NAME: *Adweek* and *Brandweek* can be accessed through their Web sites at *http://www.adweek.com* and *http://www.*

brandweek.com. Searching is free, but full access to all articles requires a subscription. *Adweek* and *Brandweek* references and articles are also found in databases such as PROMT and ABI/Inform.

SOURCE DESCRIPTION: *Adweek* and *Brandweek* are both weekly publications, and both come from VNU Business Publications. Until early 2003, the *Adweek* print edition offered six regional titles. The print edition is now consolidated into one national edition, with regionally tailored classified advertising. Regional news stories can still be viewed separately on the Web site. For this evaluation, I want to look at Adweek.com and Brandweek.com, compared with access through databases such as PROMT.

PRICING: An *Adweek* twelve-month premium subscription, including archive access, costs $238.95. *Brandweek* can be added for an additional $149. Full-text records from PROMT, File 16, can be downloaded for $3.45 each. *Adweek* is also available on Factiva back to January 1, 1991, with downloaded articles priced at $2.95 each. LexisNexis also includes *Adweek,* with coverage back to February 1989. The data format is Selected Full-Text. Pricing depends upon your individual subscription plan, but the credit card option allows searchers to purchase articles for $3 each.

SOURCE CONTENT: *Adweek* claims to have the most in-depth news coverage and industry analysis of the advertising industry from a national and international agency perspective. According to its Web site, *Adweek* covers the "players, the pitches, the deals and the decisions shaking up the advertising industry." It also covers public relations; direct marketing; and sports, event, and promotion marketing. *Brandweek* targets marketing executives and management decision makers working in product advertising, research, and promotion. It offers competitive information and insights by covering top brands and the executives who market them. According to the *Brandweek* Web site, "special emphasis is placed on breakthrough campaigns and new advertising/promotional spending."

The *Adweek* and *Brandweek* archives on the Web, which go back to 1993, can be searched using a simple keyword. Advanced Search allows you to limit a search to a specific VNU publication, searching by byline or date range, and sorting by date or keyword. Retrieved articles can be viewed and printed one by one. The Web site includes tabs to Accounts in Review, where subscribers can view a list of companies or products for which new advertising agencies are being sought, including the agency that currently holds the account and the agencies in contention. The Web site also offers a link to Industry Groups. From this page you can view lists such as *Adweek*'s 2002 Hotlists, Top 50 Interactive Agencies, *Brandweek*'s Superbrands, Top National Agencies, and Top Agencies by Region. Clicking on *Brandweek* 's Superbrands, for instance, leads to annual lists of the top two thousand brand names (in groups of five hundred), and by following the link to America's Top Brands of 2001 (1–500), we find out that McDonald's was the number one brand based on media expenditures. The site also offers articles discussing the brand categories. For instance, the Fast Food article addresses market share, product positioning, promotions, new products, and branding strategies in this category.

Subscriptions to both *Adweek* and *Brandweek* include print and online access, with the online edition providing the national edition along with articles related to the six regions. When you log in to the online version of *Adweek,* you see the headlines and breaking stories in the center, with regional news segmented along the right side of the page. The *Brandweek* home page is dominated by headlines and links to the full articles.

Adweek and *Brandweek* full-text versions are also widely available in Factiva, LexisNexis, and several Dialog databases, including File 9: Business & Industry, File 15: ABI/Inform, File 16: PROMT, File 148: Gale Group Trade & Industry, and File 553: Wilson Business Abstracts Fulltext. In File 16, for instance, full-text articles from *Adweek* go back to 1990; for *Brandweek* they go back to 1992.

SOURCE EVALUATION: *Adweek* and *Brandweek* offer a unique perspective in market and industry research. For advertising strategies, expenditures, product positioning, branding efforts, rankings, and industry overviews, these publications present depth and detail. Full access to the Web site content is available to subscribers. The Web sites are updated daily and offer standard Web site search capabilities. Unfortunately, the Web sites contain advertising banners across the top and down the sides. These banners often contain animated graphics, which can prove annoying to the searcher who spends more than a few minutes on the site.

A trial keyword search on *Pepsi* in *Adweek* retrieved thirty-four pages of articles. Although the advanced search option allows searchers to request results sorted by date, this function did not seem to work well. On one page of results there were articles from 1993, surrounded by articles from 1997 and 2001. When searching *Adweek* and *Brandweek* through an aggregator such as Dialog, the researcher has access to much more powerful search tools. Indexing allows precise limiting by date, geographic names, product names, industry names, and NAICS codes. Some databases, such as PROMT, have indexed event names, allowing retrieval related to details such as product information, market share, market size, prices, new products, or public relations.

If your organization already subscribes to either *Adweek* or *Brandweek*, you will definitely want to register to use the publication's Web site. The information available there is useful and includes graphics, charts, pictures, and tables not available through the online database aggregators. Whether or not you choose to subscribe will depend upon the anticipated frequency of use. If you are pulling articles from Dialog, Factiva, or LexisNexis on a regular basis, you may find a database subscription to be more cost-effective. If you prefer or require colorful, nicely formatted graphics, you will want to consider subscribing to the publications themselves.

SOURCE VALUE RATING: All of the data source reviewers were asked to rate each source on the basis of the following eight categories, using "10" as the highest rating and "1" as the lowest ("80" being a perfect score):

1. Relative cost-to-value:	7
2. Relative timeliness of data:	10
3. Relative comprehensiveness of data:	10
4. Ease of use:	5
5. Search options available:	3
6. Level of support services:	5
7. Level of training offered:	5
8. Amount/kinds of special services offered:	3
Total Rating:	48

CONTRIBUTOR NAME: Cynthia L. Shamel

AFFILIATION: Shamel Information Services

USEFUL TIPS

- If your organization already subscribes to either *Adweek* or *Brandweek*, you will definitely want to register to use the publication's Web site.
- For advertising strategies, expenditures, product positioning, branding efforts, rankings, and industry overviews, these publications present depth and detail.
- The Web site search capability works best when using a single keyword.

COUNTRY DATA

SERVICE/PORTAL NAME: *http://www.countrydata.com*

SOURCE DESCRIPTION: Country Data, produced by The PRS Group (*http://www.prsgroup.com*), provides a complete dataset of political, economic, and social indicators to help any company doing business in a foreign country keep up with trends that may affect current and future business. Among the target audience for this resource are purchasing agents, project planners, marketing and sales organizations, and risk management departments.

What are the current political risks to foreign investment? Are there any negative risk factors that might affect my company's upcoming supplier contract negotiations? My company has a successful business relationship in Bulgaria and would like to assess the risk of expanding into Armenia. How do the risk factors in these countries compare? These are just a few of the questions that can be answered by this resource.

PRICING: The cost for a search on Country Data is based on a pricing discount model and is the same regardless of which search method you use. The more factors you choose, the lower the per-factor cost. For example, selecting ten ICRG risk factors (see description below) costs 10 times $0.75, or $7.50. Choosing one hundred factors costs 100 times $0.32, or $32. The scale for the economic indicators is different. A link on the data-point selection page provides a complete chart of the pricing model. Note that the estimated price and the final price may not be the same. This is not a problem, since the user has the option to return to the selection screen to make any needed changes before agreeing to purchase a report.

SOURCE CONTENT: Country Data includes a variety of domestic economic indicators (e.g., GDP, real growth rate, and unemployment rate), international economic indicators (foreign direct investment, debt service ratio, and foreign trade balance), International Country Risk Guide (ICRG) ratings (foreign debt as percent of GDP, international liquidity, and exchange rate stability), Coplin-O'Leary ratings and forecasts (eighteen-month and five-year risk projections for most likely political regimes, direct investment, and export market), and social indicators (annual population growth, ethnic groups, and literacy). These are but a small sampling from the complete list of factors available. A thorough description of the data points and methodology for determining each rating is provided online. To illustrate the kind of data available through Country Data, Table 4-15 shows a one-year comparison of budget balance as percent of GDP for selected European countries.

There are two methods of obtaining data from this site. Table 4-15 was generated with a Country Data feature called ICRG (International Country Risk Guide) Data Wizard. To create the chart, the user first selects the countries to compare. Next you select the data points and then the desired time frame. The screen is updated to show an estimated price for the report. The last screen presents the final cost and requests authorization for payment. After purchasing the report, the user is asked how the list should be displayed, by country or data point.

Table 4-15. Excerpt from Sample Country Data Table: GDP Data by Country

Budget Balance as % GDP
Central government budget balance for a given year, expressed as a percentage of GDP for that year.

Country	01/2002	02/2002	03/2002	04/2002	05/2002	06/2002	07/2002	08/2002	09/2002	10/2002	11/2002	12/2002
ALBANIA	-8.0	-8.0	-8.0	-8.0	-8.0	-8.0	-8.0	-8.0	-8.0	-8.0	-8.0	-8.0
ARMENIA	-3.0	-3.0	-3.0	-3.0	-3.0	-3.0	-3.0	-3.0	-3.0	-3.0	-3.0	3.0
BELARUS	-2.0	-2.0	-2.0	-2.0	-2.0	-2.0	-2.0	-2.0	-2.0	-2.0	-2.0	-2.0
BULGARIA	-2.0	-2.0	-2.0	-2.0	-2.0	-2.0	-2.0	-2.0	-2.0	-2.0	-2.0	-2.1
CROATIA	-0.8	-0.8	-0.8	-0.8	-4.5	-4.5	-4.5	-6.6	-6.6	-6.6	-6.6	-6.6
CZECH REPUBLIC	-4.0	-4.0	-4.0	-4.0	-4.0	-4.0	-4.0	-4.0	-4.0	-4.0	-4.0	-5.5
ESTONIA	0.0	0.0	0.0	0.0	0.0	0.0	0.0	0.0	0.0	0.0	0.0	0.0
HUNGARY	-3.5	-3.5	-3.5	-3.5	-3.5	-3.5	-3.5	-3.5	-3.5	-3.5	-3.5	3.5

http://www.countrydata.com, The PRS Group. Reprinted with permission of the publisher.

The second tool for retrieving data from this site creates a report based on a single country. After selecting the country, the user is presented with a page where various risk factors can be selected. The number of factors available depends on the country chosen. Some selections allow for the addition of a time frame. Again, the screen is updated to show an estimated cost.

The data for this resource come from a variety of publicly available sources. Researchers at The PRS Group compute the factors based on this information, and the final ratings are uploaded to the site monthly. In addition to viewing and printing online, the user can download all retrieved reports as comma-delimited files.

SOURCE EVALUATION: Country Data is fairly easy to use, but a lack of consistency in design keeps the site from receiving high marks in this category. The two methods provided for creating reports work differently. When interacting with the Data Wizard, it is possible to use the common control-click keystrokes to select multiple options before adding the data points for inclusion in the final report. This is not possible when creating a report for a single country, in which case the user must add options one at a time.

The site does not offer online training. Instead, the user is directed to customer support; there is no charge for this service. I had a question while reviewing the site and contacted customer support by e-mail. I received a response the next day with the answer.

Documentation for the site is provided in a FAQ section (the link is on the PRS home page) that provides answers to questions for all of the services provided by The PRS Group. However, I found myself going in circles trying to learn more about the Country Data service. For example, under the Country Data portion of the FAQ (under the question "What data is available?") there is a link to a "complete listing" of the data available. Following this link takes the user to a page showing "some of the data" available on the site. There I found a list of about eighty data points that seemed to be complete. Although the path was a little less than intuitive, I found it easy enough to follow. However, the link should instead point to the Our Methodology page, which provides examples of how the data can be used, descriptions of the various risk factors, and an explanation of the ratings system. This is a must-read. (Note: The Our Methodology page is another of those links available from the left-side menu bar. It does look useful for understanding this data and where it comes from.)

Overall, the Country Data site is easy to use and cost-effective. The ability to select only the risk factors of interest for a particular request helps to keep costs reasonable, and the large number of factors to choose from allows for a complete look at the risks involved in doing business in a foreign country. If a company needs an in-depth view of a particular country, the Country Reports resource, also published by The PRS Group, may be more appropriate.

SOURCE VALUE RATING: All of the data source reviewers were asked to rate each source on the basis of the following eight categories, using "10" as the highest rating and "1" as the lowest ("80" being a perfect score):

1. Relative cost-to-value:	10
2. Relative timeliness of data:	10
3. Relative comprehensiveness of data:	10
4. Ease of use:	8
5. Search options available:	8
6. Level of support services:	10
7. Level of training offered:	6
8. Amount/kinds of special services offered:	10
Total Rating:	72

CONTRIBUTOR NAME: James Harrington
AFFILIATION: Fujitsu Network Communications

USEFUL TIPS

- Read the Our Methodology section of the FAQ to understand the rating system.
- To save money, make sure you thoroughly understand the question before starting your search.

EIU VIEWSWIRE

SERVICE/PORTAL NAME: *http://www.viewswire.com*

SOURCE DESCRIPTION: The Economist Intelligence Unit's (EIU) ViewsWire provides business intelligence for 195 countries. The product is targeted at busy corporate executives, business researchers, and investors. ViewsWire is a distillation of the larger Economist database of political and economic news, background, and analysis.

The EIU has been gathering and analyzing political and economic information for decades. The company is well known for publishing the weekly magazine the *Economist,* but it is also the publisher of other, less well-known periodicals, including the *Journal of Commerce.* Since 1997, the EIU has offered a large variety of reports on the Web. The EIU as a whole is a large and potentially intimidating resource, but it provides data extending back many years. ViewsWire bundles together the most relevant parts of EIU and presents them in an easy-to-navigate format. ViewsWire is a current awareness service, briefing decision makers with insightful and authoritative analysis as well as news.

PRICING: ViewsWire is available by annual subscription, with pricing based on the number of users and the number of geographic regions selected (see Table 4-16).

Table 4-16. Global Network Pricing for EIU ViewsWire

NUMBER OF USERS	ANNUAL SUBSCRIPTION COST
Up to 5	$11,950
Up to 10	$16,400
Up to 25	$21,850
Up to 50	$27,300
Up to 100	$32,750
More than 100	Call for pricing information

Subscriptions for individual regions are available at lower prices.

SOURCE CONTENT: ViewsWire is organized by country and by channel. Users can choose a country and then a channel, or vice versa. Channels include Politics, Economics, Business, Finance, and Regulations. An additional channel, EIU RiskWire, provides risk ratings for 60 of the 195 countries.

The content of ViewsWire is drawn from both the EIU database and from strategic alliances with organizations such as the British Broadcasting Corporation (BBC), the World Bank, the *Financial Times, China Online,* and the Organisation for Economic Cooperation and Development (OECD). Because ViewsWire incorporates articles from business publications, it provides stronger company and industry coverage than does the traditional EIU database. ViewsWire's main strength, however, as with EIU, lies in political and economic analysis.

Information is presented in the form of articles, tables, and graphs. Data may be downloaded in Excel format, and articles and tables may be reformatted into a printer-friendly format with a single click. ViewsWire features a powerful internal search engine, and the entire database can be searched by keyword. Limiters including country, industry, channel, category, date, and source can be used to narrow the search.

ViewsWire provides country-specific information to support organizational decision making. This database stands out above other services in two important aspects: First, it is produced by the authoritative Economist Intelligence Unit. Second, ViewsWire adds a tremendous amount of value with its insightful analysis and forecasts.

SOURCE EVALUATION: ViewsWire takes the most useful parts of a large, relatively expensive database (EIU) and distills them into a concise, powerful service. ViewsWire cuts through the clutter to the information needed by busy managers. For many organizations it is a reasonable alternative to a full EIU subscription. The various parts of ViewsWire are updated at different times. Analysis of major news events is presented within forty-eight hours, and ViewsWire provides daily updates for some items, such as stock indices and currency exchange rates.

There are many sources of country information on the Web (Country Commercial Guides from the U.S. Department of Commerce, for example), but ViewsWire takes country information an extra step and provides five-year forecasts of the data items covered. Business planners can therefore use ViewsWire as a tool to reduce uncertainty. The interface is intuitive and very easy to use. A special feature of ViewsWire is an e-mail alerting service based upon the interest profile set up by the user.

Technical support is included free of charge and is available during normal working hours. ViewsWire is well designed and straightforward to use, and training is available at no charge. Phone assistance is available during business hours, and account managers can provide face-to-face assistance when they are in the customer's geographic area. ViewsWire is unmatched in its concise, timely, and authoritative reporting.

SOURCE VALUE RATING: All of the data source reviewers were asked to rate each source on the basis of the following eight categories, using "10" as the highest rating and "1" as the lowest ("80" being a perfect score):

1. Relative cost-to-value:	8
2. Relative timeliness of data:	9
3. Relative comprehensiveness of data:	9
4. Ease of use:	10
5. Search options available:	9
6. Level of support services:	9
7. Level of training offered:	9
8. Amount/kinds of special services offered:	8
Total Rating:	71

SOURCE REVIEWS:

O'Leary, Mick. "ViewsWire Bundles Best of EIU." *Information Today* 16, no. 7 (July/August 1999): 11–12. O'Leary gives a favorable review and notes that navigating the Web site is straightforward. He writes that ViewsWire's strength lies not so much in the news it provides, but in the analysis of that news.

CONTRIBUTOR NAME: Wes Edens/Patricia A. Watkins

AFFILIATION: Thunderbird School of International Management

USEFUL TIPS

- Use British spelling when searching. For example, use "labour" instead of "labor."
- Use the advanced search feature to limit your searches to your country of interest.

ENCYCLOPEDIA OF ASSOCIATIONS (EA)

SERVICE/PORTAL NAME: Encyclopedia of Associations via Dialog (File 114); the product is also available directly via Gale as Associations Unlimited.

SOURCE DESCRIPTION: The Encyclopedia of Associations is one of the most comprehensive sources of association and organization information available. The Gale Group publishes a three-volume set annually, but the information is also available as an electronic database through Dialog as File 114. The Dialog database has the advantage over its print counterpart of providing quarterly updating as well as being searchable via a number of criteria.

PRICING: $0–$100, depending on amount of search time, File source in Dialog.

SOURCE CONTENT: The Encyclopedia of Associations database in Dialog contains detailed information on more than 135,000 non-profit membership organizations. Coverage is worldwide, representing more than 22,200 national organizations, 22,300 multinational or non-U.S. organizations, and 115,000 regional, state, or local organizations. Each association is assigned a subject based on its coverage; subject coverage categories are Trade, Business, and Commercial; Environmental and Agricultural; Legal, Governmental, Public Administration, and Military; Engineering, Technological, and Natural and Social Sciences; Educational; Cultural; Social Welfare; Health and Medical; Public Affairs; Fraternal, Nationality, and Ethnic; Religious; Veterans', Hereditary and Patriotic; Hobby and Avocational; Athletic and Sports; Labor Unions, Associations, and Federations; Chambers of Commerce and Trade and Tourism; Greek and Non-Greek Letter Societies, Associations, and Federations; and Fan Clubs. Fan Club coverage is for U.S. national organizations only. Regional, State, and Local Organizations are also assigned a U.S. regional destination, such as Great Lake States or Western States.

You can access the Encyclopedia of Associations in Dialog as File 114. A Dialog Bluesheet (*http://library.dialog.com/bluesheets/ html/bl0114.html*) outlines all of the available search fields and indexing terms. You can search by the organization's name or obtain a custom list of organizations that meet criteria in the search. For example, let's say you need to obtain a list of associations in Minneapolis that bestow awards and that also maintain a library. You would conduct the search by using the search prefix BA=, which is the index term for the field *Bestow Awards*. CY= is the search prefix for *City,* and LB= is the search prefix for *Library*. File 114 also allows word and phrase searching, and search criteria can be combined in an infinite number of ways to create lists of organizations.

The detailed entry information on each association varies. More information is available for larger organizations than for smaller ones, but even entries for small associations can include significant amounts of information. Organizations represented range in size from less than ten people to many thousands of members. Information available in a typical full-text record includes full organization name and street address, telephone number, description, number of members, number of staff, officer names, SIC code, founding year, and budget, as well as information on annual meetings or conventions, publications issued, libraries maintained, awards bestowed, and section heading code.

SOURCE EVALUATION: Although there are a few other sources for association information (e.g., see Gateway to Associations in the Key Additional Sources section), the Encyclopedia of Associations is the only one that attempts to be comprehensive. The print version is updated annually, and the online database on Dialog is updated quarterly. It is a standard source in most library reference collections and offers unique content to the market and industry researcher.

SOURCE VALUE RATING: All of the data source reviewers were asked to rate each source on the basis of the following eight categories, using "10" as the highest rating and "1" as the lowest ("80" being a perfect score):

1. Relative cost-to-value:	9
2. Relative timeliness of data:	8
3. Relative comprehensiveness of data:	8
4. Ease of use:	8
5. Search options available:	9
6. Level of support services:	9
7. Level of training offered:	5
8. Amount/kinds of special services offered:	5
Total Rating:	61

CONTRIBUTOR NAME: Jan Rivers/Patricia A. Watkins
AFFILIATION: Dorsey & Whitney LLP/Thunderbird School of International Management

USEFUL TIPS

- The Encyclopedia of Associations can be accessed and used in Dialog (File 114), both in DialogWeb and in the DialogClassic dial-up version.
- Rates charged can be found by searching File 114. Charges will also be listed for each record format (full-text, etc.) by accessing the Dialog Bluesheet or by typing the rate command in the database before searching.
- You may want to save the entire buffer when using Dialog. This provides an edited copy of the search strategy that can be shown to the client if needed.

EVENTLINE

SERVICE/PORTAL NAME: Dialog, File 165

SOURCE DESCRIPTION: EventLine is a directory listing conventions, conferences, symposia, or other events held worldwide since 1989. It is narrowly focused on medicine, biotechnology, and science events. This source is useful for marketing or sales staff looking for sales venues, for event planners, or for individuals who wish to attend an event in the medical or science fields. As a historical record, this directory verifies information on past events. It answers questions such as "How many AIDS conferences are held in North America?" and "If I plan a conference for October, what events will conflict with it?"

PRICING: $0–50, depending on the amount of time spent searching. The cost will depend upon your subscription, but costs are generally affected by how much time you spend online and how many hits you print out. Unless you have a flat-fee subscription, EventLine costs about $.58 a minute to search, and each record costs $1.50 to print out.

SOURCE CONTENT: More than 350,000 conferences, conventions, trade fairs, symposia, and exhibits events are profiled in this directory. You can search events by title, venue, date, country, contact name, subject, and type of event. In addition to this basic information, contact information for the organizer of the event is included. Events are never deleted.

The data serves marketing, sales, and competitive-intelligence needs. A common use of this directory is to create lists of events with exhibitor areas or trade shows that offer opportunities to sell or buy products related to medicine or science. For example, regional manufacturers could use EventLine to find national events in their region to attract national customers in order to expand. Another use of the source would be to identify educational opportunities. Perhaps a company is considering a new line of business, or an employee is given responsibility for an industry in which he or she has little background. In either case, attending the key conference in the industry would provide an immersion experience, with information and personal contacts not available from other sources. Because people are usually familiar with important events in their own area or specialty, this source is most useful for finding events outside of one's usual sphere of knowledge. It is also unique in offering historical information on past events, providing details of events and a record of onetime commemorative events.

A similar source in print format is *Trade Shows Worldwide*, published by Gale and priced at $350. This source covers all subject areas and thus has wider scope than EventLine. The Gale source is more limited geographically, however, covering only the United States and Canada, and it does not cover the more esoteric events such as symposia. As a resource for event planners, the Gale source provides more detail on how to exhibit, fees, number of exhibitors, square footage of exhibit space, and the number of hotel rooms used in conjunction with the event. For example, a city planner could learn whether the city's hotel space was sufficient to accommodate certain conferences.

MediConf (*http://www.mediconf.com*) is similar to EventLine in its coverage of global events and conferences in the science and medical fields. Produced by Fairbase Database in Hanover, Germany, MediConf contains information similar to that in EventLine: event name, dates, location, description, and organizer contacts. You can access it via the Web or via Dialog. On the Web version, MediConf is devoted to forthcoming events and lists only ten thousand events, compared with EventLine's thirty-five thousand. Access costs $49 annually.

SOURCE EVALUATION: EventLine is a comprehensive source from a reputable science publisher. The search capabilities are powerful on any of the vendors of this source. For event planners, the Gale source gives more useful information on hotels or other services likely needed for the event.

SOURCE VALUE RATING: All of the data source reviewers were asked to rate each source on the basis of the following eight categories, using "10" as the highest rating and "1" as the lowest ("80" being a perfect score):

1. Relative cost-to-value:	7
2. Relative timeliness of data:	8
3. Relative comprehensiveness of data:	7
4. Ease of use:	7
5. Search options available:	10
6. Level of support services:	10
7. Level of training offered:	10
8. Amount/kinds of special services offered:	5
Total Rating:	64

CONTRIBUTOR NAME: Brenda Reeb/Patricia A. Watkins

AFFILIATION: University of Rochester/Thunderbird School of International Management

HOOVER'S ONLINE

ALTERNATE/PREVIOUS DATA SOURCE NAMES: Hoover's

SERVICE/PORTAL NAME: *http://www.hoovers.com*

SOURCE DESCRIPTION: Hoover's Online delivers company information in the form of short company capsules and longer company profiles. It also contains industry snapshots, market intelligence, and sales prospecting tools. Significant portions of Hoover's database (company capsules) are available for free, and the more in-depth sections are offered on a subscription basis. Hoover's targets sales, marketing, business development, and other professionals who need to retrieve a standard bucket of company, industry, and competitive information on a regular basis. It also works well for interviewees, small businesses, and personal investors.

PRICING: Hoover's is very reasonably priced. With three pricing structures in place, Hoover's Lite, Pro, and ProPlus (in addition to Hoover's Corporate), a user can choose the level of access. Options begin at $50 per month or $400 per year for individual subscriptions to Hoover's Lite. A Hoover's Pro subscription starts at $1,995/year for a 1–5 seat license, and Hoover's Pro Plus starts at $4,995/year for a 1–5 seat subscription. Hoover's offers a large amount of information for free, and icons indicate what is available for no cost and what is available to subscribers with their fee.

SOURCE CONTENT: Hoover's Online contains four linked parts that are described below: Companies & Industries, IPO Central, News Center, and Information Marketplace.

1. **Companies & Industries.** Hoover's covers more than 18,000 public and private companies worldwide, 300 industries, and 180,000 corporate executives, as well as over 12 million companies from Dun & Bradstreet and 9,000 non-U.S. firms from Mergent. From a company capsule, one can find the top competitors and access Information Marketplace, News, Investor Information (SEC filings), and Key Executives. Company profiles contain in-depth company descriptions, financial comparisons with competitors, and industry benchmarks. Each industry snapshot contains a description of the industry along with a list of trends provided by Plunkett Research, a glossary of industry terms, and lists of associations, selected Web sites, and print resources. The Hoover's Industry Snapshots are an excellent source for an overall look at an industry and its players.

2. **IPO Central.** Here users can search for IPOs (initial public offerings) by company name or ticker symbol. Subscribers can also search for IPOs by location, underwriter, industry, filing or trading date ranges, offering amount, price range, or annual sales. Once IPOs are identified, Hoover's links to the Companies & Industries section of the database.

3. **News Center.** This section can be searched by keyword, ticker symbol, date, or phrase. Archives are searchable for up to ninety days. News items are selected by Hoover's editors and are derived from NewsEdge, so they are primarily press releases and articles from *Fortune, Business Week, Forbes Magazine*, and the *Wall Street Journal.* The News page also links to company press releases.

4. **Information Marketplace.** This section includes over forty-five thousand reports from more than ninety publishers, including Dun & Bradstreet, Datamonitor, Freedonia, Harris, Jupiter, and Reuters. These reports are available for fees ranging from $5 for a D&B Credit Report to approximately $500 for an industry report. The reports are described in enough detail to make a purchase decision.

SOURCE EVALUATION: Hoover's licenses a good deal of content and puts it together in an easy-to-understand format. However, this licensed content is available in many other sources. The narratives on companies and industries are what the Hoover's brand is known for, forming the strongest part of this resource. They are well written and interesting and provide useful information, and unlike more analytical sources, they are jargon free. The profiles are well written, with an eye toward providing a clear description of the issues that companies and industries face. Hoover's narratives are also licensed to other information providers, such as Bloomberg and LexisNexis.

Dun & Bradstreet acquired Hoover's in March 2003. This will add more companies to Hoover's roster, but the acquisition is not expected to significantly change Hoover's Online. Hoover's is now part of Dun & Bradstreet's E-Business Solutions Group.

SITE DESIGN REVISED: Hoover's launched a redesigned site just as this volume was going to press. Following are the highlights as reported by Hoover's public relations director:

Improved Site Design

- The site is cleaner and less cluttered, making content and tools easier to find.
- A clear log-in page for free versus paid users more clearly differentiates the user experience, content access levels, and quantity/type of advertising.
- The user can more quickly understand all options for finding information using the new search box on the streamlined home page.
- Company and industry records share consistent, clear organization, including new record navigation in blue.
- A new, green toolbox on every page showcases all relevant tools for finding, manipulating, and downloading information.
- Intuitively renamed features and tools reflect the content or the function performed; for example, Advanced Company Search is now Build Company List.
- A new Financials page for each company, listing auditor, stock price, and other popular elements on a single page, thus saving time.
- Fewer ads on the subscriber site. Subscriber pages are personalized with customer's name, and they consistently contain only one standard ad in the same place on each page.
- Instead of getting a simple "denial of access" page, users will hit "incentive" pages that detail what they're missing and provide an example.

Enhanced Tools and Content

- Industry coverage expands from three hundred Hoover's defined industries to over six hundred. New industry records offer basic information, news, and industry codes for more than six hundred industries. More than six hundred newly created industry codes were classified in an orderly and systematic process to make searching companies and products much easier. Includes the addition of NAICS Codes, Industry Keyword Search, and access to industry news.

- Even more parameters have been added to advanced searches, such as Build Company List and Build Executive List.
- Links to external content are clearly identified and open in a new browser window so you don't lose your place.
- A report repository exists on each content page, with relevant pay-per-view third-party reports.
- More search results are downloadable, and users can choose the data elements to include in the download.
- Deeper subsidiary information is available, with a new hierarchical display that shows indirect relationships.
- ProPlus with Downloads features additional fields for searching (Net Income Range, Net Income Growth, Industry Keyword, and SIC or NAICS Codes) in addition to the expanded Hoover's Industry Names list.
- The Small Business Finder features additional fields to further filter and refine your search (SIC, NAICS, Metro Area, Asset Range, Company Type, and/or Fiscal Year-End).
- Users can set up news alerts for any of more than six hundred industries and can set up multiple ticker symbol alerts through one interface.

New Tools and Content

- A unique "reverse" search capability called Find Similar Companies locates companies with similar attributes.
- Users can easily track companies and industries with the Add News Alert tool, available on company or industry records.
- Every industry can be found with a specific keyword using the new Industry Keyword search.
- Users can browse lists of companies organized by stock index, geography, industry, and more.
- An extensive database of over forty thousand pay-per-view third-party reports can be searched using Report Search. All pay-per-view third-party reports are grouped together intuitively on one page.
- SIC and NAICS codes are offered for industries and for Hoover's companies.
- Users can see how a company has changed over time with the new archived Products and Operations Charts.
- Applicable 10-K filings can be quickly found using a stand-alone 10-K page.

SOURCE VALUE RATING: All of the data source reviewers were asked to rate each source on the basis of the following eight categories, using "10" as the highest rating and "1" as the lowest ("80" being a perfect score):

1. Relative cost-to-value:	9
2. Relative timeliness of data:	8
3. Relative comprehensiveness of data:	7
4. Ease of use:	8
5. Search options available:	6
6. Level of support services:	7
7. Level of training offered:	6
8. Amount/kinds of special services offered:	9
Total Rating:	60

SOURCE REVIEWS:

Fulton, Marsha L., Denise G. Rabogliatti, and Jan M. Rivers. "Company Directories: Past, Present, and Future." *Searcher* (September 2002): 39+. Compares three resources: Directory of Corporate Affiliations through Dialog and LexisNexis, Hoover's and Hoover's through LexisNexis, and Standard & Poor's via Dialog and LexisNexis.

O'Leary, Mick. "Business Site Seeing: The New Hoover's: Complete Company Content." *Link-Up* (May/June 2002). Analysis of *http://www.hoovers.com* site.

"What Does Hoover's Pro Offer Information Pros?" *Information Advisor* (September 2002): 6–8. Discusses the Companies and Industries section of Hoover's, along with the sales prospecting tools offered to Hoover's Pro subscribers.

CONTRIBUTOR NAME: Meryl Brodsky/Patricia A. Watkins
AFFILIATION: Consultant/Thunderbird School of International Management

USEFUL TIPS

* To start working in Hoover's, explore the Help Center and the FAQ section (in Help).
* Become familiar with the link for Companies & Industries, and investigate Industry Snapshots.
* Practice using the Search drop-down menu, which allows a variety of searches by Company Name, Ticker, Keyword, and other fields.

USADATA

ALTERNATE/PREVIOUS DATA SOURCE NAMES: USADATA's Direct Marketing Portal

SERVICE/PORTAL NAME: *http://www.usadata.com*

SOURCE DESCRIPTION: USADATA is a direct marketing portal that provides an automated, self-serve process for direct mail marketing. USADATA offers two customized corporate portal products: the Customer Acquisition Portal and the Customer Retention & Cross Sell Portal. The Customer Acquisition Portal has two components: Consumer Prospecting and Business Prospecting. Companies can choose to place a link to the portal on their internal Web site (or intranet) or they can access these prospecting tools through the USADATA Web site. The target audience for the Customer Retention & Cross Sell Portal is the large corporation with a decentralized sales staff.

PRICING: The cost of data from USADATA varies. Mailing lists and mailers are priced per record by type of data, ranging from $50 through $1,501–$2,000 and up. Customized corporate is available on request.

SOURCE CONTENT: USADATA offers two customized corporate portals, the Customer Acquisition Portal and the Customer Retention & Cross Sell Portal, which may be made available on a company's Web site or through an intranet. These portals provide access to consumer or business lists that have been created especially for the company based on targeted criteria and selected geographic locations. Direct mailings may be generated and personalized for the individual company.

Targeting criteria include the following:

1. Consumer Mailing Lists
   - Geographic Area Selects: state, city, county, ZIP code. Additional criteria through data specialist: area code, MSA, DSA, radius around an address.
   - Demographics, Lifestyle, Behavior Selects: age, sex, estimated income (HH), home owner/renter, home market value, length of residence, dwelling type. Additional criteria through data specialist include, but are not limited to, lifestyles/hobbies/interests, marital status, property detail, presence of children, presence of children by age, race/ethnicity, religion, mail order buyers, donors and contributors, opportunity seekers, new home owners/movers, pool owners, RV/mobile home owners.

2. Business Mailing Lists
- Geographic Area Selects: state, city, county, ZIP code. Additional criteria through data specialist: area code, MSA, DSA, radius around an address.
- Business Selects: SIC code, employee size, sales volume, sales growth, contact names where available. Additional criteria through data specialist include, but are not limited to, fax number, contacts by job title, contacts by job function, franchise/branch affiliation, home-based businesses, ethnic-owned businesses, public/private indicator, year established, multiple contacts at same location, owner's sex.

The resulting Consumer Lists include name, address, and telephone number of each prospect. Business Lists are available in Basic or Advanced formats, and the Advanced format contains additional data elements.

Implementation and support of the corporate portals is provided through USADATA's Client Partner Group, which offers training to the corporate client and customer service to the end user.

SOURCE EVALUATION: The Customer Acquisition Portal is surprisingly easy to use to create your own lists and mailings, although many targeting criteria are available only by calling a data specialist. Results are sent via e-mail, in comma-delimited ASCII text format, and may be downloaded into Excel, usually within two hours of submitting the criteria. The mailing lists and mailer costs seem very reasonable. Complete price lists are found in the Order Lists & Data section of the Web site. Payment may be made by credit card, or corporate accounts may be established.

Although the Acxiom data underlying the USADATA portal does appear to be fairly comprehensive, the source of the demographic information and how recent it is are not clear, so it is difficult to judge the reliability of the data. Data source information indicates that data come "from more than fifteen of the nation's top data sources," but none of these sources are named at the site. A ProQuest database search finds articles discussing USADATA's resource partnerships with, among others, Arbitron, Scarborough Research, Hoover's, MediaMark Research, and Seagate Software.

One negative about the USADATA Web site itself is the absence of a search option. The site is easily navigated using the section title links found at the top of the page, but neither these links nor the site map give the user insight into the content of each section.

Finding a useful tutorial and guided tour required diligent exploration of the site, and I would not have known these existed at all had I not methodically clicked every link I found on each page. A site map is included, but the tour and tutorial do not appear there; the map includes only two "levels" of the site.

SOURCE VALUE RATING: All of the data source reviewers were asked to rate each source on the basis of the following eight categories, using "10" as the highest rating and "1" as the lowest ("80" being a perfect score):

1. Relative cost-to-value:	10
2. Relative timeliness of data:	8
3. Relative comprehensiveness of data:	9
4. Ease of use:	10
5. Search options available:	3
6. Level of support services:	8
7. Level of training offered:	8
8. Amount/kinds of special services offered:	9
Total Rating:	65

SOURCE REVIEWS:

> Mason, Kate. "Jiffy Lube Employs Direct Mail Portal." *Target Marketing,* September 2001.

CONTRIBUTOR NAME: Polly D. Boruff-Jones/Patricia A. Watkins
AFFILIATION: IUPUI University Library/Thunderbird School of International Management

USEFUL TIPS

- A helpful list of Frequently Asked Questions pertinent to the direct mail portal is hidden under the heading Order Mailing Lists.
- Before ordering from the prospecting portal, take advantage of the Learning Center tutorial and the Guided Tour, also found under Order Mailing Lists.

KEY ADDITIONAL SOURCES

The following source annotations are presented in alphabetical order. They range in scope from large database aggregators to single directories. Each is a valuable addition to the market and industry researcher's toolbox.

- *Association of Independent Information Professionals* (*http://www.aiip.org*). The AIIP Web site includes a free online searchable directory to its members. AIIP members, who represent more than twenty-two countries, are small-business owners working to meet the information needs of clients in all industries and in companies of all sizes. Members provide secondary and primary research, as well as library and information management services on a contractual basis. In addition to the online searchable directory, the association offers a referral program to aid in finding the members best able to provide the required research assistance.

- *Bizjournals.com.* This site offers access to job postings and business directory listings. More unique, though, is the site's access to more than fifty regional business newspapers, from Albany to Wichita. A drop-down menu allows you to select the city of interest and search the archives of that paper. Another drop-down menu offers News by Industry. Free registration is required to view articles.

- *Baker Library Industry Guides* (*http://www.library.hbs.edu/industries*). The librarians at the Harvard Business School Baker Library maintain this excellent resource, primarily for students and alumni. The site includes an outline of information, followed by sources recommended for analysis, profiles, statistics, lists, associations, and news. Another page on the site includes links to Industry Guides for thirteen key industries, suggesting what to look for and where to look.

- *Dialog DataStar* (*http://www.dialog.com/products/productline/datastar.shtml*). According to the Web site, "DataStar offers a comprehensive content collection with a special focus on pharmaceutical, biomedical, biosciences, chemical, computing, engineering and healthcare-related industries. DataStar also includes broad coverage of companies, and industry and business news." DataStar encompasses hundreds of databases and is a valuable resource for global company information, including the Kompass database of 1.5 million companies in seventy countries.

- *ECNext Knowledge Center* (*http://www.ecnext.com/commercial/knowledgecenter.shtml*). This site offers free searching of market intelligence from more than five hundred publishers covering "every major industry." Sources include periodicals, trade news-letters, and research reports. With free registration, researchers may purchase reports online and receive them immediately.

- *F & S Indexes* (*http://www.galegroup.com*). According to the Gale Group Web site, this source offers a compilation of company, product, and industry information from financial, news, trade magazine, and special report sources. The database covers acquisitions and mergers, new products, technological developments, and social and political factors. This source is available by subscription from the publisher, Gale, or through aggregators such as Dialog.

- *Gateway to Associations* (*http://info.asaenet.org/gateway/Online-AssocSlist.html*). The American Society of Association Executives makes its online directory searchable for free. Thedirectory includes listings for more than 6,500 associations. For a more comprehensive directory of associations, use the Encyclopedia of Associations, which contains more than 135,000 nonprofit membership organizations.

- *Marketing and Advertising Reference Service & Industry Group Reports (MARS).* Another Gale Group product, MARS covers multiple industries and contains advertising and marketing information on consumer products and services. It is useful for market share, market size, and new product information, and information on ad campaigns and advertising strategies. MARS is available on LexisNexis and on Dialog.

- *New York AMA GreenBook* (*http://www.greenbook.org*). Published by New York AMA Communications Services, the New York AMA GreenBook is a worldwide directory of marketing research companies and services. The GreenBook assists the researcher in finding a primary research firm to conduct additional research when secondary and online sources do not supply the needed information.

- *Standard & Poor's Industry Surveys* (*http://www.standardandpoors. com*). Many researchers consider this the first source to go to for industry overviews and information. S&P analysts study and compile information on fifty-two major industries, offering information on trends, new developments, historical perspectives, and regulatory issues. They include statistical data, charts, and graphs to illuminate the commentary. Reports are available by subscription, or you may be able to access an online version through a corporate or academic library. For a preview and to view a sample report, go to Advisor Insight at *http://www. advisorinsight.com.* Click on Preview and then Sample Report.

- *U.S. Business Reporter* (*http://www.activemedia-guide.com*). U.S. Business Reporter is a relative newcomer on the business research scene, originating in 1998. The resources are a bit rudimentary at this point, but the selection of company, marketing, economic, and business statistics documents seems to be growing. The expanding list of industry reports includes nearly fifty publications. Flat-fee subscriptions beginning at about $100 annually are available.

Appendix

The source listings and source value rating surveys provided in this Appendix are, by nature, very time sensitive and will certainly be dated to some extent at publication. Here is a very brief overview of the origin of each appendix.

A. **Directory of Online Business Data Sources:** All of the data sources (databases) that are referred to in this volume and/or other volumes in the Business Research Solutions Series are listed alphabetically by name with the name of the publisher immediately underneath. The contact information is often slanted to public relations rather than sales or support but each publisher handles outside queries in a different fashion.

B. **Directory of Online Business Data Publishers:** All of the publishers of business data sources are listed by publisher name in this directory followed by the names of the data sources (databases) that are owned and distributed by that publisher. The contact information that follows is identical to that in the first directory discussed above.

C. **Business Data Source Rating Survey:** This presentation of source ratings is in the same form as the survey in Chapter Four but has been extended to include *all* 102 business data sources covered in *all* volumes of the Business Research Solutions Series. The reader is cautioned, again, that these ratings reflect only the opinions of the contributor/reviewer and should not be viewed as the results of a large-scale national survey. Please also refer to the data source ratings section in the introduction to Chapter Four of this volume.

D. **Contributor Biographies:** The biographies of contributors to all the volumes in the Series are included to the extent that was possible. Much of the credit for the problems and solutions and the data source reviews goes to the creative group of experts.

Appendix A:
Directory of Online
Business Data Sources

10k Wizard
10k Wizard Technology LLC
Elise Soyza
Director, Marketing
elise@10kwizard.com
(214) 800-4565
1950 Stemmons Freeway,
Suite 7016
Dallas, TX 75207

ABI/Inform
ProQuest, Inc.
Tina Creguer
Marketing/Communications
Director
tina.creguer@il.proquest.com
(800) 521-0600 x3805
300 N. Zeeb Road, P.O. Box 1346
Ann Arbor, MI 48106

Accounting & Tax Database
ProQuest, Inc.
Tina Creguer
Marketing/Communications
Director
tina.creguer@il.proquest.com
(800) 521-0600 x3805
300 N. Zeeb Road, P.O. Box 1346
Ann Arbor, MI 48106

Accurint
Seisint, Inc.
Cathy Demarco
cdemarco@accurint.com
(561) 893-8008
6601 Park of Commerce
Boulevard
Boca Raton, FL 33487

Adweek
VNU eMedia
Deborah Patton
Media Relations
Dpatton@vnubusinessmedia.com
(646) 654-5755
770 Broadway, 7th Floor
New York, NY 10003

AICPA
*American Institute of Certified Public
Accountants*
Edward J. Novack
Product Marketing Director
edward.novack@CPA2Biz.com
(201) 521-5714
1211 Avenue of the Americas
New York, NY 10036

Alacra
Alacra, Inc.
Carol Ann Thomas
Marketing Manager
carolann.thomas@alacra.com
(212) 804-1541
88 Pine Street, 3rd Floor
New York, NY 10005

BigCharts
MarketWatch.com, Inc.
123 North 3rd Street
Minneapolis, MN 55401

Bloomberg Professional
Bloomberg L.P.
Leslie Van Ordsdel
Bloomberg Professional
Product Training
lvanorsdel@bloomberg.net
(212) 318-2244
499 Park Avenue
New York, NY 10022

Bondtrac
Bondtrac, Inc.
Dan Powers
President
dan.powers@bondtrac.com
(800) 555-6864
210 Park Avenue, Suite 2200
Oklahoma City, OK 73102

Brandweek
VNU eMedia
Deborah Patton
Media Relations
Dpatton@vnubusinessmedia.com
(646) 654-5755
770 Broadway, 7th Floor
New York, NY 10003

Briefing.com
Briefing.com
Cassandra Bayna
Media Relations
cbayna@briefing.com
(312) 670-4463 x232
401 N. Michigan Avenue,
Suite 1680
Chicago, IL 60611

Budget and Economic Outlook
U.S. Congressional Budget Office
William J. Gainer
Associate Director for
Management
(202) 226-2600
Ford House Office Building,
4th Floor
Second and D Streets SW
Washington, DC 20515

Bureau of Economic Analysis (BEA)
U.S. Bureau of Economic Analysis
Larry R. Moran
Media contact
LARRY.MORAN@BEA.GOV
(202) 606-9691
1441 L Street NW
Washington, DC 20230

Bureau of Labor Statistics
U.S. Bureau of Labor Statistics
Katharine G. Abraham
Commissioner
blsdata_staff@bls.gov
(202) 606-7800
2 Massachusetts Avenue, NE
Washington, DC 20212

Bureau of the Census
U.S. Census Bureau
Stephen Buckner
Media contact
stephen.l.buckner@census.gov
(301) 763.2135
U.S. Census Bureau
Washington, DC 20233

Bureau of the Public Debt online:
Treasury Bills, Notes, and Bonds
U.S. Bureau of the Public Debt
Van Zeck
Commissioner
OAdmin@bpd.treas.gov
Bureau of the Public Debt
200 3rd Street
Parkersburg, WV 26106

Business & Industry
Thomson Learning
Jennifer Bernardelli
Product Manager, Gale
Jennifer.Bernardelli@gale.com
(800) 877-4253 x1514
Gale Group
27500 Drake Road
Farmington Hills, MI 48331

Business Dateline

ProQuest, Inc.
Tina Creguer
Marketing/Communications
Director
tina.creguer@il.proquest.com
(800) 521-0600 x3805
300 N. Zeeb Road, P.O. Box 1346
Ann Arbor, MI 48106

Business Wire

Business Wire, Inc.
Sandy Malloy
Senior Information Specialist
sandy.malloy@businesswire.com
(415) 986-4422 x512
44 Montgomery Street,
39th Floor
San Francisco, CA 94104

CBS MarketWatch

MarketWatch.com, Inc.
Dan Silmore
Director, Public Relations
dsilmore@marketwatch.com
(415) 733-0534
KPIX Building
825 Battery Street, 3rd Floor
San Francisco, CA 94111

CCH Tax Research Network

CCH Incorporated
Leslie Bonacum
Media Relations
bonacuml@cch.com
(847) 267-7153
2700 Lake Cook Road
Riverwoods, IL 60015

Chilling Effects

Electronic Frontier Foundation
Wendy Seltzer
Founder
wendy@seltzer
Electronic Frontier Foundation
454 Shotwell Street
San Francisco, CA 94110

CLAIMS/U.S. Patents

IFI Claims Patent Services
Jim Brown
Customer Service
(302) 633-7200
3202 Kirkwood Highway,
Suite 203
Wilmington, DE 19808

Closed End Fund Center

Mutual Fund Educational Association
Brian M. Smith
Media contact
bsmith@cefa.com
(816) 413-8900
P.O. Box 28037
Kansas City, MO 64188

Corporate Affiliations

LexisNexis
Judi Schultz
Senior Public Relations Manager
judith.schultz@lexisnexis.com
(937) 865-7942
LexisNexis Group
P.O. Box 933
Dayton, OH 45401

Country Data

PRS Group, Inc., The
Adrian Shute
Vice President Marketing/Public
Relations
ashute@prsgroup.com
(315) 431-0511
6320 Fly Road, Suite 102,
P.O. Box 248
East Syracuse, NY 13057

CyberAlert

CyberAlert, Inc.
Joel Crosley
Director, Business Development
jcrosley@CyberAlert.com
(800) 461-7353
Foot of Broad Street
Stratford, CT 06615

D&B—Dun's Electronic Business Directory
Dun & Bradstreet, Inc.
Julie C. Hiner
Public Relations, U.S.
hinerj@dnb.com
(973) 921-5608
One Diamond Hill Road
Murray Hill, NJ 07974

D&B—Dun's Financial Records Plus
Dun & Bradstreet, Inc.
Julie C. Hiner
Public Relations, U.S.
hinerj@dnb.com
(973) 921-5608
One Diamond Hill Road
Murray Hill, NJ 07974

D&B—Dun's Market Identifiers
Dun & Bradstreet, Inc.
Julie C. Hiner
Public Relations, U.S.
hinerj@dnb.com
(973) 921-5608
One Diamond Hill Road
Murray Hill, NJ 07974

D&B Key Business Ratios (KBR) on the Web
Dun & Bradstreet, Inc.
Julie C. Hiner
Public Relations, U.S.
hinerj@dnb.com
(973) 921-5608
One Diamond Hill Road
Murray Hill, NJ 07974

D&B Million Dollar Database
Dun & Bradstreet, Inc.
Julie C. Hiner
Public Relations, U.S.
hinerj@dnb.com
(973) 921-5608
3 Sylvan Way
Parsippany, NJ 07054

DailyStocks.com
DailyStocks, Inc.
info@dailystocks.com
New York, NY 10006

Datamonitor Market Research
Datamonitor/Reuters
info@datamonitor.com
106 Baker Street
London W1M 1LA, UK

Derwent Patents Citation Index
Derwent Information
sales@derwentus.com
(703) 706-4220
14 Great Queen Street
London WC2B 5DF, UK

Dialog
Thomson Legal & Regulatory
Sandy Scherer
Director, Corporate Communications, Dialog
sandy.scherer@dialog.com
(919) 461-7354
The Dialog Corporation
11000 Regency Parkway, Suite 10
Cary, NC 27511

Disclosure Database
Thomson Financial
Kerri Shepherd
Manager, Public Relations
kerri.shepherd@tfn.com
(646) 822-2077
195 Broadway, 8th Floor
New York, NY 10007

Economic Indicators
Council of Economic Advisors
wwwadmin@gpo.gov
(888) 293-6498
Office of Electronic Information Dissemination Services
732 N. Capitol Street
Washington, DC 20402

Economy.com
Economy.com, Inc.
Monica Mercurio
Director, Customer Service
mmercurio@economy.com
(610)241-3362
600 Willowbrook Lane
West Chester, PA 19382

EIU ViewsWire
Economist Intelligence Unit
Jisla Escoto
Senior Contract Administrator
jislaescoto@eiu.com
(212) 554-0600
111 West 57th Street
New York, NY 10019

Encyclopedia of Associations (EA)
Thomson Learning
Jennifer Bernardelli
Product Manager, Gale
Jennifer.Bernardelli@gale.com
(800) 877-4253 x1514
Gale Group
27500 Drake Road
Farmington Hills, MI 48331

EventLine
Elsevier Science B.V.
Eric Merkel-Sobotta
Director, Corporate Relations
PressOffice@elsevier.com
31 20 485-2994
P.O. Box 211
NL-1000 AE Amsterdam,
Netherlands

Experian Business Credit Profiles
Experian
Donald Girard
Public Relations Director
donald.girard@experian.com
(714) 830-5647
505 City Parkway W, 3rd Floor
Orange, CA 92868

Factiva
Factiva
Gina Giamanco
Global Public Relations
gina.giamanco@factiva.com
(609) 627-2342
105 Madison Avenue, 10th Floor
New York, NY 10016

FactSet
FactSet Data Systems, Inc.
Betsy Fischer
Media Relations
efischer@factset.com
(203) 863-1500
One Greenwich Plaza
Greenwich, CT 06830

Fastcase
Fastcase, Inc.
Edward Walters
Media Relations
ed.walters@fastcase.com
(202) 466-5920
1916 Wilson Boulevard, Suite 302
Arlington, VA 22201

Federal Reserve Board
U.S. Board of Governors, Federal Reserve System
Jennifer J. Johnson
Secretary
(202) 452-3000
20th Street and Constitution
Avenue NW
Washington, DC 20551

Financial Accounting Research System (FARS)
Financial Accounting Standards Board
Ron Guerrette
Vice President, Publishing
rpguerrette@f-a-f.org
(203) 847-0700 x237
FASB Research Systems
401 Merritt 7, P.O. Box 5116
Norwalk, CT 06856

Financial Accounting Standards Board (FASB)
Financial Accounting Standards Board
Sheryl L. Thompson
Public Relations Manager
slthompson@f-a-f.org
(203) 847-0700
401 Merritt 7, P.O. Box 5116
Norwalk, CT 06856

Financial Forecast Center
Institute of Business Forecasting
ibf@ibf.org
(516) 504-7576
P.O. Box 670159
Flushing, NY 11367

Financial Times
Financial Times Electronic Publishing
Gregory Roth
Public Relations Manager, U.S.
Gregory.Roth@ft.com
44 171 8257777
Fitzroy House
13-17 Epworth Street
London EC2A 4DL, UK

FindLaw
Thomson Legal & Regulatory
(650) 210-1900
1235 Pear Avenue, Suite 111
Mountain View, CA 94043

First Research
First Research, Inc.
Bobby Martin
bmartin@firstresearch.com
(888) 331-2275 x1

FreeEDGAR
EDGAR Online, Inc.
Jay Sears
Senior Vice President, Business & Strategy Development
sears@edgar-online.com
(203) 852-5669
50 Washington Street, 9th Floor
Norwalk, CT 06854

Gale Group Business A.R.T.S.
Thomson Learning
Jennifer Bernardelli
Product Manager, Gale
Jennifer.Bernardelli@gale.com
(800) 877-4253 x1514
Gale Group
27500 Drake Road
Farmington Hills, MI 48331

Gale Group New Product Announcements/Plus (NPA/Plus)
Thomson Learning
Jennifer Bernardelli
Product Manager, Gale
Jennifer.Bernardelli@gale.com
(800) 877-4253 x1514
Gale Group
27500 Drake Road
Farmington Hills, MI 48331

Gale Group Newsletter Database
Thomson Learning
Jennifer Bernardelli
Product Manager, Gale
Jennifer.Bernardelli@gale.com
(800) 877-4253 x1514
Gale Group
27500 Drake Road
Farmington Hills, MI 48331

Gale Group Trade & Industry Database
Thomson Learning
Jennifer Bernardelli
Product Manager, Gale
Jennifer.Bernardelli@gale.com
(800) 877-4253 x1514
Gale Group
27500 Drake Road
Farmington Hills, MI 48331

Global Insight
Global Insight, Inc.
Ken McGill
ken.mcgill@globalinsight.com
(610) 490-2644
1000 Winter Street, Suite 4300N
Waltham, MA 02451

GPO Access
Superintendent of Documents, U.S.
Government Printing Office
gpoaccess@gpo.gov
(888) 293-6498
U.S. Government Printing Office
732 North Capitol Street, NW
Washington, DC 20401

Hoover's Online
Dun & Bradstreet, Inc.
Lisa Glass
Public Relations Manager
lglass@hoovers.com
(512) 374-4662
5800 Airport Boulevard
Austin, TX 78752

INPADOC/Families and Legal Status
European Patent Office
Elena Sereix
Database Online Services
maes@epo.e-mail.com
(431) 521 26 40 51
Information Service
Schottenfeldgasse 29 Postfach 82
A-1072 Vienna, Austria

Internal Revenue Service:
The Digital Daily
Internal Revenue Service, Department
of the Treasury
Robert E. Wenzel
Commissioner
1111 Constitution Avenue NW,
Room 1552
Washington, DC 20224

International Accounting
Standards Board
International Accounting Standards
Board
Tom Seidenstein
Media contact
tseidenstein@iasb.org.uk
44 20 7246 6410
30 Cannon Street
London EC4M 6XH, UK

Investext
Thomson Financial
Kerri Shepherd
Manager, Public Relations
kerri.shepherd@tfn.com
(646) 822-2077
195 Broadway, 8th Floor
New York, NY 10007

IPO Express
EDGAR Online, Inc.
Jay Sears
Senior Vice President, Business
& Strategy Development
sears@edgar-online.com
(203) 852-5669
50 Washington Sreet, 9th Floor
Norwalk, CT 06854

IPO.com
IPO Group, Inc.
DeWayne Martin
Publisher
dmartin@ipo.com
(212) 918-4510
48 Wall Street, Suite 1100
New York, NY 10005

KnowX
ChoicePoint Asset Company
Jane Rafedie
jane.rafeedie@choicepoint.com
(404) 541-0300

Law Digest
LexisNexis
Judi Schultz
Senior Public Relations Manager
judith.schultz@lexisnexis.com
(937) 865-7942
LexisNexis Group
P.O. Box 933
Dayton, OH 45401

Lawyers.com
LexisNexis
Judi Schultz
Senior Public Relations Manager
judith.schultz@lexisnexis.com
(937) 865-7942
LexisNexis Group
P.O. Box 933
Dayton, OH 45401

Legal Information Institute (LII)
Legal Information Institute/Cornell Law School
Thomas R. Bruce and
Peter W. Martin
Co-Directors
lii@lii.law.cornell.edu
Cornell Law School
Myron Taylor Hall
Ithaca, NY 14853

LexisNexis
LexisNexis
Judi Schultz
Senior Public Relations Manager
judith.schultz@lexisnexis.com
(937) 865-7942
LexisNexis Group
P.O. Box 933
Dayton, OH 45401

LexisNexis (legal)
LexisNexis
Judi Schultz
Senior Public Relations Manager
judith.schultz@lexisnexis.com
(937) 865-7942
LexisNexis Group
P.O. Box 933
Dayton, OH 45401

LexisNexis (public records)
LexisNexis
Judi Schultz
Senior Public Relations Manager
judith.schultz@lexisnexis.com
(937) 865-7942
LexisNexis Group
P.O. Box 933
Dayton, OH 45401

LexisONE
LexisNexis
Judi Schultz
Senior Public Relations Manager
judith.schultz@lexisnexis.com
(937) 865-7942
LexisNexis Group
P.O. Box 933
Dayton, OH 45401

Lipper Horizon
Reuters
Camilla Altamura
Media Relations Manager
Camilla.Altamura@lipper.reuters.com
(877) 955-4773
3 Times Square, 17th Floor
New York, NY 10036

Litigation Stock Report
Thomson Media
Paul E. McGowan
Editor-in-Chief
pmcgowan@lsrmail.com
(804) 282-7026
P.O. Box 18322
Richmond, VA 23226

LIVEDGAR
Global Securities Information, Inc.
Bob Brooks
Marketing/Public Relations Director
bbrooks@gsionline.com
(202) 628-1155
419 7th Street NW, Suite 300
Washington, DC 20004

LLRX.com
Law Library Resource Xchange LLC
Sabrina Pacifici
President/CEO
spacific@earthlink.net

Loislaw
Aspen Publishers
Marc Jennings
Publisher
marc.jennings@
aspenpublishers.com
(646) 728-3001 x423
1185 Avenue of the Americas
New York, NY 10036

Market Share Reporter
Thomson Learning
Jennifer Bernardelli
Product Manager, Gale
Jennifer.Bernardelli@gale.com
(800) 877-4253 x1514
Gale Group
27500 Drake Road
Farmington Hills, MI 48331

MarketResearch.com
MarketResearch.com, Inc.
Robert Granader
CEO
rgranader@marketresearch.com
(301) 468.3650 x216
11810 Parklawn Drive
Rockville, MD 20852

Markets & Industry Library on LexisNexis
LexisNexis
Judi Schultz
Senior Public Relations Manager
judith.schultz@lexisnexis.com
(937) 865-7942
LexisNexis Group
P.O. Box 933
Dayton, OH 45401

MarkMonitor
MarkMonitor, Inc.
Elisa Cooper
Director of Marketing
elisa.cooper@markmonitor.com
(208) 389-5779
12438 W. Bridge Street, Suite 100
Boise, ID 83713

Mergent Online
Mergent FIS, Inc.
Kimberly Pile
Human Resources
hr@mergent.com
(800) 342-5647
60 Madison Avenue, 6th Floor
New York, NY 10010

MindBranch
MindBranch, Inc.
Sharon Oakes
Director, Marketing
soakes@mindbranch.com
(413) 458-7673
160 Water Street
Williamstown, MA 01267

Morningstar
Morningstar, Inc.
Martha Conlon Moss
Corporate Communications
martha.moss@morningstar.com
(312) 696-6050
225 W. Wacker Drive
Chicago, IL 60606

MSN Money
Microsoft Corporation
Microsoft Corporation
One Microsoft Way
Redmond, WA 98052

Multex Fundamentals
Multex, Inc.
Samantha Topping
Media contact
stopping@multex.com
(917) 294-0329
100 William Street, 7th Floor
New York, NY 10038

National Law Library
Juri Search
Satish Sheth
President
ssheth@jurisearch.com
(877) 484-7529
4301 Windfern Road, Suite 200
Houston, TX 77041

News on LexisNexis
LexisNexis
Judi Schultz
Senior Public Relations Manager
judith.schultz@lexisnexis.com
(937) 865-7942
LexisNexis Group
P.O. Box 933
Dayton, OH 45401

OneSource
OneSource Information Services
Ed Hutchinson
Director, Public Relations
Edward_Hutchinson@
onesource.com
(978) 318-4300
300 Baker Avenue, Suite 303
Concord, MA 01742

PatentWeb
Information Holdings, Inc. (MicroPatent)
Laura Gaze
Marketing/Communications
Director
lgaze@micropatent.com
(203) 466-5055 x205
MicroPatent USA
250 Dodge Avenue
East Haven, CT 06512

PatSearch FullText
Information Holdings, Inc. (MicroPatent)
Laura Gaze
Marketing/Communications
Director
lgaze@micropatent.com
(203) 466-5055 x205
MicroPatent USA
250 Dodge Avenue
East Haven, CT 06512

Profound
Thomson Legal & Regulatory
Sandy Scherer
Director, Corporate Communica-
tions, Dialog
sandy.scherer@dialog.com
(919) 461-7354
The Dialog Corporation
11000 Regency Parkway, Suite 10
Cary, NC 27511

PROMT
Thomson Learning
Jennifer Bernardelli
Product Manager, Gale
Jennifer.Bernardelli@gale.com
(800) 877-4253 x1514
Gale Group
27500 Drake Road
Farmington Hills, MI 48331

Reuters Business Insight
Datamonitor/Reuters
info@datamonitor.com
106 Baker Street
London W1M 1LA, UK

RMA's Annual Statement Studies
Risk Management Association, The
Kathleen Beans
Public Relations Manager/
Senior Writer
kbeans@rmahq.org
(215) 446-4095
1650 Market Street, Suite 2300
Philadelphia, PA 19103

SAEGIS
Thomson Legal & Regulatory
Scott Rutherford
Senior Marketing Communica-
tions Specialist
Scott.Rutherford@t-t.com
(617) 376-7667
Thomson & Thomson
500 Victory Road
North Quincy, MA 02171

SDC Platinum
Thomson Financial
Kerri Shepherd
Manager, Public Relations
kerri.shepherd@tfn.com
(646) 822-2077
195 Broadway, 8th Floor
New York, NY 10007

SmartMoney
Dow Jones & Company, Inc. & Hearst
Communications, Inc.
Amy Knapp
Public Relations
aknapp@smartmoney.com
(212) 649-2765
250 W. 55th Street, 10th Floor
New York, NY 10019

Standard & Poor's NetAdvantage
McGraw-Hill
Burt Shulman
Vice President, Marketing
Services & Publishing
burt_shulman@
standardandpoors.com
(212) 438-1288
55 Water Street
New York, NY 10041

The Virtual Chase
Ballard Spahr Andrews & Ingersoll LLP
Genie Tyburski
Web Manager, The Virtual Chase
tyburski@virtualchase.com
(215) 665-8500
1735 Market Street, 51st Floor
Philadelphia, PA 19103

The Wall Street Transcript
The Wall Street Transcript
Andrew Pickup
CEO/Publisher
pickup@twst.com
(212) 952-7437
67 Wall Street, 16th Floor
New York, NY 10005

TheStreet.com
TheStreet.com
Wendy Tullo
Media contact
wendy.tullo@thestreet.com
(212) 321-5000
14 Wall Street
New York, NY 10005

Thomas Register
Thomas Publishing Company
Ruth Hurd
Publisher
RHURD@trpublication.com
(212) 290-7277
TR User Services
Five Penn Plaza, 12th floor
New York, NY 10001

Thomas: Legislative Information on the Internet
Library of Congress
thomas@loc.gov
(202) 707-5000
101 Independence Avenue, SE
Washington, DC 20540

Thomson Analytics
Thomson Financial
Kerri Shepherd
Manager, Public Relations
kerri.shepherd@tfn.com
(646) 822-2077
195 Broadway, 8th Floor
New York, NY 10007

Thomson Research
Thomson Financial
Kerri Shepherd
Manager, Public Relations
kerri.shepherd@tfn.com
(646) 822-2077
195 Broadway, 8th Floor
New York, NY 10007

Trademark Applications and Registrations Retrieval (TARR)
U.S. Patent and Trademark Office
James E. Rogan
Director
usptoinfo@uspto.gov
General Information Services
Division(800) 786-9199
Crystal Plaza 3, Room 2C02
Washington, DC 20231

Trademark Electronic Search System (TESS)
U.S. Patent and Trademark Office
James E. Rogan
Director
usptoinfo@uspto.gov
(800) 786-9199
General Information Services
Division
Crystal Plaza 3, Room 2C02
Washington, DC 20231

Trademark.com
Information Holdings, Inc. (MicroPatent)
Laura Gaze
Marketing/Communications
Director
lgaze@micropatent.com
(203) 466-5055 x205
250 Dodge Avenue
East Haven, CT 06512

TRADEMARKSCAN
Thomson Legal & Regulatory
Scott Rutherford
Senior Marketing Communications Specialist
Scott.Rutherford@t-t.com
(617) 376-7667
Thomson & Thomson
500 Victory Road
North Quincy, MA 02171

U.S. Copyright Office
U.S. Copyright Office, Library of Congress
Marybeth Peters
Register of Copyrights
101 Independence Avenue, SE
Washington, DC 20559

U.S. Copyrights
Thomson Legal & Regulatory
Sandy Scherer
Director, Corporate Communications, Dialog
sandy.scherer@dialog.com
(919) 461-7354
The Dialog Corporation
11000 Regency Parkway, Suite 10
Cary, NC 27511

U.S. Patents Fulltext
Thomson Legal & Regulatory
Sandy Scherer
Director, Corporate Communications, Dialog
sandy.scherer@dialog.com
(919) 461-7354
The Dialog Corporation
11000 Regency Parkway, Suite 10
Cary, NC 27511

U.S. Securities and Exchange Commission
U.S. Securities and Exchange Commission
Harvey L. Pitt
Chairman
help@sec.gov
(202) 942-7040
Office of Investor Education and Assistance
450 Fifth Street, NW
Washington, DC 20549

USADATA

USADATA, Inc.
Dominic LeClaire
Director of Marketing
dleclaire@usadata.com
(212) 679-1411 x222
292 Madison Avenue, 3rd Floor
New York, NY 10017

USPTO

U.S. Patent and Trademark Office
James E. Rogan
Director
usptoinfo@uspto.gov
(800) 786-9199
Office of Electronic Information
Products
Crystal Plaza 3, Suite 441
Washington, DC 20231

Value Line

Value Line
David Henigson
dhenigson@valueline.com
(212) 907-1500
Institutional Services
220 E. 42nd Street
New York, NY 10017

VersusLaw

VersusLaw, Inc.
Jim Corbett
Vice President, Business
Development
jcorbett@versuslaw.com
(888) 377-8752 x3024
2613 - 151st Place NE
Redmond, WA 98052

Wall Street City ProStation

Telescan, Inc.
Dan Olson
Media contact
dan@investools.com
(281) 588-9700
5959 Corporate Drive,
Suite LL250
Houston, TX 77036

Wall Street Journal (WSJ)

Dow Jones & Company, Inc.
Aaron Bedy
aaron.bedy@dowjones.com
(609) 520-7889
P.O. Box 300
Princeton, NJ 08543

Westlaw (legal)

Thomson Legal & Regulatory
Ruth Orrick
Senior Vice President, Corporate Communications
ruth.orrick@westgroup.com
(651) 687-4099
West Group
610 Opperman Drive
Eagan, MN 55123

Westlaw (public records)

Thomson Legal & Regulatory
Ruth Orrick
Senior Vice President, Corporate Communications
ruth.orrick@westgroup.com
(651) 687-4099
West Group
610 Opperman Drive
Eagan, MN 55123

**White House Economic Statistics
Briefing Room**

White House, The
feedback@whitehouse.gov
(202) 456-1414
1600 Pennsylvania Avenue, NW
Washington, DC 20500

Yahoo! Bond Center

Yahoo! Inc.
Chris Castro
Chief Communications Officer,
Senior Vice President
(408) 349-3300
701 First Avenue
Sunnyvale, CA 94089

Yahoo! Finance

Yahoo! Inc.

Chris Castro
Chief Communications Officer,
Senior Vice President
(408) 349-3300
701 First Avenue
Sunnyvale, CA 94089

Zacks

Zacks Investment Research

support@zacks.com
(800) 767-3771
155 N. Wacker Drive
Chicago, IL 60606

Appendix B: Directory of Online Business Data Source Publishers

10k Wizard Technology LLC
10k Wizard
  Elise Soyza
  Director, Marketing
  elise@10kwizard.com
  (214) 800-4565
  1950 Stemmons Freeway,
  Suite 7016
  Dallas, TX 75207

Alacra, Inc.
Alacra
  Carol Ann Thomas
  Marketing Manager
  carolann.thomas@alacra.com
  (212) 804-1541
  88 Pine Street, 3rd Floor
  New York, NY 10005

American Institute of Certified Public Accountants
AICPA
  Edward J. Novack
  Product Marketing Director
  edward.novack@CPA2Biz.com
  (201) 521-5714
  1211 Avenue of the Americas
  New York, NY 10036

Aspen Publishers
Loislaw
  Marc Jennings
  Publisher
  marc.jennings@
  aspenpublishers.com
  (646) 728-3001 x423
  1185 Avenue of the Americas
  New York, NY 10036

Ballard Spahr Andrews & Ingersoll LLP
The Virtual Chase
  Genie Tyburski
  Web Manager, The Virtual Chase
  tyburski@virtualchase.com
  (215) 665-8500
  1735 Market Street, 51st Floor
  Philadelphia, PA 19103

Bloomberg L.P.
Bloomberg Professional
  Leslie Van Ordsdel
  Bloomberg Professional Product
  Training
  lvanorsdel@bloomberg.net
  (212) 318-2244
  499 Park Avenue
  New York, NY 10022

Bondtrac, Inc.
Bondtrac
  Dan Powers
  President
  dan.powers@bondtrac.com
  (800) 555-6864
  210 Park Avenue, Suite 2200
  Oklahoma City, OK 73102

Briefing.com
Briefing.com
  Cassandra Bayna
  Media Relations
  cbayna@briefing.com
  (312) 670-4463 x232
  401 N. Michigan Avenue,
  Suite 1680
  Chicago, IL 60611

Business Wire, Inc.
Business Wire
Sandy Malloy
Senior Information Specialist
sandy.malloy@businesswire.com
(415) 986-4422 x512
44 Montgomery Street, 39th Floor
San Francisco, CA 94104

CCH Incorporated
CCH Tax Research Network
Leslie Bonacum
Media Relations
bonacuml@cch.com
(847) 267-7153
2700 Lake Cook Road
Riverwoods, IL 60015

ChoicePoint Asset Company
KnowX
Jane Rafedie
jane.rafeedie@choicepoint.com
(404) 541-0300

Council of Economic Advisors
Economic Indicators
wwwadmin@gpo.gov
(888) 293-6498
Office of Electronic Information
Dissemination Services
732 N. Capitol Street
Washington, DC 20402

CyberAlert, Inc.
CyberAlert
Joel Crosley
Director, Business Development
jcrosley@CyberAlert.com
(800) 461-7353
Foot of Broad Street
Stratford, CT 06615

DailyStocks, Inc.
DailyStocks.com
info@dailystocks.com
New York, NY 10006

Datamonitor/Reuters
Datamonitor Market Research
Reuters Business Insight
info@datamonitor.com
106 Baker Street
London W1M 1LA, UK

Derwent Information
Derwent Patents Citation Index
sales@derwentus.com
(703) 706-4220
14 Great Queen Street
London WC2B 5DF, UK

Dow Jones & Company, Inc.
Wall Street Journal (WSJ)
Aaron Bedy
aaron.bedy@dowjones.com
(609) 520-7889
P.O. Box 300
Princeton, NJ 08543

Dow Jones & Company, Inc. & Hearst Communications, Inc.
SmartMoney
Amy Knapp
Public Relations
aknapp@smartmoney.com
(212) 649-2765
250 W. 55th Street, 10th Floor
New York, NY 10019

Dun & Bradstreet, Inc.
D&B—Dun's Electronic Business Directory
D&B—Dun's Financial Records Plus
D&B—Dun's Market Identifiers
D&B Key Business Ratios (KBR) on the Web
D&B Million Dollar Database
Julie C. Hiner
Public Relations, U.S.
hinerj@dnb.com
(973) 921-5608
3 Sylvan Way
Parsippany, NJ 07054

Hoover's Online
Lisa Glass
Public Relations Manager
lglass@hoovers.com
(512) 374-4662
5800 Airport Boulevard
Austin, TX 78752

Economist Intelligence Unit
EIU ViewsWire
Jisla Escoto
Senior Contract Administrator
jislaescoto@eiu.com
(212) 554-0600
111 West 57th Street
New York, NY 10019

Economy.com, Inc.
Economy.com
Monica Mercurio
Director, Customer Service
mmercurio@economy.com
(610)241-3362
600 Willowbrook Lane
West Chester, PA 19382

EDGAR Online, Inc.
FreeEDGAR
IPO Express
Jay Sears
Senior Vice President, Business
& Strategy Development
sears@edgar-online.com
(203) 852-5669
50 Washington Sreet, 9th Floor
Norwalk, CT 06854

Electronic Frontier Foundation
Chilling Effects
Wendy Seltzer
Founder
wendy@seltzer
Electronic Frontier Foundation
454 Shotwell Street
San Francisco, CA 94110

Elsevier Science B.V.
EventLine
Eric Merkel-Sobotta
Director, Corporate Relations
PressOffice@elsevier.com
31 20 485-2994
P.O. Box 211
NL-1000 AE Amsterdam,
Netherlands

European Patent Office
INPADOC/Families and Legal Status
Elena Sereix
Database Online Services
maes@epo.e-mail.com
(431) 521 26 40 51
Information Service
Schottenfeldgasse 29 Postfach 82
A-1072 Vienna, Austria

Experian
Experian Business Credit Profiles
Donald Girard
Public Relations Director
donald.girard@experian.com
(714) 830-5647
505 City Parkway W, 3rd Floor
Orange, CA 92868

Factiva
Factiva
Gina Giamanco
Global Public Relations
gina.giamanco@factiva.com
(609) 627-2342
105 Madison Avenue, 10th Floor
New York, NY 10016

FactSet Data Systems, Inc.
FactSet
Betsy Fischer
Media Relations
efischer@factset.com
(203) 863-1500
One Greenwich Plaza
Greenwich, CT 06830

Fastcase, Inc.
Fastcase
Edward Walters
Media Relations
ed.walters@fastcase.com
(202) 466-5920
1916 Wilson Boulevard,
Suite 302
Arlington, VA 22201

Financial Accounting Standards Board
*Financial Accounting Research System
(FARS)*
Ron Guerrette
Vice President, Publishing
rpguerrette@f-a-f.org
(203) 847-0700 x237
FASB Research Systems
401 Merritt 7, P.O. Box 5116
Norwalk, CT 06856
*Financial Accounting Standards
Board (FASB)*
Sheryl L. Thompson
Public Relations Manager
slthompson@f-a-f.org
(203) 847-0700
401 Merritt 7, P.O. Box 5116
Norwalk, CT 06856

Financial Times Electronic Publishing
Financial Times
Gregory Roth
Public Relations Manager, U.S.
Gregory.Roth@ft.com
44 171 8257777
Fitzroy House
13-17 Epworth Street
London EC2A 4DL, UK

First Research, Inc.
First Research
Bobby Martin
bmartin@firstresearch.com
(888) 331-2275 x1

Global Insight, Inc.
Global Insight
Ken McGill
ken.mcgill@globalinsight.com
(610) 490-2644
1000 Winter Street, Suite 4300N
Waltham, MA 02451

Global Securities Information, Inc.
LIVEDGAR
Bob Brooks
Marketing/Public Relations
Director
bbrooks@gsionline.com
(202) 628-1155
419 7th Street NW, Suite 300
Washington, DC 20004

IFI Claims Patent Services
CLAIMS/U.S. Patents
Jim Brown
Customer Service
(302) 633-7200
3202 Kirkwood Highway,
Suite 203
Wilmington, DE 19808

**Information Holdings, Inc.
(MicroPatent)**
*PatentWeb
PatSearch FullText
Trademark.com*
Laura Gaze
Marketing/Communications
Director
lgaze@micropatent.com
(203) 466-5055 x205
250 Dodge Avenue
East Haven, CT 06512

Institute of Business Forecasting
Financial Forecast Center
ibf@ibf.org
(516) 504-7576
P.O. Box 670159
Flushing, NY 11367

Internal Revenue Service, Department of the Treasury
Internal Revenue Service: The Digital Daily
Robert E. Wenzel
Commissioner
1111 Constitution Avenue NW, Room 1552
Washington, DC 20224

International Accounting Standards Board
International Accounting Standards Board
Tom Seidenstein
Media contact
tseidenstein@iasb.org.uk
44 20 7246 6410
30 Cannon Street
London EC4M 6XH, UK

IPO Group, Inc.
IPO.com
DeWayne Martin
Publisher
dmartin@ipo.com
(212) 918-4510
48 Wall Street, Suite 1100
New York, NY 10005

Juri Search
National Law Library
Satish Sheth
President
ssheth@jurisearch.com
(877) 484-7529
4301 Windfern Road, Suite 200
Houston, TX 77041

Law Library Resource Xchange LLC
LLRX.com
Sabrina Pacifici
President/CEO
spacific@earthlink.net

Legal Information Institute/Cornell Law School
Legal Information Institute (LII)
Thomas R. Bruce and Peter W. Martin
Co-Directors
lii@lii.law.cornell.edu
Cornell Law School
Myron Taylor Hall
Ithaca, NY 14853

LexisNexis
Corporate Affiliations
Law Digest
Lawyers.com
LexisNexis
LexisNexis (legal)
LexisNexis (public records)
LexisONE
Markets & Industry Library on LexisNexis
News on LexisNexis
Judi Schultz
Senior Public Relations Manager
judith.schultz@lexisnexis.com
(937) 865-7942
LexisNexis Group
P.O. Box 933
Dayton, OH 45401

Library of Congress
Thomas: Legislative Information on the Internet
thomas@loc.gov
(202) 707-5000
101 Independence Avenue, SE
Washington, DC 20540

MarketResearch.com, Inc.
MarketResearch.com
Robert Granader
CEO
rgranader@marketresearch.com
(301) 468.3650 x216
11810 Parklawn Drive
Rockville, MD 20852

MarketWatch.com, Inc.
BigCharts
123 North 3rd Street
Minneapolis, MN 55401
CBS MarketWatch
Dan Silmore
Director, Public Relations
dsilmore@marketwatch.com
(415) 733-0534
KPIX Building
825 Battery Street, 3rd Floor
San Francisco, CA 94111

MarkMonitor, Inc.
MarkMonitor
Elisa Cooper
Director of Marketing
elisa.cooper@markmonitor.com
(208) 389-5779
12438 W. Bridge Street, Suite 100
Boise, ID 83713

McGraw-Hill
Standard & Poor's NetAdvantage
Burt Shulman
Vice President, Marketing Services & Publishing
burt_shulman@
standardandpoors.com
(212) 438-1288
55 Water Street
New York, NY 10041

Mergent FIS, Inc.
Mergent Online
Kimberly Pile
Human Resources
hr@mergent.com
(800) 342-5647
60 Madison Avenue, 6th Floor
New York, NY 10010

Microsoft Corporation
MSN Money
Microsoft Corporation
One Microsoft Way
Redmond, WA 98052

MindBranch, Inc.
MindBranch
Sharon Oakes
Director, Marketing
soakes@mindbranch.com
(413) 458-7673
160 Water Street
Williamstown, MA 01267

Morningstar, Inc.
Morningstar
Martha Conlon Moss
Corporate Communications
martha.moss@morningstar.com
(312) 696-6050
225 W. Wacker Drive
Chicago, IL 60606

Multex, Inc.
Multex Fundamentals
Samantha Topping
Media contact
stopping@multex.com
(917) 294-0329
100 William Street, 7th Floor
New York, NY 10038

Mutual Fund Educational Association
Closed-End Fund Center
Brian M. Smith
Media contact
bsmith@cefa.com
(816) 413-8900
P.O. Box 28037
Kansas City, MO 64188

OneSource Information Services
OneSource
Ed Hutchinson
Director, Public Relations
Edward_Hutchinson@
onesource.com
(978) 318-4300
300 Baker Avenue, Suite 303
Concord, MA 01742

ProQuest, Inc.
ABI/Inform
Accounting & Tax Database
Business Dateline
Tina Creguer
Marketing/Communications
Director
tina.creguer@il.proquest.com
(800) 521-0600 x3805
300 N. Zeeb Road, P.O. Box 1346
Ann Arbor, MI 48106

PRS Group, Inc., The
Country Data
Adrian Shute
Vice President Marketing/Public
Relations
ashute@prsgroup.com
(315) 431-0511
6320 Fly Road, Suite 102,
P.O. Box 248
East Syracuse, NY 13057

Reuters
Lipper Horizon
Camilla Altamura
Media Relations Manager
Camilla.Altamura@lipper.
reuters.com
(877) 955-4773
3 Times Square, 17th Floor
New York, NY 10036

Risk Management Association, The
RMA's Annual Statement Studies
Kathleen Beans
Public Relations Manager/
Senior Writer
kbeans@rmahq.org
(215) 446-4095
1650 Market Street, Suite 2300
Philadelphia, PA 19103

Seisint, Inc.
Accurint
Cathy Demarco
cdemarco@accurint.com
(561) 893-8008
6601 Park of Commerce
Boulevard
Boca Raton, FL 33487

Superintendent of Documents, U.S. Government Printing Office
GPO Access
gpoaccess@gpo.gov
(888) 293-6498
U.S. Government Printing Office
732 North Capitol Street, NW
Washington, DC 20401

Telescan, Inc.
Wall Street City ProStation
Dan Olson
Media contact
dan@investools.com
(281) 588-9700
5959 Corporate Drive,
Suite LL250
Houston, TX 77036

The Wall Street Transcript
The Wall Street Transcript
Andrew Pickup
CEO/Publisher
pickup@twst.com
(212) 952-7437
67 Wall Street, 16th Floor
New York, NY 10005

TheStreet.com
TheStreet.com
Wendy Tullo
Media contact
wendy.tullo@thestreet.com
(212) 321-5000
14 Wall Street
New York, NY 10005

Thomas Publishing Company
Thomas Register
Ruth Hurd
Publisher
RHURD@trpublication.com
(212) 290-7277
TR User Services
Five Penn Plaza, 12th floor
New York, NY 10001

Thomson Financial
Disclosure Database
Investext
SDC Platinum
Thomson Analytics
Thomson Research
 Kerri Shepherd
 Manager, Public Relations
 kerri.shepherd@tfn.com
 (646) 822-2077
 195 Broadway, 8th Floor
 New York, NY 10007

Thomson Learning
Business & Industry
Encyclopedia of Associations (EA)
Gale Group Business A.R.T.S.
Gale Group New Product Announce-
ments/Plus (NPA/Plus)
Gale Group Newsletter Database
Gale Group Trade & Industry Database
Market Share Reporter
PROMT
 Jennifer Bernardelli
 Product Manager, Gale
 Jennifer.Bernardelli@gale.com
 (800) 877-4253 x1514
 Gale Group
 27500 Drake Road
 Farmington Hills, MI 48331

Thomson Legal & Regulatory
Dialog
Profound
U.S. Copyrights
U.S. Patents Fulltext
 Sandy Scherer
 Director, Corporate Communica-
 tions, Dialog
 sandy.scherer@dialog.com
 (919) 461-7354
 The Dialog Corporation
 11000 Regency Parkway, Suite 10
 Cary, NC 27511
FindLaw
 (650)210-1900
 1235 Pear Avenue, Suite 111
 Mountain View, CA 94043

SAEGIS
TRADEMARKSCAN
 Scott Rutherford
 Senior Marketing Communica-
 tions Specialist
 Scott.Rutherford@t-t.com
 (617) 376-7667
 Thomson & Thomson
 500 Victory Road
 North Quincy, MA 02171
Westlaw (legal)
Westlaw (public records)
 Ruth Orrick
 Senior Vice President, Corpo-
 rate Communications
 ruth.orrick@westgroup.com
 (651) 687-4099
 West Group
 610 Opperman Drive
 Eagan, MN 55123

Thomson Media
Litigation Stock Report
 Paul E. McGowan
 Editor-in-Chief
 pmcgowan@lsrmail.com
 (804) 282-7026
 P.O. Box 18322
 Richmond, VA 23226

**U.S. Board of Governors, Federal
Reserve System**
Federal Reserve Board
 Jennifer J. Johnson
 Secretary
 (202) 452-3000
 20th Street and Constitution
 Avenue NW
 Washington, DC 20551

U.S. Bureau of Economic Analysis
Bureau of Economic Analysis (BEA)
 Larry R. Moran
 Media contact
 LARRY.MORAN@BEA.GOV
 (202) 606-9691
 1441 L Street NW
 Washington, DC 20230

U.S. Bureau of Labor Statistics
Bureau of Labor Statistics
Katharine G. Abraham
Commissioner
blsdata_staff@bls.gov
(202) 606-7800
2 Massachusetts Avenue, NE
Washington, DC 20212

U.S. Bureau of the Public Debt
Bureau of the Public Debt online:
Treasury Bills, Notes, and Bonds
Van Zeck
Commissioner
OAdmin@bpd.treas.gov
Bureau of the Public Debt
200 3rd Street
Parkersburg, WV 26106

U.S. Census Bureau
Bureau of the Census
Stephen Buckner
Media contact
stephen.l.buckner@census.gov
(301) 763.2135
U.S. Census Bureau
Washington, DC 20233

U.S. Congressional Budget Office
Budget and Economic Outlook
William J. Gainer
Associate Director for
Management
(202) 226-2600
Ford House Office Building,
4th Floor
Second and D Streets SW
Washington, DC 20515

U.S. Copyright Office, Library of Congress
U.S. Copyright Office
Marybeth Peters
Register of Copyrights
101 Independence Avenue, SE
Washington, DC 20559

U.S. Patent and Trademark Office
Trademark Applications and Registra-
tions Retrieval (TARR)
Trademark Electronic Search System
(TESS)
USPTO
James E. Rogan
Director
usptoinfo@uspto.gov
(800) 786-9199
Office of Electronic Information
Products
Crystal Plaza 3, Suite 441
Washington, DC 20231

U.S. Securities and Exchange Commission
U.S. Securities and Exchange
Commission
Harvey L. Pitt
Chairman
help@sec.gov
(202) 942-7040
Office of Investor Education and
Assistance
450 Fifth Street, NW
Washington, DC 20549

USADATA, Inc.
USADATA
Dominic LeClaire
Director of Marketing
dleclaire@usadata.com
(212) 679-1411 x222
292 Madison Avenue, 3rd Floor
New York, NY 10017

Value Line
Value Line
David Henigson
dhenigson@valueline.com
(212) 907-1500
Institutional Services
220 E. 42nd Street
New York, NY 10017

VersusLaw, Inc.
VersusLaw
Jim Corbett
Vice President, Business Development
jcorbett@versuslaw.com
(888) 377-8752 x3024
2613 - 151st Place NE
Redmond, WA 98052

VNU eMedia
Adweek
Brandweek
Deborah Patton
Media Relations
Dpatton@
vnubusinessmedia.com
(646) 654-5755
770 Broadway, 7th Floor
New York, NY 10003

White House, The
White House Economic Statistics
Briefing Room
feedback@whitehouse.gov
(202) 456-1414
1600 Pennsylvania Avenue, NW
Washington, DC 20500

Yahoo! Inc.
Yahoo! Bond Center
Yahoo! Finance
Chris Castro
Chief Communications Officer,
Senior Vice President
(408) 349-3300
701 First Avenue
Sunnyvale, CA 94089

Zacks Investment Research
Zacks
support@zacks.com
(800) 767-3771
155 N. Wacker Drive
Chicago, IL 60606

Appendix C: Business Data Source Rating Survey

Table C.1. Data Source Ratings – Alphabetical by Data Source

DATA SOURCE	1. RELATIVE COST-TO-VALUE	2. RELATIVE TIMELINESS OF DATA	3. RELATIVE COMPREHENSIVENESS OF DATA	4. EASE OF USE	5. SEARCH OPTIONS AVAILABLE	6. LEVEL OF SUPPORT SERVICES	7. LEVEL OF TRAINING OFFERED	8. AMOUNT/KINDS OF SPECIAL SERVICES OFFERED	TOTAL
10k Wizard	9	10	10	10	10	10	5	9	73
ABI/Inform	6	10	7	10	10	8	8	10	69
Accounting & Tax Database	5	8	8	4	6	7	7	7	52
Accurint	10	9	7	9	9	7	9	9	69
Adweek	7	10	10	5	3	5	5	3	48
AICPA	8	9	8	7	6	7	5	3	53
Alacra	8	8	8	7	7	8	7	7	60
Bloomberg Professional	8	10	9	6	10	10	10	9	72
Bondtrac	5	10	10	10	10	10	10	10	75
Brandweek	7	10	10	5	3	5	5	3	48
Briefing.com	8	10	8	9	7	8	8	8	66
Budget and Economic Outlook	10	10	10	10	5	5	5	5	60
Bureau of Economic Analysis (BEA)	10	10	10	8	5	7	6	8	64
Bureau of Labor Statistics	10	10	10	6	8	8	7	8	67

Table C.1. Data Source Ratings – Alphabetical by Data Source (cont.)

DATA SOURCE	1. RELATIVE COST-TO-VALUE	2. RELATIVE TIMELINESS OF DATA	3. RELATIVE COMPREHENSIVENESS OF DATA	4. EASE OF USE	5. SEARCH OPTIONS AVAILABLE	6. LEVEL OF SUPPORT SERVICES	7. LEVEL OF TRAINING OFFERED	8. AMOUNT/KINDS OF SPECIAL SERVICES OFFERED	TOTAL
Bureau of the Census	10	10	10	6	7	8	8	8	67
Business & Industry	7	6	8	8	8	7	8	6	58
Business Dateline	5	9	8	9	9	8	7	6	61
Business Wire	5	10	5	7	5	5	5	5	47
CBS MarketWatch	10	9	9	9	8	8	8	8	69
CCH Tax Research Network	7	9	8	10	10	9	8	8	69
Chilling Effects	9	6	7	8	8	7	5	9	59
Corporate Affiliations	5	7	7	9	10	10	9	9	66
Country Data	10	10	10	8	8	10	6	10	72
D&B—Dun's Electronic Business Directory	7	7	6	2	9	8	8	8	55
D&B—Dun's Financial Records Plus	7	7	6	2	9	8	8	8	55
D&B—Dun's Market Identifiers	7	7	6	2	9	8	8	8	55

Table C.1. Data Source Ratings – Alphabetical by Data Source (cont.)

DATA SOURCE	1. RELATIVE COST-TO-VALUE	2. RELATIVE TIMELINESS OF DATA	3. RELATIVE COMPRE-HENSIVENESS OF DATA	4. EASE OF USE	5. SEARCH OPTIONS AVAILABLE	6. LEVEL OF SUPPORT SERVICES	7. LEVEL OF TRAINING OFFERED	8. AMOUNT/ KINDS OF SPECIAL SERVICES OFFERED	TOTAL
D&B Key Business Ratios (KBR) on the Web	6	7	8	7	6	7	3	6	50
D&B Million Dollar Database	5	7	8	9	7	7	3	5	51
Datamonitor Market Research	7	6	9	8	6	6	5	5	52
Dialog	8	9	9	7	10	10	9	8	70
Disclosure Database	7	8	9	9	7	7	5	7	59
Economic Indicators	7	8	6	5	3	4	5	5	43
Economy.com	8	10	8	9	7	8	8	8	66
EIU ViewsWire	8	9	9	10	9	9	9	8	71
Encyclopedia of Associations (EA)	9	8	8	8	9	9	5	5	61
EventLine	7	8	7	7	10	10	10	5	64
Experian Business Credit Profiles	3	8	5	6	6	7	6	9	50
Factiva	9	10	10	8	7	6	6	9	65
FactSet	7	10	10	7	5	8	8	8	63
Fastcase	7	7	6	7	8	9	5	6	55

Table C.1. Data Source Ratings – Alphabetical by Data Source (cont.)

DATA SOURCE	1. RELATIVE COST-TO-VALUE	2. RELATIVE TIMELINESS OF DATA	3. RELATIVE COMPRE-HENSIVENESS OF DATA	4. EASE OF USE	5. SEARCH OPTIONS AVAILABLE	6. LEVEL OF SUPPORT SERVICES	7. LEVEL OF TRAINING OFFERED	8. AMOUNT/KINDS OF SPECIAL SERVICES OFFERED	TOTAL
Federal Reserve Board	10	10	8	10	10	6	5	10	69
Financial Accounting Research System (FARS)	9	8	9	6	7	4	4	5	52
Financial Accounting Standards Board (FASB)	10	10	8	10	5	8	5	3	59
Financial Forecast Center	10	10	8	10	5	8	5	8	64
Financial Times	8	10	6	7	7	2	5	5	50
FindLaw	10	8	10	7	8	2	5	7	57
First Research	5	8	8	8	5	5	5	5	49
FreeEDGAR/EDGAR Online/EDGARpro	6	9	7	6	7	8	8	6	57
Gale Group Business A.R.T.S.	7	10	7	6	6	7	8	5	56
Gale Group New Product Announcements/Plus (NPA/Plus)	7	10	9	8	9	9	8	7	67

Table C.1. Data Source Ratings – Alphabetical by Data Source (cont.)

DATA SOURCE	1. RELATIVE COST-TO-VALUE	2. RELATIVE TIMELINESS OF DATA	3. RELATIVE COMPREHENSIVENESS OF DATA	4. EASE OF USE	5. SEARCH OPTIONS AVAILABLE	6. LEVEL OF SUPPORT SERVICES	7. LEVEL OF TRAINING OFFERED	8. AMOUNT/KINDS OF SPECIAL SERVICES OFFERED	TOTAL
Gale Group Newsletter Database	7	8	7	6	6	8	9	9	60
Gale Group Trade & Industry Database	8	9	6	8	9	4	5	5	54
GPO Access	5	7	6	6	8	1	3	6	42
Hoover's Online	9	8	7	8	6	7	6	9	60
Internal Revenue Service: *The Digital Daily*	10	10	10	8	8	8	5	8	67
International Accounting Standards Board	9	9	8	10	6	7	5	3	57
Investext	7	7	8	6	8	7	6	7	56
KnowX	5	7	6	8	5	5	2	4	42
Legal Information Institute (LII)	10	10	10	10	9	8	5	9	71
LexisNexis	8	9	8	7	8	8	7	7	62
LexisNexis (public records)	7	9	10	7	10	8	8	9	68
LexisONE	5	7	4	5	7	1	2	5	36
Lipper Horizon	5	10	10	6	7	8	7	8	61

Table C.1. Data Source Ratings – Alphabetical by Data Source (cont.)

DATA SOURCE	1. RELATIVE COST-TO-VALUE	2. RELATIVE TIMELINESS OF DATA	3. RELATIVE COMPREHENSIVENESS OF DATA	4. EASE OF USE	5. SEARCH OPTIONS AVAILABLE	6. LEVEL OF SUPPORT SERVICES	7. LEVEL OF TRAINING OFFERED	8. AMOUNT/KINDS OF SPECIAL SERVICES OFFERED	TOTAL
LIVEDGAR	9	9	9	8	9	8	9	9	70
LLRX.com	10	9	9	10	8	8	5	10	69
Loislaw	10	10	9	8	8	9	7	9	70
Market Share Reporter	10	5	10	10	10	10	8	10	73
MarketResearch.com	8	9	9	10	10	10	7	8	71
Markets & Industry Library on LexisNexis	8	10	10	7	8	10	10	10	73
MarkMonitor	10	10	10	10	9	9	9	10	77
Mergent Online	6	9	9	8	7	8	9	6	62
MindBranch	9	8	9	9	7	10	2	7	61
Morningstar	10	10	10	9	9	8	9	9	74
MSN Money	9	8	8	7	7	4	1	3	47
Multex Fundamentals	6	8	10	7	8	5	5	5	54
National Law Library	4	3	4	4	5	2	4	2	28
News on LexisNexis	8	8	7	7	8	7	6	8	59
OneSource	8	8	8	10	9	8	8	9	68
Profound	9	10	9	9	9	9	10	10	75
PROMT	8	10	7	7	7	6	6	7	58
Reuters Business Insight	7	6	7	8	5	9	9	7	58

Table C.1. Data Source Ratings – Alphabetical by Data Source (cont.)

DATA SOURCE	1. RELATIVE COST-TO-VALUE	2. RELATIVE TIMELINESS OF DATA	3. RELATIVE COMPREHENSIVENESS OF DATA	4. EASE OF USE	5. SEARCH OPTIONS AVAILABLE	6. LEVEL OF SUPPORT SERVICES	7. LEVEL OF TRAINING OFFERED	8. AMOUNT/KINDS OF SPECIAL SERVICES OFFERED	TOTAL
RMA's Annual Statement Studies	10	8	6	9	4	7	3	7	54
SmartMoney	7	10	8	6	7	5	5	6	54
Standard & Poor's NetAdvantage	8	10	8	7	8	7	6	8	62
The Virtual Chase	10	9	9	8	9	7	9	9	70
The Wall Street Transcript	8	10	8	9	9	8	8	10	70
TheStreet.com	9	10	9	6	8	8	8	9	67
Thomas Register	10	8	9	9	7	10	2	10	65
Thomas: Legislative Information on the Internet	10	10	10	10	10	8	5	8	71
Thomson Research	5	10	10	7	8	6	5	8	59
Trademark Applications and Registrations Retrieval (TARR)	10	8	9	10	8	8	5	5	63
Trademark Electronic Search System (TESS)	9	8	9	9	10	7	5	5	62

Table C.1. Data Source Ratings – Alphabetical by Data Source (cont.)

DATA SOURCE	1. RELATIVE COST-TO-VALUE	2. RELATIVE TIMELINESS OF DATA	3. RELATIVE COMPRE-HENSIVENESS OF DATA	4. EASE OF USE	5. SEARCH OPTIONS AVAILABLE	6. LEVEL OF SUPPORT SERVICES	7. LEVEL OF TRAINING OFFERED	8. AMOUNT/ KINDS OF SPECIAL SERVICES OFFERED	TOTAL
Trademark.com	8	9	10	8	9	8	9	8	69
TRADEMARKSCAN	9	9	10	10	8	10	10	5	71
U.S. Copyright Office	9	10	9	7	7	1	5	10	58
U.S. Copyrights	10	9	9	9	8	10	10	1	66
U.S. Securities and Exchange Commission	10	10	8	9	5	6	2	2	52
USADATA	10	8	9	10	3	8	8	9	65
USPTO	10	10	10	7	9	8	7	10	71
Value Line	9	9	9	10	5	10	10	9	71
Yahoo! Finance	9	10	9	9	9	5	5	6	62
Zacks	10	9	9	10	10	5	5	10	68

Note: Reviewers were asked to rate each research data source on the basis of a "10" being the highest, most complimentary, rating and "1" being the lowest or least complimentary ("80" being a perfect score).

Table C.2. Data Source Ratings – Ranked by Overall Rating

DATA SOURCE	1. RELATIVE COST-TO-VALUE	2. RELATIVE TIMELINESS OF DATA	3. RELATIVE COMPRE-HENSIVENESS OF DATA	4. EASE OF USE	5. SEARCH OPTIONS AVAILABLE	6. LEVEL OF SUPPORT SERVICES	7. LEVEL OF TRAINING OFFERED	8. AMOUNT/ KINDS OF SPECIAL SERVICES OFFERED	TOTAL
MarkMonitor	10	10	10	10	9	9	9	10	77
Bondtrac	5	10	10	10	10	10	10	10	75
Profound	9	10	9	9	9	9	10	10	75
Morningstar	10	10	10	9	9	8	9	9	74
10k Wizard	9	10	10	10	10	10	5	9	73
Market Share Reporter	10	5	10	10	10	10	8	10	73
Markets & Industry Library on LexisNexis	8	10	10	7	8	10	10	10	73
Bloomberg Professional	8	10	9	6	10	10	10	9	72
Country Data	10	10	10	8	8	10	6	10	72
EIU ViewsWire	8	9	9	10	9	9	9	8	71
Legal Information Institute (LII)	10	10	10	10	9	8	5	9	71
MarketResearch.com	8	9	9	10	10	10	7	8	71
Thomas: Legislative Information on the Internet	10	10	10	10	10	8	5	8	71
TRADEMARKSCAN	9	9	10	10	8	10	10	5	71

Table C.2. Data Source Ratings – Ranked by Overall Rating (cont.)

DATA SOURCE	1. RELATIVE COST-TO-VALUE	2. RELATIVE TIMELINESS OF DATA	3. RELATIVE COMPRE-HENSIVENESS OF DATA	4. EASE OF USE	5. SEARCH OPTIONS AVAILABLE	6. LEVEL OF SUPPORT SERVICES	7. LEVEL OF TRAINING OFFERED	8. AMOUNT/ KINDS OF SPECIAL SERVICES OFFERED	TOTAL
USPTO	10	10	10	7	9	8	7	10	71
Value Line	9	9	9	10	5	10	10	9	71
Dialog	8	9	9	7	10	10	9	8	70
LIVEDGAR	9	9	9	8	9	8	9	9	70
Loislaw	10	10	9	8	8	9	7	9	70
The Virtual Chase	10	9	9	8	9	7	9	9	70
The Wall Street Transcript	8	10	8	9	9	8	8	10	70
ABI/Inform	6	10	7	10	10	8	8	10	69
Accurint	10	9	7	9	9	7	9	9	69
CBS MarketWatch	10	9	9	9	8	8	8	8	69
CCH Tax Research Network	7	9	8	10	10	9	8	8	69
Federal Reserve Board	10	10	8	10	10	6	5	10	69
LLRX.com	10	9	9	10	8	8	5	10	69
Trademark.com	8	9	10	8	9	8	9	8	69
LexisNexis (public records)	7	9	10	7	10	8	8	9	68
OneSource	8	8	8	10	9	8	8	9	68
Zacks	10	9	9	10	10	5	5	10	68

Table C.2. Data Source Ratings – Ranked by Overall Rating (cont.)

DATA SOURCE	1. RELATIVE COST-TO-VALUE	2. RELATIVE TIMELINESS OF DATA	3. RELATIVE COMPRE-HENSIVENESS OF DATA	4. EASE OF USE	5. SEARCH OPTIONS AVAILABLE	6. LEVEL OF SUPPORT SERVICES	7. LEVEL OF TRAINING OFFERED	8. AMOUNT/KINDS OF SPECIAL SERVICES OFFERED	TOTAL
Bureau of Labor Statistics	10	10	10	6	8	8	7	8	67
Bureau of the Census	10	10	10	6	7	8	8	8	67
Gale Group New Product Announcements/Plus (NPA/Plus)	7	10	9	8	9	9	8	7	67
Internal Revenue Service: The Digital Daily	10	10	10	8	8	8	5	8	67
TheStreet.com	9	10	9	6	8	8	8	9	67
Briefing.com	8	10	8	9	7	8	8	8	66
Corporate Affiliations	5	7	7	9	10	10	9	9	66
Economy.com	8	10	8	9	7	8	8	8	66
U.S. Copyrights	10	9	9	9	8	10	10	1	66
Factiva	9	10	10	8	7	6	6	9	65
Thomas Register	10	8	9	9	7	10	2	10	65
USADATA	10	8	9	10	3	8	8	9	65
Bureau of Economic Analysis (BEA)	10	10	10	8	5	7	6	8	64

Table C.2. Data Source Ratings – Ranked by Overall Rating (cont.)

DATA SOURCE	1. RELATIVE COST-TO-VALUE	2. RELATIVE TIMELINESS OF DATA	3. RELATIVE COMPRE-HENSIVENESS OF DATA	4. EASE OF USE	5. SEARCH OPTIONS AVAILABLE	6. LEVEL OF SUPPORT SERVICES	7. LEVEL OF TRAINING OFFERED	8. AMOUNT/KINDS OF SPECIAL SERVICES OFFERED	TOTAL
EventLine	7	8	7	7	10	10	10	5	64
Financial Forecast Center	10	10	8	10	5	8	5	8	64
FactSet	7	10	10	7	5	8	8	8	63
Trademark Applications and Registrations Retrieval (TARR)	10	8	9	10	8	8	5	5	63
LexisNexis	8	9	8	7	8	8	7	7	62
Mergent Online	6	9	9	8	7	8	9	6	62
Standard & Poor's NetAdvantage	8	10	8	7	8	7	6	8	62
Trademark Electronic Search System (TESS)	9	8	9	9	10	7	5	5	62
Yahoo! Finance	9	10	9	9	9	5	5	6	62
Business Dateline	5	9	8	9	9	8	7	6	61
Encyclopedia of Associations (EA)	9	8	8	8	9	9	5	5	61
Lipper Horizon	5	10	10	6	7	8	7	8	61
MindBranch	9	8	9	9	7	10	2	7	61
Alacra	8	8	8	7	7	8	7	7	60

Table C.2. Data Source Ratings – Ranked by Overall Rating (cont.)

DATA SOURCE	1. RELATIVE COST-TO-VALUE	2. RELATIVE TIMELINESS OF DATA	3. RELATIVE COMPRE-HENSIVENESS OF DATA	4. EASE OF USE	5. SEARCH OPTIONS AVAILABLE	6. LEVEL OF SUPPORT SERVICES	7. LEVEL OF TRAINING OFFERED	8. AMOUNT/ KINDS OF SPECIAL SERVICES OFFERED	TOTAL
Budget and Economic Outlook	10	10	10	10	5	5	5	5	60
Gale Group Newsletter Database	7	8	7	6	6	8	9	9	60
Hoover's Online	9	8	7	8	6	7	6	9	60
Chilling Effects	9	6	7	8	8	7	5	9	59
Disclosure Database	7	8	9	9	7	7	5	7	59
Financial Accounting Standards Board (FASB)	10	10	8	10	5	8	5	3	59
News on LexisNexis	8	8	7	7	8	7	6	8	59
Thomson Research	5	10	10	7	8	6	5	8	59
Business & Industry	7	6	8	8	8	7	8	6	58
PROMT	8	10	7	7	7	6	6	7	58
Reuters Business Insight	7	6	7	8	5	9	9	7	58
U.S. Copyright Office	9	10	9	7	7	1	5	10	58
FindLaw	10	8	10	7	8	2	5	7	57
FreeEDGAR/EDGAR Online/EDGARpro	6	9	7	6	7	8	8	6	57

Table C.2. Data Source Ratings – Ranked by Overall Rating (cont.)

DATA SOURCE	1. RELATIVE COST-TO-VALUE	2. RELATIVE TIMELINESS OF DATA	3. RELATIVE COMPRE-HENSIVENESS OF DATA	4. EASE OF USE	5. SEARCH OPTIONS AVAILABLE	6. LEVEL OF SUPPORT SERVICES	7. LEVEL OF TRAINING OFFERED	8. AMOUNT/ KINDS OF SPECIAL SERVICES OFFERED	TOTAL
International Accounting Standards Board	9	9	8	10	6	7	5	3	57
Gale Group Business A.R.T.S.	7	10	7	6	6	7	8	5	56
Investext	7	7	8	6	8	7	6	7	56
D&B—Dun's Electronic Business Directory	7	7	6	2	9	8	8	8	55
D&B—Dun's Financial Records Plus	7	7	6	2	9	8	8	8	55
D&B—Dun's Market Identifiers	7	7	6	2	9	8	8	8	55
Fastcase	7	7	6	7	8	9	5	6	55
Gale Group Trade & Industry Database	8	9	6	8	9	4	5	5	54
Multex Fundamentals	6	8	10	7	8	5	5	5	54
RMA's Annual Statement Studies	10	8	6	9	4	7	3	7	54
SmartMoney	7	10	8	6	7	5	5	6	54
AICPA	8	9	8	7	6	7	5	3	53

Table C.2. Data Source Ratings – Ranked by Overall Rating (cont.)

DATA SOURCE	1. RELATIVE COST-TO-VALUE	2. RELATIVE TIMELINESS OF DATA	3. RELATIVE COMPRE-HENSIVENESS OF DATA	4. EASE OF USE	5. SEARCH OPTIONS AVAILABLE	6. LEVEL OF SUPPORT SERVICES	7. LEVEL OF TRAINING OFFERED	8. AMOUNT/ KINDS OF SPECIAL SERVICES OFFERED	TOTAL
Accounting & Tax Database	5	8	8	4	6	7	7	7	52
Datamonitor Market Research	7	6	9	8	6	6	5	5	52
Financial Accounting Research System (FARS)	9	8	9	6	7	4	4	5	52
U.S. Securities and Exchange Commission	10	10	8	9	5	6	2	2	52
D&B Million Dollar Database	5	7	8	9	7	7	3	5	51
D&B Key Business Ratios (KBR) on the Web	6	7	8	7	6	7	3	6	50
Experian Business Credit Profiles	3	8	5	6	6	7	6	9	50
Financial Times	8	10	6	7	7	2	5	5	50
First Research	5	8	8	8	5	5	5	5	49
Adweek	7	10	10	5	3	5	5	3	48
Brandweek	7	10	10	5	3	5	5	3	48

Table C.2. Data Source Ratings – Ranked by Overall Rating (cont.)

DATA SOURCE	1. RELATIVE COST-TO-VALUE	2. RELATIVE TIMELINESS OF DATA	3. RELATIVE COMPRE-HENSIVENESS OF DATA	4. EASE OF USE	5. SEARCH OPTIONS AVAILABLE	6. LEVEL OF SUPPORT SERVICES	7. LEVEL OF TRAINING OFFERED	8. AMOUNT/ KINDS OF SPECIAL SERVICES OFFERED	TOTAL
Business Wire	5	10	5	7	5	5	5	5	47
MSN Money	9	8	8	7	7	4	1	3	47
Economic Indicators	7	8	6	5	3	4	5	5	43
GPO Access	5	7	6	6	8	1	3	6	42
KnowX	5	7	6	8	5	5	2	4	42
LexisONE	5	7	4	5	7	1	2	5	36
National Law Library	4	3	4	4	5	2	4	2	28

Note: Reviewers were asked to rate each research data source on the basis of a "10" being the highest, most complimentary, rating and "1" being the lowest or least complimentary ("80" being a perfect score).

Appendix D:
Contributor Biographies

Melissa Barr
Cuyahoga County Public Library

Melissa Barr is the legal resources specialist and reference librarian at the Maple Heights Regional Library, part of the Cuyahoga County Public Library system in Northeast Ohio. She serves as a building steward for the Cuyahoga County Library Union (Service Employees International Union, District 1199) and as an SEIU/1199 delegate to the Cleveland Federation of Labor. She is a member of the Ohio Regional Association of Law Libraries, the American Association of Law Libraries (AALL), and two AALL Special Interest Sections: Research Instruction & Patron Services and Legal Information Services to the Public.

Melissa earned a B.A. in English from Heidelberg College in Tiffin, Ohio (1977), a paralegal certificate from Ohio Paralegal Institute in Cleveland, Ohio (1982), and an M.L.S. from Kent State University (1997). She has also attended Baldwin Wallace College in Berea, Ohio; Central Texas College in Killeen, Texas; Bad Kreuznach, West Germany; Cuyahoga Community College in Parma, Ohio; and Cleveland State University, where her interests ranged from criminal justice to business communications, cultural anthropology, and Web page design.

After completing a tour of duty in the U.S. Army, Melissa started out in the legal field as a file clerk for a law firm and then moved on to work as a paralegal, bankruptcy liaison clerk, legal secretary, recruiting coordinator, and law library assistant. She also worked as a research assistant for a consulting company that prepared economic damage claim reports for court cases. While attending graduate school at Kent State University, Melissa was employed as the waste tracking coordinator at a hazardous waste recycling plant. She joined the Cuyahoga County Public Library staff in 1999. Melissa is the author of "Democracy in the Dark: Public Access Restrictions from Westlaw and LexisNexis," which appeared in the January 2003 edition of *Searcher: The Magazine for Database Professionals*.

Kathy Biehl
Independent Researcher

Attorney and freelance journalist Kathy Biehl is coauthor of *The Lawyer's Guide to Internet Research* (Scarecrow Press, 2000). She has reviewed online legal research resources as a columnist for LLRX.com, the Internet Legal Research Newsletter, and Pro2Net (now Smart Pros). In addition to legal and Internet writing, she has contributed more than eight hundred articles on a spectrum of general interest topics to national and regional publications. She is the winner of the 2002 Lone Star Award in magazine column writing presented by the Houston Press Club. Biehl earned a B.A. from Southern Methodist University with highest honors and a J.D. from the University of Texas School of Law with honors. She taught business law at Rice University and legal research and writing at the University of Houston Law Center. A member of the State Bar of Texas, she maintained a private law practice for nineteen years before turning to full-time research and writing.

Polly D. Boruff-Jones
IUPUI University Library

Polly Boruff-Jones is an assistant librarian at University Library on the Indiana University Purdue University Indianapolis (IUPUI) campus, where she serves as the reference team leader and business subject specialist. She received both her B.A. and M.L.S. degrees from Indiana University, Bloomington.

Ms. Boruff-Jones's primary areas of research are integration and assessment of information literacy in the business school undergraduate curriculum and management of virtual reference services in academic libraries.

Meryl Brodsky
Consultant

Meryl Brodsky is currently working as an independent consultant after working as a librarian at Ernst & Young LLP for four years and Cornell University for ten years. She has an M.B.A. from the Business School at Cornell and an M.L.S. from Southern Connecticut State University. She specializes in the financial services industry and particularly likes to analyze and compare databases. She is a member of the Special Libraries Association and the American Library Association.

Helen P. Burwell
Burwell Enterprises

Author and online expert Helen Burwell is well known for providing consulting services to the information industry and international business community. Since 1984, as president of Burwell Enterprises, Inc., she has helped corporate clients develop successful strategies for electronic retrieval of competitive intelligence information.

Ms. Burwell is editor and publisher of *The Burwell World Directory of Information Brokers,* an annual annotated directory of nearly one thousand companies that provide information retrieval and consulting. Now in its fourteenth edition, *The Burwell Directory* is widely used by business and industry for outsourcing information research. The directory is also available on the Internet at *http://www.burwellinc.com.*

Ms. Burwell holds a master's degree from Louisiana State University's School of Library and Information Science, which named her its 1996 Outstanding Alumna for her contributions to the information profession. In 1998, the Association of Independent Information Professionals, an international organization comprising information consultants, online searchers, document delivery services, and other information professionals, presented Ms. Burwell with the President's Award for outstanding service to the profession.

In recent years Ms. Burwell has been an invited guest speaker both at the European Information Brokers Meeting in Frankfurt, Germany, and at the first Asian and Pacific Rim Conference and Exhibition on Electronic Commerce in Shanghai, China. Regular speaking engagements in the United States have included national conferences and large trade shows such as the National Online Meeting, Online World, and the Society of Competitive Intelligence Professionals.

Ms. Burwell is the author of *Online Competitive Intelligence,* published by Facts On Demand Press in 1999 and 2000. The second edition will be released in January 2004.

Cindy Carlson
Fried, Frank, Harris, Shriver & Jacobson

Cindy Carlson is the electronic resources librarian for the Washington, D.C., office of the law firm of Fried, Frank, Harris, Shriver & Jacobson and has over fifteen years of experience working in libraries. She writes a monthly column, "Notes from the Technology Trenches," on electronic research, training, and legal information technology for LLRX.com, the Law Library Resource Exchange. An occasional contributor to other publications covering information research, she has also spoken at several conferences concerning Internet resources in business and legal research. She leads the Legal Research Training Focus Group of the Law Librarians' Society of the District of Columbia.

Elena Carvajal
Ernst & Young

Elena Carvajal is an information professional at Ernst & Young's Center for Business Knowledge. She has over twenty years of experience as a librarian, researcher, analyst, and communications specialist. Prior to joining Ernst & Young, Carvajal worked at EDS in a variety of roles, including research analyst for the corporate library and market analyst and industry relations/public relations specialist for the travel and transportation industry. She also served as marketing communication specialist for the Executive Communications Group at EDS.

Ms. Carvajal earned her B.A. in English and her M.L.S. from the University of North Texas. She has previously served on a number of committees and programs for the American Library Association, where her contributions include editing "COGnotes," the conference newsletter, and presenting a workshop entitled "Wrestling with the Future" at an ALA LITA Pre-Conference. She is a member of the Special Library Association.

Donna Cavallini
Kilpatrick Stockton LLP

Donna F. Cavallini has over fifteen years experience in the legal profession in a wide variety of settings, including academic and governmental and in both large and small law firms. Currently, she serves the attorneys of the law firm of Kilpatrick Stockton

LLP as manager of competitive knowledge, a position that combines the disciplines of knowledge management and competitive intelligence and focuses on the practice areas of corporate/securities, intellectual property, and technology law. Before joining the firm in 1996, Ms. Cavallini was library program administrator for the Florida Attorney General's Office, and prior to working for the state of Florida, she was solo librarian for a medium-sized firm in Tallahassee, Florida. She is a regular contributor to information professional Listservs and newsletters, including LLRX and The Virtual Chase, and she has been a speaker for professional groups both large and small. Ms. Cavallini received a B.A. in Classics from Washington University and a J.D. from St. Louis University.

Dudee Chiang
Amgen, Inc.

Dudee Chiang currently works as the library business analyst at Amgen, Inc., the world's largest biotechnology company. Prior to her current position, she worked as the database information consultant at Amgen Library, and she held various positions at the Norris Medical Library and Leavey Library at University of Southern California. She holds an M.S. degree and a certificate of advanced studies (C.A.S.) in Library and Information Science from the University of Illinois at Urbana-Champaign, and she also has a M.B.A. degree from the Pepperdine University. She is an experienced professional in information retrieval, end-user training, and resource evaluation; in recent years, she has taken on project management responsibilities for implementing technologies within the library environment, including Web and portals. She is always looking for new challenges in her work

Wes Edens
Thunderbird School of International Management

Wes Edens is on the faculty of the International Business Information Centre at Thunderbird, the American Graduate School of International Management, in Glendale, Arizona. In addition to duties as a full-time international business researcher, Wes evaluates and selects electronic resources for Thunderbird, ranked number one in the world for international business by *US News & World Report* and the *Wall Street Journal*. He holds a B.S. in

Business Administration and a M.L.S. degree, both from the University of Arizona, and is an M.B.A. candidate at Arizona State University.

Prior to coming to Thunderbird, Mr. Edens was business librarian/bibliographer for the University of North Dakota in Grand Forks. He has also worked as a reference librarian for Pima Community College in Tucson, Arizona.

Mr. Edens's publications include: "An International Information Gateway: Thunderbird's Intranet for Teaching, Learning and Research" (with Carol Hammond, Ann Tolzman, and Cate Cebrowski) in *Advances in Library Administration and Organization,* October 1997; and "World Database of Business Information Sources on the Web," a review for the November/December 1998 issue of *Business Information Alert.* In addition, he was interviewed by Mary Ellen Bates in the 2001 book, *Super Searchers Cover the World: The Online Secrets of International Business Researchers,* published by Eight Bit Books.

He is a member of the Special Libraries Association and the Arizona Libraries Association. He is married with three children and is an avid reader, stargazer, and amateur radio operator.

David Ernsthausen
Kenan-Flagler Business School

Since 1997 David Ernsthausen has been the faculty teaching and research support librarian of the University of North Carolina at Chapel Hill's Kenan-Flagler Business School. He consults with faculty and students about which resources are most likely to provide useful answers for their research. He also presents guest lectures for classes in the M.B.A. and bachelor's degree programs. Prior to 1997 he worked for seven years as a reference librarian at Wake Forest University, working mainly with the undergraduate business students and faculty. He has an M.B.A. from the Babcock Graduate School of Management at Wake Forest University and a M.L.S. degree from Indiana University.

Michelle Fennimore
Competitive Insights

Michelle Fennimore is the principal of Competitive Insights, a market research company specializing in competitive intelligence, company, and industry research. Its services range from online research and one-on-one interviews to custom-designed market research studies, including mail and telephone surveys. Ms. Fennimore's work focuses primarily on marketing and advertising issues, as well as business development and expansion. Prior to founding Competitive Insights, she spent nine years in New York City, marketing national brands for global advertising agencies including J. Walter Thompson, Saatchi & Saatchi, and Grey Advertising.

James Harrington
Fujitsu Network Communications

Jim Harrington earned his M.L.S. from the State University of New York at Buffalo. He began his career assisting libraries in the setup and implementation of a variety of automated services for both staff and end users, primarily dealing with system design and training. For the past four years, he has worked as the corporate librarian for Fujitsu Network Communications, providing library services primarily for the marketing and sales organizations.

Michelle Hartstrom
Columbia Financial Advisors, Inc.

Michelle Hartstrom is a financial analyst with over ten years of experience in the valuation of closely held business interests. In her analysis of client companies, she researches economic and industry information, financial market data, public company information, and merger and acquisition data. She performs financial analysis for clients for a variety of purposes including ESOP, litigation, gift and estate tax, and management planning. In addition to the financial analysis aspect of her work, verbal and written communication is an integral part of each project she performs.

Prior to joining Columbia Financial Advisors, Inc., Ms. Hartstrom worked for Willamette Management Associates in its Portland, Oregon office. She has earned accreditation as a senior appraiser in business valuation from the American Society of Appraisers and a certification in financial management from the Institute of Management Accountants. She earned a B.S. in Business Administration with high scholarship from Oregon State University. Her concentrations of study were financial management and international business, and she minored in behavioral science.

Jean M. Heilig
Jones International University

Jean M. Heilig is the director of the online library at Jones International University (JIU), the first completely online university to achieve regional accreditation. Ms. Heilig has been working full time for the university since January 2003. Prior to that, she worked part time for the university and part time for Jones e-global library (a licensed product), where she was the senior director of Research and Information. At both Jones e-global library and the JIU library she has been involved with resource development and review as well as the selection and evaluation of database vendors and content providers. She participates in client (student, faculty, and staff) outreach, support, and training and also monitors copyright issues, national and international digital library initiatives, advances in electronic publishing, and similar issues that affect the competitive environment of e-global library. Prior to joining Jones in 1999 she was the program coordinator for the Library and Information Services graduate program at the University of Denver (DU), where she managed all program logistics, budget, personnel, and student advising.

Ms. Heilig obtained her master's degree in library and information services from the University of Denver (1999), her master's degree in business administration from the University of Colorado – Denver (1992). She also holds a certificate in competitive intelligence from Drexel University (2002). In addition to her work with JIU, she is an adjunct faculty member in the Library and Information Science master's degree program at DU.

Karl Kasca
Kasca & Associates

Five years ago Karl Kasca formed his own company, Kasca & Associates, which provides top-level information research results to business and legal decision makers. His company specializes in business research and competitive intelligence, as well as market, product, and industry trends, and due diligence—information useful to businesses and attorneys in making decisions and acting on them.

Mr. Kasca was formerly with a Fortune 500 company with over sixteen years experience performing operational and financial internal audits as well as vendor and conflict-of-interest/fraud examinations in diverse business situations. As a result, he has become very experienced at finding creative approaches and solutions to problems/questions as well as performing insightful analyses of results.

Wendy S. Katz
Factscope LLC

Dr. Wendy Katz owns Factscope LLC, a research consulting firm based in Lexington, Kentucky. Dr. Katz received her B.S. in Conservation of Natural Resources, with highest honors, from the University of California at Berkeley in 1977. She has seventeen years of laboratory experience in biomedical research and has published research papers and literature reviews in *Cell* and other peer-reviewed journals. She earned her Ph.D. in Biology from the Massachusetts Institute of Technology in 1989, where her research focused on structure-function analysis of proteins. Her postdoctoral research at the California Institute of Technology used tools of molecular genetics to study how cells in a developing animal know where they are. Dr. Katz joined the Department of Biochemistry in the University of Kentucky College of Medicine in 1995 and both continued her research and taught graduate biochemistry there from 1995 to 2000. She has a long-standing interest in animal training and behavior modification and in her free time teaches dog obedience classes.

Hal P. Kirkwood, Jr.
Purdue University

Hal P. Kirkwood is currently an assistant professor of Library Science at the Management & Economics Library at Purdue University. He acts as the instruction coordinator for the Management & Economics Library, conducting workshops and class sessions on the multitude of business databases available. He has written extensively in publications such as *Online, Journal of Business & Finance Librarianship, FreePint,* and the *Bulletin* of the Business & Finance Division of Special Libraries Association. Professor Kirkwood has presented at Online World, Internet Librarian, and the Special Libraries Association's Annual Conference. His research interests are in teaching business information to M.B.A.s, Web design and usability, and concept mapping.

Jan Knight
Bancroft Information Services

Jan Knight is owner of Bancroft Information Services. As an independent research consultant, she provides a variety of business intelligence and market research services to a diverse list of companies, including publishers, corporate trainers, software companies, biotechnology firms, marketing strategists and sales consultants. Much of her work involves providing industry profiles, market studies, and competitor profile reports. Clients often commission her services when working on initial business plans, marketing strategies, or new product development.

Originally from England, Ms. Knight has a professional background in advertising, marketing, and publishing. She holds an M.A. in Information Resources & Library Science from the University of Arizona and a B.A. in Humanities/Renaissance Studies from the University of California, Berkeley. She regularly attends local business events and has spoken to various business groups on the topic of "Jump-Starting Your Own Market Research via the Internet." Her Web site provides more information on services as well as client testimonials. It can be found at: *http://www.bancroftinfo.com.*

Margery A. Mackie
Mackie Research LLC

Margery A. Mackie is an independent business researcher located in Portland, Oregon. Her firm, Mackie Research LLC, specializes in online industry research and overview writing. Other services include regional economic profile research and writing, environmental research, and specialized industry data searches. Ms. Mackie is also a contributor to "The CyberSkeptic's Guide to Internet Research," a monthly newsletter. Prior to launching her business, Margery worked in a variety of private sector, nonprofit, and government settings, always enjoying the research and reporting aspects of her work the most. She is a member of the Association of Independent Information Professionals and the National Association for the Self-Employed, and she holds an environmental planning degree from Stanford University.

Matthew J. McBride
Information Consultant

Matthew J. McBride is the president and principal information consultant of CInC, Inc. He holds an M.S. in Plant Pathology from the University of Minnesota and a B.S. in Molecular Biology from Purdue University. Matthew is currently completing his M.L.S. degree at Drexel University. He has worked as a biological research scientist for a major chemical company and as an information consultant for The Dialog Corporation. He has over seven years of experience searching commercial systems and databases for scientific, technical, and intellectual property information.

Karin Mohtadi
KZM LLC

Karin Mohtadi has participated in business valuations and business research during the last eight years. Currently she researches economic and industry information, public company information, and merger and acquisition data. As a financial analyst conducting business valuations and other analysis, she worked for clients for a variety of purposes, including buy-sell agreements, damages and lost profits analyses, economic damage analysis, enhanced earnings, employee stock ownership plans, litigation support, and gift and estate tax.

Prior to forming KZM LLC, Ms. Mohtadi worked for Veber Partners LLC, an investment bank in Portland, Oregon. Prior to that she worked for Willamette Management Associates in its Portland, Oregon, office. She holds a M.S. in Economics as well as a B.A. in both Economics and French from Portland State University.

Rita W. Moss
University of North Carolina at Chapel Hill

Rita Moss's education includes a B.A. from the University College of North Wales, Bangor, United Kingdom, with a double major in Social Theory and Institutions and History, an M.Ed. from the same institution, and an M.L.S. from the University of North Carolina at Chapel Hill received in 1988. She has worked since 1991 as a business and economics librarian at the University of North Carolina at Chapel Hill. For the past twelve years she has also conducted workshops on business information resources for

Southeastern Library Network and for North Carolina Libraries for Virtual Education, as well as giving several presentations at workshops offered by the North Carolina Library Association.

Ms. Moss recently finished revising the second edition of the *Handbook of Business Information* for Libraries Unlimited.

Robin Neidorf
Electric Muse

Robin Neidorf has provided research, writing, and consulting services through her company, Electric Muse, since 1996. She works with clients in the fields of nonprofit management, health care, business consulting, law, investment services, public policy, education, and market research to help them find and use information to communicate more effectively in print, electronic formats, and face to face. Ms. Robin holds a master's degree in nonfiction writing from the Bennington Writing Seminars and teaches research, writing, and public relations through the University of Minnesota's Compleat Scholar program. Her articles and essays have appeared regionally and nationally in such publications as *Ms.* magazine, *Minnesota Law & Politics, Corporate Report,* and *Ventures* magazine, and she is the coauthor of *e-Merchant: Retail Strategies for e-Commerce* (Addison Wesley, 2001). Ms. Robin often speaks to groups on market research, communications, public relations, life-work balance, and other topics. She is a member of the Association of Independent Information Professionals and Business/ Professional Women USA.

Judith M. Nixon
Purdue University

Judith Nixon has worked at the Purdue University Libraries since 1984, first as a consumer and family sciences librarian and since 1993 as a management and economics librarian. Prior to this she worked as a reference librarian at the University of Wisconsin, Platteville and at the Cedar Rapids Public Library.

Ms. Nixon is widely published in the field. Her works include *Industry and Company Information,* which she coauthored with Craig A. Hawbaker (Ann Arbor, MI: Pierian Press, 1991), and *Lodging and Restaurant Index,* a quarterly periodical index (West Lafayette, IN: RHIMI, Purdue University, 1985–1993), as well as numerous journal articles. Her awards include the John H. Moriarity Award for Excellence in Library Service to the Faculty and Students of Purdue University (1989) and the Gale Research Award for Excellence in Business Librarianship (1994).

Ms. Nixon has a master's degree in Library Science from the University of Iowa (1974) and a B.S. in Education from Valparaiso University (1967). She is a member of the American Library Association, the Reference and User Services Association, and the Business Reference and Services Section.

Judith Parvez
Tax Analysts

Judy is a senior information specialist at Tax Analysts. Prior to that, she was employed as a tax librarian and tax knowledge manager for several professional services firms. She is a member of the Special Libraries Association and has served as moderator of the Tax Roundtable – Legal Division.

Judy received a Bachelor of Administration/Library Science degree from the University of Wisconsin, Eau Claire.

Marcy M. Phelps
Phelps Research

Marcy Phelps is the founder and president of Phelps Research, located in Denver, Colorado. Her company offers business and market research to management, marketing, and financial services professionals. Marcy specializes in providing clients with industry profile reports and has particular expertise in online database searching. Phelps Research also offers company profiles, competitive intelligence, litigation support, regional economic overviews, comparable company research, and merger and acquisition research. Ms. Phelps has a master's degree in Library and Information Services from the University of Denver as well as a degree in Mathematics from the State University of New York at New Paltz. She currently holds memberships in the Association of Independent Information Professionals, the Business Marketing Association, and the Metro Denver Chamber of Commerce. A first-degree black belt in Taekwondo, Ms. Phelps enjoys golf and mountain biking in her spare time.

Brenda Reeb
University of Rochester

A native of rural southern Illinois, Brenda Reeb earned her B.A. in history from Loyola University of Chicago in 1987. During her senior year in college she wrote her first paper on a microcomputer, using MS-DOS and WordPerfect. She earned her M.L.S. from Simmons College in Boston in 1991. In 1993 Ms. Reeb relocated to Rochester, New York, to serve as the management librarian at the University of Rochester. With no prior business background, she was hired primarily for her computer skills. Now the director of the Management Library, she manages a staff of three, serving the William E. Simon School of Business and the economics department at the university.

After nearly a decade of business library reference work, Ms. Reeb remains fascinated by the ways students engage business sources, particularly in an online environment. She coordinates several Web interface design projects in the library and maintains a private consulting practice in user-centered design. She is a member of the American Library Association and the Association for Women in Computing.

While living in Boston, Ms. Reeb became an avid bicycle commuter, which she continues to this day, although she no longer rides in the winter.

Jan Rivers
Dorsey & Whitney LLP

Jan Rivers is reference/electronic services librarian for Dorsey & Whitney LLP. Prior to joining Dorsey, Ms. Rivers worked for Arthur Andersen LLP, where she was a manager in the Risk Management Services Group, as well as a project manager and team leader for Andersen's AskNetwork e-Products Consulting Team and a regional leader in the firm's Business Information Network. She managed projects relating to the firm's intranet and Internet sites, and she developed databases and electronic information products for groups within the firm. She also conducted in-depth research and analysis for firm personnel and leadership worldwide. Before joining Arthur Andersen, Ms. Rivers worked for the Hennepin County Public Library System. She has also presented at Intranets 2000 and at Computers in Libraries and has been published in *Searcher* and *Intranet Professional.*

Roger V. Skalbeck
George Mason University School of Law

Roger Skalbeck is the technology librarian at George Mason University School of Law. Mr. Skalbeck has worked in law libraries for almost a decade, including work in five law firms in three jurisdictions. Mr. Skalbeck has analyzed and reviewed numerous legal resources and technologies, and he frequently participates in conferences focused on law libraries and legal technology. He received his B.A. from Macalester College and his M.L.I.S. from Dominican University, and he is currently pursuing a J.D. at George Mason University School of Law.

Jen Venable
Purdue University

Jen Venable is the assistant management and economics librarian and an assistant professor at Purdue University. She holds a B.A. in News-Editorial from Oklahoma State University (1994) and an M.L.I.S. from the University of Texas at Austin (1997).

Ms. Venable has been working in libraries in the academic, public, and private sectors since the age of nineteen. She began her professional career as a reference librarian for Queens Borough Public Library (QBPL) system in New York City. After working in the branch libraries, she became a business reference librarian and later assistant manager of the business research department for QBPL. After three years in New York, she moved back to Austin as the solo librarian for Hoover's, Inc., a business information database company. Jen worked for a year in the dot-com industry; she then accepted a position at the Management and Economics Library at Purdue University, where she works today.

Patricia A. Watkins
Thunderbird School of International Management

Patricia Watkins is a business information service and resources librarian in the International Business Information Centre at Thunderbird, the American Graduate School of International Management in Glendale, Arizona. In her position she consults regularly with executives from a variety of fields worldwide to help find solutions to their business intelligence needs. Prior to her current position, she was manager of Information Resources at MORPACE International, a Michigan-based market research firm partnering with the automotive industry.

Raised in Dearborn, Michigan, Watkins now lives in Phoenix. Before relocating to Arizona in 2001, she spent a career in advertising, marketing, and market research within the automotive industry. She was founding partner and senior project director with Creative Marketing Consultants, a Southfield, Michigan-based primary market research company whose clientele included General Motors Corporation. Prior to that, she worked with the Polk Company, Campbell-Ewald Advertising, and Ward's Automotive Research. In 2000, Watkins earned a master's degree in Library and Information Science from Wayne State University in Detroit. Her undergraduate degree is in political science from the University of Michigan.

Ms. Watkins served on the board and is a past-president of Women in Communications of Detroit. She is active in several information and library organizations: the Society of Competitive Intelligence, Arizona Women in International Trade, the American Library Association, the Arizona Library Association, the Mountain Plains Library Association (MPLA), and the Special Libraries Association. She was recently chosen to attend the inaugural MPLA Leadership Institute in Abiquiu, New Mexico. She is currently involved with research on the history and economic impact of immigration between Arizona and Mexico.

Susan F. Weiler
Weiler Information Services

Susan F. Weiler is the owner of Weiler Information Services (WIS), an information brokerage business that since 1989 has provided customized business research to companies that do not have in-house libraries or information centers. Weiler Information Services provides customized business research services to a variety of organizations, including executive recruiting firms, consulting firms, financial services firms, telecommunications equipment and service firms, and manufacturers of consumer packaged goods.

Ms. Weiler holds a masters degree in Library and Information Sciences from Simmons College and has extensive experience as an information specialist and corporate reference librarian. Prior to founding WIS, she was employed by Bain & Company, an international strategic management consulting firm. Ms. Weiler is a frequent writer and speaker on topics relating to the library and information industry.

Ms. Weiler is a member of the Association of Independent Information Professionals (AIIP), New England Online Users Group, and the Special Libraries Association. She serves as a trustee of the Walpole Public Library in Walpole, Massachusetts, a member of The Dialog Corporation's Customer Advisory Board (2001–2003), and served as a director-at-large and vendor relations chairperson of the AIIP Board (1999–2002).

Samuel Werberg
FIND/SVP, Inc.

Sam Werberg joined FIND/SVP, Inc. as a research consultant in the Technology, Information and Communications Group in August 2000, after serving as an information specialist in Morocco for three years with the U.S. Peace Corps. Prior to that he worked for an information broker in Austin, Texas, where he covered the semiconductor and telecom industries.

For FIND/SVP, Mr. Werberg covers Artificial Intelligence, Consumer and Business Internet Usage Patterns, Enterprise Content Management, Information Services, Knowledge Management, Semiconductors, and Wireless Technologies and Communications. Mr. Werberg has also worked in academic libraries in Texas and New York and currently volunteers in the Queens Public Library in Astoria, New York.

Mr. Werberg received a B.S. in Sociology from Hamilton College and an M.L.I.S. from the Graduate School of Library and Information Science at the University of Texas at Austin.

Kim Whalen
Emory University

Kim Whalen is a business librarian at Emory University's Goizueta Business School. She has a B.A. in business administration with a major in marketing from Illinois Institute of Technology (1990) and an M.L.I.S. from the University of Pittsburgh's School of Information Sciences (2002).

In addition to her responsibilities within the Goizueta Business Library, Ms. Whalen is the liaison to Goizueta's Career Management Center. Through the development of Web research tools, group instructional sessions, and one-on-one consultations, she assists job-seeking students with their research of companies, industries, and geographic areas.

Prior to earning her master's degree, Ms. Whalen spent over eleven years in Chicago's nonprofit sector. Positions with the University of Chicago Graduate School of Business, Illinois Institute of Technology, Advocate Health Care Foundation, and the City of Chicago developed her nonprofit marketing, public relations, and program administration experience. She is an active member of the Special Libraries Association and the American Library Association and currently serves on the SLA Georgia Chapter Membership Committee.

INDEX

10-K. *See* annual report
10k Wizard, 60, 222, 271, 382, 396
   content, 272–273
   description, 272
   evaluation, 274
   pricing, 272
   reviews, 274
   value rating, 274
10-Q. *See* quarterly report

A

Abbott, Langer & Associates, 193
ABI/Inform. *See* ProQuest
Academics, 61–62
Access, 56
access, long-term, 48
Accounting & Tax Database, 382
Accurint, 382
ACS. *See* American Cancer Society
Adweek, 224, 354–355, 382
   content, 355–356
   description, 355
   evaluation, 356–357
   pricing, 355
   useful tips, 358
   value rating, 357
aggregator, 22, 63, 219–223
AIIP. *See* Association of Independent
   Information Professionals
Alacra, 23, 63, 198, 223, 382, 396
   content, 278–281
   description, 275–277
   evaluation, 281–283
   pricing, 277–278
   reviews, 283
   useful tips, 284
   value rating, 283
AlltheWeb, 41–42, 90
AltaVista, 136
alternative phrases, 144
American Cancer Society (ACS), 137, 138
American College of Cardiology, 59
American Heart Association, 59
American Institute of Certified Public
   Accountants, 382, 396
American Medical Association, 32
American Society of Association Executives
   (ASAE), 33, 95
Amgen, Inc., 426
annual report, 58, 129, 132, 133
ASAE. *See* American Society of Association
   Executives
Ask Jeeves, 325
askSam, 126, 196, 198, 199–201
Aspen Publishers, 396
Association of Country Club Executives, 95
Association of Independent Information
   Professionals (AIIP), 29, 49, 67, 377

B

Baker Library Industry Guides, 22, 377
Baker Thomsen Associates Insurance
   Services, 193
Ballard Spahr Andrews & Ingersoll, 396
Bancroft Information Services, 130, 143,
   312, 431
Barr, Melissa, 422
Bates Information Services, 65, 243
Bates, Mary Ellen, 8, 50, 65, 243
BEA. *See* U.S. Bureau of Economic Analysis
Biehl, Kathy, 423
BigCharts, 382
BioInformatics, 129, 130
Biological Abstracts, 13
Biotechnology Association, 59
Bio Whittaker, 129
Bizjournal, 60, 145, 147, 377
BLA Biologics, 180–188
Black's Law Dictionary, 29
BLDSC. *See* British Library Document
   Supply Centre
Bloomberg Professional, 383, 396
BLS. *See* U. S. Bureau of Labor Statistics
Boeing, 162
Bondtrac, Inc. 383, 396
Boolean logic, 44, 200
Boruff-Jones, Polly D., 376, 423
Boston University School of Public
   Health, 147
Brandweek, 224, 354–355, 383
   content, 355–356
   description, 355
   evaluation, 356–357
   pricing, 355
   useful tips, 358
   value rating, 357
Briefing.com, 383, 396
British Library, Inside Conferences, 62
British Library Document Supply Centre
   (BLDSC), 62
Brodsky, Meryl, 220, 235, 243, 255, 373, 423
brokerage house reports, 63
budget. *See* research budget
Budget and Economic Outlook, 383
*Building and Running a Successful Research
   Business* (Bates), 8
BullsEye Pro, 196–197, 201
Bureau of the Census. *See* U.S. Census Bureau
Burwell Enterprises, 255, 424
Burwell, Helen, 4, 15, 123, 255, 424
Business Wire, 384, 397

C

Cambrex, 129
Carlson, Cindy, 425
Carr, Margaret Metcalf, 124, 125–126, 145,
   155, 179
Carr Research Group, 145, 155, 179

M